School, Society, & State

TRACY L. STEFFES

School, Society, & State

A NEW EDUCATION
TO GOVERN
MODERN AMERICA,
1890–1940

The University of Chicago Press   Chicago and London

Tracy L. Steffes is assistant professor of education
and history at Brown University.

The University of Chicago Press, Chicago 60637
The University of Chicago Press, Ltd., London
© 2012 by The University of Chicago
All rights reserved. Published 2012.
Printed in the United States of America

21 20 19 18 17 16 15 14 13 12   1 2 3 4 5

ISBN-13: 978-0-226-77209-7 (cloth)
ISBN-10: 0-226-77209-8 (cloth)

Library of Congress Cataloging-in-Publication Data

Steffes, Tracy Lynn.
    School, society, and state : a new education to
govern modern America, 1890–1940 / Tracy L.
Steffes.
        p. cm.
    Includes bibliographical references and index.
    ISBN-13: 978-0-226-77209-7 (cloth : alkaline paper)
    ISBN-10: 0-226-77209-8 (cloth : alkaline paper)
    1. Educational change—United States—History—
20th century. 2. Education and state—United
States—History—20th century. 3. School management and organization—United States—History—
20th century. 4. Schools—Centralization—United
States—History—20th century. 5. Education,
Compulsory—United States—History—20th
century. 6. Democracy and education—United
States—History—20th century. 7. Educational
sociology—United States—History—20th century.
I. Title.
    LC191.4.S74 2012
    379.73—dc23   2011032763

⊗ This paper meets the requirements of ANSI/NISO
Z39.48-1992 (Permanence of Paper).

For my parents, Richard and Mary Jo Steffes

CONTENTS

ACKNOWLEDGMENTS

I have accumulated many debts in the years it has taken me to write this book. I owe the largest to my parents, Richard and Mary Jo Steffes, who have been unfailing in their support, encouragement, and patience through what has sometimes felt like endless years of schooling, research, and writing. They have inspired me to work hard, to strive for balance in life, and to follow my passions even when they lead to something as foolish as graduate school in history. I am also enormously grateful to the rest of my family for their love and support, including my grandmother Elaine Steffes; my siblings, Brian, Julie, and Maryann Steffes; my best friend, Kara Brooklier, who has become family over the years; and the entire extended clan of Steffeses and Hollicks. Thanks for keeping me grounded and reminding me of what is important.

I am also indebted to the many wonderful teachers I have had over the years. Teachers at every level have inspired, encouraged, and guided me in innumerable ways: from Adele Solomon, Kimberly Voss, and John Bassett at Chippewa Valley public schools to Janet Coryell, John Houdek, and Paul Meier at Western Michigan University; to Amy Dru Stanley, Kathleen Conzen, Mae Ngai, George Chauncey, and William Novak at the University of Chicago. I owe a special debt to William Novak, my dissertation adviser, who has always pushed me to ask big questions, offered constructive feedback and practical guidance, and provided positive encouragement when I needed it most. It was Bill who started me on the path to this book. After shooting down all of my other ideas for a seminar paper, he observed that there might be potential in civics and school reform as a research topic and encouraged me to pursue it.

I am also enormously grateful to two other teachers and friends who have offered unwavering support and guidance, Jonathan Zimmerman and Carl Kaestle. With characteristic energy and generosity, Jon has read countless drafts, provided invaluable advice at crucial moments, and offered steady support and encouragement. I will consider it a great success if I can become half as good of a teacher and mentor as Jon is to all of his graduate students and adopted advisees. Carl Kaestle welcomed me to Providence with warmth and enthusiasm and has been exceedingly generous with his time, advice, and friendship. I cannot express how much I have appreciated and enjoyed our lunchtime conversations that have ranged from research and teaching, to education policy, to sailing and singing. Jon and Carl are models of how to balance rigorous scholarship, commitment to high-quality teaching and advising, and a rich and robust life outside of work. I am deeply grateful to both of them.

I have also been fortunate to have fantastic colleagues in graduate school and since who have enriched my work and my life while doing it. Thank you for great conversation, feedback, and inspiration in reading groups, work-shops, and coffeehouses and bars throughout Chicago to Joanna Grisinger, Kyle Volk, Lisa Andersen, Matthew Perry, Emily Brunner, Karrin Hanshew, Sean Forner, Moira Hinderer, Matthew Miliken, Grant Madsen, Laurel Spindel, Stephen Porter, and Erik Gellman. I also appreciate the intellectual and social community I have found since graduate school at Brown, national conferences, academic centers, and especially at the annual meetings of the History of Education Society, including but not limited to Hilary Moss, Joan Malczewski, Sarah Manekin, Leah Gordon, Daniel Amsterdam, Karen Benjamin, Marc VanOverbeke, Diana D'Amico, Heather Lewis, Amy Lippert, Jason Sharples, T. Austin Graham, Thomas Crocker, Heather Tresslar, and Coleman Hutchison.

I am also grateful to many scholars, colleagues, and friends who have offered critical feedback on this project at various stages. I owe special thanks to Michael Katz, Mitchell Stevens, Hilary Moss, Jonathan Zimmerman, Carl Kaestle, Joanna Grisinger, and the anonymous press reviewers for reading the entire manuscript and providing constructive feedback and suggestions. I am also indebted to Kyle Volk, Joan Malczewski, Luther Spoehr, Patricia Spacks, Amy Lippert, and Thomas Crocker for careful readings of the introduction and sections of the book. Thank you also to commentators and audiences at conferences and workshops who have helped me to refine my ideas along the way, especially Brian Balogh, James Sparrow, Elisabeth Clemens, Thomas Sugrue, Christine Ogren, Maris Vinovskis, Ellen Lagemann, and William Reese. In addition, I owe a special thank you to Robert Devens at the University of Chicago Press for believing in the project, offering helpful feedback, and deftly guiding it to publication.

I am also indebted to generous financial support that has enabled me to research the book and given me time to write it. I could not have completed the research without fellowships and travel grants from the University of Chicago, Brown University's Richard T. Salomon Faculty Research Fund, the Rockefeller Archive Center, and the National Parent-Teacher Association. I have also been fortunate to receive fellowships that have not only given me the support to write fulltime but also introduced me to other junior scholars that have enriched this writing. Thank you to the Miller Center for Public Affairs at the University of Virginia, the Social Science Research Council Program on Philanthropies and the Non-Profit Sector, the National Academy of Education/Spencer Foundation Postdoctoral Fellowship program, and the American Academy of Arts and Sciences Visiting Scholars program.

Brown University has been a wonderful place to research and teach. I appreciate the intellectual stimulation, guidance, support, and community provided by colleagues in the education and history departments. I am particularly grateful to Kenneth Wong, Luther Spoehr, John Tyler, Cynthia Garcia Coll, and Jin Li in education and to Nancy Jacobs, Tara Nummedal, Omer Bartov, Kenneth Sacks, and the entire Americanist history faculty: Howard Chudacoff, Linford Fisher, Elliott Gorn, Francoise Hamlin, Karl Jacoby, Seth Rockman, Robert Self, Naoko Shiwashabi, and Michael Vorenberg. Friends and colleagues outside of my departments have also made Providence a great place to live and work. Thanks in particular to Savvas Koushiappas for helping me to try to visualize state power and to Edel Minogue, Meredith Hastings, Deborah Rivas Drake, Masha Ryskin, and the whole happy-hour crew for many enjoyable nights.

Last but by no means least, I am grateful to the wonderful undergraduate students I have had at Brown with whom I have discussed many of the ideas in this book. They have made teaching a constant pleasure and learning experience. I am particularly indebted to terrific student research assistants who worked with me during summers and semesters to collect and analyze scores of court cases, newspapers, and reports: Alice Costas, Kaley Curtis, Lauren Faulkner, Jamal Hill, Mark Robbins, Kimberly Spanier, and William Tatum. Thanks to Brown's Undergraduate Teaching and Research Awards (UTRA), which made some of this work possible.

Introduction

When Edward Nolan knocked on the door of Elma De Lease in December 1916, he provoked a violent confrontation that ultimately landed them both in court. Nolan was the attendance officer for the school district in Malborough, New York, and he had received a complaint from a local teacher that twelve-year-old Edward De Lease was absent from school yet again. The boy had attended only fourteen days within the previous ten weeks. His mother claimed he had tonsillitis, but she refused to provide a doctor's note, and neighbors reported seeing the boy riding on horseback and running errands for her in town that morning, several miles away. A few decades earlier, De Lease's refusal to send her son to school would have been regarded by local school officials and the state of New York as her common-law prerogative. In 1916, however, Elma De Lease ran afoul of new state laws requiring parents to send their children to school until age fourteen. Attendance officers like Nolan, hired and supervised by local school boards, were at the center of new efforts to enforce state attendance laws in the early twentieth century, and they were invested with broad legal authority to investigate absences, apprehend truants, and prosecute parents.

Attendance officers could often use persuasion, backed by the threat of legal prosecution, to secure parents' compliance with the law, but Elma De Lease would not be persuaded to send Edward to school that day. After the verbal conflict escalated, Officer Nolan decided to break the standoff with a show of force. He grabbed Edward and tried to drag him from the house, but his mother took hold of her son and refused to let go. Unable to pry Edward from his mother's arms, Nolan wrapped a chain around Elma De Lease's arm to force her to release the boy, injuring her in the process. Two other household members—De Lease's sister and a boarder—tried to intervene, but Nolan succeeded in wresting Edward away, hauling him out of the house, and delivering him to school.

Elma De Lease responded by suing Nolan for trespassing and assault. The trial jury awarded her damages, but the New York Supreme Court overturned the decision and in a striking rebuke warned that *she* could be prosecuted for interfering with the performance of the officer's duty. According to the court, Nolan had the right and duty under the state compulsory attendance law to enter De Lease's home and take the boy into custody, for "the State is sovereign in the matter of attendance of a child at school. The dominion of the State is absolute as far as attendance upon instruction is concerned during the ages prescribed."[1]

While the physicality of the encounter was exceptional—most attendance officers did not have to literally wrestle children out of the arms of their parents—the principle it articulated was not. Public schools were state institutions, state courts throughout the nation ruled at the turn of the century, and state legislatures had a compelling interest in and expansive authority over them on behalf of the public welfare. Officer Nolan's insistence that Elma De Lease send her son Edward to school according to state statute reflected a new, more assertive claim of state authority over local schools and over children themselves in the early twentieth century.

State constitutions had long invested state legislatures with legal responsibility to maintain public schools, but throughout the nineteenth century legislatures had discharged this duty by empowering local districts and giving them wide latitude to manage their own schools. Beginning at the turn of the century, however, and especially after World War I, state legislatures and growing state departments of education were pressured from above and below to take a stronger role in governing public schools. Reformers operating at local, state, and national levels turned to schools to address a host of concerns stemming from the great social and economic transformations of the era, including problems of social cohesion and community, changes in the nature of work, and growing economic stratification brought about by industrialization and urbanization. In the process they defined children's education and welfare as a public interest that transcended the family and community and justified new state interventions. Professionalizing educators and an array of groups from outside the school pressured state legislatures to expand state and county supervision of schools, increase state fiscal support, articulate new statutory requirements and minimum standards, and develop new mechanisms for standardizing schools and coordinating them into systems. They aimed to diffuse modern school reforms and to promote equal educational opportunity, which they defined as access to an adequate, minimum education for all throughout the state.

As the conflict at De Lease's doorstop shows, however, state legislatures did not always assert their authority directly. Although compulsion was a policy defined by state statute, legislatures delegated its enforcement to local school districts. Hired and supervised by the local school district, Nolan answered to local school officials who determined how vigorously to enforce the law on the basis of community sentiment. In this and other school policies, state legislatures and departments of education defined goals and standards over time and then worked with local districts, voluntary groups, and other nonstate actors to accomplish them. Local districts retained considerable authority to manage and finance their schools, and their role in implementing state policy meant that it varied across space, sometimes considerably. Yet state interventions subtly reshaped and circumscribed local control. Local schools found themselves increasingly embedded in coordinated state systems, governed by new standards and accreditation policies, dependent on state funds that came with strings attached, and beholden to state leadership and aid to implement reforms. By working with and through local districts rather than administering policies directly, state governments were often able, slowly but surely, to get local districts to invest in state goals and policies without generating hostility to state imposition.

The confrontation between De Lease and Nolan also dramatized ways in which school reform, particularly the deepening state role and claims of public responsibility, transformed the public school as a governing institution. In the nineteenth century, schooling was only one of many ways that parents educated their children and school attendance was often casual and intermittent; it supplemented education received in the home, work, church, and community to transmit literacy and basic intellectual skills and build character. The compulsory, twentieth-century state school, on the other hand, expanded public oversight over children's education and invested the school with primary responsibilities for socialization; it pursued more ambitious aims to develop and adjust youths for modern society and economy in the public interest.

Through compulsory attendance policies, state legislatures and local officials extended public power over children and households. They attached new regulations and intervened in decisions about children's education, health, labor, and welfare that had once been wholly private household matters, such as whether to send children to work or school or what constituted a legitimate illness. Elma De Lease learned firsthand that this public interest in schooling could quite literally cross the threshold of the home and challenge traditional parental authority. Often unacknowledged by reformers at the time and neglected by scholars since—but utterly unforgettable to parents like De Lease—schools were state-building projects that expanded the institutions and authority of government.

By 1916, when Nolan and De Lease fought over the state's attendance law, compulsory attendance had become effectively a national policy despite the absence of a federal government role. State legislatures in nearly every state had passed compulsory attendance statutes and in the process had borrowed statutory language, enforcement techniques, and attendance practices from examples in other places and from a burgeoning national educational policy conversation. Throughout the nation, states and localities addressed common problems and converged on common solutions. Despite legal control at state and local levels, American education came to appear so uniform, both structurally and functionally, that many Americans perceived and spoke of a national "system" in their midst.

A wide array of groups fostered this national discussion and diffusion of reforms. Professionalizing educators formed national ties through new associations, conferences, publications, networks, and university training programs, and also developed a science of education that provided a common language and models to which states and localities often turned. In addition, a variety of national actors played important roles in spreading school reforms: philanthropic foundations like the Rockefeller-funded General Education Board; reform organizations like the National Child Labor Conference; voluntary societies and interest groups including the General Federation of Women's Clubs and American Federation of Labor; and universities with national standing like Columbia's Teachers College. Some were self-conscious nation builders who saw education as a national project. Others were focused on their particular state or community or a particular reform goal—the problem of child labor or Americanization, the benefits of vocational education, the need for a modern school building—and turned to expert solutions or examples from other places. Although schooling was not a federal government project, it nevertheless became a national policy issue as national, state, and local players spread reforms around the United States and converged on shared practices in both deliberate and wholly unanticipated ways.

This emerging national policy conversation reflected a conscious and unconscious turn to schools as a national social policy strategy to address the social consequences of industrialization. While public school advocates had long touted schooling's social benefits, reformers around the turn of the century began to work in more systematic and focused ways to expand the social responsibilities of schools and define investment in education as a solution to social problems. For example, clubwomen, laborers, and medical professionals looked to public schools to safeguard children's health. They lobbied schools to add health study to the curriculum, established new health regulations such as mandatory vaccination, and added new services such as school meals, medical inspection, and supervised play. Laborers, child welfare advocates, and other reformers turned to schools to address problems of child labor, poverty, and economic instability. They supported expansion of high schools, introduction of vocational courses and guidance, and compulsory attendance policies in order to steer children away from unskilled, low-paying, dead-end jobs by equipping them to make wise decisions.

Concerns about democracy suffused many of these reform efforts throughout the period and came to the forefront of public discussion during and after World War I. Many commentators and reformers worried about how to define and protect individual freedom—the central value of democracy—in a world where individual autonomy and opportunity seemed to be retreating in the midst of increasing economic stratification, class conflict, and large-scale organization of the economy, society, and government. They increasingly looked to the already expanding and modernizing public school system to address democratic concerns about individual freedom as well as democratic community, social cohesion, and self-government. Public schools would safeguard the democratic freedom of the individual and the stability of the democratic state, reformers asserted, by guaranteeing access to educational opportunities that would equip them as workers and citizens to thrive in the new society and economy and instill civic and social values. In the postwar period, reformers mobilized behind calls to provide "equal educational opportunity": they wanted to guarantee that more students would have access to schooling and that students would undertake more schooling, all the way through high school; define minimum standards; reshape the school program to meet the needs of a diverse student body; and offer services and interventions to ameliorate barriers to attendance.

The effort seemed to bear fruit. By the end of the 1930s, Americans pointed with pride to the rapid expanse of schooling, particularly the high school or "people's college," as an expression and guarantee of American democracy. While it had been an elite endeavor in the nineteenth century, serving only 4 percent of adolescents, by 1940 public high schools educated over 50 percent of American youths. By 1940, more kids attended school for longer periods of time than ever before: elementary education was nearly universal (over 90 percent) for all ethnic groups in all regions of the country when it had previously been so only for Northern whites, and average daily attendance had nearly doubled from its 1890 levels, from 86 days per year to 152 days per year. New curricular differentiation, extracurricular activities, and pupil adjustment services purported to offer democratic adaptations to meet individual needs and recognize individual differences.[2]

Yet this vision of equal educational opportunity was limited. Not all groups were included on equal terms in this project in either theory or practice. African Americans in segregated Southern schools, for example, were usually left behind in the project of school building as resources were disproportionately distributed to white schools. Equality of opportunity, reformers were quick to point out, did not mean the *same* opportunities for all but rather access to an acceptable minimum education to prepare youths as good citizens, workers, and community members. What constituted an adequate minimum level of education for black Southern agricultural laborers was consequently different than that for white middle-class urbanites. Reformers' efforts to promote equal educational opportunity were also limited by their reliance on local control, and particularly local property tax, which virtually guaranteed educational disparities in resources because of the unequal distribution of wealth. Despite a rhetoric that sounded universalistic, reformers in practice accepted differences and inequalities in education as inevitable and acceptable.

In a period of tremendous change and uncertainty that prompted many European nations to create new social insurance programs, Americans invested heavily in schooling, fiscally and emotionally, to address the social tensions and risks of industrialization, to safeguard democracy, and to provide for the individual and collective welfare of citizens. Reliance upon schooling was a social policy choice, made sometimes consciously and sometimes unconsciously, which reflected American social policy preferences and values. This choice has often been overlooked by scholars who have tended to view American social policy as weak and laggard compared to Europe and who have sought explanations for the underdevelopment of the American welfare state. European nation-states reconciled democracy with industrial capitalism by socializing risk and constructing a social safety net for all citizens, laying the foundation of modern welfare states beginning in the late nineteenth century. Social reformers seeking to enact similar policies in the United States usually met with failure until the emergency of the Great Depression, but even New Deal policies usually described as the foundations of the American welfare state (such as Social Security) were far less universal and generous than similar policies abroad. However, in taking European policies as the normative model, scholars have overemphasized American failures to act and in the process have missed the social policy initiatives Americans *did* undertake.[3]

Americans chose education. Public schooling was arguably *the* American public investment of the early twentieth century. Americans spent generously on their schools, increasing school expenditures from $141 million per year in 1890 to $2.3 billion per year by 1940 in constant dollars, more than a sixteenfold increase. By 1940, public schooling shaped the everyday lives of 875,000 teachers and school employees and over twenty-five million children who were enrolled in school. Schooling was the largest expenditure of state and local governments, averaging between one-quarter and one-third of their combined outlays throughout the period. In 1940, when state and local governments spent $9.2 billion for all purposes, they spent $2.3 billion on public elementary and secondary education, which represented half of all social welfare expenditures as defined by the U.S. census. One of the most outstanding expressions of this public commitment was found in expansion of free public high schools. The United States was the first nation on earth to make secondary schooling a mass institution. In 1940 when over 50 percent of American adolescents attended publicly supported high schools, fewer than 20 percent of their European counterparts did so, and in 1955 when American high school attendance reached almost 80 percent, no nation in Europe surpassed 40 percent.[4]

As a social policy choice for addressing the consequences of industrial capitalism, education was a limited strategy. It channeled social problems into schools, which could not hope to fix them, and ignored the ways in which social and economic structures outside schools shaped and limited what they could do. Schools might provide students with vocational guidance and training to make wise choices, for example, but they could not solve the problems of poverty and insecurity that resulted from the large number of unskilled, low-paying, dead-end jobs that industrial capitalism produced. Schools could prepare youths for better jobs, but this did not provide any actual opportunity if racial or gender discrimination, labor market stratification, or family need prevented people from pursuing them. Rhetoric about the democratic opportunity of schooling obscured these barriers and presented schooling as a project of individual effort and merit; failures were individual rather than structural.

This book argues that school reform was a major project of national state-building, a public governing response to the tensions of democracy and capitalism in modernizing America. Enacted from the top down and bottom up in ways both planned and improvised, school reform expanded the institutions, the reach, and the authority of the state, including both state-level government and public power operating at all levels of American governance. School reform was a national but not a federal social policy: reformers defined education as a national interest, spread reforms across the nation, and produced a new national policy arena and conversation. This heavy fiscal and emotional investment in public schooling to safeguard the democratic freedom of the individual reflected an American social policy preference for bolstering individualism rather than socializing risk as a way to address the democratic and social tensions of industrialization. This choice had important consequences. It legitimated American democracy and placed responsibility for meeting social policy goals and aspirations to schools, which were often ill equipped to actually solve them. It also obscured the extent to which opportunity was stratified and unequal and schools could serve to deepen these inequities.

*

In a series of lectures titled "School and Society," delivered in 1899, philosopher John Dewey explained how his experimental Laboratory School fit into the context of wide-ranging educational reforms and experiments taking shape. "The obvious fact is that our social life has undergone a thorough and radical change," he observed. "If our education is to have any meaning for life, it must pass through an equally complete transformation." This transformation was already in progress, he noted, and could be seen in new efforts to reshape school pedagogy, curriculum, administration, and organization. These efforts to frame a "New Education," Dewey concluded, were "as much an effort to meet the needs of the new society that is forming, as are changes in modes of industry and commerce." School reform was a response to the larger social and industrial changes of the era and an effort to develop and socialize individuals for this new environment. As urbanization and industrial change transformed older agencies of socialization like the home, church, work, and small local community, Dewey argued, schools should assume more responsibility for socializing children into an ever-changing society.[5]

By framing the problem as one of "school and society," however, reformers at the time and most historians since then have missed the role of the *state* at the center of this relationship. "The state" in this context means both state-level government and the myriad ways in which public governing power was deployed in the American nation-state. The school's power as a social institution came in large part from the public power and purposes that animated it. School reform and expansion reflected a major project of state-building and governance that extended public authority into households and pursued social policy goals through education.[6]

Putting the state back into examinations of school and society recasts the history of education and the period. First, it draws attention to the legal and political framework of schooling, particularly the role of state government. In histories of education of this and other periods, local case studies have dominated and tend to narrate reform as a local story. However, state constitutions, case law, legislation, and administrative policies structured the context in which local schools operated and the rules of the game by which they played, even in cities where the state's hand was often less visible. In the early twentieth century, states took a stronger role than they ever had, promoting reforms, shaping local school policy, distributing resources, and coordinating schools across space in both overt and covert ways. To study local schools in isolation is to miss the ways in which they are embedded in a larger web of relationships that shape and constrain their choices.[7]

While state government provided the most important framework, local schools were also embedded in a larger national policy conversation that developed in this period. Local schools and state education policies did not develop independently but in active dialogue with reforms in other places and with national institutions, networks, models, and norms. Despite the remarkable convergence of school content, structures, and functions, scholars have given little attention to the national dimensions of schooling. They have ignored a striking question: how and why did American public schooling come to appear so similar across the nation despite decentralized legal control and no significant federal role?[8]

Although it has not taken up this question in education, interdisciplinary scholarship on state-building, including American political development, offers some insights to conceptualize national reform as something other than federal government policy. Scholars have investigated how the American nation-state has effectively deployed power to accomplish national policy goals through a variety of means, including complex arrangements with private actors, local and state governments, and "hidden" mechanisms like regulatory policies and tax expenditures that exist in place of direct spending and bureaucratic administration. In other words, the lack of overt federal government administration does not signal "weak" state-building or preclude national policy.[9]

This scholarship also signals the need for histories of education to consider alternative narrative frameworks for school reform. In studies of city school reform and the period more generally, historians of education have tended to tell the story of school reform as one of conflict over centralization and professional authority. In these narratives, school administrators, businessmen, and other elite reformers worked to modernize schools, create efficient organization and bureaucracy, and centralize control in the hands of professional experts and elites at the expense of decentralized, lay community control. In depicting it as a story of centralization and rationalization, however, these histories tend to understate political pluralism, grassroots reformers, and community control, and to overemphasize the autonomy and power of professional educators and businessmen to impose their agenda. They also miss a host of other policies and arrangements in the countryside, at the state level, and at the national level that do not conform to expectations about centralization versus decentralization or conflicts between different levels of government. Histories of education need to utilize new conceptual models of state-building and governance reform.[10]

Thinking about school, society, and state also raises important questions about the public and political functions of schooling and its larger significance in the period. Histories of education and histories of the period have tended to explain school reform—when general histories look at schooling at all—as part of the larger progressive reform impulse, another example of the larger search for order or transatlantic social politics of the age. Lawrence Cremin's classic synthesis, *The Transformation of the School*, situates school reform within the progressive impulse and emphasizes how larger social concerns and themes were reflected in it. While this is an important point, scholars should also ask more ambitious questions about schooling's impact and significance as a public policy and governing institution, given its tremendous size, scope, and power. The shift from schooling as a part-time, voluntary supplement to the family and community to a full-time, compulsory institution of public socialization changed the relationships between parents, children, and the state, for example, and should have consequences for how scholars understand the social history of childhood and the family, child welfare and social policies, labor history, and legal rights.[11]

Public schooling was not just one more progressive reform among many but a major—perhaps THE major—public response to tensions between democracy and capitalism. Viewing it in these terms casts new light on the major narratives of the period that put this tension at the center. Failed social insurance efforts, patchwork labor protections, ad-hoc social reforms, and halting federal administrative growth do not tell the whole story of the progressive response to the social consequences and democratic challenges of industrialization. Public school reform, which engaged the efforts of a wide swath of Americans, showed the imprint of progressive social visions of expanding public responsibility and socializing the individual. Yet much of its success came from the ways in which it simultaneously and powerfully reinforced individualism at the heart of American political culture and emphasized individual over collective responsibility. Public schools accordingly have important consequences for how scholars understand American social policy and welfare, the meaning and practice of democracy in the United States, and the continued faith in the American dream of social mobility even amid economic inequality and instability.[12]

While bringing the state back into studies of school and society helps to raise new questions about the history of education and period, putting the school back into studies of the state also sheds new light on American governance. Public schooling was the single largest investment of state and local governments throughout the period and reflected a major public commitment overall. Its size, scope, and intimate reach into the everyday lives of millions of Americans make it an important subject for scholars of policy and governance. Schooling, however, was also an important site of state formation, a place at which the institutions and authority of government expanded and where public power and individual rights were negotiated.

Schooling also offers a particularly revealing window into government and governance in America's system of federalism. State power grew in the period through the overt expansion of state government bureaucracy, but also more commonly and powerfully through voluntary associations and nonstate actors, courts and regulatory policies, intergovernmental cooperation, associationalism, state government delegation to local districts, and the policymaking efforts of private actors with nation-building aims. As a local and state project national in scope, schooling offers a window into the construction and diffusion of social policies across the nation in the absence of a strong federal role and provides insights about the strengths, weaknesses, and tradeoffs involved in this kind of policymaking. It also demonstrates how decentralization could be a source of strength in statebuilding and national policymaking. Local control was not an obstacle to be overcome, for example, but often a source of innovation and popular investment that could drive expansion of both state- and national-level policies.[13]

Bringing the school back into studies of national social policy also reshapes our questions about the development of the American welfare state. Education was an area of generous American social spending, but most studies neglect it or cast it as a peculiar exception to the dominant traditional narrative about the weak and underdeveloped American welfare state. In the introduction to a collection of essays on comparative social policy, for example, Theda Skcopol and her collaborators acknowledged that schooling was an area of exceptionally generous American social spending, then dedicated the entire volume to exploring the problem of American lag, weakness, and stinginess in social policy. Scholarship on the "hidden welfare" state has challenged the uncritical acceptance of European nations as the normative model of strong welfare states and expanded the categories and methods used to define welfare states to include mortgage credits, tax expenditures, delegation to private actors, and other alternatives to direct social spending. Yet education has remained largely outside these reconsiderations of the American welfare state.[14]

Taking education seriously as social policy and putting it within narratives of welfare state development helps to reframe the questions. Rather than explain American weakness or deviance from Europe, it challenges us to understand why Americans made the choices they did, and with what consequences. Early and generous investment in schooling may well have weakened support for other kinds of social welfare goals and policies. It also reveals important American political values, preferences, and institutional arrangements that shape social policy strategies. Like other aspects of America's public-private welfare state, education reflects preferences for equal opportunity rather than equal results, an orientation toward middle-class benefits, and an acceptance of inequities and disparities in those benefits. Rather than socialize risk and provide protections for industrial capitalism's losers, schooling instead promised opportunity for all to be winners, even if it didn't always deliver on these promises in practice. By casting the story in terms of what Americans have not done, scholars have missed the choices Americans *did* make to address the challenges wrought by industrial capitalism and perpetuated a misleading narrative of American welfare state exceptionalism.[15]

This book tells a national story that takes place at all levels of government, so consequently the book moves between national conversations, state-level reforms and policies, and local examples across the nation. It emphasizes broad national trends and patterns, gleaned from contemporaries' assessments of emerging policies and priorities as well as evidence of state and local practice in different contexts. I have combined the broad story of national developments with selected, deeper examinations of episodes in states and localities, following the story to sites of innovation or conflict. This emphasis on national patterns requires some tradeoffs in terms of depth, but breadth allows one to raise big questions and explore connections and developments across time and place.

In emphasizing shared patterns and national developments, however, I do not mean to suggest that schooling was everywhere the same. In a legally decentralized system, there were exceptions to nearly every trend, and infinite variations in how reforms played out in particular states or localities based on many distinctive political, economic, social, and cultural factors. Decentralization meant that even where common trends did emerge, there was often significant lag in the spread of school forms and policies, particularly in the South where poverty, racial politics, and an agricultural economy shaped reform priorities and reception. Nor do I mean to suggest that consensus reigned in education, even within small communities. On nearly every issue, there were dissenters and conflicts over aims, values, and means that shaped the politics of school reform and the policies that emerged. Conflict marked every aspect of school reform and appears throughout this narrative. However, my primary goal has not been to probe this conflict but rather to identify, analyze, and explain the similarities and shared patterns that emerged. Ultimately, American education was more than a bundle of discrete school systems or idiosyncratic experimentation, and this approach puts the common elements at the center.

The first three chapters of this book analyze school administration and governance reforms in cities, the countryside, and at the state level and chart the dynamics of state-building in the federalist system. They show how reformers, motivated by a sense of having to solve common problems, experimented with and disseminated new organizational, governance, and curricular reforms, a process that began before World War I but accelerated after it. They explore how school reform operated at local, state, and national levels and benefited from the energies of a wide array of actors. The first chapter explores the mutually constitutive projects of urban school reform and professionalization, both of which exerted a powerful nationalizing influence on the nature and direction of school reform. City reformers were the first to define the need for a new education and to push schools to expand their social responsibilities and activities. Chapter 2 examines rural school reform as a national project to strengthen rural communities against the forces of industrialization that was shaped by distinctive rural concerns and the rural context. The third chapter analyzes the expansion of the state government role in education, particularly after World War I highlighted the public stakes of educational failures and inequalities. It explores public debates over state and federal aid, the growth of state administration, and the complex ways that states negotiated with and utilized local control.

The final two chapters probe more deeply the ways in which the public power at the center of education reform refashioned schools into governing institutions that extended the reach and power of the state. They look at how the changes in schooling extended public authority over children and invested schools with new responsibilities to solve social problems and address democratic concerns. Chapter 4 examines the development of compulsory attendance policies and how they expanded public surveillance and regulation over children and households in new ways and redefined the relationship between parents, children, and the state. The final chapter examines the political, legal, and ideological debates over high school curriculum, as reflected in the expansion of two new modern subjects—civics and vocational training—to understand the changing aims of the school and its relationship to society and state. It explores how reformers celebrated the democratic expansion and differentiation of the high school. However, in sorting, guiding, and adjusting individuals to existing social and economic relations, the school program implicitly oriented youths toward the status quo and reproduced existing inequities at the same time it purported to enhance democratic access and opportunity for the individual.

*

American public schooling was not simply one more progressive reform. It was a singularly important national, public effort to address the social consequences of industrialization and safeguard democracy. While prefaced on public and collective responsibility and driven by concerns about social progress and welfare, public schooling was a popular solution in large part because of the ways it seemed to strengthen individualism in a new context and legitimate powerful myths about the American Dream. Americans invested in schooling to develop good democratic citizens, prepare them to succeed in the rapidly changing economic and social context, and keep the gates of opportunity propped open. Yet this turn to schooling to address the risks of capitalism, often in lieu of other social policies, obscured and reinforced structural inequalities and constraints to opportunity under a powerful language of merit and individualism. Like the territorial frontier, it provided opportunity and mobility for some while also obscuring hidden barriers and structural impediments for others, but served as a powerful site of democratic imagination and aspiration for all.

We continue to live today with many of the choices made in this period. Many of the fundamental educational structures and assumptions persist from this foundational moment of school-building, including tensions between innovation and equity in the federalist system. Furthermore, our contemporary political debates often posit the welfare state as a European invention and fail to recognize the true size, scope, and nature of American social welfare policies. If we take American investment in schooling seriously as a part of the American welfare state, it invites new questions for scholarship and public discussion about how Americans have understood and pursued collective responsibility, social welfare, opportunity, and equality.

ONE ✳ Urban School Reform, Professionalization, and the Science of Education

"The characteristic feature of the St. Louis schools," Joseph Mayer Rice reported in a series of articles for the *Forum* in 1892, is "the absolute lack of sympathy for the child." During twenty-minute recitation periods several times a day, "the children are obliged to stand on the line, perfectly motionless, their bodies erect, their knees and feet together, the tips of their shoes touching the edge of a board in the floor. The slightest movement on the part of a child attracts the attention of the teachers." While an extreme form, St. Louis recitations represented the "mechanical instruction" and "unscientific" teaching that Rice found evident in most of the more than 1,200 classrooms he visited in thirty-five cities. This unscientific "old education," Rice argued, relied on drills, recitations, and memorization because it was based on the "antiquated notion that the function of the school consists primarily, if not entirely, in crowding into the memory of the child a certain number of cut-and-dried facts." The "new education," on the other hand, drew from psychology and knowledge of the child in order "to develop the child naturally in all his faculties, intellectual, moral, and physical." While he criticized poor teaching, the ultimate blame did not lie with teachers alone or even primarily, for "the character of the instruction which the child receives represents the result of the general management of the schools." The root problem, Rice argued, was the "corruption and selfishness on the part of school officials, and unjustifiable ignorance, as well as criminal negligence, on the part of parents," which had sacrificed children to "politics." School boards elected "superintendent[s] who will make able tools" and selected teachers on the basis of "friendship, business, or politics" rather than merit. School reform had to start with the system itself.[1]

Rice's muckraking critique came at the beginning of a period of dynamic urban school reform. A pediatrician rather than a professional educator, Rice was part of a growing chorus of voices from outside of the schools that drove and supported change. Some reformers viewed the school as a purposeful modern institution for shaping individuals and society, and they supported a wide range of reforms to expand the scope and aims of public schooling and define a "new education" for modern times. Others turned to the school to address particular social problems made acute by the rapid expanse of industrial cities, including morals policing, labor conflict, city machine politics, child welfare, economic development, or Americanization.

While Rice was critical of parental apathy at the beginning of the decade, by its end, parental activism, community interest, and grassroots reform efforts had exploded around schooling. Clubwomen, labor unions, businessmen's associations, good-government clubs, fraternal organizations, parent-teacher associations, and a host of other groups lobbied school officials, mobilized campaigns for tax support and particular reforms, worked to shape public opinion, and developed new programs and experiments. Parental demand for expanded schooling and services, like kindergartens and high schools, helped drive school expansion as parents patronized new school extensions and supported them with tax increases and school board elections.

Rice's critique also pointed to two of the major lines of reform activity over the next five decades: efforts to reframe pedagogy and broaden the curriculum and aims of the school on the one hand, and efforts to remake school governance on the other. Reformers pushed the schools to embrace new pedagogical methods, subjects, and activities in order to prepare youths for the modern social world and make instruction more relevant to their lives. At the same time, reformers sought to reorganize the governance of city schools by centralizing policy in a single central school board, separating school administration from city political machines, and delegating greater management and leadership to professional superintendents and their subordinates in growing school bureaucracies. Rice made clear that he saw reform of school governance as an essential first step to improve instruction. In practice there could be significant tensions between the efforts to unleash the powers of the child and to rationalize the management of the school, but both sets of reforms worked over time to expand the role of educational expertise and professional school administrators in urban public schooling.

This chapter analyzes the mutual constitution of urban school reform and professionalization. Urban school reform was a contested, pluralistic, dynamic process and one that engaged the energies of a wide array of Americans, many of whom were directly impacted by schooling. Middle-class reformers, business allies, and professionalizing educators pushed from the top, but at the same time grassroots efforts, parental demand, and the need to secure majoritarian community consent shaped urban school reform from the bottom. City public school reform thus reflected more than the imposition of a professional project, the bureaucratic ambitions of a middle-class search for order, or the efforts of elites to impose social control on urban populations. These accounts of elite imposition tend to overestimate the ability of any one group to dictate the terms of reform on the one hand and to underestimate the role of grassroots reform and popular support on the other. Professionalizing educators were important actors in city school reform and grew more influential over time as their administrative authority expanded in city school systems; however, professionalization was an active project of the period and not a fully formed agenda to be imposed.[2]

Beginning in the late nineteenth century, universities experimented with new departments of education to meet the growing demand for school professionals and educational expertise. These early university professors had to define education as a university study and scholarly field. They drew experience and models from urban schools as well as social science disciplines to create a science of education with its own body of expert knowledge, methods, and theories. New educational experts used urban schools as laboratories to construct, test, and refine this science of education, and the results of this experimentation then influenced the reform agendas of urban schools. This new science of education and the growing university programs of training and credentialing that went with it strengthened school administrators' claims of expertise and leadership in city schools and helped to foster shared goals and identity.

This story of the mutual shaping of professionalization and urban school reform was important because it was a major component of the national diffusion of reforms. The science of education constructed new professional norms, language, and identity that tied educational experts together. It offered an authoritative body of knowledge to which local reformers could turn and thus fostered convergence on shared forms and policies across the nation. Furthermore, urban school reform helped to drive a national conversation. Cities were the first to articulate the need for a new education and to define its parameters, and they continued to shape the conversation. The innovations of city schools created models, inspiration, and pressure for other districts to follow and state legislatures to address.

Urban school reform and professionalization also shaped the growth of state power. State governments often gave urban districts wide latitude to experiment, following a strategy of unleashing local energy and encouraging local experimentation that could then be used to raise standards in the system overall. Yet the hand of state government was not absent in urban school reform. Legislatures accomplished state goals by delegating authority to city school officials in areas like attendance. They used city charters,

state aid and distribution policies, professional training and licensing requirements, and statutory requirements to encourage and shape local effort.
Over time, they took a stronger role in diffusing these urban innovations
by incentivizing or requiring other districts to follow suit, as subsequent
chapters will explore. Furthermore, as town, village, and rural districts
clamored for the educational opportunities available in the city, like access
to high schooling, they pushed state governments to take a stronger role in
enabling reform. City schools thus played an important role in promoting
state government intervention.

City schools also expanded state power by serving as sites where state
goals and public power could be extended over children in new ways. As
later chapters will explore, city schools developed more ambitious aims and
techniques over time, which reflected expanded public claims over children
and extended the reach and depth of the state into their lives. City schools
served as entry points for new public interventions and surveillance of the
household, including regulations about children's health, welfare, labor,
and education. Urban school reform and the science of education it helped
to produce thus expanded the governing power of the school and its character as a state institution.

The New Education and the Urban School

In defining child-centered pedagogy as the essence of the new education,
Rice drew from decades of arguments and experiments with centering education on the needs and interests of the child that would become known
as progressive education. In the mid-nineteenth century, the European
pedagogical theories of Johann Heinrich Pestalozzi, Friedrich Froebel, and
Johann Friedrich Herbart were imported to the United States and shaped
experimental programs, including, among others, the first American kindergartens, the object teaching of the Illinois Normal School, and the Quincy
method of Colonel Francis Parker. Supporters of these radical pedagogical
theories and experiments argued for schools that would liberate children's
natural tendencies rather than mold them to the dictates of order, restraint,
and authority and argued for active, child-centered classrooms. In the late
nineteenth century, these pedagogical innovators engaged in a vigorous
discussion about the need for a new education to challenge the mechanical
instruction of mass schooling.[3]

This discussion of the new education was transformed in the 1890s and
subsequent decades by a multitude of efforts to reshape the urban landscape and by the intellectual and material changes out of which these efforts emerged. In cities across the nation, reformers worked to change the

structure and operation of city government in order to separate politics and administration and enhance the powers of municipal self-government. Others worked to beautify the city and to expand and rationalize city services, including efforts to improve health and sanitation, regulate public utilities, expand opportunities for recreation, and promote economic development. Social settlement workers targeted problems of poverty, particularly among the growing immigrant populations, and evinced a special concern with child welfare and labor conditions. Moral reformers decried the moral perils of the city and organized campaigns to stamp out vice by policing prostitution, drinking, and working-class amusements, among other things. Clubwomen mobilized locally and nationally and targeted a range of municipal and child welfare concerns, including issues like schooling, juvenile justice, child labor, and health. Labor reformers, emanating from cities, pushed state governments to expand protections for workers and regulations on behalf of hours, wages, and working conditions. The expansion and concentration of city populations, rapid expanse of technologies, and the sheer logistics of governing shaped many of these reform efforts.[4]

More was at work, however, than just organizational challenges. As historians since the era have explored, a spirit of reform permeated cities in the 1890s through World War I in a widespread and multifaceted effort to remake urban life as well as the nation itself. Older efforts to pinpoint who the progressives were and what motivated them as a group have largely given way to explorations of what marked this *moment* as such a dynamic one of reform and how coalitions mobilized around particular issues and reforms. Looming large in these accounts are the economic, political, and social transformations that accompanied the rapid industrialization of the period, which created new conditions that provoked both anxiety and opportunities for change. The development of mass production and mass distribution, enabled by new technologies, created large-scale national corporations that outpaced the ability of law to deal with them and created major changes in how Americans lived and worked. Capital and people flowed to and concentrated in cities from the countryside and abroad, swelling urban populations. This human tide and its diversity created new problems of community in cities and also eroded patterns of authority and social relations of nineteenth-century island communities. Industrialization intensified the commodification of labor and the human toll of capitalism, which fueled a transatlantic social politics in the period to grapple with its social consequences. The depression of 1893 with its record rates of unemployment further displayed the social consequences of this large shift to wage labor and industrial capitalism. Nowhere were these changes and risks more visible than in the rapidly growing cities where extremes of wealth and poverty were concentrated and starkly juxtaposed.[5]

Intellectual and cultural shifts that accompanied these material changes, as well as new ideas, also shaped this moment of reform. Science and technology undermined old certainties and established authorities, creating both anxiety and a sense of possibility through the application of new scientific tools. The "chaos of the new freedom," as Walter Lippmann called it in 1914, produced tremendous cultural anxiety but also a sense of responsibility and opportunity. Social gospel Protestantism provided a moral imperative for many reformers to remake and regenerate society. Furthermore, the development of the social sciences and philosophical pragmatism, which emphasized knowledge as an active project of testing experience rather than a fixed entity, created new tools and questions for scientific social inquiry. The social sciences developed as academic disciplines and informed social reform, both shaped by an implicit faith in progress and an increasing awareness of social interdependence as a practical and intellectual problem of modern life. Reformers and social scientists, closely allied in the period, began to challenge the theories of autonomous individualism and laissez-faire that had been staples of classical economic theory and emphasize instead the social context that shaped individuals. Self-consciousness about living in a new modern age characterized by constant change infused many of these reforms, including schooling.[6]

In addition to the great economic, social, and intellectual changes that helped to make these challenges seem both pressing and solvable, political changes opened up space for new kinds of political mobilizations and the ad-hoc coalitions that characterized reform in the period. Historians have explored the ways in which the explosion of social concerns and frustration with the two-party system weakened it as a vehicle for expressing policy preferences and opened up new spaces for issue-oriented organizing and interest-group mobilization. The period marked a transformation in political style as older modes of partisan politics framed around party loyalty and identification were slowly replaced by more issue-oriented politics that called for citizens to exercise independent judgment and make their preferences known through public opinion. In this environment, reformers tapped into and manipulated powerful reform languages to mobilize support and build coalitions around particular issues, while often obscuring different motivations and social assumptions.[7]

In this context of economic, social, political, and intellectual changes, many reformers and intellectuals began to rethink the traditional aims and responsibilities of the school, both in theory and in practice. In a series of lectures commemorating his experimental laboratory school in 1899, John

Dewey noted that "the obvious fact is that our social life has undergone a thorough and radical change. If our education is to have any meaning for life, it must pass through an equally complete transformation." According to Dewey, traditional agencies of education and socialization, such as work and family, had been transformed and weakened by the rapid industrial changes. Schools must necessarily assume expanded responsibility for training children into membership in modern society. Dewey's colleague at the University of Chicago, the discipline-building sociologist Albion Small, repeatedly emphasized the importance of schools as social institutions, arguing that teachers were "makers of society," for "sociology knows no means for the amelioration or reform of society more radical than those of which teachers hold the leverage." For Small, like Dewey, the goal of education was "completion of the individual" and "adaptation of the individual to such cooperation with the society in which his lot is cast that he works at his best." Social scientists and philosophers began to argue that schools were particularly important institutions for securing social progress and cohesion in an era of rapid change. They elaborated on the role of schooling in promoting social interdependence, progress, cohesion, control, and efficiency.[8]

Commentators increasingly distinguished between the traditional functions of schools and the pressing need for a more expansive new education for modern times. Scott Nearing, in his 1915 book *The New Education*, argued that the old education, built for a rural, agricultural, locally oriented society was no longer adequate for the urban, industrial, interconnected mass society of the twentieth century. The task of the "new education" was to "recognize the change and to remodel the institutions of education in such a way that they shall meet the new needs of the new life." According to Nearing, "Yesterday the school fulfilled the needs of men. To-day it fails to meet a situation which reshapes itself with each rising and each setting sun." Educator Walter Barnes similarly defined the "new education" broadly in 1922, placing under its umbrella nearly every major effort to reform the school, from new pedagogical methods and curriculum to the scientific measurement movement to the reorganization of school systems. According to Barnes, "to maintain a well-balanced, close-knit, interdependent society, each member of it must be prepared by education to make his full share, to do his full work," and this was the spirit that animated the new education. The new education encompassed not only pedagogical and curricular reform, but fundamental efforts to reshape and extend the aims and operation of the school.[9]

Thus while the new education began as a discussion of pedagogical reform and educational aims among a relatively small group of radical pedagogues, it broadened around the turn of the century into a wider conversation about the social aims and responsibilities of the modern school. Some commentators would continue to use the phrase "new education" or its favored successor, "progressive education," to describe a set of radical pedagogical theories and practices, and experimental pedagogy would remain a vital area of reform and experimentation. However, other reformers, like Barnes and Nearing, began to speak of the "new education" as a many-sided effort to remake the school for modern life. It became a loose and amorphous term to describe a reformist orientation, a recognition that the "old education" of the nineteenth century focused on basic skills and casual school attendance was no longer appropriate for the changed conditions of the twentieth century. It did not reflect any consensus, however, on what this new modern education should look like, and a wide variety of groups, sometimes with diametrically opposed agendas and social philosophies, would take up its banner.[10]

This expansive view of the school was not only expressed by intellectuals or in the pages of academic and educational journals, but evidenced in myriad, concurrent reform efforts to extend the responsibilities of the school and broaden its aims, curriculum, and activities. The development of free public kindergartens in urban schools offers one example of the varied actors and new demands that propelled urban education reform. The kindergarten was imported to the United States from Germany in the mid-nineteenth century, and in the next few decades several German communities, Froebel supporters, and private groups experimented with it. While there were efforts to Americanize kindergartens and make them part of the public school system in a few cities in the 1880s, they began to spread like wildfire in the decades around the turn of the century when they were embraced and popularized by the growing women's club movement and female-dominated social settlement movement.[11]

Scholars have explored the tremendous proliferation and organization of middle-class women's organizations in the period and noted the ways in which they articulated a gendered rationale for political engagement, claiming that they were engaging in "municipal housekeeping," an expansion of their maternal role rather than a descent into the world of male politics. Education and child welfare reforms—juvenile courts, child labor restrictions, health and social services—fit neatly into this maternalist ideology and became early concerns of both, often overlapping groups. Kindergartens were taken up by many middle-class women as a reform that not only promoted child development but as a measure that could help Americanize immigrants and promote the social welfare of poor and working-class children. They were joined in this advocacy in many cities by labor organizations and socialists who viewed it as a matter of justice to the working class, either as a mode of democratic mobility or socialist evolution.[12]

Kindergartens were one of many school reforms advocated by club-women, social settlement workers, social gospel reformers, labor groups, and other allies that promoted a similar mix of humanitarian concern, paternalism, social justice, and Americanization anxieties and ultimately pushed the school to extend its reach and responsibilities. Often at their own expense, these reformers supported extensions of the school like vacation schools, playgrounds, mothers' clubs, and manual training classes like cooking or woodworking. They advocated expanding the social welfare role of the school, funding and promoting things like low-cost meals, medical inspection, and health services like free dental clinics. Furthermore, they endorsed special classes for children with special needs, including open-air classes for tubercular children and the expansion of special classes for children with physical handicaps. Many of these groups endorsed the school as an institution of the whole community, sponsoring adult education courses and promoting the wider use of the school building such as organizing it as a social center for democratic discussion and recreational activities. Like the kindergarten, many of these reforms were initially supported by private groups that introduced experimental programs and then pushed the school board to take them over when they proved popular and expand them throughout the school system. Experimental reforms then spread to other cities as reformers outside of the school, and educational professionals within it, endorsed and promoted these changes.[13]

In addition to concerns about Americanization, child welfare, and democracy, reformers pushed the schools to meet other perceived social needs arising from urbanization and industrialization. A coalition of unlikely allies, including businessmen, labor groups, social settlement workers, and moral reformers, all agreed in the early twentieth century, for very different reasons, that public schools should do more to instill the values and skills of work, including explicit job preparation. As chapter 5 will explore in more detail, these groups came together to promote vocational education first as a city project and then to lobby state and federal governments for aid. Educators were initially divided on the issue, some fearing that it would create a rival system to the public schools or would detract from traditional school goals. However, they came to embrace and even enthusiastically promote it as they began to recognize its value in holding children into high school and organizing them within it. Even more importantly, they embraced the assumption that undergirded it as their own: that one of the dominant aims of schooling was to socialize children into their adult roles, including that of worker.[14]

Vocational education was one aspect of a broader effort in the period to remake the curriculum for modern life. Schools also embraced other new school subjects and extracurricular activities and adjusted old ones in order to prepare youths for citizenship, leisure, health, avocational pursuits, gender roles, and family responsibilities. Professional educators played an important part in this conversation. They embraced and promoted these shifts, but they did so in dynamic conversation with groups outside the school rather than as an imposition of their own invention.[15]

As schools claimed greater responsibility for these reforms, professionals gained more authority over the implementation and character of innovations like kindergartens and vocational education. Yet they continued to work with voluntary associations to promote reforms and cultivate public support. In the post–World War I era, which historians have often described as a retreat from progressive reform, grassroots reformers and parents continued and in some cases even intensified their efforts. In New York City, for example, the Public Education Association increased rather than scaled back its activities in the 1920s; it sponsored new experiments in progressive education and social work and lobbied for higher teacher salaries and administrative reforms. Local school improvement clubs grew in size and often worked with school officials for education reform. The National Congress of Parents and Teachers, or PTA, expanded to over one million members during the 1920s. Administrators turned to these organizations in the interwar years to try to combat fiscal retrenchment efforts brought about first by soaring school costs and then economic depression through publicity and community outreach. Parent-teacher associations, one administrator noted, "secure agencies of publicity not always open to the superintendent" and "disseminate data and help to counteract unfavorable opinion, as well as build up constructive favorable sentiment." An Illinois school principal agreed that the groups "both reflect and mold public opinion" and "their most important function should be the education of the community regarding its own schools."[16]

In addition to organized groups outside of the school, family demand was an important driving force of these efforts, for the tremendous expansion in school enrollments and the popularization of particular reforms like manual training classes and kindergartens helped to propel their institutionalization. Families voted with their feet, sending their children to school in such large numbers that they threatened at times to overwhelm the capacity of the system. Voluntary attendance, extending into high school and fueling demand for its expansion, was a crucial driving force of both the expansion of the school and its reorganization, and it too reflected a more expansive set of expectations. This demand was shaped by a number of factors including growing cultural and emotional value of children and rising educational norms, the growing prosperity of the period that made extended schooling more feasible, and changes in the economy that pushed children out of the labor market and expanded white-collar jobs for which extended schooling and educational credentials were useful or necessary.[17]

Thus schooling was a popular reform target that intersected with a host of social concerns. The school itself, many argued, was an important social institution that could and should play a larger role in adjusting and integrating children into modern society. As chapter 5 will explore, it was the site of competing social goals and projects. An array of reformers looked to school reform to pursue specific social goals like protecting children, policing morals, expanding democracy, furthering socialist revolution, protecting adult labor, promoting economic development, or Americanizing immigrants. Schools were powerful sites for addressing these and other social issues because of their tremendous size and scope as a public project, because of their access to children, and because by nature they involved shaping behavior and transmitting values. In order for schools to be successful sites for other reforms and effective institutions of socialization, many reformers shared Rice's conviction that their organization and governance must be transformed.

Administrative Reform

Rice's critique of the interjection of politics into school management and his argument that professional expertise and merit should run the schools reflected a growing critique in the 1890s of school governance and city governance more generally. Urban governance, including schools, had been showing signs of strain from the rapid expansion of city populations and demand for new services. The organizational challenges of scale combined with rapid advances in technology created demand for new regulations and rationalization of services, including water, sewage, electricity, transportation, zoning, health, and sanitation. In schooling, the rapid increase in enrollments created chronic problems. City schools turned away children, crowded them into classrooms that topped sixty students, rented and erected temporary structures, held classrooms in hallways and basements, and resorted to shortened sessions. In 1881 alone, for example, New York City reportedly turned away nine thousand students and Philadelphia over twenty thousand because of lack of space.[18]

Large cities in the second half of the nineteenth century had devised new ways to manage these growing urban challenges, including ward-level and centralized political machines that provided services and distributed benefits. Although some historians have argued that they did a fairly good job of meeting these needs considering the scale of the challenges, a rising chorus of voices at the time charged that political machines, with their webs of patronage and their emphasis on loyalty over merit, created waste, inefficiencies, and at times gross mismanagement of city services. Elite liberal reformers in previous decades had mobilized attacks on partisan politics and supported reforms like civil service examinations. In the 1890s these "good government reformers" attracted new middle-class supporters and mobilized powerful drives to remake urban governance. In 1894 when the National Municipal League was founded, it joined eighty local organizations, 75 percent of which were formed within the past four years.[19]

The National Municipal League organized national conferences in the 1890s and sponsored a model program by the end of the decade that articulated a national theory of municipal government to help guide local efforts. At the heart of this program was an effort to make city government more efficient and nonpartisan by separating "politics"—meaning largely patronage—from the administration of city services. This required enhancing executive authority, clearly separating executive and legislative functions, and staffing city offices with professionals based on merit rather than loyalty, as well as enhancing the power of city government over its own affairs—home rule from state governments. To that end, they supported innovations like city managers, commission plans of government, municipal research bureaus, civil service reform, strong mayoral powers, and charter revisions that enhanced municipal autonomy.[20]

The public school system was a particularly strong bulwark of the patronage system because it often had the largest budget and workforce of any city activity. In most cities, schooling was decentralized; effective governance of schools was lodged in the wards. Into the early twentieth century in Pittsburgh, for example, the city had a central school board but its authority was weak. The real power in school governance was held by thirty-nine ward school boards, each with the authority to independently raise local taxes, choose and supervise teachers, and build and maintain schools. In Pittsburgh and other cities, positions in teaching, supervision, and janitor service as well as school contracts could be used to reward political loyalty, to provide jobs for the unemployed, or to line the pockets of ward politicians.[21]

Examples of the infiltration of politics, including sensational charges of corruption, rocked many cities in the 1890s and helped propel school administrative reforms. In San Francisco, teaching jobs reportedly sold for up to $200 each under Blind Boss Buckley's administration. Likewise, in St. Louis, newspapers catalogued a host of outrageous instances of school board members using their position for personal gain: Edwin O'Connor, a member of the Building Committee or "Contractor's Roost," as it came to be known, awarded all bids for supplying and installing school furnaces to his own firm, and the school board president, Charles Miller, rejected bids at market value for an attractive piece of school property and then sold it to his own firm for half its value. In 1891, eleven of the thirteen board members seeking reelection were contractors, including one member with no other visible means of support than his unpaid board of education position.[22]

In cities across the nation in the 1890s, good government reformers succeeded in mobilizing support for far-reaching changes in school governance as part of larger efforts to reform city government. Cleveland offered an early model in government reform, and school administration specifically, that was held up by other cities as an example and that influenced subsequent discussions. In 1892, Cleveland adopted the Federal Plan of city government after a public outcry against corruption and patronage. The new state-granted city charter made the mayor a strong chief executive, limited the city council to legislative powers, and created a centralized system of departmental administration with executives selected by the mayor. Many of the same principles were applied to school administration: the new charter centralized educational governance in the hands of a small, central school board elected at large rather than by ward, and it invested strong executive authority in the superintendent of public instruction and a school business director. The Cleveland Plan for school administration, as it came to be known, fulfilled four major precepts of good government: elimination of politics from selection of school boards, small school boards elected on a citywide rather than ward basis, complete separation of school administration from municipal business, and departmentalized administration of schools by strong executive officers.[23]

Good government movements, often bolstered by exposes of corruption, gained traction in other cities in the next two decades. Most embraced the fundamental principles articulated in Cleveland and then enshrined in the National Municipal League's model bill, but experimented with different means for achieving them. These experiments generated a national conversation about administration. In schooling, this conversation occurred in pages of popular monthlies but also in emerging professional spaces for educational leaders like *Educational Review* and at the annual meetings of the elite National Education Association. In these forums, long-reigning city superintendents like Aaron Gove of Denver and James Greenwood of Kansas

City discussed these experiments with college men like Harvard president Charles Eliot and Columbia's Nicholas Murray Butler as well as interested laymen like Rice and social gospel minister Washington Gladden.[24]

They converged on some shared principles by the early twentieth century that influenced the development of school administration as a field and helped to shape administrative reform, which was in most places a slow and accretive process. These principles included: a small, central school board of five to seven members elected at large in nonpartisan elections in order to raise the caliber of board members and reduce their tendency to micromanage school governance; a professional superintendent as chief executive with strong authority over business and instructional decisions and with salary, tenure, and experience to reflect this stature; clear delineation of responsibilities between legislative school boards and executive superintendents; and independence from city administration and financial control, including nonpartisan elections and independent authority over school funds and budgets. School administrative reformers turned to state legislatures for charter revisions and statutory authority to reorganize urban schools and to maintain independence from municipal government.[25]

These reforms, even where they were successful in the 1890s, did not go uncontested. In Chicago, for example, the organized opposition of teachers and labor succeeded in blocking administrative reform for nearly twenty years. Influenced by reforms elsewhere, Mayor Harrison appointed a commission, led by University of Chicago president William Rainey Harper, to study the schools. Consulting experts in other cities, the Harper Commission released a final report in 1899 that made the case for centralizing school administration and enhancing the power of the superintendent. The editors of the *Dial* judged it to be "one of the strongest educational documents that we have ever seen" and argued that it was "so enlightened, so far in advance of anything that has heretofore come within the range of practical possibilities" that it "cannot fail to impress all who examine it."[26]

Despite how good government reformers sung its praises, the recommendations were rejected by state legislators and by the voters of Chicago in four separate legislative battles over charter revision. The opposition to the bill was led by the well-organized and powerful Chicago Teachers' Federation, which, like teacher organizations in many other cities, objected generally to the centralization of administration in the hands of the superintendent and specifically to provisions relating to teachers that they feared would undermine seniority and security. They were joined in opposition by the Chicago Federation of Labor, which marshaled ethnic, working-class fears that the reorganization was an attack on the ward system in an attempt by elites to gain control of city politics. Studies of other cities have shown different mixes of supporters and opponents of administrative school reform; in Pittsburgh, for example, teachers allied with school administrators, and in San Francisco, large segments of the working class supported reform that was linked to anti-Catholicism. Still in other places, like St. Louis, administrative reforms enjoyed a fairly broad range of public support.[27]

Even when administrative change was enacted, it did not usually lead to the efficiency and harmony sought by reformers. Clashes between school boards and superintendents persisted, and school boards, much to the chagrin of superintendents, did not relinquish their control fully or quietly. So-called lay meddling persisted as one of the chief complaints of school superintendents. In a quintessential example, Baltimore centralized its schools under a new charter in 1898 and hired a professional superintendent of national stature who proceeded to enact major reforms and assert his new authority in ways that alienated many teachers. An opposition movement mobilized among teachers and community members that eventually succeeded in electing school board candidates to oust him and reverse his actions. Many other superintendents found that they still lacked much of the authority they had sought. Actual changes in their relationship with school boards were slow and uneven and had to be won in practice over time.[28]

Yet administrative reform advanced, piecemeal and contested, but unmistakably toward greater centralization and professionalization in the decades that followed the turn of the century. School boards centralized and reduced the number of members, changed the modes of selecting members, and delegated most administrative responsibilities to superintendents and their growing staffs. The job of superintendent, while never free from politics, rose in prominence as its responsibilities grew. On average, superintendents' tenure became more secure, their modes of selection shifted from election to appointment, and their average level of education, special training, and credentials rose.[29]

Furthermore, the organizational changes and increased responsibilities of the school propelled a whole host of specialists and new administrative positions in the schools, many of which developed their own professional identities and specialized associations, conferences, and journals. By 1931, for example, a survey of Chicago's city system found that it had twenty assistant, district, and deputy superintendents; 394 supervisors and principals; a legal department of fourteen members; a business manager with a large clerical staff; and a host of specialized offices including the Bureau of Child Study (for testing), Visiting-Teacher Service, Bureau of Vocational

Guidance, Bureau of Curriculum Study, Bureau of Census and Attendance, Bureau of Operative Engineering, Factory and Repair Division, and Office of Substitute-Teachers. The survey commission urged even further expansion, citing the need for a permanent research bureau, director of finance, and director of plant, among others.[30]

These changes shaped the ways in which communities interacted with their schools. Changes in the size and election of school boards shifted their composition, displacing neighborhood elites with metropolitan elites, men of citywide stature and considerable means. While the working class had never been well represented with seats on ward boards, the changes in school governance did affect how parents and communities could access the schools and influence school policies. The centralization of decision making and decrease of patronage cut off some avenues of influence and in some cases made it harder for minority groups or individual parents to influence school policy. Hungarian parents in a Chicago neighborhood where they were a majority might more easily convince ward trustees, one of whom might be a Hungarian entrepreneur, to offer Hungarian language instruction in their local school. In a new centralized system they were a minority that had to appeal to a central school board or bureaucracy composed of people of a different class and ethnic background. As Paul Peterson and others have shown, the school system had an institutional interest in accommodating groups with some clout and organization—like Poles in Chicago or Germans in St. Louis—but could usually ignore groups without political power, such as African Americans in most cities at the time.[31]

However, organizational changes also opened up new opportunities for some groups to influence school policy, particularly groups that were well organized and had citywide influence or visibility. Women's groups, for example, largely supported administrative reorganization because they could lobby central school officials more effectively than ward boards. In schooling and other city services, organized groups might have better access in a centralized nonpartisan bureaucracy than under the ward system. They also had a greater opportunity to promote major, systemwide changes. Citywide public school associations in places like New York and Philadelphia formed as interest groups to work for educational reform with centralizing school boards and bureaucracies rather than individual schools.[32]

Hence school government reform, born out of broader good government movements, changed the terrain of school politics and over time increased the power of professionals. It also provided impetus for the expansion of the university study of education, which helped to raise the stature and change the nature of education professionalization.

Defining a Field: The Search for Educational Expertise and Authority

In the 1890s when urban reformers were challenging the schools to assume new responsibilities and transforming their governance, they called for professionalism rather than politics to run the schools. At the time, the model of professional expertise was the experienced educator and administrator, like long-reigning city superintendents Aaron Gove of Denver and James Greenwood of Kansas City, who had made careers in education at a time when most men had retreated from the field or stayed only temporarily on the way to other pursuits. Their professional authority came from personal qualities of leadership, their reputations as liberally educated men, and their experience in education or business, rather than any specialized training or knowledge. They created professional identities by building decades-long careers in education and forging relationships in groups like the National Education Association with other city superintendents, normal school presidents, college presidents, and elite educators. A 1902 study of school administration enumerated the main qualifications for the job of city superintendent: good moral character, good physique, administrative ability, common sense, experience in school work, and a liberal education with some professional training. This last qualification—some professional training—reflected a fairly new qualification and was still vaguely defined. Yet within a few decades it would become a defining element of educational professionalism, as universities developed education programs that offered new training, credentials, and expertise to school leaders.[33]

Although some universities had experimented in haphazard ways with teacher training earlier, president James Angell of the University of Michigan appointed the first permanent chair of education in 1879. Angell was an institution builder and he saw the expansion of secondary education and growing demand for urban educational leadership as an opportunity to attract students, including women, whose college attendance would soar by the end of the century and could be partially contained within education departments. Furthermore, as part of its admissions process, the university was beginning to inspect and accredit secondary schools, and Angell could delegate this responsibility to the new education department. Finally and not insignificantly, Michigan was a public university with an obligation to supply teachers to the state's public schools, and Angell championed the university's foray into education as a public service. These same motivations—attracting students and resources, institution building, public service, and delegating institutional responsibilities for the public schools—

would also propel the establishment of small education departments at dozens of additional universities by 1900.[34]

President Angell appointed William H. Payne, former superintendent of Adrian, Michigan, schools, as chair of the science and art of teaching and charged him with defining it as a subject worthy of university study. This was a hard sell for many college faculty members. Some argued that teaching was an art that could not be taught; preparation for the elite domains of education, including high school and college teaching and city school administration, came from a general liberal education and natural talent. Other faculty argued that teaching was insufficiently intellectual and professional to warrant college study, shaped by their disdain for the practical-methods training and precollegiate studies at normal schools and their view of teaching as a highly feminized, low-paying, unstable vocation.[35]

Consequently, Payne was faced with defining the new department's aims and courses in ways that legitimated it as a university subject and differentiated it from low-status normal schools. To this end, Payne framed the goals of the new department as training educational leaders for higher positions of public school service, developing education as a profession, and promoting the study of educational sciences. He emphasized the historical, philosophical, and theoretical aspects of education and offered courses in the history of education, school supervision, comparative education systems, and principles of teaching and governance. Payne also rejected the idea that education was an art that could not be taught and worked to define principles that could define it as a science.[36]

Despite faculty resistance and the practical challenges of building a respectable field virtually out of scratch, educational offerings continued to expand within institutions and spread to others in the late nineteenth and early twentieth centuries. In 1900, twenty-four universities reported departments of education, often one- or two-person enterprises. By 1910 the number had grown to 156 universities, and by 1933, there were four hundred departments and an additional hundred schools of education in the United States. In large part, this expansion was fueled by insatiable student demand. Students flocked to education courses, including both full-time university students and school teachers who enrolled part-time in special evening, weekend, and summer classes. In some universities, education enrollments surpassed all other liberal arts studies and became a major supplier of graduate students. In 1907, for example, over one-third of undergraduate liberal arts students and half of graduate students at New York University registered for education courses. In part these programs were fueled by expanding public school opportunities in high school teaching, special subjects, and administration. At Harvard, for example, male high school teachers were the main clientele of education courses, and they used them to build professional ties and credentials in order to move out of teaching and into supervising, administrative, and leadership positions. Studies of other institutions similarly showed that university training provided important mobility from secondary school teaching to administration and college teaching.[37]

At leading universities, new professors of education worked to define education as a field of research and professional graduate training in order to elevate it in the eyes of their faculty colleagues and establish its authority in the world of practice. The most important of these efforts was at Columbia's Teachers College, although other elite programs developed at Chicago, Stanford, Harvard, Minnesota, and Wisconsin. Teachers College was established in 1887 and within a decade it had affiliated with Columbia University, shifted its focus to graduate programs, and attracted the largest education faculty in the nation—eighteen professors. By 1910, its faculty had quadrupled and included most of the largest names in education research, and it had become unquestionably the nation's premiere education program both in terms of intellectual production and the size and influence of its graduates. Other elite programs similarly shifted to graduate study, focusing on professional training in administration and school leadership or producing education researchers and scholars rather than teacher training. The 1924–25 course bulletin at University of Chicago, for example, listed twenty-one possible careers for its graduates, none of which included teaching below the college level.[38]

In order to develop graduate study, new education professors had to define education as a distinct field of research, scholarship, and expertise. In delineating a field, some professors followed Payne's efforts to develop theoretical aspects of education, including new courses and scholarship on the philosophical, historical, and normative dimensions of education. John Dewey, a philosopher at Chicago and Columbia, explored epistemology, pedagogy, and democracy through theory and the experimental practice of his Laboratory School. Paul Monroe of Teachers College and Ellwood Cubberley of Stanford sought to build a scientific history of education as a foundational part of the field. Other scholars drew inspiration from the emerging social sciences, including sociology, anthropology, and, above all, psychology. David Snedden of Teachers College, for example, applied and extended the insights of his mentor, sociologist Edward Ross, to explore the school's role in promoting social control and social efficiency. G. Stanley Hall, an early psychologist, developed "child study" as a scientific observation of biological and cultural child development, ideas that also influenced anthropology.[39]

Psychologist Edward Thorndike of Teachers College would prove to be the most influential, however, in shaping the field of education. Thorndike's research involved controlled experimentation of stimuli and response, which he used to challenge traditional theories of learning and to argue that educational science should be framed around empirical investigation of intelligence and mental processes, individual differences, and measurable outcomes. He developed and applied new tools of scientific measurement to the study of learning, including applied quantitative techniques and new tools to assess achievement and intelligence. Thorndike and his students developed the first standardized scales and measures to evaluate handwriting, composition, spelling, and math achievement, among other subjects, and he helped to spearhead the testing movement. By 1928, the director of the University of the Illinois Bureau of Educational Research estimated that over 1,300 tests had been developed and over thirty million were being administered annually, including both achievement tests and new IQ tests to measure general intelligence.[40]

In addition to his work measuring general intelligence and individual learning, Thorndike helped to develop and popularize new methods of statistical inquiry to evaluate schools themselves. In 1907 he studied school-leaving, or "elimination," using attendance statistics as an index of how successful schools were at holding pupils during and after the compulsory attendance ages. Other scholars saw the possibilities in these statistical measures and built upon them. George Strayer of Teachers College trained with Thorndike and went on to develop a host of measurement techniques for school surveying, including building scorecards. Leonard Ayres of the Russell Sage Foundation developed age-grade analysis to analyze and expose maladjustment in the schools, and he produced rankings of "educational efficiency" based on ten quantifiable measures. These and similar new measurement techniques became key components of school surveying and educational administration, a field in which Ayres and Strayer became towering figures.[41]

Quantitative analysis—or measurement, as education scholars called it—offered important benefits for education research and professional development. As Leonard Ayres noted, measurement's emphasis on objective investigation over subjective generalization, proved that "education is emerging from among the vocations and taking its place among the professions." Numbers, as many scholars have shown, often have a peculiar kind of validity as scientific truth and consequently appealed to education scholars and administrators as a way to bolster their authority as experts. University of Wisconsin professor Edward Elliott noted that measurement helped to "create a new kind of confidence on the part of the public in the work of the public schools." Relatedly, measurement had the power to render many aspects of education as knowable and comparable in new ways. Boston superintendent Stratton Brooks observed that "the school administrator is confronted with a very difficult situation, in that his cost is measurable and his product is not measurable." New quantitative measures of student learning and school quality helped to measure that product, to demonstrate results and "prove" the value of schools to budget-conscious school boards and the public.[42]

Yet as scholars have also shown, quantification is a social process that shapes how one understands, categorizes, and values things. As the next section will show, quantification in school surveying and administration had the unintended effect of privileging some values over others and of reorienting the field of education along empirical lines. Education became the science of tabulating, measuring, comparing, and analyzing education practice as it existed, moving away from questions of value to accept and propagate existing practices.[43]

Consequently measurement catapulted to the center of the emerging science of education by 1910, shaping not only educational research and literature but also professional programs for training educational leaders. While there were occasional voices of caution, university programs of school administration and professionals in the field made substantial use of the new techniques of measurement and its findings to identify and sanction best practices and develop models and norms for school administration programs. These programs grew in size and prestige by the 1920s because of their post-baccalaureate status, purportedly scientific approach, and preparation of the top of the professional hierarchy in education. University education schools and departments responded to and intensified professional specialization, developing new programs to train and credential specialists in fields like attendance, vocational guidance, rural education, and special subjects like domestic science and the arts. Elite institutions like Teachers College also trained educational researchers, such as statisticians and testing experts, to staff city, state, federal, and foundation research bureaus and to teach education at colleges and normal schools. As administrative programs expanded and professional training in education slowly became the norm for city superintendents and administrators, it increasingly became a prerequisite for the job. Many cities and states developed special certificates for administrators and made them mandatory after World War I.[44]

By defining education as a specialized field of knowledge and legitimating it in the university context, elite education programs also helped to extend the university's role in teacher education and advance teacher professionalization. While elite programs focused on research and leadership training, hundreds of colleges and universities across the nation developed teacher education programs that benefited from education's new prestige, literature, and institutional support. Teachers flocked to full-time, evening, and summer courses to advance their careers and elevate teaching as a profession. They were steadily rewarded for this investment, as salaries became increasingly tied to level of education and training in the postwar era. City teachers joined local, state, and national professional associations, including the NEA, which welcomed them in large numbers and encouraged their participation in new ways during and after World War I. They worked collectively to improve salary, benefits, and tenure, as well as supported educational reforms more generally. Many city teachers developed strong professional identities and made lifelong careers in education.[45]

However, teacher professionalization was still on the whole a weak and uncertain project. While city teachers were the most elite, the profession as a whole was still characterized by relatively high rates of turnover and by insecurity, low salaries, and low status. Teaching remained a feminized semiprofession, much like social work and nursing, and it was unable to claim the authority, expertise, and autonomy required to convincingly assert practitioners as professionals. Teachers were also at odds with superintendents and administrators whose own professional identity was shaped in large part by their superiority over teachers, both in terms of expert authority and in their actual place in the employment hierarchy.

School administrators and other educational experts did recognize, however, that their own professional authority, like it or not, was inextricably tied with teachers, and they invited them into the National Education Association and other professional organizations. Teacher professionalism held benefits for administrators; it elevated the status and practice of education as a whole, provided allies in reform efforts and public relations, and undermined unionization. Consequently, they supported efforts to raise the level of education, salaries, and benefits of teachers and encouraged them to identify as education professionals, but made clear that they were to be junior and largely silent partners in the professional enterprise.[46]

The School Survey: The Mutual Shaping of Urban Schools and Expertise

Urban school reform was an important catalyst and laboratory for the development of education science. This education science helped to further urban school reform by enhancing the expertise of professionals, legitimating certain reforms, and helping to spread them. This mutual shaping of urban schools and professionalization can be seen in the development and application of the school survey in the 1910s and 1920s. Through the school survey, educational experts developed and applied new scientific tools and came into close contact with practice in the schools. Expert-conducted school surveys served both important field-building purposes and also influenced urban school reform across the nation.

The school survey as tool of education research and local reform began in 1910 when the school board of Boise invited renowned Indianapolis superintendent Calvin Kendall to inspect the city's schools and make recommendations for their improvement. While local investigation of schools was nothing new, what marked Boise and subsequent surveys as distinct was the ways in which they brought in outside experts and employed scientific research methods. The surveys drew inspiration from social survey methods in sociology but rapidly developed a distinctive set of educational measurements, categories, and methods. Kendall's survey, compared to two more scientific ones the following year in New Jersey, was fairly simple. He visited the city's schools for a week, during which time he observed classrooms, examined school records, and interviewed school administrators. In his final report, Kendall evaluated five factors that he viewed as indicators of a good school system: the school plant, the teacher, the course of study, the organization of the schools, and the attitude of the community. Based on his observations, he found each of these satisfactory in Boise and praised the city's schools. He recommended minor enhancements to the existing program rather than any fundamental changes, including, among other things, the expansion of playground facilities, manual training, and new programs of medical inspection and physical training. Surveyors frequently suggested these new extensions of the school promoted by grassroots reformers.[47]

Subsequent surveyors similarly had to define which factors were crucial for successful schools, yet they shifted from the subjective opinions of experienced superintendents like Kendall to what they deemed a more objective and scientific basis, including new quantitative comparisons. Two surveys in New Jersey the following year pioneered some of these new techniques and assumptions and became widely emulated models. In 1911, Harvard education professor Paul Hanus investigated the Montclair schools. In addition to the interviews and observations that Kendall had used, Hanus turned to statistics to evaluate the school, including quantitative comparisons of school data with other cities and an age-grade distribution analysis to investigate school retardation. Later that year, Yale education professor Ernest Moore conducted a ten-week study of the "educational efficiency" of the East Orange schools. In addition to statistical comparisons with other cities and a study of retardation, Moore introduced achievement tests as measures of school efficiency. Moore asked students to solve four basic math problems and write a composition and he evaluated the results himself, concluding that the students were fine at math, good spellers, and needed work on handwriting form. Subsequent surveys would systematically deploy pupil testing, although they turned to the rapidly proliferating standardized achievement tests designed by Thorndike and his students in order to get more objective and comparable scores. While rudimentary, the New Jersey surveys introduced new statistical and comparative techniques and charted out key ways to define and measure educational efficiency that would be refined by other experts.[48]

School surveying developed rapidly in the next two decades as a research conversation. Innovations introduced into one survey were adopted and expanded in others, and in the process of experimentation new forms of evaluation were created and tested. Surveying was adopted as a technique to study state systems, universities, and county school systems, although city surveys remained the most dominant subject. Surveys expanded from one-man enterprises into team efforts, often engaging expert consultants from several universities and foundations as well as local professionals and support staff. For example, the 1915 survey of Cleveland led by Leonard Ayres utilized twenty-two education experts, and George Strayer's 1920 Baltimore survey employed 110 people. Foundations like the Russell Sage, General Education Board, and Carnegie Corporation developed survey divisions because they recognized their potential to shape education policy and elevate standards. The United States Bureau of Education, state departments of education, and municipal research bureaus also performed school surveys, and large-city school systems developed their own self-study methods over time. However it was university programs of education that supplied the largest number of experts to conduct school surveys. Leading education schools developed special surveying departments. The largest and most influential was Teachers College's Division of Field Studies established by George Strayer in 1921, which trained an entire generation of surveyors. In 1928 alone, eleven of the twelve major surveys were led by men who had been trained in the division, and the staffs of nearly all of the surveys were populated by Teachers College graduates.[49]

In addition to fostering a research conversation across space and diffusing innovations, school surveys performed essential education field-building functions. To start, they provided a place to apply and refine educational research and put it in the service of school administration. Surveys gave a boost to the testing movement, for example, and developed new ways to utilize the tests for administrative purposes. In the 1915 survey of Cleveland, psychologist Charles Judd of the University of Chicago supervised a massive pupil-testing project with a team of specialists and produced a separate volume on achievement testing. Judd analyzed the test results in novel ways. He not only used the standardized tests to compare the aggregate results against other cities as others had done, but he also compared the work of individual schools, grades, and classrooms within the system and used the results to diagnose weak spots in instruction and curriculum. Silent-reading tests showed wide variation in student performance that he attributed to teachers, and Judd recommended stronger instructional supervision for weak teachers in these areas. Testing was not the only area of educational research to benefit from application in surveys: curriculum research, statistical tools like age-grade analysis, and psychological experiments in learning and adjustment, among others, were first refined in surveys and introduced to local school administrators.[50]

In addition to serving as sites where educational research could be applied, surveying helped to stimulate new research tools and administrative practices that exerted a standardizing influence. Finding tremendous heterogeneity of practice, surveyors developed scales and measures to evaluate business practices and then constructed standards to make them more efficient, standardized, transparent, and comparable. For example, school surveys began to evaluate the quality of the physical plant around 1913. They elaborated standards for things like classroom lighting and temperature, the size of classrooms and school lots, the number of toilets, and the ratio of window to floor space. In his 1916 study of Framingham (MA), George Strayer collected the standards that had been developing in different surveys and consulted with other experts to design a building scorecard. On the basis of a thousand-point scale, it assigned points for meeting specific criteria in categories like design, equipment, sanitation, and ventilation. Scores were aggregated to classify a building as excellent, satisfactory, unsatisfactory, or obsolete. Building scorecards were used in nearly all later surveys, and Strayer published the scorecard so that researchers and school systems could use them for self-study. The scorecards helped to create common categories and standards for school construction that were adopted by city school officials throughout the nation and later by state school building codes. They could also provide leverage for local reformers to press for new school construction by offering objective, expert opinion that school buildings were substandard. In this and other areas, surveyors created methods, and sometimes marketed blank forms, that helped to standardize business practices and to render school data more readily comparable across space, including pupil record cards and classification schemes, standardized accounting and budgeting procedures, and uniform statistical reporting forms.[51]

Educational surveys also helped experts to identify, sanction, and diffuse best practices that developed out of urban school experimentations and grassroots efforts. In his 1914 study of Portland (OR), Ellwood Cubberley devoted an entire chapter to health work, one of the first to give it such attention; he recommended that the system transform its basic medical inspection into a full health program that would include physical education, hygiene classes, supervised playgrounds, school meals, and the creation of special classes for defective students like the mentally slow and tubercular. He defined this ideal health program by compiling examples from new experiments in several cities, many of which were sponsored by clubwomen and other groups outside the school. In subsequent surveys, Cubberley and other surveyors would systematically investigate city schools' health work, producing a body of research about innovative practices and converging on a set of recommendations, many of which would be adopted after World War I when health moved to the forefront of public debate. Health policy was only one of many such efforts. Educational survey experts converged on best practices and principles in administrative organization, business administration, school extensions, and curricular aims and offerings, among other things, drawn from examples they saw when they investigated schools.[52]

In addition, school surveys helped to build up the power, prestige, and influence of major education programs like Teachers College and to strengthen professional networks. Surveying brought revenue and visibility to schools of education and helped to reinforce personal and professional relationships between universities and practitioners in the schools. In three New Jersey cities that invited George Strayer to survey, one study found that all three superintendents were Teachers College alumni and at least two of them had worked closely with Strayer, participated in the alumni association, and sponsored Teachers College extension courses in their communities. Indeed, power brokers like George Strayer or "Dad" Cubberley at Stanford maintained close ties with their graduates to the mutual benefit of both: they intervened at key points to advance their students' careers and in return were invited to consult. One student recalled of his mentor Strayer that "when you became his student and proved yourself he took a major interest in your career from then on." At the annual Department of Superintendence meetings, "he held court in the lobby of the main hotel" and "all of his students of former years at the meeting would seek a chance to report to him and he would be meeting with Boards of Education and other potential employers."[53]

At the same time, surveying cemented ties between researchers themselves. Surveys often involved large staffs drawn from several universities nationwide as well as local experts. The Cleveland survey in 1915, for example, brought together experts from the Russell Sage Foundation, General Education Board, University of Chicago, University of Iowa, Harvard University, University of Pennsylvania, and New Jersey State Department of Public Instruction. David Tyack has described this "interlocking directorate" of university education scholars, foundation leadership, and school administrators who developed personal and professional ties through professional associations, alumni networks, conferences, and consulting in the schools. Surveying was a crucial way that education professors maintained ties with their graduates, built networks with other researchers and institutions including grant-giving foundations, and elevated the reputations of themselves and their universities. This network also helps to explain the rapid convergence on norms and techniques that characterized surveys and other educational research.[54]

In addition to the field- and institution-building functions that surveys performed, they also shaped local practice. In the vast majority of cases, school surveys were initiated by superintendents or school boards to shape public opinion, either to urge reform or to legitimate controversial efforts already undertaken. In Portland (OR) in 1923, for example, the school board invited the U.S. Bureau of Education to conduct a building survey after voters rejected a bond measure to fund new school buildings. The survey used building scorecards and other surveying techniques to make the case that new school buildings were necessary, and voters responded by approving the bond issue at the next election. Likewise, a 1921 survey in Wilmington, Delaware, convinced wary voters to support administrative reorganization, including elimination of ward-based elections and an expansion of the superintendent's powers. These reforms had been discussed nationally for decades and were hardly surprising recommendations, yet it took outside experts to shine the light on Wilmington's practices for enough reform sentiment to materialize locally. In his 1929 study of city school surveys, Hollis Caswell found that an overwhelming majority of superintendents reported that the surveys had contributed directly or indirectly to important local school reforms, including, in a large number of cases, building programs, testing, health work, and self-study.[55]

In other cases, school surveys could be used to legitimate professional leadership and authority in the schools and sanction reforms already undertaken. In Hackensack, New Jersey, for example, the professional superintendent, trained at Teachers College by Strayer, instituted controversial changes in the curriculum that prompted a failed petition to unseat him and voters to reject his recommendation for a new school building. With the support of the school board, he invited Strayer and his graduate students to survey the city's schools in 1921, and the resulting report endorsed his reforms and emphasized the need for new buildings. The survey seemed to quiet opposition to the superintendent, and voters approved a new schoolhouse.[56]

Professional educators and educational experts also recognized the value in local school surveys in what they began to call "public relations" and began to build public outreach into their efforts to shape public opinion and build support for school reforms. In Butte (MT) in 1915, Strayer and the commission presented their findings to groups like the Silver Bow Trades and Labor Council, the teachers union, the chamber of commerce, women's clubs, and the PTA. In Baltimore in 1920, surveyors published one version of the conclusions for the public and another for experts. The public relations aspect of school surveying became increasingly important in the 1920s and 1930s when movements for retrenchment threatened ambitious school-building programs and the recently gained expansions of school programs. School administrators and surveyors reached out to local groups to garner support for recommended reforms or legitimate ones already undertaken.[57]

As these examples suggest, school surveying was a powerful tool of expansion. While at times surveyors adopted the language of efficiency and even promised cost-conscious school boards they could bring efficiencies, expert surveys almost always promoted expansion and not retrenchment. A 1915–16 survey in Boston by Strayer and Ayres was initiated by the city mayor and finance committee to investigate escalating costs and recommend economies. However, the surveyors used statistical data to argue that the city could afford the high costs and recommended even further expenditures including new junior high schools. Similarly, the Oakland city school board invited Ellwood Cubberley "to investigate the reasons for the increased expense and to determine if it were possible to conduct the schools more economically without loss of efficiency." Cubberley validated the new reforms, arguing that the city had previously been backward, and marshaled statistical evidence to show that the city was not overspending on schools relative to similar cities. Oakland and Boston were told to shoulder school costs because they were not comparatively too high, while a whole host of other cities were chastised for underspending compared to their neighbors. Surveys helped to render different aspects of schooling visible and comparable through statistics in new ways that could foster expansion. For cities that regarded themselves as educationally progressive, statistics could reveal areas where they lagged behind and stimulate reform by tapping into local pride, self-image, and rivalry.[58]

As these examples also suggest, surveying and the professional norms and standards they helped to define and promote in local reform also shaped local school practice in more subtle ways. Quantification and educational measurement not only invested expert recommendations with greater scientific and objective authority but also subtly reshaped over time some of the ways that people conceptualized school success. For example, the instructional effectiveness of the school—how well it taught children—was arguably the most important aspect of schooling and yet it was the most difficult to define and know. Surveyors converged on some basic measures: pupil testing; statistical measures of the student population to determine how well schools held children and moved them through the grades; the number and kinds of pupil adjustments available; and the quality of the teaching staff as measured in almost wholly quantitative terms such as the number of years of training and experience. However, these contained some unstated and potentially problematic assumptions, including the assumption that the level of training of a teacher translated into effective teaching or that the key to good instruction was differentiation. They also privileged the things they could easily count over the things they couldn't, and they rarely gave weight to less-quantifiable values like the culture of the school, its social impact, the satisfaction of the community, or the moral influence of the teacher. The 1918 survey of Gary's innovative curriculum and school organization, for example, applied extensive pupil testing and traditional survey tools to conclude that the city's ambitious efforts had been largely a failure. While there may well have been weaknesses in Gary's "work-study-play" plan and its social aims, surveyors nonetheless failed to evaluate how well it achieved these goals. They evaluated it based on what they could measure and ignored what they could not.[59]

In another example, surveys lavished incredible attention on school building scorecards and forecasting and promoted massive new school building programs. In the 1916 Salt Lake City survey, for example, Ellwood Cubberley deemed thirty of the thirty-four school buildings to be unsatisfactory, and other surveys, while not as critical, usually recommended considerable investment in school plant. The scorecard was quantification at its purest, and yet there was no effort to evaluate the criteria—was the color scheme of a high school classroom really as important as the condition of its roof (five points each) and more important than a fire alarm system (four points)? Furthermore, there was no effort to evaluate what priority buildings should have on educational spending. Nancy Adelman argues that in the three New Jersey communities she studied, surveys resulted in expensive building programs, which at least in one case and perhaps all three were unnecessary and may have done more harm than good by siphoning off limited resources. Buildings and other easily measurable and comparable metrics like per-pupil spending, teacher salaries, and attendance rates became over time some of the primary ways that school professionals and reformers talked about school improvement. Surveying and quantification thus helped to measure and compare schools in new ways that helped to drive reform and standardization, but they also shaped and at times distorted that conversation in ways that were rarely acknowledged.[60]

*

Thus, urban schooling and the professional project were mutually shaping and reinforcing developments in the early twentieth century. Urban school reform, which restructured governance to elevate professional leadership and rapidly expanded to encompass a whole host of new responsibilities and services, provided an important impetus and audience for new education expertise and credentialed professionals. It helped to spur and sustain the growth of university programs of education and prompt the development of scholarly study and research of education. Urban school systems served as laboratories for the emerging science of education and the field of school administration, its leading professional program, by providing sites where new scientific measurement techniques could be applied, tested, and refined. It also produced a mountain of data on school practices and provided the models and innovations that were studied and sanctioned by emerging experts. Consequently urban school practices profoundly shaped the increasingly empirical and measurement-oriented field of education. Educational expertise was grounded in analyzing and evaluating—in a scientific and quantifiable way—existing practices and thus moved away from considerations of educational values, goals, and philosophy.

Professionalization and educational expertise in turn enhanced the authority of urban school leaders and helped to propel and shape local reform. The superintendent became a more powerful executive in the school system due to structural reforms, including the centralization and bureaucratization of school governance, and his enhanced professional stature and expertise. However, professional authority was never as autonomous or uncontested as professionals may have liked. Lay meddling persisted in the form of challenges by school boards and parents and activism by community groups on a wide array of school policies. Schools continued to rely on the consent and support of the community through school board elections and bond issues, necessitating surveys and other tools of public relations to shape public opinion.

While professional authority was not unassailable, it was a powerful force of standardization. Education professionals helped to shape and standardize schooling through norms they sanctioned, networks they created, and conversations they engaged. For example, kindergartens, school extensions, and vocational education all originated in demands from groups outside the school. Yet in fairly short order, educational experts, including university professors and professionals in the school, made each of these reforms their own and helped deepen and expand them. As professionals were charged with implementation, they also increasingly adopted their values and practices as part of their professional identity and consistent with what made a successful school. They supported and urged extension of these programs in school surveys, education courses, and professional literature and infused new measurement techniques and professional language to justify them. Ernest Moore's 1913 survey of New York City and Ellwood Cubberley's 1914 study of Portland, for example, both praised school extensions and kindergartens supported by clubwomen, urged the cities under study to do more, and pressed others to emulate them.[61]

Urban school reform was the inspiration and laboratory for professional developments, and consequently urban examples had a large impact on education discussion nationally and on state government policy over time. The national conversation on the new education was heavily shaped by city school reformers' sense of the challenges of modern, urban life. In many ways, large cities were a reference point for education reform everywhere else. Innovations in large cities were adopted by smaller cities and towns, although sometimes the latter had more in common with cash-strapped and sparsely populated rural schools than they did with metropolises. State legislatures and departments of education used city school innovations to set goals and standards for schooling elsewhere at the same time that they continued to encourage further city experimentation.

While urban schools served as important impetus for national reform, school reform outside of the cities was not simply urban schooling writ large. The experience of schooling and school reform in small towns, villages, and the countryside—where the majority of children were educated through much of the period—was also shaped by a distinctive set of rural concerns and conditions. Furthermore, rural schooling, as the next two chapters will explore, profoundly shaped the development of state policies and national patterns. Our urban-focused narratives of education reform in the period have consequently told only part of the story.

TWO ✳ *The Rural School Problem and the Complexities of National Reform*

"The most important educational problem before America today is the rural school problem," announced Minnesota state superintendent J. W. Olsen to the National Education Association (NEA) in 1902. According to Olsen, "rural-school advancement has not kept pace with the wonderful progress in our city schools," which he argued was "due to the natural ultra-conservatism of our rural population, to the abandonment for the city and the west of farms in the eastern states, and to conditions inherent in the isolated one-room schoolhouse itself." These conditions included low-quality teachers, the lack of age grading and organization, and an environment that "is too narrow to broaden the intellectual horizon of the pupil."[1] As city schools expanded their aims and activities to offer a new education for modern life, educators like Olsen as well as many farmers' advocates began to worry that rural children were being left behind. Olsen's diagnosis of the "rural school problem"—the disparity between rural and urban schools—came at a moment when a number of commentators across the Atlantic were starting to worry about the impact of urbanization and industrialization on the countryside and its implications for the economic progress and moral strength of the nation.

What began as a sporadic set of critiques of rural schools and concerns about the countryside developed by the second decade of the twentieth century into a nationwide movement for rural school reform. A 1908 National Country Life Commission appointed by President Theodore Roosevelt drew together a host of groups interested in the problem of rural life and helped to articulate an agenda for reform that centered on strengthening rural social institutions, including the rural school. In the decades that followed, reformers mobilized at local, state, and national levels to redirect rural schools, both as community institutions and sites of modern, rural-focused instruction. They worked to improve school buildings, increase school support and term length, expand the rural focus and activities of the school, make the school a social center, improve teaching and supervision, and increase the efficiency of rural school administration. In doing so, they borrowed ideas from city schooling, like consolidation and administrative reorganization, and they drew from experiments in rural communities to foster a national conversation about rural schooling. They worked to strengthen professional leadership and supervision in the countryside while mobilizing community support for and participation in rural school reforms like consolidation, fundraising, and agricultural clubs and instruction. At the heart of the project of rural school reform was an effort to define a new vision of modern rural society and individuals.

City schooling played an important role in conceptualizing a rural school problem and generating reform ideas; however, rural school reform was not simply the result of urban models imposed on the country. Historical accounts have tended to overstate the goal and success of administrative centralization in rural school reform, one scholar going so far as to claim that by 1921, "earmarks of a bureaucratic and centralized administration worthy of any large corporation were to be found" throughout the countryside. They have tended to describe rural school reform as a story of centralizing, bureaucratic reformers and education professionals who tried to seize control away from communities and impose their authority.[2]

As a framework for understanding rural school reform, however, centralization and bureaucracy have limited explanatory power. Unlike the city that comprised a single school district, local control in the countryside was fractured among many legal jurisdictions, each invested with its own corporate authority. State legislatures were wary of imposing policies without rural support because of the political leverage of rural districts and strong traditions of local district control and neighborhood autonomy. Education professionals in the countryside had much weaker social authority, actual coercive power, formal training, and limited staffs that made bureaucratic centralization an unrealistic goal. Furthermore, given the aims of many country life reformers to strengthen rural community, community consent and participation was more than a strategic necessity or obstacle to be overcome, but a major reform goal.

This chapter explores the development of a nationwide movement for rural school reform as part of a larger effort to address the crisis of country life in an industrializing, urbanizing nation. It explores how rural school reforms developed and diffused within and between states not through bureaucratization and professional imposition but through a more complex negotiation of lay and professional actors working at different levels in the federalist system. Reforms were developed from both the bottom up and top down, and they traveled across space through the dynamic interplay of local lay reformers, local professional leaders, state government officials, and self-consciously national actors like philanthropies and federal agencies. Simple accounts of centralization versus decentralization have obscured an important array of rural school reforms and the importance of decentralization for developing and diffusing these reforms. Local control was not an obstacle to overcome for rural school reform, but a powerful site of energy and innovation that helped to drive it.[3]

Rural schooling was not simply a template on which urban reforms were written, but also made important, unique contributions to the transformation of education in the period. It prompted the most searing discussions of state and national responsibility for education and the role of local control in a modern school system, raising issues about local district weakness and compatibility with the new education that progressive cities did not raise. Rural school reform was a major impetus for the growth of the state government's role in education and a source of inspiration for the governance that emerged, as this chapter begins to explore and the next one analyzes in greater depth. Furthermore, rural schools educated roughly half the nation's children in the period—and in some states considerably more than half—making it important for its very size and scope, a major component of the national story of American education, not a minor aside.

Defining the Rural School Problem

Although it was increasingly defined as a problem by the early twentieth century, the one-room rural school district was a celebrated institution throughout the nineteenth century, a powerful symbol of Americans' relentless mobility, community building, and local democracy. The district system developed out of the New England town system as settlers moved away from town centers and established their own independent schools. Legally recognizing what was already happening in practice, the Massachusetts legislature in 1789 authorized settlers to establish school districts through popular vote and invested each district with corporate powers to elect trustees, define its territory, tax and bond residents, contract with teachers and suppliers, and make all reasonable rules to govern the school. Annually elected trustees on the school board were responsible for the maintenance of the school throughout the year, but the most important school decisions were made directly by the community at the annual school meeting, where they set the tax rate, determined term length, awarded contracts, selected the teacher, and discussed any changes to the course of study.

Communities maintained nearly absolute control over all aspects of schooling, and parental input and community surveillance shaped schools' character and values. School districts both reflected and helped to define community. Voters could establish new school districts and redraw boundary lines, which they did to maintain or shift ethnic, religious, or political majorities, to claim valuable pieces of taxable property, or to delineate a new rural community as settlers dispersed. In the late nineteenth century, some states began to experiment with township trustees, county superintendents, and other kinds of officials to perform clerical functions like collecting information and distributing school funds. In most cases, however, their authority was weak and their functions limited. Districts managed their own schools. According to many observers, the school district, the smallest unit of self-government in the United States, reflected the strengths of American democracy: it was highly local and participatory, it was community oriented, and it expanded access to schooling far across the frontier. Fewer commented on how it also mirrored its weaknesses, namely the privileging of the majority over the minority in ways that were often exclusionary and that could disregard the rights of minorities. African Americans, for example, were usually marginalized from white majorities' vision of citizenship and excluded from public schools in both the North and South before the Civil War.[4]

The district system was adopted throughout New England and carried westward with settlers until it became the basis of public school control in most Northern states and territories, which first permitted, and over time increasingly required, that localities establish schools. In the South, public common schooling made few inroads in the countryside before Reconstruction, when African Americans, federal officials, Northern missionaries, and Republican Southern legislatures built schools and school systems. Reconstruction state constitutions and statutes provided a legal framework for public funding and control of schools, which unleashed the energies of communities, often led by African Americans eager for education. When Democrats returned to power in state legislatures, they scaled back support for public schools, including statutory and constitutional limitations to district control and taxation, which hampered rural school development by making it reliant on paltry sums from the state or the private donations of the community. The poverty of the region, white ambivalence about public schooling, and a widespread hostility to black education severely constrained public school development in the rural South until the end of the century when a powerful movement for white school modernization swept the region, tied to the rising tide of white supremacy.[5]

While the extreme decentralization of the district system in the North was seen by many Americans as a source of its strength, some worried that it created weak schools. In his 1856 report, Indiana state superintendent Caleb

Mills argued that "small districts insure small and ill-furnished structures, short terms, incompetent teachers and corresponding instruction, lifeless schools and unawakened intellects, general apathy and partial disgust at the whole system." Educators like Horace Mann similarly urged the abolition of small one-room school districts and their reintegration into town school systems, arguing that they were expensive schools for the meager results they produced. In the late nineteenth century, New England state legislatures, faced with declining rural populations, permitted and then required the abolition of small outlying districts and their reincorporation into town school systems.[6]

The experiments in New England garnered increasing attention by other state superintendents and the National Education Association (NEA) around the turn of the century, as concerns about declining rural population spread westward. Superintendents in New York, Indiana, Nebraska, and a host of other states complained about schools of twenty, ten, and even five students. In 1894, the New York state superintendent, for example, reported nearly 7,500 schools with fewer than twenty students in average daily attendance, nearly half of those with fewer than ten students. The Ohio state superintendent argued to the NEA in 1901 that these statistics "simply confirm the claim that the city is being developed, in a measure, at the sacrifice of the rural community, the hamlet, and the village."[7]

In 1895, at the urging of Iowa state superintendent Henry Sabin, the NEA appointed a Committee of Twelve on Rural Schools to investigate. The final report two years later articulated these concerns about the small rural school and argued that it had structural limitations that made it inescapably weak: its isolation, small tax base, and small student population kept its quality low. These schools were forced to hire cheap, untrained, inexperienced teachers and to offer only rudimentary instruction, with none of the attention to health, citizenship, and other emerging subjects of the new education. Drawing from the experience of New England states and the emerging models of urban school administrative reform, the Committee of Twelve recommended that students of small schools be transported to larger ones and that larger units of school administration replace the district when feasible. These changes, it argued, "would conduce to effectiveness and simplicity of organization; to economy in the use and distribution of funds; to the equalization of the burdens of taxation; and to a system of supervision which would produce better results from the instruction given in the rural schools." According to the report, rural communities should be responsible for providing a minimum level of support for their schools, but it recognized that revenue from outside of the community might be necessary. Country children, it argued, must "have all the opportunities of education and culture that the city affords" and this may require county or state taxation, for "wealth is massed in our populous centers." These recommendations—school consolidation, district reorganization, and financial support—would become central school reform goals of rural reformers, especially professional educators, by World War I.[8]

In addition to laying out some of the chief professional recommendations for rural school reform, the Committee of Twelve report hinted at a concern that moved to the center of discussion in the early twentieth century: the growing disparity between urban and rural schools. For the urban-oriented NEA, the real problem with small rural schools was that they offered rudimentary instruction at a moment when the goals of education were expanding and city schools were modernizing.

Educators were not the only ones concerned that rural schools were being left behind. In 1905 the *Prairie Farmer* declared that "the country girl and boy have as good a right to the privileges and advantages of the best schools equal with their city bred cousins." The Wisconsin-based *Hoard's Dairyman* decried the "cheap miserable character" of rural schools, and others noted disparities in things like term length, teacher training and experience, and spending per pupil.[9]

Farm journals and rural residents often singled out two things for particular complaint: the lack of practical, rural-focused instruction and the lack of high school opportunities in the countryside. As early as the 1870s, the National Grange argued for agricultural education in rural schools. By the early twentieth century it was joined by farmers' institutes, agricultural colleges, farm journals, and groups like the Farmers Union. *Prairie Farmer* reported on the "general awakening all over the land to the importance of interesting the boys and girls of the rural district in agricultural education" and called common schools to "Teach Agriculture Now." In addition to the practical knowledge and energy it would give to the schools, supporters argued that agriculture would instill pride in the country and show children "there is opportunity on the farm for the exercise of brain as well as brawn." Many critiqued the "away-from-the-farm influence of rural education," arguing that the town-focused curriculum in rural schools "bears no relation to the life they are to lead, but actually attracts them towards a town career." Rural education should be rural focused and give children appreciation and practical instruction for life on the farm. Furthermore, as high schools became increasingly available in towns and cities throughout the North, many rural residents worried that this provided another lure for farmers to move to towns or to send their children to board there for schooling, which one critic warned "not only unfits him for his mode of life; it gives him contempt for it." Children should not have to leave the farm for the same educational opportunities that were becoming widely available in cities and towns.[10]

Many of the discussions about rural education emphasized the need to "keep the boy on the farm" or stem the "drift to the city," a demographic shift that troubled many observers in the United States and in industrializing nations across the Atlantic. They worried rural depopulation would weaken agricultural production that was necessary to feed growing city populations and fuel manufacturing and trade, as well as undermine rural society. It was these concerns about the impact of industrialization and urbanization on rural life and its consequences for the nation that prompted President Theodore Roosevelt to appoint a Country Life Commission (CLC) in 1908. Influenced by advisors like Gifford Pinchot and Liberty Hyde Bailey, both of whom he appointed to the commission, Roosevelt saw the country-life problem as part of the larger issue of conservation, including conservation of the environment, the nation, and the race. Roosevelt explained in the preface to the CLC report that the nation relied on the country "to continue to feed and clothe the hungry nations; to supply the city with fresh blood, clean bodies, and clear brains that can endure the terrific strain of modern life" and to be "the stay and strength of the nation in time of war, and its guiding and controlling spirit in time of peace."[11]

Yet while the country was the strength of the nation and supported the cities with physical, moral, and racial strength, rising rates of rural migration reflected a dangerous imbalance. Sir Horace Plunkett, an Irish country life specialist and advisor to both Roosevelt and the Country Life Commission, explained that "the moral and physical health of the modern city depends upon the constant influx of fresh blood from the country," but the current flood of migration was threatening to deteriorate the countryside and lead to "National degeneracy." CLC chairman Liberty Hyde Bailey used similar imagery of the city draining the countryside of vitality, arguing the "city sits like a parasite, running out its roots into the country and draining it of its substance. The city takes everything to itself—materials, money, men—and gives back only what it does not want." Commentators like Bailey and Plunkett worried that cities were attracting too many native, white, yeoman farmers and replacing them with transitory, low-order tenants and "foreign-born farmers" with a "low standard of living."[12]

In the letter of appointment to Chairman Bailey, Roosevelt outlined the purpose of the CLC as the problem of farmers' welfare: "how can the life of the farm family be made less solitary, fuller of opportunity, freer from drudgery, more comfortable, happier, and more attractive?" Roosevelt noted that "no nation has ever achieved permanent greatness unless this greatness was based on the well-being of the greater farmer class," and the nation needed to find ways to safeguard their welfare, "material and moral." The investigation, which included a series of public hearings, community meetings, and surveys of over half a million rural residents, drew a range of different groups interested in rural life together. The commission's members represented all regions of the country and many of the leading agencies interested in rural improvement: the federal government, agricultural colleges and experiment stations, the farm press, and farmers' organizations. In the course of its investigation, it worked with other groups deeply interested in the problem of rural life and supportive of the rural reform efforts it generated, including women's clubs, educators, ministers, sociologists, agrobusiness interests, philanthropists, and state and local government officials.[13]

The final report, released the following year, defined the country life problem as a social one that could be solved by building up social institutions like the rural school. It argued that "the underlying problem is to develop and maintain on our farms a civilization in full harmony with the best American ideals," which required "nothing more or less than the gradual rebuilding of a new agriculture and a new rural life." To slow the drift to the city and make rural life more profitable and satisfying for farm families, the report argued, rural life had to offer the things the city offered: economic success, a higher standard of living, rich social life and recreation, and intellectual and cultural stimulation. Rural schools could help with all of these things by building up the cultural and intellectual resources of the community and helping to form the social basis of cooperation needed in economic endeavors. Schools could be sites for disseminating better agricultural and business methods, as well as health and home practices that would improve the quality of life and standard of living in the countryside. To do this, however, "the school must be fundamentally redirected, until it becomes a new kind of institution." Agriculture and the needs of country life should color the work of the rural school. The starting point for this redirected education must be to "arouse all the people to the necessity of such education, to coordinate the forces that are beginning to operate, and to project the work beyond the schools" to reach adults in the community.[14]

The Country Life Commission provided a wave of publicity for rural issues and a major stimulus for rural reform efforts. In the decade after the report, hundreds of popular scholarly books and articles appeared on the rural life problem. In rural communities across the nation, reformers formed hundreds of local rural betterment leagues, village improvement societies, and farmers clubs and "redirected" tens of thousands of rural schools and churches. Country life reformers founded regional and national organizations to address the problem, including Rural Life Conferences, the Farmers Improvement Society, the International Congress of Farm Women, and the National Corn Association. While the Country Life Commission helped draw together groups and invest country life with national significance, a tension remained at the center of the country life movement between those who viewed it primarily as a social problem and those who viewed it as an economic one. The president of the National Grange, for example, argued that "so much talk about 'betterment' and 'uplift' in connection with the farmer class makes me just a little bit weary," for it "implies a whole lot that is not true." The real problem was economic, he argued, and "the only 'uplift' that is needed is to 'uplift' from the back of agriculture the trusts, combinations and special privilege interests."[15]

However, country life reformers of all stripes could find some common ground on the issue of rural school reform. Rural schooling could build community, foster love of country life, and teach practical rural skills and knowledge that could help keep boys on the farm and strengthen the basis of both economic cooperation and social uplift. In many of the rural school reforms that emerged, farmers groups and rural residents played key roles. Like in the city, perceptions of economic and social changes drew a range of groups to demand that the public school broaden its aims and activities and embrace new social goals and responsibilities. In reformers' vision, schools must educate citizens in new ways to prepare them to meet the challenges of rural life in the modern world.

Professional Leadership and Community Building in Rural School Reform

In the decade after the Country Life Commission, a variety of rural reformers took up this project of redirecting rural schools in order to build up rural life and improve educational opportunities for rural children. Many argued that one of the outstanding needs of rural education was to reorganize the curriculum and activities of the school to reflect the practical needs and realities of country life, including agriculture and the farm home. Like the new education in the city, one educator noted, "the new rural school must, therefore, have the new educational aim—that of adjusting our boys and girls to their present environment and of developing them into the highest type of manhood and womanhood, physically, mentally, and morally." Rural schools should have practically oriented instruction that began with the immediate environment and prepared children for healthy, productive, satisfying lives on the farm. Over the next decade, rural school reformers worked to enhance professional leadership and mobilize community support to give, as one normal school leader argued, "new meaning and a new influence to the rural school" and to provide, as another noted, "distinct social service" to the community.[16]

At the time of the Country Life Commission report, the efforts of a few pioneering communities to solve the rural school problem served as inspiration that shaped national reform after it. County superintendent O. J. Kern, for example, wrote in 1906 about his efforts in Winnebago County, Illinois, to promote "a new educational ideal in the country school" that "will lead the boys and girls to see more of the 'divine joy of living' in the country" and "meet the new conditions of life." He aimed to enhance the rural focus of the schools and connect them to the community. To that end, he developed a traveling county library stocked with books about agriculture and country living, and he promoted school garden work to beautify school grounds and promote practical agricultural instruction. Working with the State Agricultural College, Kern created the Winnebago County Farmer Boys' Experiment Club to hold older boys in school and promote scientific agriculture. The college sent each boy—thirty-nine of them in the first year and over five hundred within five years—literature about the latest developments in agricultural research and outlined experiments to perform at home, such as testing whether sugar beets would grow in the state or experimenting with high-yield engineered corn seed. The boys demonstrated their results at the annual county farmers' institute, which helped to advertise new methods to farmers, interest them in the school, and connect it to the life of community. In these and other efforts, Kern outlined innovative new practices and encouraged teachers, school boards, and school patrons in each district to adopt them. They spread through the county as some schools followed his lead and served as positive examples for neighboring schools.[17]

Many of Kern's efforts were borrowed or adapted from experiments in other states and communities. Women's clubs financed traveling libraries in several other states, including South Carolina, Tennessee, and Texas. State legislatures also began to promote the work, such as North Carolina, which began to offer state matching funds for rural school libraries in 1901. In Canada, Europe, and some American cities, communities experimented with school garden work and Southern school improvement leagues had taken up the project of school beautification and improvement of rural schoolhouses. Boys' and girls' clubwork was making strides under the watchful eye of county superintendents and local farmers' clubs in Iowa, Illinois, Indiana, and especially Nebraska, where a new statewide series of boys' corn-growing and girls' cooking contests was stimulating great interest in vocational instruction. Within a few years, this clubwork would be supported by the U.S. Department of Agriculture and expanded by its farm demonstration agents. Enterprising county superintendents similarly worked to vitalize the school and build community interest in it through activities like countywide spelling contests, educational rallies, school fairs, and school exhibitions at farmers' institutes and county fairs. In the wake of the Country Life Commission, reformers promoted these kinds of innovations to improve rural school facilities, promote practical, rural-focused instruction, and bring the school into closer cooperation with other rural life institutions like farmers' institutes, agricultural colleges and extension work, and rural community organizations.[18]

The growing Southern education reform movement also shaped the national discussion of rural schooling after the CLC investigation. At the turn of the century, New South economic boosters, educators and middle-class professionals, and women's groups fashioned a powerful movement for white school modernization by framing it as a project of regional development and linking it to the rising tide of white supremacy. They worked with Northern philanthropies, including the Peabody Fund, which had financed Southern educational institutions since Reconstruction and the newly created General Education Board (GEB) funded by the Rockefeller Foundation to promote educational modernization. After meeting in annual conferences for three years, they created the Southern Education Board (SEB) in 1901 to spearhead educational campaigns for the region. These school reform efforts gained traction as political candidates, like "education governor" Charles Aycock of North Carolina, ran on platforms that linked support for white public schooling and black disenfranchisement. Restrictions on black voting limited the threat of black political power and made siphoning resources into white schools easy and seemingly justifiable, thereby easing some of the fears that public education would provide too much aid to African Americans. The educational qualifications for voting also increased working-class white demands for schooling.[19]

Southern education reform held lessons and built a foundation for later reform by combining top-down organization and bottom-up mobilization of community groups. The SEB sent organizers to every Southern state to organize educational campaigns, speakers, and publicity, but they were most successful in the places where voluntary groups took up the work. In North Carolina, for example, SEB state organizers helped to plan and coordinate a campaign, but its ultimate success was due to the extensive mobilization of women's clubs around school reform, particularly the Women's Association for the Betterment of Public School Houses (WABPS). WABPS developed county- and district-level clubs across the state, which did most of the work of mobilizing community support for school reform, including campaigning for higher taxes to extend school terms and improve school buildings. Its federated organization and statewide reach helped to make North Carolina one of the leading southern states in school reform.[20]

In other places, reforms also advanced farthest when top-down organization was married with local, voluntary groups that could build local interest and support for school reform. In Kentucky, the General Federation of Women's Clubs brought in a field agent from North Carolina to organize school improvement leagues in 1907. She created an executive committee and recruited a corps of women volunteers to create county school improvement leagues and to do publicity work, including write letters and newspaper articles. Within three years, 112 out of 119 counties in the state had school improvement leagues, which played an important part in the state's 1908 Whirlwind Campaign and supported local school reform over the next decade.[21]

In the decades after the Country Life Commission investigation, efforts to "redirect" rural schools within Northern and Southern communities often relied on similar combinations of professional leadership and local effort. The work of Jessie Field, the "Corn Lady" of Page County, Iowa, shows how a progressive educational leader and community could work together to define a modern, rural school. First as a teacher and then as a county superintendent, Field's motto was that "we must teach a country child in terms of country life" and she convinced teachers, school boards, and patrons to embrace that philosophy. A visitor to Page County in 1912 described the "wholesome country atmosphere that characterized all the schools we visited." He observed practical, rural-oriented study in all the schools: nature lessons about apple harvesting, math problems framed around corn measurement, reading lessons about birds, and opening musical exercises that included "Iowa" and "Whistling Farmer Boy." This work in the classroom was connected to the home and other rural agencies; students joined agricultural clubs, demonstrated their work at the annual county farmers' institute, and attended short boys' farm and girls' golden maid camps run by the agricultural college.[22]

Field reached out to teachers in order to improve instruction and build support for her progressive reform vision. In addition to her regular school visits and summer teachers' institutes, Field organized a Progressive Teachers Club, which met regularly to discuss country life, rural education, and the relationship between the two. Members had to pledge their commitment to relating the school to country life. The regular meetings helped to inspire and nurture reform zeal among teachers, develop common lines of activity, and enhance professional training and identity. The club began with a dozen teachers, and within a few years every one of the 130 teachers of the county had applied for membership and endorsed Field's agenda.[23]

In a pattern emulated in other self-defined "progressive" communities, county superintendents Kern and Field were dynamic educational leaders who inspired teachers, students, and school patrons to enact changes to improve instruction and connect the school and community. As elected county superintendents, they were responsible for rural supervision, which entailed visiting schools, holding annual teachers' institutes, disseminating educational materials and advice, and providing general instructional leadership. However, both were superintendents in states with strong district systems, which meant that they had no actual authority to manage teachers. Teachers answered to the district school boards and patrons who hired them, fired them, and paid their salaries. Any influence the superintendents had over school practice came from their powers to persuade teachers, trustees, and patrons to follow their advice and to more generally shape public opinion and educational expectations within the community. Implementation came from teachers, students, and district schools. Both Kern and Field were successful because of their personal qualities of leadership, the high educational aspirations of their communities, and the willingness of some patrons to experiment and demonstrate results to others.[24]

At the time of the Country Life Commission report, most states had county or township superintendents with responsibilities for supervision, but for every Kern or Field who was an effective educational leader, there were dozens of others who lacked the interest, skills, or community support required to promote reform. Observers recognized that rural supervision presented daunting challenges for even the most motivated and able county superintendents. In addition to the lack of administrative authority over personnel or finances, county superintendents in most states had to contend with a host of other challenges that made their jobs more difficult than those of their city counterparts. They had a far greater number of teachers and schools under their supervision sprawled over great distances—hundreds to thousands of square miles over sometimes difficult terrain and poor roads.

Even the most energetic superintendents could provide little regular contact with teachers. One 1911 survey found that county superintendents in North Carolina and Tennessee spent less than two hours on average in each school during the entire year, and a similar study in 1916 found that to be average across forty states. And yet rural teachers needed much more guidance and support than city teachers, educational experts pointed out, because they were on average much younger, more inexperienced, less educated, and less professionally trained. They also faced the very difficult task of organizing instruction in all subjects for students of all ages. County superintendents also had other duties that limited their ability to supervise teachers closely, including responsibilities to collect and disseminate school statistics, settle disputes between district officials, and answer questions and correspondence from the state, other districts, and patrons. In most cases they did all of this alone, for the overwhelming majority of county superintendents did not have any staff, even clerical, to help them with their work.[25]

Educational scholars and reformers complained incessantly about the low quality of county superintendents and poor support for their work. In subsequent decades they argued for reforms, with varying degrees of success, to raise qualifications, lengthen terms, improve salaries, add staff, and change the method of selection to attract a higher caliber of professional educator. In New Jersey, for example, a 1916 state law offered aid for each county to hire one or two supervising teachers to offer instructional support to rural teachers. In the next five years these supervisors reported organizing activities like health pageants and clubs, physical education classes, summer teachers' institutes, weekend extension classes, demonstration teaching, student achievement tests, and pupil record-keeping systems. A number of other states in both the North and South authorized counties to hire supervising teachers or clerical assistants to aid the county superintendent, and some states followed New Jersey's example and offered state aid along with requirements for minimum professional training.[26]

In some states, county supervision, encouraged often by state aid, made notable progress. By 1922, Ohio, West Virginia, Wisconsin, and New Jersey had one or more county supervisors in every county. However, in other places, professional assistance to county superintendents depended on community willingness to expend the funds for additional staff, and this commitment was uneven. In 1922, several states reported five or fewer county supervisors in the entire state, including Colorado, Florida, Kansas, Michigan, New Mexico, and Washington. Ten years later a survey of nearly 2,000 counties across the nation found that only 23 percent reported one or more supervisory assistants and 41 percent reported one or more fulltime clerical assistants. Thus despite efforts to encourage and promote professional supervision, it remained fairly spotty in most places and highly uneven within and between states.[27]

In the South, philanthropies encouraged rural supervision by funding county industrial teachers in the hopes it would lead to greater public investment. In Putnam County, Georgia, for example, the Peabody Fund offered the county school board a trained, experienced supervisor for white rural schools in 1909 to promote practical, vocational education. In similar ways to her Northern counterparts, this supervisor visited classrooms and advised teachers, taught demonstration lessons, organized canning and school improvement clubs, started a library fund, and helped raise money for a new schoolhouse. Although the community had been skeptical, it was not long, authorities reported, before "she was very much in demand, freely sent for and entertained. She was not an instructor but a visitor, adviser, and leader." She reportedly awakened the "social interest" of the community and inspired neighboring counties to apply to the Peabody Fund for a similar teacher. These supervisory teachers, North and South, were supposed to cultivate the trust and respect of teachers and communities. One state official warned new supervising teachers in South Carolina that they must establish "friendly personal relationships" and their attitude toward the teacher "must be not that of the boss, but of the friend and helper who has come in an unobtrusive way to assist her in solving the difficult problems which she has met in her classroom."[28]

While philanthropies encouraged counties to employ supervisors for white rural schools to emphasize rural-focused, agricultural work, they also extended this support to African American schools, although on a less generous basis. Philanthropies invested the most resources in white school reform, and disparities between white and black schools grew dramatically as a result. In one of the most extreme examples, South Carolina black schoolchildren received about one-sixth the school funding that white children received in 1900, and by 1915 the disparity had doubled to one-twelfth the amount of public funds. In a 1904 internal memo labeled "confidential," the GEB explained the approach that guided it for the next several decades: noting that "as a matter of absolute justice [Negroes] ought to participate proportionately with the whites," it nevertheless concluded that "an attempt on our part to compel such proportionate participation would in all probability defeat all our effort and work to the injury of negro public school education." Since white public sentiment was so hostile, the survey concluded, the best strategy for the organization was to encourage "cooperative effort among [African Americans]," for whites tended to be won over, they reasoned, "wherever negroes evince a disposition to help themselves."[29]

However, they also promoted the expansion of black schooling in ways that built on African Americans' "disposition to help themselves." This interest in black education reflected the belief among many white reformers that African Americans, as a major social group and labor force in the region, would either drag down progress or help lift it up. One Southern reformer complained that "the Negro is not getting a fair deal in the South" but was quick to point out, "now of course you know I have no sentimental stuff in me about the Negro, but I have a lot of economic stuff in me about the necessity of training him." The training they envisioned—industrial education—would produce better workers and neighbors and contribute to the development of the region by instilling values and practices of work. African Americans were consequently not left out of the school reform project entirely. Yet their marginalization illustrates both their lesser status as citizens in the eyes of most white reformers and these reformers' limited vision; they accepted racial inequality and other kinds of stratification as natural even as they made fervent calls to equalize opportunity between rural and urban schools.[30]

Spurred by philanthropic aid, black communities invested generously in their own schools despite the burdens of "double taxation"—paying for schools with both public taxes and then again with private donations. As many historians have shown, black communities were often able to shape this support to their own ends, including to promote educational expansion and traditional academic subjects, strengthen community, and foster resilience in the face of segregation and discrimination.[31]

Supervising industrial teachers, commonly known as Jeanes teachers, illustrate some of the ways that black communities and philanthropies leveraged one another to expand black schooling. Funded by the Anna T. Jeanes Fund and later the General Education Board, Jeanes teachers were usually African American women who worked for the county superintendent to promote industrial education and organize industrial clubs. Although their stated purpose was to supervise industrial education, Jeanes teachers operated like supervising teachers elsewhere: they offered instructional support and professional development for teachers in all subjects, organized community activities, and promoted a wide range of school improvement efforts. One Tuskegee graduate employed as a Jeanes teacher in Virginia explained to her supervisors why she had spent so much of her time fundraising rather than teaching industrial education: "It's impossible to do this work [industrial teaching] under the conditions that prevailed for the poor schools. In one school in attempting to show 25 children who occupied a backseat in a crowded room how to do the work I found the apron being scorched by the stove that's in the middle of the room. Much of this work cannot be done without more suitable buildings." Industrial education was not even possible, many Jeanes teachers argued, without far-reaching improvements in black schools, including better buildings, longer terms, and more fiscal support.[32]

Jeanes teachers not only mobilized black communities for school improvements, but helped to expand white community fiscal support in ways that expanded the public infrastructure of black schooling. Jeanes teachers often led efforts to secure other forms of philanthropic aid for communities, including Rosenwald school buildings or Slater Fund county training schools. Both of these programs, like the Jeanes Fund itself, were designed by philanthropists to build on black "self-help" and stimulate white fiscal support; philanthropic aid had to be matched with private donations and public funding, and any new buildings or staff had to be absorbed into the public school system. Jeanes teachers, new school buildings, and other philanthropic projects were often taken over by county school boards and consequently expanded public oversight and responsibility for black schools. Despite the intentions of many philanthropists to promote industrial education as a project of cultivating labor skills and discipline, Jeanes teachers and other philanthropic projects helped to build public infrastructure of black schools in ways that could have wholly unintended effects.[33]

In addition to county-level rural supervision, school reformers sought to enhance local leadership and community reform efforts by building new forms of state rural supervision. Drawing from their experience with the Southern Education Board, the Peabody Fund and the General Education Board began to fund new state supervisors of rural schools, white and black, in 1909 and 1910, respectively. Under agreement with state superintendents, the state rural supervisors were official members of the state department of education who worked underneath the state superintendent and had all of the authority of that office, but made monthly reports to the philanthropies that paid their salaries and expenses. In many Southern states these supervisors were the first professional additions to the state department of education and consequently played an important role in the institutional development of the office. They also stimulated Northern states to take up rural supervision. Wisconsin was the only Northern state department of education with a state rural supervisor on staff at the time that philanthropies began to fund them in the South. However, within ten years nearly every state had created the position.[34]

After staggered beginnings and some initial efforts to define their work, the new agents of rural white schools met in conference in 1911 and pledged themselves to develop "a new type of school for the development of Country Life" with four major goals for the coming years: to define rural content for the schools, promote school consolidation, enhance professional supervision at the county level, and expand tax support for schools. The new state agents of Negro rural schools set more modest goals, given the hostility they faced. They aimed to investigate black school conditions—which in some states were virtually unknown when they took office—and to build up

interest and support within black and white communities for black education, including teacher training, industrial education, and improvement of
schoolhouses. [35]

Like county superintendents in most states, these new state supervisors' effectiveness rested on their leadership abilities and local consent. In
1910, the new Georgia state rural supervisor of white schools described the
lengths to which he went to build trust and cultivate popular support:

> The cultivation of popular sentiment has been the most delicate and most
> arduous part of the work. In the pursuit of this end, I have made formal
> speeches and informal speeches (sometimes as many as three speeches in
> a day), I have attended school commencements and exhibitions, picnics,
> casket dinners, barbecues and box suppers. I have eaten the best food in
> Georgia, and some not so good; I have drunk lemonade, pink and amber;
> I have hobnobbed with all kinds and ages of people. I have ridden in farm-
> ers wagons, spent the night in their homes, and have used every means
> possible to get their views and give them mine, and even more to get their
> good will.

In their monthly reports, other rural school supervisors described similar
types of outreach to secure the goodwill of county superintendents, local
trustees, and school patrons. W. K. Tate of South Carolina, for example,
detailed his activities in the first quarter of 1912: he visited 52 schools in
27 counties; spent 23 days with county superintendents; aided 15 local tax
campaigns and 8 consolidation efforts; held 21 meetings with trustees,
28 meetings with citizens, and 7 meetings with teachers; made 26 public addresses and 19 illustrated lectures; furnished 7 newspaper articles; mailed
12,000 pamphlets and 6 circular letters; and traveled 4,500 miles. Given the
enormity of their task, state supervisors usually focused their efforts, at least
initially, in places where they were invited. They delivered public addresses
and met with local officials and lay groups, for example, when invited by
districts that were considering tax increases or new high school buildings.
As one state agent explained, "coming as the representative of the State Department of Education, equipped with the facts and figures from the larger
world, the supervisor is often the decisive factor in the election."[36]

State supervisors of black schools similarly focused their efforts on communities where white educational leaders or school patrons showed some
willingness to work on behalf of black education, since they had little authority to coerce participation. N. C. Newbold, the North Carolina state
agent, reported with excitement in January 1914 that the new superintendent of Ansen County, "a young man, native born in his county, well edu-

cated, enthusiastic, and a man of ideas," had invited him to spend a week visiting schools and meeting with patrons. Encouraged by the superintendent's interest in black schools, Newbold reported it was "one of the best week's work I have done for this or any other cause." Newbold's excitement revealed the rarity of this experience, for as another supervisor noted, county superintendents "know less and care less about their Negro schools than their white schools."[37]

The South Carolina agent described the early years of his work when "It was difficult to get a county superintendent to visit the Negro schools with the state agent. He always found some other pressing duty that prevented him from visiting these small, rural schools. In fact he would tell you he did not know where they were located." Attitudes changed slowly over time, he reported, as more white county superintendents were willing to provide some leadership to black schools, often in no small part because of the work of Jeanes teachers and because of concerns in some communities about black outmigration and its labor implications. It remained a delicate project of cultivating support, however. Newbold's efforts to encourage black teachers' institutes in North Carolina provoked an angry response from the Wilson County superintendent, who accused the state agent of trying to take over "the whole show" of supervision and declared, "I am not going to surrender to any outside person."[38]

As part of their work, state agents encouraged county superintendents to take a strong role as professional supervisors and leaders. L. C. Brogden of North Carolina explained how he worked with county superintendents to model effective supervision. When he visited a county, the state agent of white schools helped the county superintendent to formulate a set of standards and then visited schools with the local official. Brogden worked with the superintendent to analyze the strengths and weaknesses of each school, formulate strategies for improvement, and discuss methods for ongoing supervision and feedback, such as written records or follow-up meetings with teachers. State rural supervisors' monthly reports were filled with examples of this careful professional guidance, since many of the elected superintendents had little or no professional educational training or experience. In these visits, state agents also tried to persuade county superintendents to promote school consolidation, employ supervising teachers, hold a teachers' institute, improve a school building, or give more attention to black schools. In both the North and South, state agents of rural schools defined their roles in terms of providing service to local supervisors, school boards, teachers, and patrons.[39]

Consequently, in the state- and county-level rural supervision that developed after the Country Life Commission report in the North and South, professional leadership and community mobilizations worked in tandem for rural school reforms. These were not urban bureaucracies in the countryside, for even in their most ambitious dreams, rural school supervisors could never have exercised the close supervision and management authority over teachers that were possible in city environments. While professionals might organize the community and provide the vocabulary for reform, community support and participation were essential. In most places, rural supervisors, state and county, had supervisory responsibilities but not administrative authority; they lacked coercive authority and control over fiscal resources, and consequently they had to persuade and advise rather than manage and compel. The relatively high proportion of women holding these positions, particularly in the West, further underscores their relatively low status as actual administrators.[40]

Rural superintendents, supervisors, and teachers worked to build professional identity and encourage particular reforms, but they directed their efforts toward mobilizing and supporting local reform sentiment and community efforts. For many school reformers, the rural school problem could not be solved without elevating the school to an important place in the community, aligning it with other agencies of rural development, and redirecting its activities to prepare children for rural life. Commitment to community building was not just a pragmatic necessity but a philosophical commitment.

Consolidation and the Structural Weaknesses of Small Rural Schools

At the same time that they worked to build up community support, to adapt and integrate the rural school with rural life, and enhance professional leadership and supervision, rural school reformers also promoted consolidation as a key solution to the rural school problem. One enthusiastic supporter proclaimed that "of all the plans, suggestions, and experiments proposed and tried to redirect, revitalize, revivify, reorganize, rebuild, and enrich the rural school to meet the educational demands of the twentieth-century farmer, the consolidated school stands supreme as the only complete and adequate method to meet that need." Many reformers argued there were limits to what could be done in the confines of very small schools. Consolidated schools would enable longer terms, better teachers, modern buildings, and high school grades because they amassed resources—money and people—in a way that small schools and school districts could not. Consolidation was efficient because it eliminated redundancies and replaced small, cheap structures and poor teachers with fewer, higher-quality ones. More importantly, consolidating schools meant consolidating small districts, which enlarged the territory and tax base, thereby spreading out cost and opportunity more widely and equitably.[41]

The first consolidations, around the turn of the century, usually involved closing one or more small schools and transporting students to a larger village or town school for economic reasons. In Louisiana, for example, the state's first consolidation occurred in 1902 when a parish school board decided to transport students to a neighboring school rather than rebuild the one recently destroyed by a hurricane. Similarly in Ohio, the state's first consolidation occurred in Kingsville Township when a small district with a declining population needed a new school building and patrons and trustees decided it would be more cost effective to transport students to the town school than to build a new one.[42]

In some cases, communities not only transported students to existing schools but constructed new buildings for consolidation. Massachusetts went farthest in this, having been the first state in the nation both to authorize transportation of pupils at public expense and to reestablish town school board control of outlying rural districts. In 1896, the town of Warwick, Massachusetts, decided to consolidate the nine small schools under its care and build one well-equipped, three-room modern school located at the center of town. Without much tax increase, the school board was able to lengthen the school term by 50 percent and replace the nine young, inexperienced teachers with three better-paid "normal school graduates of exceptional ability" and special visiting teachers in music and drawing. At a 1902 NEA meeting, school administrators discussed it as an efficient reform, one that provided higher-quality schooling at similar cost.[43]

By the time of the Country Life Commission report, many school reformers began to see consolidations, like the one at Warwick, as a potential solution to the rural school problem. Rather than emphasize the cost savings of consolidation, however, they began to explore its potential to provide a modern rural education and close the gap with urban schools. According to supporters, consolidation did three things that even the most engaged rural community could not do effectively with a small school: it provided high school opportunities, it mobilized a broader tax base on behalf of schooling, and it provided economies of scale that could be used to enhance quality. Educating children in small one-room schools, one educator argued, "is like attempting to carry on our manufactures in thousands of primitive and poorly equipped shops, each employing but a few workmen, instead of conducting such industries in well-equipped factories manned with hundreds or thousands of skilled mechanics." Consolidated schools, reformers argued, allow for "well-equipped" modern facilities under the leadership of highly trained, professional educators and expanded opportunities, including rural-focused vocational education and high school grades. Consolidation was "a movement to restore to the country child something like equal rights with the city child."[44]

Reformers rejected the idea that closing small schools would weaken community—a concern of many rural residents—and argued that it would enlarge and enrich community. The Kansas state superintendent argued, "the central school has more dignity, more character, more force than the rural school, and evokes more pride, interest and support on the part of the people." Mabel Carney, a normal school professor and later rural specialist at Teachers College, likewise reasoned that the consolidated school could be a "center for redirected education and community building" and "the most immediate and effective local agency in the solution of the farm problem." School consolidation could enlarge and enrich the boundaries of rural community and provide greater social, cultural, and intellectual stimulation.[45]

In order to provide a rural-focused modern school, reformers recommended that consolidations be effected in the open country rather than village and town centers whenever possible. In 1916, USBE rural specialist Katherine Cook visited one of these ideal open-country consolidations in Colorado and described its benefits. At a time when most rural schools were one- or two-room wooden buildings, Cook reported, the rural Cache LaPoudre Consolidated School was "a substantial brick structure of two stories with a commodious basement" that contained such modern facilities as a manual training shop, sewing room, library, auditorium, playrooms, kitchen, and indoor restrooms. Its teaching staff was composed of nine highly trained and professional teachers by the standards of the day; all but one was a college or normal school graduate. The school also offered the first high school opportunities in the area. Its 4.5-acre property contained athletic fields for baseball, basketball, and football, demonstration farms, orchards, playgrounds, and a barn, all of which supported community activities and vocational instruction. The school was a community center, Cook reported, and hosted activities throughout the year, like community singing, lyceums, holiday socials, lectures, political meetings, plays, and public auctions. Cook noted that "It is not difficult to see how community spirit is preserved and promoted in the district, co-operation between parents and teachers encouraged, school pride strengthened, and the spirit of fellowship" maintained. Consolidated schools like this one, she argued, were solving the rural school problem by building rural community and offering a thoroughly modern education that prepared young people for productive, healthy, satisfying lives in the country.[46]

Education experts like Cook were fairly united on the benefits of consolidation and worked to convince school reformers and communities to support it. The NEA Committee of Twelve had endorsed consolidation in 1897 and NEA members discussed it at nearly every annual meeting, particularly after the Department of Rural Education was formed in 1907. Emerging new textbooks and courses in rural supervision in university schools of education and normal schools similarly promoted rural school consolidation as the epitome of modern rural education. At the same time, state superintendents and federal officials continued to advocate consolidation by publishing histories of consolidation, examples of ideal consolidated schools, and statistical studies that supported it, and they urged consolidation to county superintendents and district officials. Philanthropies also made consolidation a major item on the agenda of rural school agents; it was one of the four major goals outlined in the first conference of rural school agents for white schools and the subject of extensive reporting and correspondence by agents. The Southern Education Board also sponsored a tour for Southern state superintendents and rural school supervisors in the fall of 1910 to introduce them to the work of leading consolidated rural schools in Canada, Ohio, Indiana, Maryland, and Virginia. The eighteen state officials in attendance reportedly went back to their home states as enthusiastic supporters.[47]

For all the professional enthusiasm, however, consolidation in most places required local consent and popular support to enact. Small schools were often independent school districts and consequently consolidation required redrawing district lines and reallocating the corporate powers and property of two or more districts. This consolidation required state authorization, and between the late nineteenth century and World War I, every state established procedures for consolidation and authorized publicly funded transportation of students. While state laws varied in the particulars, the majority made school consolidation a local decision subject to special, popular election. Reformers had to collect a designated number of signatures to get the issue on the ballot, often one-quarter of eligible voters, and a special election followed to decide the issue. In most states a majority vote was required in each affected district, although some states set the bar higher (a three-quarters majority) or lower (a majority of the entire affected area).

State legislatures did not have to defer to local districts. As the next chapter will explore, state courts by 1910 had consistently and decisively established that schooling was a function of the state and school districts were legally quasi-corporations, mere functionaries of the legislature's plenary authority with no inherent rights. In other words, legislatures could create, abolish, or alter school districts as they saw fit and could consolidate districts without local consent, if they chose. Yet state legislatures were loathe to take the decision away from local communities and officials, deferring both to the political power of rural localities and culture of local control. They sometimes offered incentives, like special aid for consolidation or transportation, but they usually left the decision to affected communities.[48]

In some states, most notably in the South, which had stronger traditions of county governance, states gave popularly elected county school boards authority to initiate consolidation, instead of or in addition to special-election procedures. Yet even in those places, popular support and community consent was usually required in practice because elected county officials tried to defer to majority sentiment on what was often a passionate local issue. For example, Maryland county school boards, which were widely regarded as the strongest in the nation, could legally change district boundaries and consolidate schools. However when the Montgomery County school board was considering a proposal to close small schools at Montrose, Goshen, and Claysville and transport students to Rockville, a delegation of opponents from the affected schools appeared before the county board and it agreed to shelve the proposal indefinitely.[49] Likewise in Utah, county commissioners could consolidate districts, but when the Sevier County superintendent suggested consolidation in 1908, the county commissioners asked every district to hold a special caucus to determine its stance on the issue. When the majority of districts voted against it, the commissioners refused to consolidate. The issue came up for public debate again in 1911 and the commissioners again deferred to district votes against it, not moving to consolidate until a major public campaign by consolidation supporters succeeded in convincing a majority of communities to support it.[50]

Consequently, professional educators and allied school reformers who were committed to consolidation had to win majority community support. As in other types of rural school reform, local reform groups were often important allies and in some cases even the guiding force. In Putnam, Illinois, for example, a model open-country consolidated school was erected after the local Grange proposed it and rallied support for an election, hoping it would stem the drift to the city and raise educational quality. More typical, however, was Preble County, Ohio, where the county superintendent worked overtly and behind the scenes to rally support for consolidation. Describing his successful efforts, he explained that he "sought the help of the school officials, the teachers, and some influential patrons" to organize petition drives so that "elections were called upon petition of the people" and had wider support and legitimacy. After the petition for an election was successful, "our policy was to conduct an educational campaign for about ten days immediately preceding the election" to show the people the advantages of consolidation. To that end, teachers and patrons conducted house-to-house canvases, held public meetings with speeches by prominent local leaders and representatives of the state education department, and sent mass mailings with detailed information about the proposed consolidation. He reported that as a result of the campaign "consolidation became the fashion in our county" and ten special elections succeeded within five months.[51]

As the example of Preble County suggests, consolidation in one community could sometimes prompt similar moves in nearby communities. In Randolph County, Indiana, for example, consolidation spread through example. In 1905, the first consolidation in the county occurred when the board of health condemned a small school and trustees decided to erect a new building and combine with another district. Enrollment boomed, causing school officials to expand the building and add a high school program. Neighboring districts, impressed by the example, decided to try consolidation, including the county's first open-country consolidation, which proved so popular that neighboring districts voted to close their small schools and transport students to the new school. These examples inspired more consolidation as communities that regarded themselves as educationally progressive embraced it as a modern reform. By 1923, it had swept the entire county; 134 small one-room schools had been replaced by twenty consolidated schools, fourteen of which were located in the open country.[52]

Yet while neighboring communities could inspire consolidation by example, they could also prompt it as a defensive move. The community that grew up around Buck Creek church in Iowa in the 1910s and 1920s, for example, created a consolidated school, even though most patrons were satisfied with their small schools. The issue was under consideration in neighboring districts and they feared losing valuable taxable property.[53]

Consolidation advanced in patchwork fashion within and between states, sweeping through the nation in the 1910s and 1920s. A 1930 U.S. Bureau of Education study found that "remarkable progress" had been made in school consolidation since 1918, when records were first kept. Approximately forty thousand one-room schools had been abandoned and over twelve thousand new consolidated schools constructed throughout the nation. In seventeen states it represented a 25 percent reduction in one-room schools. Consolidation tended to make the most progress, experts noted, in states with stronger degrees of town, township, or county administration of schools where those officials could help to mediate or decide thorny issues like school location, district boundaries, and asset and liability redistribution. Illinois and Indiana were often held up as exemplars of the difference that the administrative unit made: both states had similar geography and population, high levels of literacy, strong educational leadership, and reputations for being educationally progressive, yet in 1917 Indiana, with the township system, reported 706 consolidated schools while Illinois's district system counted less than forty.[54]

With their town and county oversight, New England and the South had the highest rates of consolidation, although in the latter it was confined almost entirely to white schools. White school officials and voters were reluctant enough to provide adequate small schools for African Americans; they had little interest in ensuring long terms, high school access, and other more expansive educational aims embodied in consolidation plans. In the West, sparse population and geography combined to keep consolidations more limited overall, although they could be found in virtually every state, while in the Midwest and mid-Atlantic, where the district system was strong, results were varied. State aid could provide incentives for consolidation, like in Minnesota, while alternative provision for rural high school opportunities could decrease the incentive for consolidation, like in Illinois, which created a system of township high schools to provide rural access.[55]

School consolidation was an uneven process, not only between states and regions but within them. Consolidation was controversial even where it was enacted, and many communities rejected it or failed to even seriously consider it because of local opposition. Resistance to school consolidation often centered on objections to cost, concerns about transportation, disputes over logistical details like schoolhouse location or district boundaries, or principled defenses of the one-room school as both a community and educational institution. While school reformers often dismissed opposition as based on ignorance or selfishness, resistance often reflected larger concerns about self-government and autonomy. Rural residents feared losing control of their children's education within a larger community, as well as the impact that school closings would have on the rural neighborhood, which in many places was an important site of community and identity. Resistance sometimes also reflected a great deal of skepticism of the new education itself and the project of modernizing schools.[56]

Consequently, as consolidation spread throughout the nation, it did so in an uneven, ad-hoc way, which eliminated tens of thousands of small schools but left hundreds of thousands virtually untouched. While it solved the rural school problem for some districts, it could exacerbate it for others. Consolidated districts could monopolize the most valuable pieces of property and most educationally engaged communities, leaving neighboring areas to languish with low property values or weak public interest in schooling. Under uneven patterns of consolidation, the strong districts got stronger and the weak got weaker, simply replacing, as one educator put it, the "wild, chaotic variety" of the district system on a slightly larger scale. School administrators had recognized this problem since the NEA's Committee of Twelve first argued that consolidation of small schools should go hand in hand with the reorganization of larger administrative units. Throughout the first two decades of the twentieth century they urged more centralized planning of consolidation and schooling more generally, but after a decade of consolidation and resurfacing concerns about inequities around World War I, their recommendations for administrative reorganization got a stronger hearing.[57]

In one of their most ambitious plans for administrative reorganization of rural schools, educational experts urged that the district system be abolished altogether and replaced by the county as the unit of local control. Simply consolidating small districts into slightly larger districts did not solve the fundamental problem, they argued. Rural schools needed a higher level of planning, coordination, fiscal support, and efficiency that could only come by more rational organization over larger areas. This would spread out the costs and benefits more equally across space and allow for economies of scale. Experts converged in the decade after the Country Life Commission on the "county unit" as a solution, urging that county school boards, county superintendents with professional staffs, and county taxation should replace existing districts. This would provide a rural version of city systems, with centralized, corporate-style administration. Indiana state superintendent Benjamin Burris succinctly summed up the advantages that would come from it: "It provides professional leadership and professional management of schools, a sound school organization and efficient business administration, equalized educational opportunities over a larger area and for larger numbers of children, and equitable local school tax burden." Administrators claimed to see the county unit emerging in practice in a handful of Southern and Western states with county school boards or county taxation for school support, but closer scrutiny often revealed that districts maintained most of the power in those places. In school surveys, professional discussions, and administration texts, educational scholars recommended that weak existing county structures be reorganized into powerful units of local school control and established where they did not exist.[58]

Professional educators found it much more difficult to rally public opinion behind county units, and in all but a few places educational experts' calls to centralize and professionalize local school administration were decisively rejected. In Indiana, for example, the GEB conducted a state survey of the public schools in 1923 and recommended that the existing township trustees be replaced by the county unit for local school administration. After the legislature rejected a proposed bill prepared by the GEB, the survey director suggested that "the fight here suggests a problem of study." Noting that the county unit was much discussed but rarely enacted, survey director Frank Bachman suggested that the GEB fund a demonstration project to document the benefits of the county unit plan to the people of Indiana and the nation. He received enthusiastic support from LaGrange County superintendent Hilda Hughes, a graduate of Northwestern University who had studied with rural specialist Mabel Carney at Teachers College. Hughes volunteered her county for the experiment, noting that "We County Superintendents are regular 'copy-cats,'" and she predicted that "practically every detail demonstrated here would be copied in other counties" and could "influence the entire middle west."[59]

In late 1923 the GEB organized county unit demonstration projects in LaGrange and Johnson counties. Under an agreement reached with the state superintendent and local township trustees, each county received two rural supervisors, a business manager, clerical assistance, and extra support from the state department of education. The GEB defined four areas of emphasis for the two-year project: improvement of business administration, school organization, classroom work, and publicity. In each of these areas, the new county agents sought to centralize and professionalize administration and employ the latest technologies of school administration: uniform county-wide salary schedules, cooperative buying for school supplies, improved methods of school accounting, school consolidation, pupil testing to measure achievement, introduction of health work, and the professional supervision of classroom work. The highly trained and specially chosen county supervisors worked to improve classroom work through active oversight of rural teachers. At four different times during the two-year project, county supervisors administered tests to the demonstration counties and two non-demonstration counties to "prove" the superiority of the county unit system. Publicity was a central goal of the project, and Bachman noted that "if the effects do not reach beyond these two counties, the demonstrations will not be worth while from our point of view." In addition to publishing the results of testing that showed that students in demonstration counties accomplished more work, the county supervisors worked to build up local public support and demonstrate classroom results through parent-teacher associations and special events throughout the year.[60]

Yet despite the so-called proof that the county system was superior, neither county continued the work after the two-year project ended and neither Indiana nor any neighboring state adopted the county as the unit of local school control as the GEB had hoped. The GEB blamed this failure on self-interested township trustees, arguing that they mobilized popular sentiment against the plan in order to protect their own position. However, in attributing opposition solely to trustee self-interest and farmers' ignorance, supporters of the county unit system profoundly misunderstood the depth and rationale of local resistance. Rural residents of Indiana and in many other states rejected the county unit system of school administration because they correctly perceived that it inaugurated a major change in the nature of local control. Township trustees in Indiana and district officers in other states were highly prized agents of local self-government that were close to and rooted in the small rural communities of which they were part. Counties were not natural units of community, and for many rural residents they were simply too large and too far removed from the lives of rural people to be effective sites of "local" control. As one observer noted, the county "is so arbitrary and impersonal in its geographical boundaries that it is not suited to community needs" and "the school must be governed and supervised by some form of community unit."[61]

Some opponents argued that efficiency was not a worthwhile tradeoff for self-government. A 1926 Indiana University Extension Division *Bulletin* acknowledged that the county unit system might result in greater efficiency and better educational results, but argued that there were other important values in education that were not worth sacrificing: "Can the interest of the people in their own affairs and their participation in them, which constitute the very essence of democracy, be given up for a bureaucracy of control, no matter how efficient, if it marks the end of local self-government?" Against a similar torrent of criticism that county units sacrificed local democracy for the sake of efficiency, administrative scholars argued that the schools would still be "managed for the people, by the people, and of the people" and that the change represented *more* democracy rather than less because it meant "equal educational opportunities, the very essence of democracy." However, these arguments were not persuasive to the majority of state legislators or rural residents.[62]

The rejection of the county unit in Indiana was emblematic of its fate elsewhere. Rural patrons were afraid that it would undermine local effort, initiative, and interest, and this had been such an important motor of school reform, historically and in the recent past. Consequently, the county system, as envisioned by educational experts, was adopted wholesale in very few states. Even those states celebrated as most closely approximating county systems tended to retain strong elements of local control.

Yet while counties rarely became the *local* unit of school control, they became an important *intermediate* unit that exercised a growing range of administrative functions. In both Wisconsin and Ohio, for example, expert-conducted state school surveys in 1912 and 1914, respectively, recommended the establishment of strong county school boards to govern the schools. Due to popular resistance in both states, state legislatures modified these plans by creating new boards but significantly weakening their authority to ensure that districts retained the balance of power in management of the schools. Many states went in the direction of Wisconsin and Ohio in the 1920s by embracing limited forms of county administration, including greater oversight over fixing and changing school boundaries, greater responsibilities for examining and certificating teachers, power to select textbooks, and supplementing local taxes with county ones, among others. Many of these new county functions, observers noted, resulted less from pressures from above to impose it and more from voluntary delegations and acquiescence from districts below, which recognized the desirability of greater standardization in the county. District trustees, for example, were often happy to pass responsibility to examine and certificate teachers to county officials so long as they retained the power to hire the teacher of their choice. They benefited from the larger pool generated by county certification as teachers were able to teach in any school in the county.[63]

While state legislatures and local communities in most places rejected the radical redefinition of local control embodied in the county unit system and insisted on greater decentralization, they recognized that rural schools suffered from structural limitations that could not always be addressed through purely local efforts. Consolidation and other efforts to redirect rural schools were creating model rural schools in some places, but exposing the extent to which many other districts were unable or unwilling to reform on their own. While some states had begun to notice the problem before World War I, in its aftermath states wrestled with the issue of "weak" districts—ones with property valuation too low to support adequate schools—and "unthinking" districts, where "local pride or local intelligence is dead." As the next chapter will explore, states began to experiment with new forms of state aid and minimum standards and to wrestle in a more sustained way with the issue of state and federal responsibility for education. They built upon the arrangements and policies that deferred to and mobilized local effort but also began to grapple with how to exert more pressure and compulsion on the lagging minority.[64]

National Rural School Reform in America's System of Federalism

Historians have been limited by a framework in which the bureaucratic impulse—top down, centralized, coercive, professional, insulated from popular control—is taken as the only framework for understanding school reform and state development more generally. Yet, rural school reform was not achieved through the bureaucratic imposition of authority, either at the state level or at the local level. Some reformers, like Ellwood Cubberley and Indiana state superintendent Benjamin Burris, may have wished to create centralized bureaucracies in the countryside by refashioning the county as the unit of local school control in order to approximate the city's efficient organization, professional leadership, centralized planning, and aggregation of resources. These plans were rarely realized in practice and even in their most ambitious dreams, reformers like Cubberely and Burris had to realize that county administration was an imperfect analog for city bureaucracy because of its territorial expanse, limited resources, weaker professional leadership, traditions of community governance, and very different demographic characteristics.

Despite the bureaucratic ambitions of some professional educators, rural school reform as it emerged in practice in the early twentieth century was a much messier affair, one that involved a variety of actors working at multiple levels, from both the top down and bottom up. In school consolidation, for example, state legislatures shaped the rules of the game and offered incentives for consolidation while state departments of education encouraged it through publications and direct outreach to communities. Philanthropies, U.S. Bureau of Education officials, and educational experts all strenuously urged consolidation and used research, incentives, conferences, personal networks, and expertly sanctioned models to promote it. Ultimately, however, it was a local decision, either through popular vote or the decision of popularly elected local officials, and it was successful when local educational leaders, local groups like women's clubs or farmers' organizations, and popular sentiment crystallized around it.

In this and other types of reform—building improvements, curricular reforms, and expanded school activities, among others—rural school reform in America's federalist system worked through the complex interplay of government and nongovernmental actors operating at local, state, and national levels, and sometimes each simultaneously. Federated women's clubs, for example, could be powerful forces of reform, like in North Carolina, because their organization enabled them to lobby simultaneously at district, county, and state levels. National and state actors provided important stimulation, leadership, and coordination but in most reforms the fragmentation of school control among different levels of government and the strong traditions of and deference to community control meant that local consent was vital for rural school reform.[65]

Reform spread across space not because of the centralized, bureaucratic decision-making and imposition, but because of the exchange of ideas, dynamics of emulation and competition, and the cooperative efforts of actors at different levels working to solve common problems. Industrial clubwork offers one of many examples of how experimentation in a few localities could become a nationwide reform. In the first decade of the twentieth century, county superintendents and farmers' groups, like the Texas Farmers Union, developed boys' and girls' industrial clubs. County superintendents, rural teachers, and local school improvement clubs were inspired by examples in other places to try the work in their own communities and they sometimes built upon those examples, such as the Nebraska state superintendent who added state contests to the clubwork. As the country life problem became a topic of national conversation, these experiments and trends garnered attention from agricultural colleges, professional educators, farmers' groups, and federal officials who further publicized and promoted the work. National agencies like the USDA and philanthropic foundations organized and funded efforts to diffuse the clubs more broadly. The USDA wrote bulletins and materials for club use and instructed county demonstration agents to organize them, while the GEB helped to fund this work and diffuse it further by offering Jeanes teachers additional salaries to organize clubs for African American children. What began as the innovative experiment of a few local leaders had become by World War I a nationwide reform that was actively promoted by state and national agencies, had penetrated into communities across the nation, and touched the lives of hundreds of thousands of children.[66]

In both the implementation of reforms locally and the diffusion of rural reforms across space, education professionals played important roles, although their influence through expertise and leadership was both similar and different than in the urban context. Rural professionals' claims to expertise and status were more tenuous than their urban counterparts; rural educational expertise was located not just, or often primarily, in university schools of education but also in agricultural colleges and normal schools, which served a largely rural clientele. Professional superintendents in the field might be university-trained educators or popularly elected laypeople, and in most cases they lacked the administrative authority to implement and enforce changes. Consequently, rural educators and supervisors, at both local and state levels, positioned themselves as leaders, mentors, and guides whose role was to assist school boards and patrons to improve their schools. Their leadership could be decisive for laying out a reform vision and mobilizing the community around it, as seen in many of the examples in this chapter of consolidation and curricular reforms, but it rarely was sufficient alone to bring about changes.

Like their urban counterparts, rural school supervisors were connected to larger professional networks and expertise that shaped their visions of reform, including state education associations, regional country life associations and conferences, and local groups like the Page County Progressive Teachers Club. While rural school administration remained a much less developed specialization than urban administration, it nonetheless produced a growing body of expertise and professional norms, drawn from theory and practice, which helped to shape reform goals of innovative leaders like Field and lay groups like school-improvement associations.

In a system of federalism with top-down and bottom-up reform, some national actors played particularly important roles in coordinating and shaping an agenda across space. One of the most influential and self-conscious of these national actors was the General Education Board and its allied, interlocking network of philanthropic foundations. The new breed of scientific philanthropies, like the GEB, provided leadership, resources, and coordination for social inquiry and experimentation in a wide array of social policy areas. One scholar has called them "parastates," institutional sites of national authority outside the traditional political system that self-consciously aimed to discern and pursue the "true" national interest. Other historians have similarly emphasized the important role that private philanthropies played in developing national social policy in the decades before the Great Depression in the absence of a strong federal government role. Some have described this as "private" leadership for "public" policy in ways that blurred the boundaries between them. However, it can also be seen as emblematic of the complex relationship between "public" and "private" in American political development and an example of the tendency to govern through private actors.[67]

Philanthropies worked to extend public infrastructure and stimulate public policy along particular lines; they funded, for example, new public officers including farm demonstration agents, state supervisors of rural education, and county supervising teachers. This private funding expanded public infrastructure of schooling and public responsibility. Nowhere was this more clear than in African American schooling; philanthropic aid helped leverage black community donations and public school officials' financial support to build over five thousand schools across the South, dozens of new secondary schools (county training schools), and thousands of Jeanes teachers in places that would not have supported them otherwise. The Florida state superintendent in 1917, for example, requested a state agent for black schools because, he explained, "it is impossible for me to get an appropriation for $1 for the bettering of conditions in negro education" from the state legislature, and he noted that at the county level, "negro schools are poorly supervised" because "county superintendents seem to think that it will popularize them with the voters to give as little attention as possible to negro schools." The only way to begin work on behalf of black education and "break down this ignorant and foolish prejudice against negro education," he reasoned, was to leverage outside resources.[68]

In addition to the role that they played in promoting public policy and infrastructural development in particular places, philanthropies played a key role in setting a wider agenda and coordinating reform across space. Philanthropies promoted projects throughout the nation that aimed to introduce new practices locally and provide broader models to shape the national conversation on rural school reform, including state rural supervisors in Maine and Oklahoma, county unit demonstration in Indiana, state school surveys in Maryland and Kentucky, Jeanes teachers in North Carolina and Georgia, and even the Country Life Commission investigation itself.

Yet they focused most of their resources on the South, where the most need and opportunity for impact existed. They aimed to bring the South into the mainstream of the nation and to demonstrate the efficacy of reforms so that they could be adopted elsewhere, such as state supervisors and consolidation. Philanthropies helped to create a tight-knit network of school reformers in the South and throughout the nation with a shared agenda through conferences, publications, and the constant oversight and communication they fostered. Philanthropies held conferences and sponsored professional development for their agents to help them define common goals, exchange ideas and experiences, and connect them with other stakeholders like universities, voluntary associations, and governors. With their resources and their national reach and ambitions, philanthropies helped to shape and promote a common agenda for rural school reform by stimulating its implementation in particular places and providing mechanisms and coordination for reforms to spread across the nation.

Although philanthropies were the most overt nation-builders, other national actors helped to mobilize educational expertise around rural school reform and diffuse solutions across space, including federal governmental agencies like the U.S. Bureau of Education. Although the USBE has often been dismissed by scholars as relatively insignificant since it lacked the coercive authority of European national ministries of education, its primary function—to gather and disseminate information on education—played an important, underappreciated role in the national diffusion of rural school reform. The USBE helped to make rural school conditions visible in new ways. After the Country Life Commission report, the USBE requested detailed information about rural school conditions for the first time, information that many states did not collect or analyze. Using this new data, it released the first major study to quantify the urban-rural disparity at the heart of the "rural school problem" in 1912, and six years later additional requests for detailed information on one-room and consolidated schools allowed it to quantify and begin to chart trends over time in both. In rendering school conditions more legible and comparable, the USBE helped to identify needs and chart national trends. It allowed each state to put itself into larger context, which often provided incentive for individual states to reform.[69]

With administrative scholars focusing most of their attention on urban schools, USBE specialists Katherine Cook and A. C. Monahan helped to define "rural supervision" as a field of study in a pioneering series of bulletins. They were the first to take a heterogeneous set of local, county, and state practices and try to define it as a movement; they defined its parameters and history, investigated and compared current practices, identified promising trends, and made recommendations for the future. USBE publications and conferences—they held a series on rural education throughout the 1910s and 1920s—helped to diffuse new research in rural education conducted by the USBE and other experts and to bring together professionals and lay people interested in reform.[70]

In a federalist system with diffuse, fragmented authority and strong traditions of deference to local control, rural school reform was a slow, uneven, messy process. Some states, counties, and localities embraced some or most of the "progressive" educational reforms of rural schools, and they did so according to widely different timetables, while others rejected most or all efforts to reform their schools. Reformers could point with pride to some localities that were solving the rural school problem, providing innovative ideas and experiments that adapted the rural school to the community and provided a "modern" rural-focused training of youths that prepared them for their future roles. The strength of American federalism, many reformers noted, was that local pride, initiative, and experimentation provided a dynamic engine of reform, both for producing new ideas and diffusing them. Localities copied, adapted, and competed with one another. Furthermore, this local effort and initiative meant that communities were invested in rural schooling and the reforms were popular, strong, and durable.

Yet when they looked across the country landscape, reformers also saw many places that could not or would not reform their schools. The drawback to this kind of slow, bottom-up state building, some reformers came to realize, was that it exacerbated inequalities within the countryside as some localities lagged behind. In the wake of World War I, this increasingly became a problem that transcended the locality itself and could not be ignored, as the next chapter will explore, and reformers struggled to find ways to both maintain the dynamic power of local school reform and provide the aid or compulsion necessary to get the most laggard to follow.

THREE ✳ *Redefining State Responsibility in Education*

In 1918, Payson Smith, state superintendent of Massachusetts, addressed his colleagues at the Department of Superintendence meeting of the National Education Association (NEA) on the topic of "centralizing tendencies in educational administration." Too often Americans approached education, Smith argued, with "traditional conceptions of responsibility, individual and local, presenting education as a personal privilege and not as a need of the state." It was time to overcome "a parochial or neighborhood conception of responsibility" and "to think in terms of larger units and to widen the boundaries of our responsibility." The war had exposed widespread educational failures that had underscored the fact that "wherever education breaks down, whether by reasons of poverty, neglect, or indifference, there democracy is in danger." It was becoming apparent, he argued, that due to "inequality in the distribution of wealth and educational problems," expanded state responsibility and action were necessary. We should "tax wealth wherever it is for the education of children, wherever they live, for the solution of our educational problems, wherever they are found, for the production of that equality of educational opportunity without which democracy can never realize itself to the full."[1]

Providing democratic equality of educational opportunity in the form of equal access, Smith argued, was the chief goal of state action. However, he warned that states must be careful to build upon local support and consciousness of expanded responsibility, or state policies might be viewed as "the officious action of an outside body not answerable to the people" and therefore be "mischievous" and "demoralizing." It was important, he argued, for local and state officials to govern as "co-working agencies, each to supplement the other, created to make effective the ideals and purpose of the people in education."[2]

Smith's call for a stronger state government role to safeguard equal opportunity by addressing inequities wrought by social, economic, and demographic changes reflected a larger discussion that defined the post–World

War I era about the state role in and responsibility for education. For decades states had been experimenting with new types of supervision, regulation, and aid to promote local educational reform and address particular needs and demands. However, World War I prompted many Americans to reassess education and its relationship to democracy, in light of failures the war exposed in literacy, health, and patriotism of the citizenry and the striking inequalities it exposed across space, the consequences of which took on new significance in wartime. In the postwar era, reformers and policymakers articulated a stronger state interest in schooling and state responsibility to better equalize opportunities and costs. They pursued equalization through new state fiscal policies, expanded state administration, and new minimum standards. Yet in theory and in practice, equalization did not mean the same for all. Rather, reformers defined equal educational opportunity as access to an adequate minimum education that was differentiated and defined by one's race, gender, and place, among other considerations.

The discussion that followed Smith's address at the NEA reflected some of the tensions and debates that characterized this discussion of the state role in the postwar era. Many audience members agreed with Smith's call for expanded state responsibility. North Carolina state superintendent James Joyner described the growth of the state role in education as "the logical evolution of an expanding civilization and an enlarged conception of democratic obligation." Because of growing inequities in the distribution of wealth, population, and intelligence, he argued, some state centralization was necessary to achieve the "fundamental principle of democracy": "equal educational opportunity."[3]

Not everyone was as enthusiastic about the growing state role, however. Wisconsin state superintendent C. P. Cary warned that centralization means "red tape, politics, compulsion, loss of public interest; it means a handed-down-from-above type of education" that will impair democracy, not expand it. Democracy, he argued, "is a moving affair, a going concern, a growing concern, a matter of personal interest and intelligence on the part of every citizen" that comes from participation in affairs and "keeping the schools close to the people." While "autocratic efficiency" might have some benefits, he argued, "the efficiency of Germany is not worth what it costs." Implicit in Cary's critique was a different definition of core democratic values. While Smith and Joyner emphasized equal opportunity as the centerpiece of democracy, Cary defined it as self-government. Centralized control undermined participation in schooling by the people and thus threatened not only to diminish local autonomy and self-government but also to undermine the democratic values it fostered in the individual, including personal and social responsibility. Too much centralization, he argued, was bad for education and bad for democracy itself.[4]

Although Cary critiqued the emphasis on equality of opportunity and educational efficiency over self-government, he and Smith shared common ground that reflected a near-consensus in the larger postwar reform conversation. Like Smith and Cary, most educators, policymakers, and reformers viewed local participation and investment in education as crucial to its success and viewed state bureaucratic centralization with suspicion. The key question, most agreed, was how to maintain local control, effort, and responsibility while also ensuring, for the good of the state, that all children had access to minimum school opportunities. State legislatures and administrators tried to embrace both goals and balance them when in tension, with policies that defined equalization as a minimum standard of education pursued in cooperation and conversation with local districts. States used aid, standards, and supervision to prod, reward, and subtly shape local effort and to encourage local support for and identification with state policies. Rather than usurp control, states often utilized the dynamics of federalism to spur reform, including the dynamics of local competition and the influence of national organizations, networks, and models. In the process they succeeded in exerting leadership, constructing and elevating statewide standards, and drawing once disparate schools into more tightly coordinated relationships.

Scholars have largely neglected this state role, in part because by design it did not hew to the models of bureaucratic governance or reflect an overt upward shift in control from districts to the state level. The state role was often subtle, modest, and even hidden, working as it did with local districts to achieve goals in ways that guided them to embrace state policies as their own and obscure state coercion and pressure. Guiding and shaping local action, rather than taking overt control, sometimes obscured the hand of the state, but it made it no less present or powerful.[5]

State Government Promotion of Local Schooling before World War I

In 1890, the Indiana Supreme Court considered a legal challenge to the new statewide textbook-adoption law by a township school trustee who argued that it violated local rights of self-government. While previously township trustees—the local school officials in Indiana—had selected books and negotiated the price at which parents could buy the text from the publisher, the new law directed the state board of education to select textbooks for five-year adoption in the public schools and sell to parents at cost. Responding to complaints from parents and school officials about price gouging, bribery, frequent re-adoptions, and other unscrupulous practices by textbook publishers, state legislatures in a dozen states created similar laws in the late nineteenth century that aimed to control costs and protect parents as consumers. A handful of states paired statewide adoption with state laws mandating that school districts provide free textbooks to students. In the overwhelming majority of states, however, textbook consumers were parents who had once sent their children to school with whatever textbooks the family owned, but increasingly had to purchase required texts for a standardized curriculum.[6]

Haworth's challenge to the textbook law on the grounds that it violated rights of local self-governance reflected a popular understanding that schools were local institutions and the state role was a limited one, an understanding reinforced by state policy in the nineteenth century. Although under state constitutions, state legislatures were responsible for maintaining a system of common schools, they had discharged this duty, as they did in so many other areas of public policy in the nineteenth century, by delegating the task to localities. In schooling, this meant leaving finance, governance, and management largely to local school districts. State legislatures created and shaped the legal framework of schooling; they established procedures for the formation of school districts, defined their powers and duties, permitted and then required local taxation for school purposes, created rules for local certification of teachers, and defined new township, county, and state supervisory positions, among others.[7]

However, state legislatures shaped the rules of the game most often with an eye to releasing local energy and promoting local innovation. For example, when some localities petitioned for power to form special taxing districts to support a high school or other school improvements, or requested new city charters to reorganize and expand schooling, legislatures usually obliged. Legislatures also sought to promote local effort through distribution of benefits and general encouragement of education. They funded state normal schools, for example, to promote teacher training and created state permanent school funds from the proceeds of federal land sales that were distributed to districts on the basis of school-age population.[8]

Consequently, for most Americans in the nineteenth century, the state role was all but invisible. Schooling was a local institution, controlled by the community, financed almost entirely through local property tax, managed by the locally elected school board, and oriented toward the needs and demands of local families. Occasional efforts by state legislatures to change school rules or define state goals were often met with tremendous controversy in the nineteenth century. Charges of "state centralization" surrounded efforts to establish state superintendents in New England and the Midwest, for example, even though the positions were limited to collecting and distributing information about the schools and had no administrative authority or staff. In several states the office of state superintendent was established, left vacant, abolished, and reestablished, sometimes several times, before it became a permanent position due to this resistance. Likewise, proposals to establish township or county school positions, in addition or in lieu of district ones, frequently met with substantial opposition. In Indiana, township control over schools was established after decades of discussion and debate. However, in nearby Wisconsin it was adopted only on a voluntary basis, and rarely at that, and in Michigan it was consistently rejected by the legislature.[9]

In the decades after the Civil War, these state interventions to shape the framework of schooling and prescribe state goals increased in response to myriad pressures, but in practice they usually continued to delegate and defer to local management of schools. Over a dozen states, for example, passed their first compulsory attendance laws in the midst of Reconstruction-era discussions about the national dangers of ignorance. In 1890, the U.S. commissioner of education reported they were "dead letters" since no local districts chose to enforce them; it was not until the twentieth century when child labor reformers pressured districts for local enforcement and lobbied for stronger state laws to strengthen that enforcement that attendance laws developed as a policy. Similarly, state legislatures in many states added curriculum requirements in the nineteenth century that operated in most cases as moral suasion or suggestion rather than actual requirement. The Women's Christian Temperance Union (WCTU) engineered a successful lobbying campaign that convinced legislators in thirty-three states by 1890 to require scientific temperance instruction in the schools. States recommended instructional materials, but with no commitment or apparatus for enforcement, local teachers and school boards chose whether and how to incorporate the new subject. Many simply ignored it, prompting the WCTU to mobilize grassroots campaigns to pressure local schools to implement the state requirement.[10]

Textbook adoption, already a highly charged political issue, was a particularly contentious area of state policy precisely because the new state requirements came with stronger enforcement mechanisms and state officials proved more willing to use them. In Indiana, the new state statute prescribed penalties for local officials who failed to comply with the law that could be, and was, enforced through the courts. It was this stronger assertion of state regulation over schooling that provoked Haworth's challenge to the law on the grounds that it violated rights of local self-government.

In its opinion in *State v. Haworth*, the Indiana Supreme Court offered a lengthy, substantive analysis about state power in education and the relationship of state legislatures and local districts. Rejecting Haworth's claim that schools were local institutions, the court drew from an assortment of recent state cases and legal treatises to argue that "essentially and intrinsically, the schools in which are educated and trained the children who are to become the rulers of the commonwealth are matters of state, and not of local, jurisdiction." In schooling, the court argued, "the state is a unit, and the legislature the source of power." As the "central power" in schooling, the state legislature had "unrestricted discretion and an unfettered choice of methods" on how to deliver schooling. It could delegate authority to the state board of education or to county, city, township, or district organizations and "may change plans as often as it deems necessary or expedient." In other words, the state legislature, whose power over schools was "plenary," retained supreme authority over schools, regardless of past deference or delegation to local townships.[11]

This definition of schools as state rather than local institutions and the state legislature as the supreme authority in schooling had important consequences for state-local relations. In *Haworth* and subsequent cases, state courts agreed that the school district was a "subordinate agency of the state doing the work of the state," as the Oklahoma Supreme Court framed it; the district was merely a "quasi-corporation" exercising only the authority given to it by the legislature. Consequently local districts could not challenge legislative moves to consolidate school districts, reorganize administrative units, or reallocate resources. Local school trustees had no vested right to school property or existing arrangements and no right to self-government since schools were inherently state institutions. This definition of schools as state rather than local institutions also shaped the relationship between schools and city governments. A California court rejected a city treasurer's attempt to claim excess school funds for municipal government, noting that "school moneys never lose their character of public moneys belonging to the state." In this and other cases, state courts gave school districts considerable autonomy from city government by defining them as state rather than municipal institutions. They were therefore independent from city government and municipal control unless the state legislature explicitly decided otherwise.[12]

The court's analysis about the nature of state authority over schools in *Haworth* was adopted and extended by state courts throughout the nation in the next two decades. The Tennessee Supreme Court, for example, quoted *Haworth* at length in responding to a similar challenge in 1899 to the state's new textbook-adoption law. Noting that the court's reasoning in *Haworth* "is so satisfactory and conclusive that we cannot perhaps do better than give a synopsis of it," the Tennessee Supreme Court affirmed that education was foremost a state, not local, matter and that the state legislature was the supreme power in schooling. Like the Indiana court in *Haworth*, the Tennessee court held that education was a state function because the state constitution made it one, but it also went further by framing education as a function of the state's police power, or inherent lawmaking authority to regulate on behalf of the health, safety, and welfare of the people. The object of education, the court reasoned, was to "provid[e] and secur[e] a higher state of intelligence and morals" that would "prevent crime" and "conserve the peace, good order, and well-being of society." Protection, it argued, was "the highest exercise of the police power of the state, whether done by punishing offenders or educating the children." Other state courts agreed, for example a Kentucky court of appeals, defining education as a "prerogative of sovereignty" for the protection of the state, no less important than the power to raise troops in wartime, for "upon preparation of the youngest generations for civic duties depends the perpetuity of this government." This expansive state interest in and authority over schooling, rooted in the very sovereignty of the state, provided a powerful rationale for state educational regulations and foreclosed most legal challenges by localities and, as the next chapter will explore, by parents.[13]

State police power was a powerful legal framework for state regulation of schooling as state and federal courts gave it an expansive reading in the late nineteenth and early twentieth centuries. State police power, courts and legal treatises agreed, was an inherent lawmaking power of the state to regulate on behalf of the public health, safety, and welfare, and was limited only when it conflicted with other provisions of state and federal constitutions. In the period, a deeply contentious question, legally and politically, was the extent to which the Fourteenth Amendment and its protection of individual rights, like freedom of contract, imposed limits on state police power. Many progressive critics at the time and historians since have portrayed the Supreme Court as hostile to state social regulations. They have emphasized judicial obstructionism based on court decisions in a handful of high-profile cases, like *Lochner v. New York*, which struck down protective labor legislation limiting bakers' working hours to sixty per week. However these rejections of state police power regulations were the exception rather than rule. A 1911 study of all 560 cases in which a state economic or social regulation was at issue between 1887 and 1911 found that the U.S. Supreme

Court struck down only three as unconstitutional. Despite the persistent narrative of judicial obstructionism, federal and state courts sustained the overwhelming majority of social and economic regulations and new administrative forms and functions, including in education. Consequently, state legislatures had extensive legal authority in education, as courts found few limits to their inherent power to legislate on its behalf.[14]

In the next two decades, state courts across the nation applied and expanded these education decisions with a surprising degree of consistency, given the varied state constitutions, statutes, and circumstances. Except for a few highly charged areas of policy with idiosyncratic state provisions— most notably Bible reading in the public schools—state courts drew from and articulated a set of general legal principles about the school and the state that amounted to a national body of education case law. By the start of World War I, it was well settled across the nation that education was a state function, schools were state institutions, and education fell within the purview of state police powers as a fundamental state interest.[15]

While the legal articulation of the state legislature's power over education was expansive, state legislatures in the decades before World War I tended to aid and incentivize local effort and build on local efforts and support. States empowered cities and reform-minded rural districts to innovate by authorizing new arrangements like city charters and district consolidation and by offering special aid and supervision. For all the cries of "state centralization" in a few highly charged policy areas like textbook regulation, the state role in the early twentieth century grew steadily and usually quietly as legislatures continued to frame state policies and add new tools to release local energy, often in response to local demands and national pressures.

Two major new areas of state policy—rural school reform and high school reform—reflected the growing role of state legislatures and departments of education in helping local districts meet the challenges of the new education and were also key sites where states experimented with new techniques and authority. As the previous chapter explored, state legislatures and superintendents focused new attention on rural schools before World War I in response to national and local pressure to modernize them. Sporadic concerns about the disparity between rural and urban schools developed into a national school reform movement after the 1909 Country Life Commission report framed schooling as a solution to the broader country life problem, namely the impact of industrialization on the countryside. Rural school reformers, mobilizing at local, state, and national levels, worked to modernize rural schools by building local support for reform and enhancing professional leadership. However, they also turned to the state for assistance. Reform-minded localities and reform organizations lobbied state legislatures for laws and policies to enable local reform, including laws to authorize district consolidation, free public transportation, and county rural supervisors. They also urged new state aid and leadership, including state rural supervisors and targeted grants-in-aid for school libraries, consolidation, vocational education, and transportation, among others.

These new policies combined traditional state goals with new techniques. They aimed to release local energy and stimulate local reform, but they also carried with them new and subtle forms of state influence. State rural supervisors, for example, framed their roles as mentors and boosters for local reform that worked with local officials on a largely voluntary basis. However, these new agents of the state department of education guided districts to state and professional standards and reform priorities. They encouraged districts to consolidate, for example, or to add new agricultural subjects and activities to the curriculum by building popular support, appealing to the professional identity of school officials, and using the example of other localities to stoke local pride and competition for the purposes of reform. Likewise, targeted state aid for rural school libraries was voluntary and aimed to stimulate local effort by matching local contributions with state funds. This state money often came with some requirements, however, such as rules about the size of the library, access policies, and library maintenance, that stemmed from legislative concerns that state money be spent well. State aid reflected stronger efforts to influence and shape local practice—defining minimum standards and incentivizing particular practices—and also gave states greater power to apply pressure if they chose to do so.[16]

Rural school standardization programs offer a telling example of the ways in which state leadership shaped local practice toward state goals while building on local effort and control. Beginning around 1910, dozens of states developed rural standardization programs using rural scorecards. The scorecards, filled out by local or county school officials, gave points and recognition to schools that met prescribed standards. In Virginia, for example, the first rural scorecard in 1915 awarded points for things like teacher's professional membership in an association (3 points), seven-month or longer school term (3 points), average daily attendance of 80 percent (2 points), neat grounds and shade trees (2 points), two sanitary outhouses (2 points), window shades (1 point), and state aid library (8 points). Schools that achieved 90 out of 100 possible points were designated a standard school, entitled to a framed diploma, and recognized in an annual published registry. Participation was voluntary and in most states the reward was simply bragging rights, although by the mid-1920s a handful of states like Iowa tied state aid to standard schools. Observers noted that in the thirty-four states that used them by 1925, rural scorecards gave small schools standards to which they could aspire. The scorecards, adopted on a voluntary basis, thus appealed to local pride and helped foster adherence to state-defined standards without a sense of state imposition.[17]

State legislatures and departments of education also responded to myriad demands for expanding opportunities, defining common goals, and addressing challenges of the new education in high school policies. In the late nineteenth century, as high schools developed rapidly in cities, state legislatures faced pressure from towns, villages, and rural districts that could not afford to build them to make high school opportunities more widely available. To that end, legislatures authorized a variety of legal forms and practices including new types of districts, county and township high schools, and laws that required home districts to pay tuition of students that had to transfer to another district for high schooling.[18]

At the same time, nearly half of state legislatures by 1916 encouraged high school building by offering state matching aid tied to minimum standards. In South Carolina, for example, state-aided high schools had to establish an eight-month school term, hire teachers with first-grade certificates, and maintain a minimum level of attendance. High school aid funds had the largest impact in the South, where high schooling lagged far behind the rest of the nation by the early twentieth century. Virginia's high school aid fund, for example, stimulated a nearly eightfold increase in high schools within five years: when it was established in 1905 there were only forty-four public high schools in the state, including only ten four-year schools, but in 1910 the number had grown to 341 high schools, including eighty-three four-year schools.[19]

Another major set of pressures around high schools emanated from universities and high school administrators who wrestled with the problem of "articulation"—the coordination of high schooling and college. Traditionally, college entrance had been determined by institution-specific exam, but both high school and college administrators had an interest in facilitating college attendance by making the process less idiosyncratic. The University of Michigan, led by institution-builder James Angell, was among the first to experiment with a new method to try to increase its applicant pool: beginning in 1871 it sent faculty to inspect and approve high schools so that graduates could enter the university without examination. By 1890, about half of the students entered the university through eighty-two approved schools. The accreditation model was adopted by other universities by the turn of the century with great variation in the standards and process for approval. Universities struggled to articulate standards beyond the vague and subjective "satisfactory" rendered by Michigan faculty, and they met with one another and representatives from high schools to articulate national principles for curriculum content and standards. They organized forums like the NEA Committee of Ten (1893) and formed regional associations, including the New England Association of Colleges and Preparatory Schools (1885) and North Central Association (1895), to coordinate high school and college standards.[20]

Although most of the activity in establishing accreditation and curricular standards for high schools developed at universities and in professional, voluntary associations, state departments of education were slowly drawn into the work. Regional accreditation agencies, like the North Central Association, began to accredit high schools for their members but set such high standards that they approved only a small fraction of schools. This left most local communities, which were making a costly investment in high schools, without the guidance they needed for college articulation and without standards to govern the large majority of students not bound for college. Furthermore, it left each university with the onerous burden of inspecting and accrediting the growing number of high schools. Under pressure from local communities and universities, states began to develop systems of classification and employ high school supervisors to visit schools and encourage higher standards that could be articulated with college. In 1889 Wisconsin appointed the first state high school agent, and by 1920, twenty-seven state departments of education assumed responsibility for high school supervision, most after 1905, when the General Education Board (GEB) helped stimulate and redefine the work.[21]

Beginning in 1905, the GEB funded "professors of secondary education" in Southern states to work with universities and state departments of education to promote high school development, advise and supervise localities, and accredit high schools for the university. Much as it would shortly do with state rural supervisors for black and white schools, the GEB defined the "main and principal work" of the new agents to be building local infrastructure and support for reform. The new agents were told to ascertain where "the conditions are favorable for the establishment of public high schools" and assist and advise local leader so as "to create in such communities a public sentiment that shall permanently sustain such high schools." In contrast to the first high school inspectors in the North who initially emphasized inspection, the GEB agents framed their work, in the words of one agent, as "high school propaganda," which required encouraging local support and effort. In his first three years on the job, for example, Bruce Payne of Virginia reported making hundreds of visits to communities to give public addresses, meet with school and town officials to broker deals, and advise local officials in applications for state aid. He and his successor,

Charles Maphis, had authority to accredit schools for the university, but rather than frame their work as inspection they emphasized guidance, including advice to local officials on the course of study and other aspects of schooling, often at the invitation of local officials.[22]

This style shaped state high school work outside of the South as other states began to decrease the emphasis on inspection and instead frame the work of high school agents as supervision, leadership, and service. One history of state administration in Minnesota reported that the high school agent's reputation at the turn of the century was one of "dictatorial, uncompromising 'snooper,'" but over time he assumed the role of "leadership" and used "influence and expertise in improving schools to greater levels of excellence." Like rural supervisors emerging at the same time, high school supervisors thus supported local school administration while working to shape it.[23]

Although high school supervisors and aid encouraged and supported local effort, state accreditation of high schools also expanded the authority of the state in myriad ways. It required states to define clear minimum standards for approval in areas like curriculum, teacher qualifications, building facilities and equipment, and school size. In many places, states categorized schools, based on size, and elaborated differentiated standards for approval. As states began to elaborate standards they also began to shape and standardize curriculum through state high school courses of study. In Louisiana, for example, high schools seeking state approval had to have a nine-month school term, two or more certified teachers, minimum laboratory facilities and equipment, recitation periods of forty minutes or more, and obedience to the state course of study. This approval not only accredited the high school for colleges but determined the level of state aid it would receive. Over time these standards were raised, and state aid for high school support in Louisiana and other states reinforced these minimum standards, as did federal vocational aid after 1917, which flowed through state departments of education. Experts argued that classification was a spur to local effort, for much like rural school scorecards, it gave local schools standards to aspire to and stoked local pride and competition for improvement.[24]

Thus, in the early twentieth century, state legislatures experimented with new legal rules, targeted aid, and state supervision in uneven and piecemeal ways to address particular needs. High school and rural school reform were two of the largest new areas of state action, both of which were driven in large part by local pressure from districts that sought expanded opportunities as well as institutions like universities and philanthropies with state and national concerns. While experimenting with new forms and techniques, the growing state role still largely reflected the traditional goal of promoting local schooling and unleashing the energy of local districts, with some additional new influence and oversight. Yet they had broad legal authority to do more.

Some of the limitations of this approach were already becoming clear before World War I as many districts could not or would not reform their schools and inequalities within the countryside grew. In creating a sense of national crisis about school failure across space, the war reshaped the conversation and prompted states to claim more expansive responsibility to ensure a minimum level of educational quality. The myriad experiments before World War I were extended more broadly and deeply throughout the nation after the war, as states redefined the responsibility of the state in education.

World War I, Equal Educational Opportunity, and the Nation-State Interest in Schooling

On the eve of American entry into World War I, state legislatures and departments of education throughout the nation were expanding their functions, rationales, and responsibilities in incremental and idiosyncratic ways. American mobilization for the war transformed the role of state government in education. A series of lessons drawn from this experience fueled postwar reforms to provide more centralized leadership and aid. While some observers were impressed by the power and promise of schooling to mold the citizenry—through both examples of American citizen mobilization and German nationalism—most commentators were struck instead by the educational failures that the war exposed. To many observers, the war revealed dangerous civic failures, including wartime slackers, dissidents, and hyphenated Americans with divided national loyalty that all demonstrated the schools' failure to Americanize immigrants and teach citizenship to all. One educator argued in 1918 that the war highlighted "the need for a more intensive study of the problems of modern democracy" in order "to develop in the average citizen a sense of his own obligation as a member of representative democracy to render continuous service for the common good."[25]

Furthermore, the release of statistics on draft rejections painted a shocking picture of the citizenry and highlighted the national costs of educational failures: 25 percent of the 2.7 million men examined for the draft were found to be illiterate and nearly 30 percent were discharged as physically unfit for military service, many from problems that could have been remedied in childhood. An additional 30 percent of draftees, men who were supposed to be in their physical prime, had documented physical defects, which raised concerns about the overall health and vigor of the citizen body.[26]

While these educational failures were troubling, one of the most jarring revelations for many Americans was the extent to which they were found among native-born, white, rural youths. Native-born white Americans constituted 60 percent of the illiterates, and over three-quarters of these illiterates came from rural communities, demonstrating the continued salience and costs of the rural school problem. The hundreds of thousands of unhealthy and illiterate young men unable to defend their nation in war, observers noted, represented a major failing of the schools and drew attention to the tremendous disparities across space in the quality and reach of the school. One commentator in the *New Republic* called "the inequality of achievement of the schools throughout the country" the "most striking revelation in education during recent years." The California state superintendent told a conference of school administrators in 1920 that "the war has clearly demonstrated that education can no longer be regarded as a matter of purely local concern." The draft lessons should not be forgotten, he warned, for "men who must be educated in time of war so that they shall be fit to fight for their country ought to be educated in time of peace so they may live for their country."[27]

Other commentators agreed that the war drove home the importance of education for the state and nation, one text noting in 1920 that "The child in the little miserable mining town is just as truly a national asset as is the child born on Fifth Avenue in New York." The war revealed that "it cannot be left wholly to the community to say what kind of school it will have. The state has a stake in the schools of every community, and the Nation has an interest in the schools of every state." Education transcended the family and community to have significant state and national implications.[28]

The wartime lessons about the disastrous national consequences of weak schools and inequality across space convinced a number of groups to support federal intervention. In 1918, Senator Hoke Smith of Georgia introduced legislation drafted by the NEA to create a federal department of education and give federal aid to states to support teachers' salaries, literacy, and Americanization, and promote health and physical education. Smith had previously cosponsored two successful bills for federal grants-in-aid to agricultural extension (Smith-Lever Act, 1914) and vocational education (Smith-Hughes Act, 1917) and viewed the proposed Smith-Towner Act as "good business" and "preparedness for war as well as peace." He explained to the *Forum* that money for educational training "is the best investment bound to earn ten-fold and even a hundred-fold. It produces wealth. It develops citizens. And it guards against discontent by satisfying the aspirations of the people." Others similarly argued that education served important national purposes and it should therefore receive federal support because it was "unfair to ask local communities to bear the entire burden of a problem which is state and national."[29]

The NEA, which had recently undergone a large membership drive and created a special legislative lobbying division, became the driving organizational force for federal aid as it was debated, rejected, and reintroduced into every session of Congress for the next decade with minor changes in name and provisions. Other supporters of the bill included women's organizations like the National Federation of Women's Clubs, organized labor including the American Federation of Labor, and fraternal and nationalist organizations like Scottish Rite Masons who all testified before Congress and supported lobbying efforts. While supporters of the first Smith-Towner Bill in 1918 framed it in nationalist terms and supported federally imposed minimum standards to accompany the aid, the outcry against federal control made them shift their rhetorical strategy and write into the text of subsequent versions that federal aid would respect state autonomy and not impose federal control.[30]

In addition to arguing for the national interest in education, supporters argued that federal aid was necessary because it alone could provide the equality of educational opportunity necessary for democracy. Teachers College professor William Bagley argued that only through federal aid could "the gross inequalities of educational opportunity now existing thruout the country be significantly reduced and in no other way can the nation be assured of the high level of trained and informed intelligence which effective democracy needs above all else." Scholars backed up the claims with new studies about disparities in wealth within and between states. An NEA study, *The Ability of States to Support Education*, concluded that "some states must bear tax rates five and six times as great as other states to provide a given school opportunity for their children" and that "the states differ widely in their economic ability to support education." The "accomplishment of a great national purpose" like education, others argued, should not "depend upon burdening the people of one state many times as heavily as those of another state."[31]

Federal aid was necessary to alleviate unequal burdens and promote equal opportunity, for, as one educator explained, some states were too poor and others were "negligent and do not recognize their responsibility." He argued that "the nation cannot afford to let children suffer through an accident of birth because of either the poverty or the negligence of their state. The children are citizens of the United States as well as of the state of their birth, and the nation should see to it that they have the proper educational advantages." This call for equalization of educational opportunities and burdens through federal funding became a dominant rationale for federal aid in the 1920s and again when the issue resurfaced the next decade.[32]

Opponents of federal aid argued that it would lead to federal control and would undermine local autonomy and democracy. The newly formed National Catholic Welfare Council (NCWC) spearheaded opposition to the bill, objecting to its centralization, its impact on private schools, the anti-Catholic undertones of nationalist rhetoric, and the anti-Catholic activism of many of the bill's supporters. It was joined in opposition at congressional hearings and in public debates by business groups including the National Association of Manufacturers and veterans' associations like the Sentinels of the Republic. A host of educators dissented from the NEA position, including Columbia University president Nicholas Murray Butler.[33]

Opponents of federal aid criticized the claim by the bill's supporters that federal money would not usurp state and local control. One educator noted that history proved this wrong, including recent federal vocational aid, for it showed "the increasing power and control in management acquired by those who have the funds to distribute." Over time, he argued, states will become "merely automatic agencies for carrying out federal ideas" and there would be "federal influence through federal standards—all-pervading and all-controlling." Another educator reasoned that federal subsidies required one "to choose between the two horns of a vicious dilemma": "either he must advocate a policy of granting subsidies without provision for their supervision, accounting, and control, or he must advocate a policy of granting subsidies with definite provision for some control over their uses." One would potentially waste money and fail at its goals while the other would undermine local and state autonomy.[34]

Federal money and influence would erode local autonomy and responsibility, opponents argued, and thereby undermine education and democracy itself. Many opponents saw it as part of a broader and more troubling trend toward "federalization" and "bureaucracy," which stifled community and individual self-reliance. A *Boston Herald* editorial warned that the bill was a "step towards tyranny through socialism—a long step towards the disintegration of our federated republic," and the *Boston Transcript* similarly critiqued it as a "bill to Europeanize the educational system of the United States." Federal centralization "would end in the destruction of the very substance of Americanism, which is individualism, self-reliance, initiative, and responsibility," another educator reasoned.[35]

Catholic leaders made this argument persistently. Catholic University professor Rev. James Ryan argued that the proposed bill would lead to "federalized education" and was a step toward "autocracy" and "socialism." He warned that federal aid would "paralyze local initiative and impose upon every community a set of rigid standards wholly unadaptable to local needs and conditions." Ryan argued that "with all its blunderings and mistakes, educational liberty is to be preferred either to the rule of autocracy, no matter how benign, or of a bureaucracy, no matter how efficient." A Catholic University graduate student agreed that education reform must come from "voluntary co-operation and local initiative" rather than "excessive legislation," because "coercion may prove effective, but it is not the instrument of a free people." Catholics and many other opponents of the federal aid warned that American democracy and freedom—defined by local autonomy, self-government, and responsibility—would be demoralized by federal intervention.[36]

Although proponents of federal aid to education pressed the issue throughout the 1920s, they ultimately could not convince the majority of federal legislators and overcome deeply held suspicions that federal aid would come with federal control. Yet the discussion around federal aid and national responsibility shaped educational reform at the state level. The debate forcefully raised the problem of equality of educational opportunity, and while Congress rejected a federal solution, state legislators and departments of education increasingly embraced a state responsibility to equalize school burdens and opportunities in the larger state interest. Many opponents of federal aid supported these state-level solutions in part as an alternative to federal intervention. Legislatures expanded state aid and used it for equalization purposes after the war and at the same time established a host of new minimum standards tied to this aid. State legislatures, for example, addressed concerns about low teacher supply and quality by enacting new minimum teacher salary schedules that tied salary to minimum professional qualifications and used it in calculations of state aid.[37]

A few states had experimented in limited ways with state aid for districts with low property valuation before the war, but an emerging cadre of school finance experts helped them to transform piecemeal experimentation and theoretical commitments to financial equalization into a major state policy in the 1920s and 1930s. The conversation was carried out in state survey consulting work, philanthropically funded national investigations, and university-based research studies, including the Educational Finance Inquiry (1921–24) sponsored by the GEB and American Council of Education, and a series of state finance studies by Fletcher Swift and his graduate students at the University of Minnesota. The largest and most influential body of work, however, was done by Paul Mort and his Teachers College graduate students who defined methods for equalization, including measurements for local need and ability to pay and formulas to develop a state minimum, or foundation, program. Mort directed the National Survey of School Finance (1931–33) funded by Congress, trained scores of graduate students, and consulted on dozens of influential state finance surveys from the 1920s through the 1960s. He developed the Mort Plan, a weighted-per-pupil formula for state foundation plans, which was adopted by dozens of states in the interwar years and became the dominant model for state funding after World War II.[38]

In making the case for equalization and defining new methods, scholars documented tremendous disparities between localities in their school spending and tax burden, rooted in the unequal geographic distribution of wealth. In 1922, for example, Swift documented that counties in Colorado varied in wealth from $22,000 to $1,800 per school child while within counties the disparity in ability to pay was even greater: in Conejos County, wealth per child varied from $617 to $26,500, resulting in tax burdens seven times greater or more in some districts than others within the county. Likewise in Georgia, a 1925 study that prompted a new state equalization funding plan found that the wealthiest county had an assessed valuation of $153,286 per teacher while the poorest had a valuation of only $13,693 per teacher, making it over eleven times more able to support schools. In study after study, scholars quantified differences in spending, term length, and teacher salaries within states and linked them to disparities in property valuation. The problem was structural, they argued, for many communities were putting in maximum local effort, as defined by a heavy tax burden, but were still only able to afford cheap schools. At the same time property-rich districts were able to have high-quality schools with very little local effort. It was "the height of absurdity," Fletcher Swift argued, to expect local units to "offer educational opportunities approaching any degree of equality" when they were "so unequal in wealth, and consequently in ability to finance schools."[39]

While some scholars in the interwar years argued for reorganization or abolition of districts in favor of county units to address this problem, most converged on state aid as a solution. They argued both for a higher proportion of school funding to come from the state and for this funding to be collected and distributed in a manner to equalize burden and opportunity. In these studies, scholars defined equalization, as did Paul Mort, as "a minimum satisfactory offering with a burden falling equally on all parts of the state." This meant, as one scholar explained, "the state should see that all subdivisions are required to operate the public schools for a minimum number of days, to pay a minimum annual salary to teachers and administrators of given qualification, and to set aside for the support of the public schools a minimum tax rate on the local assessment" and then "the state should make up difference between cost and what can be raised locally." In other words, states should prescribe minimum standards for things like term length and teacher salaries, and if localities were unable to afford the minimums with reasonable local tax rates, the state should assist.[40]

However, scholars were quick to point out, equalization did not mean trying to erase differences or provide the same education for all, and they suggested that such an approach would be foolhardy and even dangerous. One scholar explained that "the arguments for state equalization, if pushed to their logical conclusion, might seem to require the state to provide all support, to bring about absolute uniformity of burdens, and to secure identical opportunities for all children." However, this was "absurd," he argued, "unsound theoretically" and "impossible practically." The goal was "satisfactory school facilities for the general good," a "sane middle ground" that aims to "remove the most extreme conditions and to leave to communities a margin for individuality."[41]

This margin for individuality meant that localities should be free to exceed the minimum state program, for local effort was a driving force of educational innovation. Mort argued that "the progress of education within a given state depends largely upon the willingness of individual communities to move beyond the established level set by the state. A continually changing social order demands this constant experimentation and change in educational programs." States must help offset the cost of a minimum program while not monopolizing all taxing power or retarding local initiative. Consequently, while scholars argued forcefully for an increased state share in school funding and for changes in the method of distribution to take greater account of local need and ability to pay, they also maintained that local school finance should remain a crucial part of school support. One finance scholar warned that any plan without substantial local support would "rob the community of its right and power of initiative and its feeling of personal interest in the school because of its personal investment."[42]

A few reformers tried to expand and reframe the language of equalization to demand that states do more to close gaps and address systematic inequities, including racial and socioeconomic ones. Nolan Irby, for example, wrote his dissertation at Peabody College for Teachers on the need for educational equalization in Arkansas and was one of few white finance scholars to quantify the racial disparity in school facilities and to make the case for equalizing black schools with white ones. African American scholars, including the USBE specialist of Negro Education, similarly used the language of equalization to argue for greater investment in black schools in the South. In addition, some New Deal officials, including Harry Hopkins, tried to expand the conception of equalization to target socioeconomic gaps and urge more fundamental redistribution of school opportunities—in other words to press for equalization as a guarantee of the same funding and standards rather than merely a minimum level. For the most part, however, the widespread commitment to local effort and control mitigated against a definition of equalization as the same education for all. Consequently, although the language of "equal educational opportunity" seemed universalistic, in practice policymakers and experts framed it as creating a floor below which no locality should be permitted to fall rather than as an effort to close gaps.[43]

This educational floor was differentiated by race, which had the contradictory impact of both institutionalizing racial disparity in the short term and providing long-term impetus for black school improvement. Louisiana, for example, had a separate and lower teacher salary schedule for black teachers than white ones, and Maryland mandated a minimum term length of forty days longer for white schools than black ones. The establishment of minimum standards therefore wrote racial inequities into the law, inequities widely in practice but usually off of the statute books in most Southern states. Even though the standards lagged behind those for whites, they did draw attention to black schools that were far below the minimum standards and put pressure on localities to raise teacher salaries and lengthen school terms. In states like North Carolina, which was concerned about black out-migration and regarded itself as educationally progressive, these standards drew new attention to and improvement efforts for black schools. Furthermore, these state minimum standards provided strong legal arguments, and often irrefutable evidence, of educational inequality for the NAACP's legal campaign for school equalization that began in the late 1930s.[44]

In the majority of states after the war, legislatures increased state aid for schooling and embraced equalization as a goal of state fiscal policy, experimenting with different ways to address local need without undermining local effort and responsibility. Some grafted equalization onto existing state aid and others reconstituted the entire basis of school funding. In New York, for example, the 1925 Cole law adopted the recommendations of two survey commissions to increase state support for local districts and establish a series of equalization quotas that distributed state aid based on local need as measured by the value of taxable property and number of teachers employed. In Maryland, the state instituted a far-reaching equalization law in 1922 that required all counties to levy the same minimum tax and then paid the full remainder of the cost required to lift each locality up to the state's minimum requirements for term length and teacher salaries. The law therefore guaranteed that every school in the state would achieve a certain minimum standard and that every community would bear a minimum burden regardless of property valuation, thereby helping equalize costs and opportunities, but it also allowed each locality to exceed that minimum effort.[45]

By 1928, thirty-four states provided equalization funds or grants to localities and two additional states mandated county-level equalization. The specifics of the plans varied as did the amount of state aid that went toward the goal of equalization, with some states using the majority of state aid for this purpose and others devoting relatively little state funds. However, the trend toward equalization was clear, and growing, by the early 1930s.[46]

The emergency of the Great Depression intensified trends toward state aid and equalization. The crisis for schools was overwhelming. At the same time that youths were thrown out of the labor market and attended schools in record numbers, school budget reductions and lost property tax revenue led to severe shortfalls. Most cities slashed programs and services, increased class sizes, cut salaries, and in some cases failed to pay teachers altogether. In rural areas, thousands of schools simply closed their doors when they ran out of money. At the same time, tax reduction movements sought property tax relief through constitutional amendments, referendums, and statutes that further eroded school funding.[47]

The crisis prompted many state legislatures to increase the state share of schooling and develop new revenue sources. In West Virginia, for example, local districts paid 92 percent of the cost of schools before 1932, when popular pressure resulted in local property tax limitations. Faced with major school cutbacks, the state legislature created a new state sales tax, the revenues to be distributed to the schools to support teacher salaries according to the state salary schedule for an eight-month term. The law thus dramatically increased the state share in schooling—from 8 percent to 50 percent of school costs—and distributed it on the basis of equalization in order to guarantee a state minimum program. Likewise in Ohio, a constitutional amendment lowered the maximum tax rate on general property and created a fiscal crisis for the schools; under advice from Paul Mort, the legislature increased the state share of funding by tapping new revenue sources including sales and fuel taxes, and distributed it on the basis of equalization. It raised the state share of schooling from less than 5 percent to over 15 percent and established a state foundation program according to the Mort Plan that guaranteed a minimum, weighted-per-pupil expenditure for all children in the state.[48]

Throughout the 1930s, nearly all states established new or expanded old equalization plans and increased the amount of state aid to schools. By 1934 all but four states reported equalization funds and one-third of states, according to a national study, had substantial commitments to equalization. By 1938, the average state share of schooling had nearly doubled from 1920, reaching nearly 30 percent—within the range of 25 to 50 percent recommended by most experts. Seven states paid more than half the cost of schooling.[49]

At the same time that states assumed greater responsibility for support and equalization of school burdens and opportunities during the depression, the NEA and other supporters renewed their calls for federal aid to schools. Legislation for federal aid to K–12 schools was again introduced, debated, rejected, and reintroduced in several successive congresses. Two national commissions studied the issue and came to different conclusions: President Hoover's National Advisory Committee on Education (1931) rejected any federal aid other than small, temporary assistance, while Presidential Roosevelt's Advisory Committee on Education (1938) recommended substantial federal responsibility for schooling despite the president's reluctance to spend political capital on it. The politics of the federal aid debate were similar to the previous decade, with Catholics again emerging as the primary voice of opposition and the NEA as the main proponent of the bill. However, race played a more central role in the debate as Southern white support decreased because of fears that it would undermine segregation, a fear exacerbated by developments in the New Deal coalition, new USBE attention to black education and equalization, and the mobilization of the NAACP and African American educators to press for equitable distribution of federal resources.[50]

The arguments on behalf of federal aid were also similar to the previous decade, although the Depression replaced the lessons of World War I as the crisis that dramatized national interest, the necessity of federal action, and the democratic imperative of equal educational opportunity. John Norton of Teachers College, for example, argued that the crisis demonstrated the need "to proclaim the principle of a national minimum or foundation program of financial support for the education of every child, whether he happens to live in Maine, Arkansas, or California." The depression highlighted in even more dramatic fashion than had the war the fiscal inequities between the states as they struggled to deal with the crisis, renewing calls for the federal government to equalize costs and opportunities. Furthermore, popular support for New Deal policies legitimated federal intervention in a host of social policies once deemed the exclusive domains of states and localities and led many proponents to sense an opportunity for education. One proponent of federal aid explicitly invoked schooling as a "public works" that should be part of the New Deal, for "if such federal participation is warranted for roads, dams, and waterworks, it is equally justified for schools," for education "stands first" in importance among public projects.[51]

Opposition to federal aid again hinged on the fact that federal aid must necessarily come with some federal oversight and a fear that excessive centralization was un-American and undemocratic. Some opponents warned that centralized schools were the weapon of dictators and fascists and that Americans' decentralized system, which had grown up from the people— "folk-made," "folk-controlled and folk-directed"—would protect the nation from totalitarianism. While "there is a remote chance that some Hitler in some future time might be elected to high office in the United States," one educator noted, "he would have a difficult time, indeed, to win control of our schools and colleges." Opponents of federal aid again carried the day by invoking local control and state responsibility for education as the appropriate remedies for current educational weaknesses and resisted "Uncle Sam's long arm reaching into the little red schoolhouse." As in the previous decade, noisy debates over federal aid occupied Congress and national organizations at the same time that state legislators were quietly and decisively expanding state aid and responsibility in the background.[52]

Consequently in the two decades after World War I, Americans wrestled with education as a national interest, a project that transcended the family and community to affect the state and nation. While a persistent minority pushed for federal aid, the majority of Americans maintained that education was a state and local function. However, the federal debate may have softened some opposition to the expansion of the state government role. In all of these discussions, commentators on all sides agreed that local school finance played an important role in American education and that the state role had to be designed in ways that addressed some of the worst features of decentralization while not undermining the best. Even the most ardent centralizers argued that local finance invested communities in schools, literally and figuratively. Experts noted that it made communities feel more responsible for and more connected to their schools, which spurred further investment.

Yet despite these paeans to local control, a significant shift took place after World War I and deepened during the Depression, as states increased their responsibility for school funding and embraced the theory and practice of equalization. In the modern world, with its interdependence and its unequal distribution of wealth, states defined a new responsibility to promote equal educational opportunity—defined as a minimum, differentiated guarantee of schooling opportunities—to all students regardless of their place of birth in the interests of state and national welfare, progress, and security. They did so by increasing the state share of school finance, distributing funding to meet local needs and promote equalization, and tightening state regulations over local school finance. They also set out to develop and promote state minimum standards for school buildings, curriculum, attendance, and teachers. The greater fiscal role of the state proved to be a powerful engine for these developing state standards, and state leaders struggled with how to use this authority to promote progress and lift up the bottom without alienating local effort, responsibility, and support.

Postwar State School Administration

In the context of wartime lessons about educational failure and debates about federal aid, state legislatures adopted reforms to address the specific shortcomings exposed by World War I and to expand state administration generally. Legislatures embraced the goal of equalization and defined new minimum standards in a host of areas, using new state fiscal policies and state administration, particularly experts in the state department of education, to give meaning to those standards.

In a wave of state legislation in the five years following World War I, most states investigated and made changes to state administration, ranging from minor to major. Legislatures created or strengthened state boards of education, expanded the size and responsibilities of state departments of education, created or strengthened county superintendents and boards as an intermediary between the state and locality, and delegated a range of new responsibilities to state officials, including authority over teacher certification, building plans and specifications, and calculation and distribution of growing state aid. In New Hampshire, the state legislature appointed a lay commission to recommend new state legislation which resulted in the so-called Great School Law of 1919. This radical centralization of the state's schools provided for a powerful new state board of education, statewide supervision, special state aid and an equalization fund, and a host of new requirements and state minimum standards for attendance, medical inspection, term length, local tax rate, and teacher certification, among other things. Likewise in Alabama, the legislature invited the U.S. Bureau of Education to conduct a survey of the state's school system in 1919 and on the basis of its recommendations created a strong state board of education and reorganized and expanded the state department of education into ten divisions. In dozens of other states, expert, legislative, and lay bodies investigated the school system at the end of the war and recommended strengthening aspects of state administrative structure and authority.[53]

While some states appointed legislative or citizen committees to study the schools, many others turned to the USBE philanthropic foundations like the GEB, which had the resources and expertise to conduct major investigations of the state system as a whole. From 1916 to 1923, these agencies conducted over a dozen major state investigations that encouraged policymakers and citizens to define and conceptualize the schools as part of a system and to emphasize the connections and coordination, or lack thereof, between its parts. These expert surveys along with dozens of smaller studies helped to define expert norms and principles in the emerging field of state administration and encourage and diffuse reform. As they did in cities, states surveys usually resulted in adoption of at least some of the recommendations as experts shone a light on weaknesses in the state system and provided concrete suggestions for improvement. Emerging state scholarship also encouraged the diffusion of reform by fostering comparison and competition between states. Leonard Ayres of the Russell Sage Foundation developed a widely cited state school index that evaluated and ranked states at different points in time according to ten measures of educational efficiency. A 1922 Pennsylvania fiscal study was not alone in using the state's low ranking on the Ayres index and slippage over time as justification for major reform.[54]

Through surveys and studies, experts converged on a set of recommendations for state administration. Echoing their recommendations for city school governance, scholars urged that states create a strong, centralized state board of education to define education policy and invest a nonpartisan, expert state superintendent and his staff with strong authority to execute and administer state policy. They criticized the practice in most states of electing the state superintendent by popular vote and urged higher salaries, minimum professional credentials, and greater administrative discretion for the official. They also criticized the tendency of states to divide educational authority among several state boards and agencies and urged that the state boards of education, which ranged in practice from weak ex-officio boards to powerful policy setters, be strengthened and centralized. At the same time, experts recommended statewide supervision through county boards and superintendents, as either a local or intermediary unit of school control, and defined their proper scope of authority and relationship to other levels. In a host of other emerging state policy areas, they defined best practices, including finance, teacher certification systems, and rules regarding school terms and attendance.[55]

Although the unmistakable trend immediately after the war and in the two decades that followed was to strengthen and expand state administration, state policymakers, influenced by popular pressure, were cautious and inconsistent in their incorporation of expert recommendations. The war created popular sentiment for reform but it did not erase anxieties and resistance to state centralization and bureaucracy. In Delaware, a 1919 GEB survey recommended a major centralization of the state's school system, including controversial proposals to create strong county boards that assumed important local responsibilities like selecting teachers. Downstate rural interests strenuously objected but in the wartime zeal for reform, the recommendations narrowly passed in what the GEB director described as an "eyelash finish." Two years later, however, opponents gained the majority in the legislature. It scaled back some of the controversial changes in county authority in order to return more power to districts. In Indiana, the legislature passed a new teacher certification law in 1923 on the basis of a GEB-conducted survey, but rejected the other two bills prepared by the foundation embodying important recommendations: a bill to replace local trustees with a county unit of control, which foundered on defenses of local self-government, and a bill to strengthen and centralize the state board of education, which became embroiled in concerns about state political corruption.[56]

In these and other state administrative reforms, experts played a role in defining and promoting models, some of which were adopted by legislatures, but they lacked the political clout and allies they had in city administrative reform. Many legislators and their constituents, particularly those from politically strong rural districts, preferred divided authority and popular checks on state administrative apparatus to prevent overcentralization and political corruption. By 1940, for example, 75 percent of states still elected the state superintendent rather than appointed the position despite persistent expert critiques, and over half maintained weak state boards or had them share authority with other agencies.[57]

Despite some ambivalence about centralization, state departments of education grew steadily in size, accumulated more authority and responsibilities, and exercised more discretion in the interwar years by framing their work as supervision rather than control. While in 1890, there had been only 129 state department of education staff in the *entire nation*, by 1940 several states alone counted larger staffs. The average size of state departments of education grew from less than three people in 1890 (typically a state superintendent and one or two clerks) to almost thirty-four in 1920 to almost seventy by 1940. The largest increases came during and after World War I as a result of postwar reorganizations and federal vocational aid, which funded a large number of state vocational curriculum supervisors. The General Education Board also helped to expand the size of Southern departments; as it had done to spur rural and high school supervision, the foundation offered funds for agents and divisions of school buildings, research, and finance in the 1920s and 1930s with the hope—often realized—that state legislatures would take over funding and continue the work.[58]

Behind this average growth, however, lay tremendous variations. New York boasted a mammoth staff of 751 by 1940 and was the first state in the nation to build a special building to house the department. In Montana, Idaho, Wyoming, and a handful of sparsely populated Western states, state administration was on the other extreme, averaging staffs of under twenty and delegating a great deal of authority to county and local officials or other institutions. In Colorado, for example, the state department numbered only fifteen by 1940. It was one of the only states without a high school supervisor in the department, and those functions were performed instead by the state university.[59]

The Depression deepened these trends; although a few states scaled back the department of education during the emergency, most actually expanded its size and responsibilities. For example, in Louisiana the legislature increased the share of state aid and promoted equalization during the Depression that necessitated adding personnel to the state department of education to calculate, manage, monitor, and distribute these funds. In many states New Deal aid helped to expand and bolster responsibilities of state departments and officials, including in some cases adding staff and functions such as general supervision over federally aided programs. State department officials sometimes acted as local agents of New Deal agencies; the Ohio state superintendent, for example, chaired the Ohio schools division of Federal Emergency Relief Administration (FERA) and was responsible for supervising adult education, vocational education, and nursery schools funded through the program. State departments also used federal aid to leverage desired state changes and strengthen state policies and standards. In Virginia, the state department of education used federal aid to conduct building surveys and promote high school consolidation, while in many other states the Works Progress Administration (WPA) funded construction of thousands of schoolhouses in accordance with state plans, standards, and regulations, sometimes for the first time.[60]

Although the size, organization, and power of the state department staff varied across the states, they converged on basic goals and functions by the early 1930s. Building on prewar models, departments defined their work in terms of supervision that entailed leadership and cooperation to guide local practice: instructional supervision for rural schools, high schools, elementary schools, vocational subjects, and special subjects like physical education; supervision of teacher credentialing and teacher training (including normal schools and summer teachers' institutes); and supervision over building plans, health standards, and pupil personnel services (including attendance, welfare work, and child labor). Some of these supervisory functions represented new areas of state and local effort, such as vocational supervision, while others marked a growth of state responsibility in an area once controlled exclusively by local districts where greater standardization was desired, such as teacher certification. State legislatures expanded the supervisory responsibilities of state departments of education and over time gave the state superintendent greater autonomy to hire staff and initiate and organize new activities.[61]

In defining the ideal state role and its relationship to local districts, administration scholars and officials in the field consistently framed it as a cooperative relationship. Although growing staffs and state aid gave them stronger tools to promote state policies and compel local compliance, state department officials usually chose to wield these weapons gently. They built on models of rural supervision that had developed before the war, framing their work as mentoring, service, and leadership to guide local effort. The Massachusetts state superintendent argued that the goal of state supervision should be "to capitalize the success of their most adequately administered local school systems" and "to stimulate the local administrative authorities" and not to impose "a dead level of uniformity" by "exercising authority" and "securing control." In other words, it should not operate like a bureaucracy that imposed its will on local districts, but rather work with and through local control to utilize the strengths of decentralization while also compensating for some of its failings.[62]

In addition to their very real concerns about local hostility and the politics around state centralization, state administrators were also steeped in the same assumptions that guided fiscal policy: local support, effort, and initiative were the driving forces of educational progress, and the state role should be to unleash and guide those forces, stepping in only when necessary to aid or prod them to achieve a minimum standard. The central puzzle about the state role, many experts and practitioners emphasized, was how to bring about enough centralization to secure the benefits of minimum educational advantages and raise the quality of schools while not reaching the point at which "the people will cease to think of the schools as theirs to support and to plan for." Administrative expert Ellwood Cubberley warned that "to attempt to standardize everything after one pattern should not be the purpose of the State," for "out of freedom to exercise initiative nearly all our educational progress has come." Administrative scholars were critical of efforts to set too many detailed requirements that hampered local freedom and initiative because they believed progressive localities, mainly cities, should be free to experiment and exceed requirements, which would produce innovations and drive standards upward. Furthermore, this local identification and responsibility, one scholar noted, was a powerful dynamic in reform across space, for "emulation between local districts is the most powerful string on which to pull for increased facilities; to spare it entirely would indeed be foolish."[63]

As a result of political and philosophical hostility to state control, state departments of education developed policies and practices that emphasized voluntary local action over overt imposition and that framed the state role in terms of assistance and service to localities. This language of cooperation did not mean coercion was absent, and state departments of education applied different forms of pressure, especially on laggard districts. While it might be tempting to view this simply as weak state-building or the dominance of local control over state authority, this model of state administration and cooperative state-local governance could be quite successful at achieving its aims while also legitimating state leadership. States were able to define, pursue, and enact statewide policies by guiding localities toward best practices and utilizing the dynamics of local pride, competition, and innovation to pursue and over time elevate state goals. They wielded subtle forms of influence and power through these voluntary policies and cooperative efforts. State-building in education was not a zero-sum game in which authority exercised by the state was lost by the locality; rather their authority often grew together and reinforced one another. States achieved their goals in large part by putting the dynamics of federalism to work and by working with and through local control.

This cooperative relationship can be seen in compulsory attendance policy, which was one of many areas in which state legislatures and departments of education worked with localities to achieve a state policy in ways both obvious and subtle. Although compulsory attendance laws were first passed in nearly two dozen states by 1890, it was not until the early twentieth century that city districts developed new techniques and commitments to enforce and extend attendance requirements that ultimately drove changes in state policy. A growing movement for child labor reform, supported by labor organizations, middle-class clubwomen, and a variety of child welfare advocates pressured school officials in mid-sized and large Northern cities to compel attendance: if children were to be expelled from the factory, they could not be left idle in the streets.[64]

To this end, reformers and school officials developed new enforcement techniques, including methods to find and enroll youths, officers with broad legal authority to apprehend youths and prosecute parents, institutional solutions to segregate and discipline "problem" pupils, child welfare services to attack the causes of nonattendance, and systems for issuing and verifying working papers. As they worked to strengthen enforcement, city reformers lobbied state legislatures to strengthen attendance laws, tighten loopholes, and authorize or mandate new enforcement methods. Consequently, before World War I, the efforts of localities—especially large cities—drove the conversation on attendance and prompted the gradual extension, tightening, and enforcement of state statutes. They developed models that were adopted by smaller cities and towns and written into state laws. After New York City developed the continuous census as an accounting method, for example, the state legislature made its use mandatory in all cities.[65]

The crisis of school failure raised by World War I shined new light on the problem of irregular attendance and nonattendance, particularly in rural areas, and prompted a stronger state commitment to promote attendance throughout the state. Legislatures revised statutes to require longer attendance, limit legal exemptions, raise requirements to secure working papers and leave school, and target rural enforcement. While initial laws required attendance to age fourteen, by 1928, forty states had raised the compulsory period to age sixteen or higher, including six states that raised it past age eighteen for non-English speakers. Most continued to allow work exemptions after age fourteen, but many states added new educational attainment or health requirements to secure working papers, and some required part-time schooling for working youths. In addition, states lengthened the required attendance term; while initial laws usually mandated twelve weeks, by 1928, all but nine states had lengthened it to full term, in most states eight months or longer. In addition to the statutory requirements for attendance, state attendance laws and policies made changes to encourage more active enforcement. By 1928, twenty-one states permitted or required county officials to hire attendance officers and supervise attendance for rural areas that had largely neglected it because of resources, size, or the awkwardness of enforcement in small communities. In addition, most states began to distribute state aid on the basis of average daily attendance rather than enrollment or school-age census, which rewarded local efforts to improve attendance.[66]

While state legislatures bolstered the legal requirements of attendance in the postwar period, state policy in attendance was defined less by overt force than by a multifaceted effort to aid localities to reduce nonattendance. Although most state departments had authority to withhold state funds if localities did not enforce attendance policy, few if any ever exercised this power and instead worked to shape local public opinion on behalf of enforcement and aid in the development of effective methods. In New York, for example, the state attendance bureau, staffed by ten professionals by the early 1930s, worked to improve local attendance enforcement by issuing reports on attendance practices and conditions in the state, holding conferences for attendance workers, visiting local districts to consult with local officers, preparing and disseminating forms and procedures for attendance service, and carrying on a continuous campaign for educational and welfare reforms to promote better attendance.[67]

State departments often framed the work in terms of pupil personnel services and social welfare work, an effort to help localities address and remove causes of nonattendance rather than coerce them. In Pennsylvania, for example, the state department instructed its "home and school visitors" to address "the educational, psychological, medical, and social problems and needs of children who are attendance problems" and to "affect adjustments that are both educationally and socially sound." In Kentucky attendance officers were described as "ambassadors to establish the best possible relations of cooperation and helpfulness between the school and home." A variety of state aid and services also focused on promoting attendance by reducing obstacles to it. Many states mandated that districts provide free transportation and provided state aid to offset the cost in order to remove the handicap of distance. Other states provided special aid, including mothers' pensions, free textbooks, and clothing, for poor children in order to reduce poverty as both an obstacle and a legally recognized exemption from attendance requirements.[68]

Utah offers an example of the multifaceted state effort to extend and improve state attendance policy after the war. The state legislature passed an ambitious new compulsory attendance law in 1919, swept up, as many commentators noted, by the fervor of the war. The law mandated attendance until age eighteen—one of the most ambitious policies in the nation—and allowed exemptions for working children over age sixteen as long as they attended part-time schooling. The law was aspirational, since the state did not have enough high schools to accommodate all high school-age children at the time of its passage. Over the next five years, the state legislature and department of education provided aid and encouragement for high school construction, new part-time schooling programs in cities, and improved attendance methods. They did this all gradually, recognizing, as one state official noted, that "any effort to force the issue of compulsory attendance for a hurried achievement of the ends of the law would have resulted in popular protest to its standards." State education officials thus did not pressure local districts to enforce the law but offered assistance for them to meet its obligations. They also worked to build popular support, initiating a statewide educational campaign in 1920 that invited national experts to speak throughout the state to promote the new law, and they disseminated materials with slogans like "Girls and Boys: Utah's Greatest Asset" and "Education: Her Biggest Business."[69]

Although by 1924 high school attendance had doubled, a state-directed census found 11 percent of children ages fourteen to seventeen were not enrolled in school, and those who were enrolled had unexpectedly high rates of retarded school progress and irregular attendance. To address concerns raised by the study, the state department of education developed a program to implement new child accounting methods and make instructional changes to accommodate working adolescents. One-fifth of the school districts in the state volunteered to implement the program. They each received a state-aided attendance coordinator who applied new methods to find unenrolled youths, developed procedures to investigate absences, and created new classes and curricular adjustments to accommodate working students, including flexible start and end dates to match the agricultural calendar. While coordinators reported a great deal of success with persuasion, they were willing to use force, including prosecuting parents, when persuasion failed. After a five-year trial, a state survey reported the majority of school officials, parents, and children judged the program a success, and when the legislature considered a proposal that year to reduce the attendance period, local school officials overwhelmingly endorsed the current law. Consequently, Utah's state department of education worked with localities that recognized a problem and provided professional leadership and solutions to address it, gradually extending its reach to others. Offered as a voluntary service to local districts to help meet their obligation to secure good attendance, state leadership and the compulsory attendance law itself achieved great legitimacy and local support over time.[70]

Thus, attendance was a state policy, shaped by state law and by state efforts in the postwar period to increase aid, supervision, requirements, and services to make it more effective. Ultimately, however, compulsory attendance was enforced by local districts, and rather than take over administration of attendance, states worked to encourage, aid, and prod local enforcement in order to build local support and to reduce some of the broad causes of nonattendance. One attendance officer explained to the NEA that this cooperative relationship was necessary and the burden of enforcement must rest with the local district rather than the state, for although the progress might be slower, "the result will be permanent in character." Scholars were critical of Connecticut, the only state that created state rather than local enforcement of attendance. One 1926 study, for example, showed that despite Connecticut's strong educational record in other areas, it ranked twenty-first in the nation in the efficiency of its attendance service, the lowest of any New England state. It explained that state enforcement had produced "a passive attitude toward enforcement by the local officers." Experts pointed out that cooperative state and local relationships in attendance and other policies encouraged local officials and communities to assume responsibility and invest in state policies in ways that made them more durable and permanent in character. They brought state influence and expertise to bear on local schooling without the bugaboo of state centralization and bureaucracy.[71]

Yet this reliance on local initiative and responsibility had drawbacks. Tying an important state interest to local effort and discretion meant that attendance varied according to the willingness of local officials to enforce, community and parental support for attendance, and the provisions school officials made to enable attendance. It was widely known, one former state department official noted, that districts failed to enforce attendance for African Americans in the South and Mexican Americans in the Southwest. Lack of enforcement also usually indicated a lack of commitment to children's school attendance and failure to provide the services and assistance to improve it. In Delaware, for example, one-third of black children lived over two miles from an elementary school, rendering them exempt under law and largely unable to attend voluntarily when white district officials refused to provide free transportation. The deference to local control meant that tremendous variations in commitment and efficacy were tolerated across space, both within and between states, and that state officials capitulated to local discrimination and prejudice. While state departments of education were far from paragons of racial liberalism, they were for the most part educational expansionists that supported the extension of black schooling. They had to tread lightly lest they lose local confidence or draw the ire of other state government officials.[72]

In attendance policy, as in most other areas of state supervision, state legislatures, boards of education, and departments of education worked with and through local schools to promote state policies, including defining a minimum educational program in the interests of equal educational opportunity, an opportunity that was often differentiated. State department personnel framed their role in terms of service and guidance, obscuring the subtle forms of coercion and pressure that they brought to bear through things like money, classification, minimum standards, uniform records and procedures, as well as the even more subtle ways in which their professional expertise and leadership guided localities to converge on shared practices and standards. These state leaders in turn looked to one another and to nationalizing agencies, including universities, the NEA, accrediting agencies, the USBE, and the GEB, among others. By 1940, state officials and standards were more involved in local schooling than ever before in ways that were often perceived as supplemental, advisory, and enabling rather than as bureaucratic or controlling.

※

Thus the story of the state role in schooling from 1890 to 1940 was one of expansive legal authority and steadily increasing involvement by state boards of education, state superintendents and departments of education, state courts, and state legislatures. States increasingly defined an interest and responsibility for schooling that transcended the family and local community and justified a greater state role in and leadership of schools. World War I served as a key moment of reflection as it highlighted tremendous disparities and failures in education throughout the nation and drove home the larger social consequences of these failures, thereby accelerating trends underway and stimulating new efforts in finance, attendance, curriculum, and regulation of teachers. The crisis of the Depression further deepened and intensified these postwar trends.

Among the key developments in the state role in schooling was a growing commitment to equalize school burden and opportunity, defined in practice as promoting minimum school standards throughout the state. In order to spread out school burdens and opportunities more equitably, states increased their share of school funding, defined minimum and maximum local tax burdens, distributed state money with an eye to aiding financially weak districts, and tied funding to minimum standards for term length, teacher training, and building quality and equipment, among other measures. They also increased the size and authority of state departments of education to build public and local sentiment for state policies and to work with localities to meet and exceed these minimum standards. Although they used the language of "equalization," state policy did not aim to eliminate disparities or promote the same education to all, but rather to define a bottom limit below which no school could fall, a bottom limit that was often differentiated, especially by race.

Educational experts, state policymakers, and education reformers sought to aid the poorest, weakest districts—usually rural—because of the threat that total ignorance posed to the state. However, at the same time they wanted to give maximum independence and freedom to the richest and most progressive ones—usually urban—so that they might continue to innovate and eventually raise standards for all. Local pride, effort, and innovation were widely regarded as major instruments of school progress. Even the most ardent centralizers and strongest proponents of democracy as equal opportunity sought to build on this local effort and on the dynamics of competition, emulation, and pride that propelled innovation and its diffusion. Conversely, they worried that undermining local interest and responsibility would undermine education. As a result, new state equalization policies built upon and utilized local control. State equalization funds, for example, usually required a minimum amount of local effort, reflected in tax burden, and encouraged them to exceed minimums. Likewise, many state policies, like compulsory attendance, were defined and shaped by the state but implemented and enforced by the district, with state encouragement, support, and resources.

To some observers the role of the state and its deference to and cooperation with local control might seem weak and limited. And it most definitely involved tradeoffs between autonomy and a more robust sense of equal opportunity. However, to dismiss the state role as ineffective because of the strong role that districts played underestimates the extent to which states were able to legitimate schooling as a state project, define and pursue minimum standards throughout the state, and incorporate once autonomous schools into coordinated systems. Part of the strength of the state role lay in its very diffuseness and hiddenness. In providing leadership, service, and assistance that focused on building local support, state departments were often able to get localities to buy into state policies and embrace them as their own.

While variation reigned and much decentralization in decision-making continued, nevertheless schools were no longer purely of local concern or character. They answered to the state in a host of obvious and hidden ways and adhered to state standards in nearly every facet of schooling. Local decision-making, while appearing to retain great autonomy, was guided and shaped by state and professional leadership, circumscribed by state-defined standards and expert norms, and dependent on state aid and assistance. This state power animating local schools not only reshaped school governance, but also deepened the power and authority of the school as an institution in ways that carried consequences for children and their families, as the next chapter will explore.

FOUR ✳ *Public Interest and Parental Authority in the Compulsory School*

In 1893, a Massachusetts court considered whether Frank Roberts had violated the state's compulsory attendance law by sending his eleven-year-old daughter, Mary, to a private school that the local school board had refused to approve. The statute required parents to send children that had not already attained the common branches of learning to a public school, "approved" private or parochial school, or provide other equivalent instruction. In a ruling very much in line with similar cases in other states, the court ruled that Frank Roberts had *not* broken the law, for it found that "the great object of these provisions of the statutes has been that all the children shall be educated, not that they shall be educated *in any particular way*." The court located the law within a recent set of state efforts to protect children from abuse and neglect. It reasoned that the new law did not operate restraints on parents like Roberts who provided for their children's education in private schools or in the home, only those who neglected it entirely. The laws were, in the words of the court, to ensure that "all the children be educated," but they did not dictate the content or location of that education, over which parents retained considerable authority.[1]

The ruling in another attendance case four decades later came to a very different conclusion and illustrates the considerable change over time in compulsory attendance policy and in states' deference to parents regarding matters of education. In 1937 a New Jersey court weighed whether Benno Bongart had violated the state's compulsory attendance law by teaching his two children at home. In many respects, Bongart made a strong case that he was qualified to give his children the requisite "equivalent" instruction; he was a college graduate at a time when many elementary school teachers were not, had extensive high school teaching experience, and utilized the same curriculum as the public schools. However, the judge doubted whether Bongart's teaching experience and the mere teaching of public school subjects constituted "equivalent instruction." He argued that "education is no longer merely concerned with the acquisition of facts: the instilling of worthy habits, attitudes, appreciations and skills is far more important than mere imparting of subject-matter." In finding against Bongart, the judge reasoned, "I cannot conceive how a child can receive in the home, instruction and experiences in *group activity* and in *social outlook* in any manner or form comparable to that provided in the public school." The ruling was in line with recent moves by legislatures and other courts to exercise greater oversight over alternatives to the public school, including restricting home instruction. The state's expansive interest in educating children for good citizenship in particular ways—to provide instruction in "social outlook" and "group activity"—simply outweighed parents' right to direct the education of their children as they wished.[2]

The two cases point to a profound change over time in the relationship between parents, children, and the state. While in the 1890s, state legislatures imposed new requirements to ensure that parents educated their children, they deferred to parents to define an adequate education and control how it was delivered. Education, through schools or other agencies, was foremost a familial responsibility, and state policy simply ensured that parents did not neglect it. By the end of the 1930s, state governments had defined an expansive interest in children's education and elaborated state goals and minimum standards for the public schools. They assumed that public schooling was the norm and scrutinized alternatives through compulsory attendance requirements, which effectively universalized public school standards for all children of the state. Education was no longer simply a familial responsibility, but also a public interest that sometimes outweighed parents' claims to direct this education as they chose. Compulsory attendance policies both reflected and intensified the growing public responsibility for children's education and set new limits on once virtually unlimited parental autonomy.

Nearly half of states passed compulsory attendance statutes amid Reconstruction-era debates about the national consequences of ignorance. Throughout the late nineteenth century these laws operated primarily as moral suasion since little attempt was made to enforce the laws against parents or truants. During the Progressive Era, however, school reformers and child welfare activists expanded the scope of compulsory attendance and redefined its meaning. They worked to develop strong attendance and child labor laws, design new enforcement techniques, and build community support to enroll all students and discipline their daily attendance. As in many other areas of school policy, local experimentation and support helped to drive stronger state policies and diffuse reforms across the nation. With voluntary attendance and school spending growing, many communities were willing to use force on the resistant minority that evaded school or squandered the public investment through irregular attendance. In the post–World War I era, state governments extended and deepened attendance requirements and enforcement as part of the broader effort to institute minimum standards and equalize educational opportunity.

This chapter explores the ways in which the shift from the voluntary to compulsory school extended public power over children in new ways and redefined parents' rights and authority. Attendance enforcement not only targeted truants—children not enrolled in school or legally employed—but also worked over time to regularize the attendance of all enrolled students. Attendance officers and departments developed new techniques for monitoring students, investigating and evaluating absences, and applying coercion and persuasion to secure regular attendance, which included new interventions and services for families. Attendance enforcement consequently expanded public surveillance of children and households and invited school officials into intimate family decisions about children's health, welfare, and labor that were once wholly private family matters. Compulsory attendance laws also served as a mechanism through which other state policies could be applied indirectly to children. While vaccination was not compulsory for children per se, for example, it became effectively mandatory when enforced as a prerequisite for (compulsory) enrollment in school. While scholars have explored the expansion of the state as guardian over marginal children in the Progressive Era—the dependent, delinquent, abused, and neglected—too often they have left unexamined the ways in which state authority radically expanded over *all* children through the compulsory school.

This extension of public power over children did not go uncontested. Parents resisted the gradual extension of the state into decisions of the household through legal challenges, organized protest, political lobbying, and, most often, through evasion and rejection of school policies in practice. Yet the compulsory school, and the growing public claims that animated it, circumscribed parents' once nearly unlimited autonomy over children's education, health, labor, and welfare under common law and pushed courts to redefine it on new constitutional grounds. As one of the most intimate, direct sites where individuals experienced and negotiated state power on a nearly daily basis, the compulsory school was an important place where the rights of individuals, authority of the state, and the balance between them were defined.[3]

Parental Authority and the Shift from the Voluntary to Compulsory School

Until the late nineteenth century, common law and broad cultural consent invested male heads of household with nearly unlimited authority to govern their dependents, including children. This authority was considered by most Americans to be a defining feature of republican self-government, a foundation of male independence and liberty in the new republic. Under common law and the republican political system, the household structured the legal status and rights of its members, who were bound together by reciprocal obligations. Parents owed children care, protection, and support, and children in return owed their parents service and obedience. Public officials did not intervene in these household relationships under common law until the late nineteenth century, when public outcries over child abuse and neglect prompted many state legislatures to modify parental dominion by allowing states to intervene to protect children in extreme cases under the doctrine of *parens patraie*, or state as parent. Christopher Tiedeman explained in his seminal 1886 legal treatise that "the natural affection of parents for their offspring" meant that they would serve the best interests of both the child and society in raising them. Legislatures and courts should defer to parental authority in all but the most "exceptional cases," those in which "the parents are of such vile character, that the very atmosphere of the home reeks with vice and crime."[4]

Parents had a duty to educate their children under common law, legal authorities agreed, but like other common law duties it was a moral rather than a legal obligation. In 1897, the Georgia Supreme Court evaluated whether a child could demand that a parent provide education after she was expelled from school because her mother publicly ridiculed the teacher and refused to apologize. The court found that "at common law the child has no right to demand an education at the hand of the parent," for under it "the child, so far as education is concerned, is completely at the mercy of the parent." State provision of free public schools did not change this common law deference to parents, the court concluded. "The state has provided the means, and brought them within the reach of all, to acquire the benefits of a common-school education, but leaves it to the parents and guardians to determine the extent to which they will render it available to children under their charge." The voluntary public school helped parents to discharge their moral responsibility to educate if they chose to use it, but parents retained absolute control over how, where, and even whether to educate their children.[5]

This cultural and legal deference to parents shaped the voluntary school.

Parents exercised strong control over school governance, as chapter 2 explored, and made most of the important decisions that governed it. The casual nature of schooling also reinforced parental authority; it was a part-time institution and only one of many agencies through which children received education in the nineteenth century. Schools therefore worked to attract and hold students voluntarily. While parents had to agree to follow the reasonable rules of the school if they chose to send their children to it, courts maintained that parents still had strong rights to determine the nature of their children's education within it. In an 1874 case, for example, a Wisconsin judge chastised a teacher for expelling a child who had refused to study geography because of his father's wishes. Although state law required the school to teach geography, it did not compel the child to study it. The judge ruled that the father had the right to make a "reasonable selection from the prescribed studies for his child to pursue." The teacher did not have "an absolute right to prescribe and dictate what studies a child shall pursue, regardless of the wishes or views of the parent."[6]

In the nineteenth century, education remained foremost a parental responsibility. Free public schools helped parents fulfill this responsibility but did not diminish their authority or impose any obligations to use the schools. Some commentators began to bemoan this lack of obligation after the Civil War when they confronted a national crisis of ignorance in their midst caused by the millions of illiterate freedmen, a rising tide of immigration composed heavily of poor Irish Catholics, and the newly visible presence of the "dangerous classes" in growing cities. In the 1870s and 1880s, Northern Republicans proposed and passed compulsory attendance laws in dozens of state legislatures as part of a broader agenda to bolster the (Protestant) public school and energize its waning coalition as Reconstruction ended. The new compulsory attendance statutes typically required parents to send children aged eight through fourteen to school for twelve weeks per year, six weeks of which had to be consecutive, unless exempted because of distance, poverty, physical or mental handicap, or other cause. Children who were educated in private schools, the home, or who had already attained the common branches were also excluded from requirements to attend public schools.[7]

In urging his state to adopt a compulsory attendance law, Connecticut state superintendent Birdsey Northrop issued an influential report in 1872 that laid out some of the major arguments for "obligatory education." A recent trip to Europe had convinced him that attendance strengthened the nation by promoting universal education. Enforced universal education, he argued, had "fraternized the great German nation" and "improved her social life, ennobled her homes, promoted private virtue, comfort, and thrift, and secured general prosperity in peace" as well as "unequaled prestige and power in war." Northrop argued that the United States needed compulsion because of the growing ranks of "ignorant, vagrant, and criminal youth" and the expansion of the polity through immigration. "The great influx of this foreign element," he argued, "has so far changed the condition of society as to require new legislation to meet the new exigency. The logic of events demands the recognition of compulsion, for we have imported parents so imbruted as to compel their young children to work for their grog and even to beg and steal in the streets when they should be in schools." Moral suasion was not effective against these vagrant youths and "imbruted" parents, according to Northrop, and hence "where parental pride, interest or authority fail, and juvenile perverseness is otherwise incorrigible legal coercion should be employed."[8]

Northrop called for legal coercion to supplement moral suasion, a move that social reformers were making in other areas of social policy at the same time. Compulsory attendance advocates pointed to the recent growth of state police power regulation on behalf of the public welfare and argued that education was no less important. The Louisiana state superintendent argued that "dwarfed minds and imbruted hearts are considered as calamitous to a nation as deformed bodies, and the strong arm of the law should be extended to arrest and strike down the hand which should attempt to inflict such wrong upon the state." The Illinois state superintendent likened attendance laws to accepted government powers to take property for public use, draft men to war, restrict alcohol consumption, and regulate hygiene and nuisances. "They are compulsory, sternly so; they all, in one sense, abridge the personal liberty for the individual citizen; but because the *public good demands them* they are enforced." He asked, "now when the country is menaced by an evil which no quarantine can avert; when a malady is fastening itself upon the body politic that is beyond the skill of boards of health; when a shadow is settling down upon the country the end whereof may be political death, and the people see it and know it, and there is but one remedy, why should it not be applied?"[9]

Other supporters placed compulsory attendance within the new set of court and legislative protections for children. As one supporter noted, the law now stepped in to protect a child if a "parent should beat his child unreasonably, or should starve him, or should otherwise maltreat him." However, "to deprive a child of education, to cripple him for life by a lack of knowledge and of proper schooling is a worse outrage than any of these, because it injures the child in his noblest attributes, disables him where he ought to be strongest and best." The laws would not interfere with the natural rights of parents to educate their children as they saw fit, but like other new state protections for children they would intervene in cases of negligence, such as failure to provide any education at all. According to the Kentucky state superintendent, "if the parent wished to do right, and educate his child, the law is no terror to him. It only proposes to make the wrong disposed do right. It is a restraint only on wrong intent."[10]

Opponents of compulsory attendance laws usually agreed that ignorance posed a threat to the nation but they rejected compulsory attendance as the appropriate response. They argued that reformers should educate immigrant parents and improve the pull of the voluntary school before they turned to compulsion. The president of the Maryland board of education observed that "we have not yet done what we could to make schools attractive, interesting, and useful; and until that is done, we believe that it is not prudent to use force. We should rather draw than drive; we would rather allure than compel."[11]

Others rejected compulsion because they viewed it as an unacceptable invasion of the natural rights of parents. The Texas state superintendent charged that compulsion was a "radical reconstruction of the basis of American institutions" that had been founded on the assumption that "the family is the unit of our social fabric" and "antecedent to government." Education was a "right inherent in the family and the parent," not a duty or privilege granted to it by the state, he argued. A California state senator lambasted the state's 1874 compulsory attendance law as "tyrannical legislation" that fostered "anti-parental education." The law, he argued aimed to "strip every parent of the guardianship of his children and to transfer their *entire* control to an irresponsible Board of School Trustees" that could even "choose to appoint a libertine or a harlot as the tutor to your daughters" and then punish parents who seek to shield the child "from the contaminating touch of a vile teacher."[12]

This same understanding of education as a natural right of families and a process of transmitting values animated religious defenses of the autonomy of private schools. In 1889, Republican-led state legislatures in Illinois and Wisconsin ignited a political firestorm when they added a provision to the compulsory attendance law that mandated instruction of the common subjects in English. German Lutherans and Catholics mobilized in protest, and largely on the strength of this issue succeeded in ousting the legislative majorities and governors in both states. Refuting charges that they were "unpatriotic" and foes of public schooling, the religious dissenters argued that the real issue "turned upon the right of the State to govern purely private schools, and to assume education of children." Fearing that the provision would be an "entering wedge" for state regulation of the content of private schools, the religious groups asserted the natural right of parents to educate their children according to their religious values and conscience. Lutherans issued a formal statement that claimed the right to "put up our own schoolhouses, train our teachers, and support our own schools, that our children may be taught and trained in morals and religion as our consciences tell us they ought to be taught and trained." For many of these commentators education was foremost a process of transmitting religious values, and they opposed state efforts to interfere with private school content.[13]

Despite the raucous debates about compulsory attendance laws and political fallout, the new statutes were merely symbolic in the early decades. Legislatures delegated enforcement to local districts, which in most places declined to prosecute parents or arrest truants under the law. The U.S. commissioner of education reported in 1891 that the laws were "wholly inoperative" in nearly all twenty-seven states that had them due to defects in the laws, lack of definite enforcement mechanisms, neglect or opposition of school officials and teachers, and community sentiment than ran from indifference to outright hostility. The Denver superintendent explained the reasons these laws were "dead letters" on the statute books, noting that "the president of the school board, the justice of the peace, or even the superintendent of schools, living in an American community, hesitates to call upon the might of the law to coerce a neighbor in other than criminal offences." In addition to the unwillingness to police one's close neighbors, school officials also often had institutional reasons for ignoring the laws. Many urban schools lacked enough space to accommodate all the students who wanted to attend voluntarily, and teachers and principals were less than eager to deal with the disciplinary and educational issues raised by students brought into the school by force.[14]

While the commissioner judged them to be a failure, however, many of the state superintendents with whom he corresponded painted a different picture. The Illinois superintendent argued the state's compulsory attendance law had "already accomplished very great good" by exerting moral suasion that sent thousands of children to schools. The Nebraska state superintendent similarly noted that he was not in favor of "rigid enforcement of the law," but "I am in favor of the law as far as it can be carried out by means of supervision, encouragement, and moral support." The law's true function, he argued, "is not to direct officially in the social affairs or education of the individual, but rather to cooperate with and encourage all to receive the benefits of schooling." Other superintendents expressed similar satisfaction that the laws were operating as they should by creating good public sentiment and increasing voluntary school attendance. The laws should and did operate as moral suasion.[15]

This discussion about compulsory attendance effectiveness, however, came at the dawn of a new era in attendance policies. Beginning in the 1890s, anti–child labor reformers and other child welfare advocates mobilized a movement to restrict child employment and extend compulsory schooling. The diverse members of the coalition, which included clubwomen, labor unions, and good government reformers, were motivated by a mix of humanitarian concern for children, protection of adult labor, social control and policing of poor children, and social amelioration and charity impulses. They saw schooling as a necessary component to solving the child labor problem. Illinois factory inspector Florence Kelley observed in her early reports that the child labor law was effectively nullified "if the child is not kept in school, but drifts from one workshop into another, or from the factories into the streets." According to Kelley, "until there are schools for all the children, and a compulsory education law that is enforced, the factory inspectors cannot keep all the children under 14 years out of factories and workshops." The New Jersey factory inspector similarly noted that under the new labor law "about 3,000 children will be thrown out of work by the new law, and as there is no effective compulsory education law . . . half of these children will be thrown on the streets, instead of being sent to school." Compulsory attendance enforcement was a crucial strategy for decreasing child labor and ensuring that the children expelled from the factory did not end up becoming a larger problem on the street.[16]

Consequently, as part of their effort to prohibit child labor under age fourteen and regulate it until age sixteen, many reformers pressured local school officials to enforce existing laws and aided in development of new techniques of attendance administration with resources and personnel. Through lobbying of reformers, legislatures aligned labor and attendance laws to increasingly require all children to attend school regularly until age sixteen, unless they secured legal exemptions for employment. Over time they stipulated higher standards for securing these exemptions, such as completion of eighth grade or English literacy. They lodged responsibility for issuing the working papers that employers were legally required to keep on file for all adolescent workers in the hands of school officials, and used a growing force of factory inspectors and attendance officers to monitor compliance and prosecute violators. Child labor reform not only helped to bolster attendance by investing the anti–child labor organizations in compulsory school attendance reform, but it also restricted work opportunities for children and required them to go through the school to get them. As the youth labor market shrunk overall, and contracted significantly during the Great Depression, this meant that growing numbers of young people had to stay in school because they could not secure the employment necessary to claim work exemptions. In New York City, for example, almost

75,000 children secured work exemptions in 1920, but by 1935 the number had dropped to under 5,500, over a 90 percent reduction despite a growing school-age population.[17]

During the Progressive Era, child labor reform provided a strong rationale for strengthening attendance policy; however, it was not the only factor driving attendance enforcement and statutes. Some of the broader concerns that drove child labor reform also motivated a vigorous pursuit of universal education by many of the same reformers: concern about children's welfare and development; economic considerations, including labor competition and productivity; anxieties about immigration and Americanization; attempts to provide social amelioration and address the inequities of capitalism. Many education reformers in the period saw compulsory attendance as the logical next step for ensuring the universal education needed by state and society. Over the course of the early twentieth century, as state social regulation exploded and the state took an increasing role and interest in schooling, they were much less hesitant to use force against the resistant minority.[18]

Compulsion would not have been possible, however, without strong community support, including the surge in voluntary attendance into high school and the massive expansion of facilities and services that accompanied it. As more and more parents valued extended schooling for their own children and communities generously supported it, school officials became less tolerant of parents who refused its benefits. As one commentator noted, communities spending generously for schools should not tolerate the "waste" of irregular attendance in terms of lost opportunity and misspent money.[19]

Much like other education reforms, compulsory attendance laws and practices spread first across the North and West then penetrated into the South by World War I through a combination of local experimentation, emulation and diffusion, and state government promotion. Throughout the Progressive Era, cities experimented with new ways to find and enroll students and police their attendance, which smaller cities and towns emulated and modified. Urban reformers lobbied state legislatures to extend statutes and tighten loopholes through which parents and children evaded attendance in the decades before World War I. Legislatures responded with statutes that extended the compulsory period, restricted exemptions, and mandated proven practices statewide, such as requirements that each district hire an attendance officer or maintain attendance logbooks. These state laws and state department of education leadership deepened considerably after the war, as the last chapter examined, and states made new efforts to aid and encourage rural enforcement. These statutory changes, along with growing local commitment to enforcement, helped bring more kids into school for longer periods of time.[20]

Thus, in the nineteenth century schooling had been voluntary and closely controlled by parents, who enjoyed strong common law legal rights and cultural power over their children's education. Compulsory attendance laws, initially passed in many states during a heightened period of national concern about the dangers of ignorance, were rarely enforced in the nineteenth century. In the early twentieth century, attendance policy was transformed by the advent of a child-saving movement and new education reform. With new local enforcement techniques and commitments, attendance shifted from a check on parental neglect to a tool of social regulation, which policed the boundaries of work and school and established minimum schooling standards for all children. Over time, the bottom-up development of compulsory attendance policy, animated by state legislative power but driven ultimately by local efforts, extended the scope and reach of the school in ways unanticipated by the laws' initial supporters.

The Expanding Reach of the Compulsory School

Attendance laws and enforcement brought more children into school for longer periods of time; however, the impact of attendance policy went far beyond the children it enrolled in school by force. Attendance policy developed in the twentieth century away from a focus on simply policing enrollment to a broader goal of regularizing attendance for all. School officials began to monitor and discipline daily attendance in ways that required new oversight and interventions into the home. It reflected and intensified the public interest in children's education, health, and welfare and served as a mechanism through which public oversight was extended over children and their families.

At the center of attendance enforcement stood attendance officers who were legally empowered to find, apprehend, and prosecute parents and children who violated the attendance law. Early officials in late nineteenth-century cities like Boston and Chicago spent much of their time patrolling streets and neighborhoods to find and arrest truants, idle children without the restraining force of work or school. The *New York Times* relayed the "amusing" stories of one such officer who patrolled the streets of the city's Seventh Ward. In one typical example, he tried to raid a vacant house that was a known hangout for truants, but a boy "on sentry-duty sang out 'Cheese it—the cop,' and the next instant boys, legs, and coat-tails were disappearing over the fences." He could only catch one small boy who was unable to outrun the officer. In addition to patrolling the streets, early attendance officers also investigated complaints by school principals or other agencies about suspected cases of truancy. When officers found truants, they delivered them to school, pressured parents to enroll them, or turned them over to courts for commitment to an institution.[21]

In the early twentieth century, attendance officers in growing urban attendance departments expanded their work from policing idle youths on the street to improving the daily attendance of all children. They developed new procedures and techniques to discipline daily attendance, a new flexible approach that emphasized education and persuasion of parents over force, and targeted interventions to address the causes of irregular attendance. Legal penalties, including fines and imprisonment, remained an important tool in the arsenal but a last resort after all persuasives had failed. As one scholar in 1935 observed, the "modern supervisor of attendance" "knows school work; he has had social-service training; he understands the psychology of dealing with youth" and is concerned with "discovering the maladjustment" that caused irregular attendance in order to correct it. This was in contrast to the old truant officer of the turn of the century who was "in the strict sense a police officer" who "spied in back alleys, and roamed the streets constantly for the purpose of finding youths of school age not in school." This shift in emphasis from policing to attendance "service" was shaped by general trends in the urban school toward child welfare, growing community support and reformers' pressure for effective attendance policy, educational experts who emphasized the school waste that came from irregular attendance, and the professionalizing project of attendance officers.[22]

To regularize daily attendance, school officials had to develop new forms and procedures to keep track of students within the system, monitor daily attendance, and follow up unexcused absences. Since the nineteenth century, most states had mandated a periodic census of school-age children in the district as a basis for distributing common school funds. It could be used to find and enroll students when it was taken but became quickly out of date and was difficult to use for any other purpose. In the twentieth century, attendance departments took control of the census and redefined it. Developing the "continuous census," through trial and error, they began the herculean task of keeping the census up to date by tracking students as they moved into the district, transferred between grades and schools, and claimed work or other exemptions. They used it to keep permanent records about the students' daily attendance and any mitigating circumstances that shaped it, as well as collect basic demographic information including the child's name, age, residence, ethnicity, and parents' occupations. Over time, it became the repository of more and more information about students drawn from home visitations, medical inspection, school performance, mental and achievement tests, and other sources. Attendance was therefore the foundation of permanent record-keeping systems that produced information about children that could be used by the school and other public agencies for a variety of purposes.[23]

Through trial and error, attendance workers also developed basic procedures for monitoring daily attendance. Teachers submitted daily logs of attendance to the school principal, who reported any unexcused absences to the attendance department. The attendance department notified parents of the absence by mail, phone, or visit and ascertained the reason. If the reason for absence was deemed lawful—such as illness—no further action was taken, but if the absence was considered improper, the officer issued a warning to return the child to school immediately. If the absence continued or was part of a pattern of irregular attendance, the department conducted an investigation that usually included one or more home visitations and follow-up work by the attendance officer, visiting teacher, or other allied personnel. These school officials used social work techniques to assess the family situation, find the cause of absence, and develop solutions to address it, including, if necessary, prosecution. Attendance departments also investigated cases reported by other sources, including welfare societies, parochial schools, health departments, police and immigration officials, individual citizens, and parents themselves.[24]

In order to regulate attendance without alienating community support, attendance officers emphasized education, persuasion, and service as key goals of attendance policy. The New York Attendance Bureau noted that "there are numbers of parents in all parts of the city who fail to appreciate the importance of regular attendance" and "correction of this attitude is one of the most fundamental duties" of the department. In one case it cited as an example, the department investigated the irregular attendance of an African American girl. A home visit revealed that the girl was kept "up until all hours of the night singing for colored church festivals" and as a result often overslept and had fallen behind in her studies. The attendance officer gave a stern talk to the family, spoke with the child's pastor, and arranged for her to sing in the afternoons instead. Her attendance improved significantly.[25]

Similarly, attendance officers in Chicago reported the case of a German mother who kept her twelve-year-old daughter home to help with housework. Since the girl had completed the equivalent of a common school course in Germany, the mother was surprised, but "quite willing to comply with the law" when she learned that attendance was required until age fourteen. Investigators concluded that "it is easy for these parents to make sacrifices for their children to go to school, but not easy to grasp the American standard of education, which means regular attendance for at least seven years, no matter how soon the elementary arts of reading and writing may be acquired." Children missed school for a host of reasons they deemed trivial—to help a neighbor move, perform chores, watch construction in the neighborhood, to visit or travel—and officials worked to persuade parents to give school attendance high priority and reschedule these and other activities for outside of school hours.[26]

In many cases, however, attendance officers found significant obstacles to children's regular attendance, including health problems or family responsibilities shaped by economic circumstances. Chicago sociologists noted that "poverty is only too frequently the real excuse for non-attendance," because in neighborhoods where "it is a perpetual struggle to give the children enough to eat and wear there is inevitably a great waste of the children's schooling." They noted many cases in which children lacked shoes or clothing and others in which children's labor was essential for the family. In one typical case, an eleven-year-old girl missed school to care for her invalid father, her mother who had recently given birth, and six younger siblings including the newborn. The attendance officer alerted local charities in the hopes that aid would allow the girl to return to school in the future. Attendance departments in large cities utilized social work approaches to address "whatever the condition may be which prevents a child from attending school." In practice, it might mean, as New York officials noted, "outfitting a child or an entire family, with shoes or clothing; or an advance for the payment of rent; orders for groceries, and coal; cleaning up a home; removal of mother to hospital; providing cream for babies while mother is at work; composing marital differences; reclaiming a girl falling into waywardness; facilitating the granting of a widow's pension."[27]

Like other social workers in the period, they evinced a mixture of benevolence and paternalism in their home interventions, often blurring the lines between service and coercion. In one case in New York, the attendance bureau "rehabilitated" a family by threatening and cajoling a mother who had left her husband and children eight years earlier to return to the household. The parents had married young and "grown to dislike each other," but the agent worked to "persuade" them to reunite for the good of the children by threatening to take them to court for "improper guardianship" and warning the case would get "some newspaper notice." Seven months later they were all still together, and even though the youngest child was "still a little bitter, and says she will never love either of them," the agent deemed it a success.[28]

In another case, the agent intervened in the case of a "wild girl" who frequently missed school, "powdered and painted," and would not listen to her mother. The agent made several home visits and gave the girl, "R," a stern lecture about how she was "wasting and spoiling the sweetest time of her life" and was in danger of being "sent away until she was eighteen years old." She took the case to municipal court where the judge gave "R" a "terrible scolding," sentenced her to a reformatory to scare her, and then changed the sentence to probation. The attendance agent reported that the girl recognized the error of her ways and agreed to accept the agent's help to enroll her in school, get her into a club, and "introduce her to nice girls." The intervention of the agent helped to bring the girl under the control of her grateful mother. In both cases, guidance and persuasion were backed by the unmistakable threat of legal force.[29]

Thus attendance service created new commitments and practices for evaluating absences, ameliorating social barriers to regular attendance, and shaping the attitudes and behaviors of parents and children about attendance. It gave school officials, including teachers, principals, and attendance officers, the authority and responsibility to evaluate the reasons parents gave for keeping their children home from school and considerable discretion to determine which were acceptable. It necessitated home visitations and facilitated public interventions in matters related to family economy, health, and welfare that were once wholly private matters. Attendance agents often served as points of contact with other public authorities and agencies, bringing services and policing into the home that might or might not be welcomed.

The reach of attendance policy went far beyond the minority that felt its hand directly. In policing the regularity of attendance and articulating clear standards and expectations for what constituted legitimate and illegitimate absences from school, attendance service helped to institutionalize emerging new cultural norms about attendance that affected the large majority of parents who never encountered an attendance agent. Parents who once may have thought nothing of taking their child out of school for a few weeks to travel, for example, began to plan those trips for school breaks, and social pressure led many parents to change their behavior without any consciousness of being coerced or persuaded. As one educator noted, "the virtue of a compulsory attendance law lays not so much in its compelling force upon those who are penalized for offenses as in its silent operation upon those who fear open chastisement. As a result, an attendance law affects a larger percentage of our school children than is at first apparent."[30]

Consistent full-term, fulltime attendance became not only the law but the cultural expectation, and the elaborate procedures of attendance and investigation helped to reinforce this expectation. Average daily attendance rose over time, from just over 60 percent in 1880 to over 80 percent by 1925 and nearly 90 percent by 1930. In 1890 each enrolled child attended an average of eighty-six days per year and by 1940 that number had risen to 152 days.[31]

In addition to the way that it helped to institutionalize general norms and discipline behavior, attendance policy also reached all children in other ways. Attendance service was the driving force behind elaborate new systems of student records that were used to monitor, evaluate, and guide students in the school system after the war. One leading scholar in 1929 explained how attendance service was being redefined as "pupil person-nel work," which includes "those services whereby all children of school age are 'kept track of,' caused to attend school, and so studied that they are aided in making the maximum good use of the abilities which they have." Attendance service became the source of knowledge about children and their families that was used by teachers, counselors, and other school per-sonnel to make decisions about classroom placement, curriculum, services, and activities. It became a foundational part of how urban schools moni-tored, managed, and surveilled their students after World War I, and it ex-panded public oversight and knowledge of children, as the next chapter will explore.[32]

Attendance policy also intensified the public interest in children's health and welfare and provided an entry point for regulating them. Attendance enforcement brought local school officials into daily contact with poverty, health problems, and other barriers to attendance and intensified their commitment to expanding the services of the school. It also prompted some to lobby for public aid such as mothers' pensions and family health services. They argued that if the state was going to restrict labor and require atten-dance of children, it must help to ease the burden that it placed on families and ensure that all children could access opportunity for schooling equally. One reformer argued "in our democracy the right of every child to a free public education in accordance with his native ability, in order that he may have equality of opportunity in the struggle for the good things of life, is no longer questioned. If ignorance of parents or economic conditions seek to prevent, it becomes at once the duty of the state to see that every child is allowed to take advantage of this opportunity," not only in the interests of social justice but more importantly because "ignorance and social instabil-ity are too costly luxuries we can afford to do without." The U.S. Bureau of Education similarly noted in 1935 that the enactment and extension over time of compulsory attendance "places a responsibility upon the State and upon every school district within the State to provide the very best of school facilities" and has "also placed additional responsibilities on schools" to care for children who would not be there if not for compulsion, including the poor and children with special needs.[33]

The growing field of health supervision offered one example of the ways that compulsion deepened public responsibility in the school and extended the reach of public policies over children in powerful, albeit somewhat hidden, ways. One expert in school health argued that "the medical inspection movement has come as a direct corollary of the principle of compulsory education." Having assumed a great responsibility for the education of its children, the state, he argued, must go "one step farther" to safeguard the health of children in its care and ensure that no harm come to them.[34]

Health supervision developed from medical inspection, which was first introduced in the United States in 1894. At the time, Boston faced a series of epidemics and school officials borrowed medical inspection practices from examples in Europe. Medical inspection spread rapidly through the nation: by 1910, the Russell Sage Foundation reported that 331 cities conducted regular physical examinations for contagious disease and general health, including inspections of eyes, ears, throats, teeth, and vital statistics like height and weight. By 1923, over 1,100 cities reported medical inspection in the school, and thirty-nine states mandated it on a statewide basis or in particular localities, usually first- and second-class cities. Health work also expanded into rural areas through the work of state supervisors, county health agents, philanthropies, and voluntary associations that funded health campaigns against hookworm and other diseases, health demonstration projects, and training for rural educators. By 1930, a survey of rural health supervision found that over a third of counties had a full- or part-time medical inspector working in the rural schools and roughly half had a full- or part-time nurse.[35]

Growing city school health staffs, including doctors, nurses, dentists, and medical specialists like occulists, not only inspected schoolchildren but increasingly offered treatment and access to health services. By 1930, the Philadelphia Division of Medical Inspection, for example, had over two hundred medical inspectors and nurses who not only performed hundreds of thousands of examinations but also reported performing over twenty-two thousand diphtheria vaccinations and treating twenty-two thousand students in dispensaries. In many cities, nurses could take emergency cases for free, immediate treatment without parental consent, and they helped needy families secure free or low-cost treatment in other cases. Schools continued to expand and redefine the work of these growing health departments toward health supervision or "child hygiene," which emphasized a comprehensive program of prevention, health education, and sanitation to improve the health of children and their families.[36]

Schools identified health problems but defined treatment as a parental responsibility. School officials used a combination of services, education, outreach to the home, and legal threats to pressure parents to provide this treatment. When schools identified a health issue, they sent a written notice to parents and found that this notification was sufficient to secure treatment from family doctors in about 25 percent of cases. To reach the other three-quarters of parents, they used a combination of strategies. One of the most successful, they reported, was home visitation and follow-up work by nurses who worked to educate, persuade, and aid parents, including helping needy families secure medical services. In one case, a Boston visiting nurse developed a relationship with Italian parents who refused to consent to surgery to correct rickets in their daughter's legs. The mention of hospital, she noted, "aroused unknown terrors in their mind." It took several weeks of visits with the family to earn their trust and convince them to consent to the surgery, which the nurse arranged at no cost through the Children's Hospital. As trained social workers, one expert noted, visiting nurses "afford an excellent opportunity for general family service, instruction in better methods of housekeeping, better care of all the children, as well as help in the process of Americanizing many homes."[37]

In addition to home visitation by nurses, school officials also worked to shape parents' behavior through public relations campaigns and educational outreach. In Milwaukee, for example, the boards of health and education engaged in a massive public relations campaign to sell the diphtheria vaccination to a population that had at times resisted smallpox vaccination with great vigor. They framed it as an issue of good parenting, warning parents that they were culpable if their child contracted the preventable disease. They reinforced these messages with instruction in schools, attention to school sanitation and hygiene, and activities like mothers' clubs for girls, which school reformers hoped would exert influence on the housekeeping and sanitation practices of immigrant families.[38]

While school officials emphasized education and persuasion, legal force was a tool in the arsenal in many states. Unlike many European nations that paired compulsory treatment provisions with compulsory inspection, few American states had direct legal provisions mandating treatment. However, in most states school officials could utilize compulsory attendance, sanitary codes, and domestic relations law to compel action in cases in which parents neglected serious health needs or could act themselves to treat emergency cases. In 1918, a NYC nurse and attendance agent visited a mother who refused medical aid for her child after an eye specialist reported the case to the department. The mother "was told that if she interfered with the proper treatment of the child's eyes, she would have to appear in court and that the child would be placed in the Society for the Prevention of Cruelty to Children until the matter was adjusted." Threatened with legal action, the mother "consented" and the agent took the child to the doctor for treatment three times a week until the condition was corrected. In Colorado, school officials reported parents who refused to provide important medical treatment to the state Bureau of Child and Animal Protection, which used home visits and legal prosecution to secure compliance. More commonly, school officials excluded children from school until the condition was addressed, which persuaded many parents to act. If parents continued to refuse treatment and simply keep the child at home, school officials could prosecute them for violating the compulsory attendance law.[39]

Since health practices were required at school and children were mandated to attend school, these health policies became effectively compulsory in places where local officials were intent on enforcing both. Vaccination offers a striking example of this indirect regulation of children. In the United States vaccination was a hotly contested, politically divisive issue; antivaccinationists mobilized to challenge it on medical, scientific, religious, and legal grounds and argued it was an infringement of liberty. Many states mandated vaccination in times of epidemic and delegated strong powers to state and local boards of health in those cases, but stopped short of making vaccination compulsory for all citizens, as many European nations had done. By 1912, twenty-seven states required or permitted schools to make vaccination a condition of school entry, which most enforced only in times of epidemic. Parents of unvaccinated children excluded from the school sometimes brought suit against school officials to compel their admittance, but courts consistently held it was a valid state police power regulation. Courts were more divided about whether school officials or boards of health could compel vaccination without legislative mandate or without an imminent threat of disease.[40]

The deepening of compulsory attendance policy profoundly changed vaccination and raised the issue of whether parents could be held liable for violating state attendance requirements when their children were excluded from school because of their refusal to comply with the vaccination requirement. Initially, courts answered in the negative. One court noted in 1900 that vaccination remained "a matter of choice by the defendant" and "the only consequence of non-compliance was that his child should be deprived of the privilege of the schools." The parent's "sole duty" under the compulsory attendance law was to "send his son to school" and if the teacher refused to admit him because he was not vaccinated, "it added nothing to the duties prescribed by statute." In other words, if a parent was willing to send the child to school and tried to do so, but the child was refused entrance because of the parent's refusal to vaccinate, the parent did not run afoul of either state law. This was so settled that in 1911 when an attendance officer in New York initiated prosecution against a mother whose unvaccinated child had been excluded from school, the officer not only found his case dismissed but the mother sued him for malicious prosecution.[41]

However, the New York Court of Appeals signaled a major change in policy in 1914 when it sustained the prosecution of a parent under the attendance law for refusing to vaccinate his child. In a case that would be widely cited by other state courts, the court held that Hagbard Ekerold's opposition to vaccination did not excuse him from the obligations of attendance. "I do not believe that a parent may escape his duties under the Education Law by pleading simple unwillingness to have his child attend the public schools subject to the condition of vaccination," the court ruled. "Our public school system has been developed with great pains and solicitude and its maintenance and support have been recognized as so important for the welfare of the state" that the people have safeguarded and provided generously for it in the Constitution. The legislature did not make an exception for parental objection to vaccination when it passed the compulsory attendance law, and the statutes had to be construed together. "It does not require much spirit of prophecy to foresee what will follow a contrary construction of the statutes," the court ruled. "If a parent may escape all obligation under the statute requiring him to send his children to school by simply alleging he does not believe in vaccination, the policy of the state to give some education to all children, if necessary by compelling measures, will become more or less of a farce under existing legislation." *New York v. Ekerold* thus signaled a major shift in courts' treatment of vaccination and attendance statutes, one quoted and applied by nearly every other state court that followed.[42]

Thus, while state legislatures balked at making vaccination compulsory for adults in the absence of any immediate threat, states secured the vaccination of children, even against strong parental objections based on religious convictions or health concerns through the nexus of vaccination rules and compulsory attendance. The Pennsylvania case of *Commonwealth v. Gillen* shows how potent these laws could be when enforced together. William Gillen was charged by school officials with violating the compulsory attendance law of the state by instructing his two children at home. Gillen's children had been attending St. Agatha's Parochial School in Philadelphia but were excluded by the Mother Superior under pressure from the Bureau of Health because they were not vaccinated. Deeply opposed to vaccination, Gillen tried repeatedly to persuade the Mother Superior to accept the students without vaccination or find another school that would accept them. When this failed and he was unable to afford a private tutor, Gillen's wife began to instruct the children at home, which schools officials maintained did not satisfy the state's attendance law. The court, in 1916, quoting extensively from the *Ekerold* decision, ruled that Gillen's unwillingness to comply with the vaccination rule did not exempt him from attendance requirements and that the instruction in the home did not meet the statutory requirement that alternatives to the public school be by a "properly qualified private tutor" and "satisfactory to the proper county or district superintendent of schools." Without the money to hire a tutor, Gillen had no other choice but to vaccinate his children or move to another state with less stringent laws.[43]

Not all states and localities were as committed to vaccination and attendance enforcement as New York and Philadelphia. In practice, many places enforced the vaccination requirements only during epidemics, and they declined to prosecute parents who kept their children home until the threat passed. In other places, local pressure could force school boards to modify their practices. In Montclair, New Jersey, for example, 350 residents delivered an ultimatum to the school board in 1911 when it began to enforce vaccination requirements for school attendance: "'we will, one and all of us . . . move out of Montclair and out of the State of New Jersey before we allow our children to be vaccinated. There are other suburbs of New York which have not this fetish of forcing vaccination on children.'" The school board rescinded the order. School boards often refused to back down, however, and painted protesters as a small, albeit vocal minority. In Riverside, California, the next year, the school board stood firm on its vaccination order even as dozens of parents kept their elementary school children home in protest and two hundred high school boys led a protest march in front of city hall, complete with drum corps. The strength and leverage of public protest shaped school officials' responses, and political challenge could and did mediate policies in practice.[44]

Yet attendance statutes gave public officials strong legal authority if they chose to exercise it to extend policies and regulations, like vaccination, over children inside and outside the public schools. At issue in the Gillen case was expulsion from a *private* school and the legitimacy of Gillen's home instruction. The case also shows the ways in which public officials in Philadelphia monitored the attendance and health of children outside of the public schools. This was a final way in which compulsory attendance laws extended state authority and shaped schools in far broader ways than the resistant minority dragged into school by force: hidden regulation of public school alternatives and de facto minimum requirements for the education of all children. The very logic of attendance as it deepened over time necessitated that the state, in the interests of effective policy, exercise some oversight over alternatives to ensure that they met state goals in requiring attendance in the first place. One Catholic scholar explained that compulsory attendance brought with it "new powers of state control over private schools." If attendance at private schools was to be accepted as satisfying attendance laws, then "the state must have the right to investigate the manner in which these private institutions were meeting compulsory education requirements." By 1918, about half of states regulated private schools, ranging from minimal requirements for attendance record keeping to far-reaching powers to inspect and approve private schools.[45]

In a wave of legislation during and after the war, states deepened their oversight of private schools by including them in many of the new measures for health, welfare, curriculum, and Americanization and expanding the supervision of local and state officials. For example, legislatures included private schools in new curricular mandates for civics, requirements for physical education, and health measures like medical inspection. By 1924, twenty-three states mandated inspection, supervision, or approval of private schools by public officials. In one of the most extensive controls over private schools, the Nebraska legislature revised the state's attendance law in 1921 to mandate that private schools report attendance to public officials, employ teachers with state certification, and submit to two inspections per year by public authorities. While they had helped repeal much more minimal attempts at private school oversight in Illinois and Wisconsin at the end of the nineteenth century, many Catholic leaders viewed public oversight as increasingly inevitable by the 1920s. In one internal memo, National Catholic Welfare Council members noted that the "wise course to pursue would be to try to secure the passage . . . of such innocuous legislation" as found in Indiana and Massachusetts, which stipulated private school minimum standards and cooperation with public officials in order to try to stave off more aggressive inspection and regulation, like the Nebraska law.[46]

In addition to direct regulation by statutes, public school standards were applied to private schools by state courts that interpreted attendance statutes to set minimum standards for private schools and home instruction. A 1906 Pennsylvania court, for example, ruled that the attendance statute's requirement that children receive an education in "the common English branches" required private schools to offer all of the mandatory public school subjects in English, and therefore attendance at a Polish language school did not satisfy the law. Using public schools as the standard, courts demanded that alternatives to public schools mirror the public school's hours, course of study, English language, term length, and even teacher qualifications. The Pennsylvania court in the Gillen case, among others, interpreted the attendance statute to require private school teachers to hold similar credentials to public school teachers, and by 1926 four state legislatures mandated that certification for both be exactly the same. In some cases, it meant even outlawing home instruction and private tutors altogether, as the New Jersey court in the *Bongart* case did, because of doubts that it could ever truly be equal to education in a school setting. Hence, attendance statutes gave the state a rationale and means to articulate and universalize minimum standards and expectations for *all* children's education, not just those in the public schools.[47]

Thus, the impact of compulsory attendance went far beyond the children it brought into school by force. It disciplined and normalized regular attendance for all. It justified and even necessitated greater contacts between home and school, and prompted school oversight and involvement in issues of health, welfare, and work once deemed wholly private, family decisions. The compulsory school was a mechanism for extending public power and articulating minimum education standards for all children in new ways, not just those in the public school. It reflected and deepened state responsibility and public interest in children's welfare and development.

Balancing State Power and Parental Authority, Public Interest and Individual Rights

The interventions of the school into the home brought it into greater contact and conflict with parents over the course of the early twentieth century. Parents' rights had once been nearly sacrosanct under common law and in the voluntary school. However, as education was defined as a fundamental state interest, courts and public officials increasingly decided that these private parental rights had to be balanced with, and usually subordinated to, the public interest in children's education, health, and welfare. The compulsory school was a key site at which these questions of individual rights and state power collided and where courts confronted and redefined the nature of parental rights.

Supporters of compulsory attendance policies argued that education was too important of a public interest to allow parents to evade their responsibilities. Given the complexity of modern economy and society, children's education and welfare was a concern of the entire community, not a solely private concern of parents. The state had a right to protect itself from negligence on the part of parents. As one expert argued, "the children of to-day must be viewed as the raw material of the State; the schools as the nursery of the Nation. To conserve this raw material is as logical a function of the State as to conserve the natural resources of coal, iron, and water power." Another commentator similarly emphasized the social significance of individual development, arguing that "education may be thought of as social insurance." In providing education, the state was concerned about individual development, but "this interest in the individuals is not altruistic; it is selfish, as the social order may not exist or progress except as it is composed of good leaders and effective followers."[48]

Catholics were among the most vocal critics of the expanded reach of the state over public and private schools. In a memo on educational policy in 1905, the National Catholic Education Association argued that "the Modern State with which we deal bases its activities on the doctrine that human rights derive their origin and their sanction from the authority of the State." Under this doctrine, "education is regarded as the servant of the State, the child the property of the State, and a form of State worship tends to supplant religion in the minds of people who have no Christian training." This was antithetical, it noted, to Catholic belief in "natural law and the dictates of right reason." According to Catholics, parents' rights did not derive from the state but from God. "The right by which parents give life to their children includes the right to educate them," explained the National Catholic Welfare Conference. "This right is inalienable and comes from nature itself" and was tied to fundamental values. Therefore, Catholics must defend the autonomy of private schools, where parents could ground education in religious faith and guard against the "irreligious" secular public school, where, as one priest put it, "no Catholic boy's religion is safe" and many will leave "with their faith undermined or unsettled, or irretrievably lost."[49]

Catholics' defense of parental rights and values in education resonated with other religious minorities such as Jehovah's Witnesses and Christian Scientists, who found their religious values in conflict with public school policies, especially vaccination and medical inspection. One Christian Scientist mother complained that U.S. citizens were being subjected to "a medical monarchy more absolute and tyrannical than the Tzar of Russia ever inflicted upon his subjects." Another parent wrote to the *Los Angeles Times* to complain that his children had been expelled from the public school because of his objection to vaccination. He defended his stance, arguing, "I for my part will rather bring my children up according to my religion, leaving them to be honest and good, for it is the father and mother who are responsible for their health and future good." Others charged that the growing reach and services of the school "enables the family provider to shift his burdens upon the State" and "tends directly toward Socialism." These extensions of state responsibility into private decisions of the family would, some critics contended, erode parental responsibility and therefore damage the foundation of democratic self-government. A persistent minority of parents argued that school health policies invaded parental liberty, violated religious beliefs, and stretched public responsibility too far.[50]

In protesting the extensions of state power, organized groups and individual parents initiated critiques, legal challenges, and political mobilizations at local and state levels, especially around medical liberty and vaccination issues. They were able in some cases to leverage enough political pressure on local school boards or state legislatures to prevail, such as the Montclair school board that rescinded the vaccination order or the California legislature that repealed the vaccination requirement for schools altogether. Parents could evade at least some policies to which they objected by patronizing private schools or hiring private tutors, although it was an option that was increasingly regulated in many states. Most often, however, parental resistance to the expansion of public power was more individual and less organized, expressed through quiet evasion and resistance rather than outright challenge. Parents' and children's constant, creative ways of finding loopholes in the law and evading public officials and policies drove the continuous efforts by reformers to tighten and adjust the laws and enforcement.

As parents confronted public authority in the compulsory school and resisted its policies, it raised a fundamental question about the rights of parents. Courts considered this question directly in constitutional challenges to compulsory attendance at the turn of the century. In the first major challenge to attendance in a court of record, Patrick Quigley, a Catholic priest and parochial school principal, challenged the law as a violation of the parental right to direct the education of children. In its 1891 decision, the court acknowledged the long tradition of deference to parental dominion under common law but also recognized the recent trends of legislatures and courts to modify these rights in cases of custody, neglect, and abuse. While parents' legal rights deserved respect, the Ohio court ruled, the state could intervene under the doctrine of *parens patriae* when parents neglected their duties. "It is only when the parent, if I may so say, forfeits his right to the child, or at least when he shall so far forget his duty to the child as to entirely neglect to educate him, or refuse to educate him . . . that the state steps in, and by virtue of these statutes compels his attendance at school." Compulsory attendance statutes were a legitimate extension of the state's protection of children and, like those other protections, would only step into the household in exceptional cases of neglect.[51]

From 1901 to 1903, state courts in Indiana, New Hampshire, and Pennsylvania all considered and upheld the constitutionality of compulsory attendance statutes, but they began to shift their reasoning. State courts held that compulsory attendance was an exercise of state police power, the inherent and expansive power of the state to regulate on behalf of the public welfare and limited only by express constitutional prohibitions. In 1901, the Indiana Supreme Court rejected Sheridan Bailey's claim that compulsion violated natural parental rights, reasoning that "the natural rights of a parent to the custody and control of his infant child are *subordinate to the power of the state*, and may be restricted and regulated by municipal laws." One of a parent's natural duties was to educate his child, and "this duty he owes not to the child only, but to the commonwealth." If the parent neglects this duty he "may be coerced by law to execute such civil obligation," for "the welfare of the child and the best interests of society require that the state shall exert its sovereign authority to secure to the child the opportunity to acquire an education." Significantly, the court did not ground the decision in *parens patriae* to step in when parents neglected their duty as the Ohio court had done, but instead ruled that parents' responsibility toward their children was a matter of public concern, a "civil obligation" in the best interests of society that warranted state regulation.[52]

In the last two significant challenges to make it to a court of record, courts in Pennsylvania and New Hampshire agreed that attendance statutes were a constitutional exercise of state police power. Although the statute was "a decided invasion of parental domain," one court held, it was an invasion the state legislature could make under its police power because the education of citizens was "essential to the stability of the state." Finding the statute "repugnant to no provision of the constitution" and being for the general welfare, the court concluded that it must uphold the attendance law and the citizen "must yield submission and obedience."[53]

Grounding compulsory attendance in state police power legitimated expansive state power over children's education and limited the challenges that parents could bring. In these and other challenges to state police power regulations, courts ruled that parents' rights were relative and should be balanced with, and inferior to, the public interest. If the regulation enacted by the popularly elected legislature was reasonably calculated toward the public welfare and did not violate any explicit constitutional provision, it was constitutional. As they had done with "local rights" claims against the state legislature's police power, state courts ruled that "parents' rights" were not protected by any particular constitutional provision and therefore not a recognized limit on state police power.[54]

Courts also did not recognize a child's right to education as a restraint on state action. In a series of cases before the *Ekerold* decision in 1914, parents of unvaccinated children excluded from school claimed it violated the child's right to education. Courts roundly rejected the claim. The Connecticut Supreme Court explained in 1894 that schooling "is a privilege or advantage, rather than a right, in the strict technical sense of the term. This privilege is granted, and is to be enjoyed, upon such terms and under such reasonable conditions and restrictions as the law-making power, within constitutional limits, may see fit to impose." In a similar case in Ohio, the court was emphatic that the "privilege of attendance upon the public schools of the state is, and of necessity must be, subject to such reasonable restrictions and limitations as may be imposed by the proper authorities," and hence "no right conferred or secured by the Constitution was violated by that law or by the action of the school authorities based thereon." In a series of cases based on exclusion and assignment of students based on race, courts did hold that the equal protection clause of the Fourteenth Amendment required equality of privileges. African American and Native American children could not be denied schooling when the privilege was provided for white children, but courts stopped far short of calling it a right of citizenship or defining equality as access to the same schools.[55]

The fact that schooling was a privilege provided by the state for its own benefit rather than a constitutional right of the child or parent meant that interests of the individual must give way to the good of the school when they conflicted. The New Hampshire Supreme Court noted in 1912 that "entire equality of privilege in attending school is not required," and school districts had discretion to balance the interests of the few with the many. In the case, the school board refused to provide transportation for a child who resided in an isolated area because of the expense at the same time it provided transportation for all other students. The court sided with the school district, arguing that "free schooling furnished by the state is not so much a right granted to the pupils as a duty imposed upon them for the public good." While schooling might provide individual benefits, its primary purpose was "the promotion of the general intelligence of the people constituting the body politic" in order to "increase the usefulness and efficiency of citizens, upon which the government of society depends." Therefore, the "interest of the public in the intelligence of the people generally is paramount to the special interest or desire of a single individual," and the state should not attempt to overcome "the inconvenient location of his home" by "substantially reducing the efficiency of all the schools in town."[56]

In a different type of case that similarly privileged the good of the school over the particular claims of the individual, the Wisconsin Supreme Court sustained the expulsion of a "crippled and defective child" whose "physical condition and ailment produces a depressing and nauseating effect upon the teachers and school children" and "takes up an undue portion of the teacher's time." The court ruled that "the right of a child of school age to attend the public schools of this state cannot be insisted upon when its presence therein is harmful to the best interests of the school. This, like other individual rights, must be subordinated to the general welfare." The privilege or right to education, like parents' right to direct the education of their children, should be respected, courts argued, unless it conflicted with the public interest. Parents' and children's rights were relative, not absolute, limits on state power.[57]

In addition to challenges to state legislation and policies, parents engaged with myriad everyday conflicts with school officials over school rules and policies that raised questions about parental rights and control. Since the inception of public schools, courts had held that children who attended the school must submit to all reasonable school regulations and could be punished or expelled for violating its rules even if they did so at the direction of their parents. When parents challenged school rules, courts declared that their role was limited to determining whether the regulation was reasonably calculated to promote the order, efficiency, and government of the school. In nineteenth-century cases, courts substantiated rules that punished absences and tardiness, established conditions for attendance, and proscribed corporal punishment for insubordination. They rejected rules that went beyond this, such as school rules that required students to pay for school property that they damaged, expulsion of students who refused to take up certain studies or activities, and a rule that required students to bring in wood for the fire. In the latter case, the Wisconsin Supreme Court chastised school officials and noted that they had "sadly misconceived their powers and duties," for although school officials could make rules, they "are not uncontrolled in the exercise of their discretion and judgment." Rules must be "reasonable or proper, or, in the language of the state, *needful*, for the government, good order, and efficiency of the schools."[58]

Over time, as the state interest and role in schooling expanded, courts showed greater and greater deference to school officials to determine what was reasonable, or needful, for the good government of the modern school. They sanctioned a number of rules that went much further in regulating the conduct of pupils and were even more tangentially related to the good government of the school than collecting firewood. They upheld as reasonable, for example, rules prohibiting the use of cosmetics, regulating student dress, prohibiting membership in fraternities and sororities, prohibiting students from leaving school during the day to eat lunch with parents, and regulating student speech and activities even outside of school hours and away from school property.[59]

Setting a far-reaching standard, the Wisconsin Supreme Court in 1908 sanctioned the suspension of a student who wrote a poem lampooning school rules that she submitted to a local newspaper. The court ruled that students could be suspended for "an offense committed outside of school hours, and not in the presence of the teacher" if it would have a "direct and immediate tendency to influence the conduct of other pupils while in the schoolroom, to set at naught the proper discipline of the school, to impair the authority of the teachers, and to bring them into ridicule and contempt." According to the court, teachers should been given great deference in determining what would impair the school because of their special familiarity with "the disposition and temper of the children under their charge." Other state courts similarly upheld student expulsions for conduct outside of school hours and off of school property that violated school rules or undermined the authority of the school; students were expelled for organizing a weekend football game, breaking a town ordinance against public drunkenness, and failing to wear school uniforms on the weekend.[60]

Courts did set some limits. The Supreme Court of Mississippi rejected a school regulation in 1909 that required children to stay in their homes from 7 to 9 p.m. every night to study. Sixteen-year-old Henry Germany was expelled from school for violating the rule when he attended a religious service with his father during the hours mandated by the school for home study. The court rebuffed the "misguided zeal" of school officials who overstepped their authority to pass a rule that "invades the home and wrests from the parent his right to control his child around his own hearthstone." School authorities could make laws that extended outside of school hours and into the home, the court ruled, but only around matters "which would per se have a direct and pernicious effect on the moral tone of the school, or have a tendency to subvert and destroy the proper administration of school affairs." Other states drew the line differently, however. In Georgia nine years later a court declared that a school rule that prohibited students from attending moving pictures on weeknights was reasonable and sustained the expulsion of a girl who attended a movie with her parents' permission.[61]

Thus, by World War I, it was well settled by state courts that schools were state institutions performing a fundamental state interest, that school officials had wide discretion to make and enforce rules for the management of the school even if it impinged on parental authority, and that neither parental rights nor a child's right to instruction were constitutionally recognized limitations to state police power. The once nearly unlimited realm of parental dominion under common law and the customary deference of schools to parental values and interests had been transformed by compulsory attendance and by the growing claims of public interest in education it represented. In practice, different states and communities showed more or less deference to parents in the compulsory school based on politics, culture, traditions, and the particular parents in question. However, courts clearly held that the public interest represented by the school was superior to the private rights of parents.

This steady erosion of the ground on which common law parental authority stood became an avalanche in the immediate aftermath of World War I. Wartime anxieties about American democracy and national progress spilled into a series of postwar efforts to broaden and deepen the reach of the school and to extend state oversight, as the last chapter explored. Anxieties about Americanization and a resurgent anti-Catholicism fueled a wave of statutes and controls over private schools, including laws to establish state supervision and apply minimum standards. State legislatures in Nebraska, Ohio, and Iowa forbade the teaching of German in the elementary schools. In Oregon a popular referendum supported by the Masons and the Ku Klux Klan went so far as to amend the state's compulsory attendance law to require all children to attend public schools, effectively rendering private schools illegal.[62]

Catholics mobilized politically in the wake of World War I to fight state and federal initiatives that they argued invaded family governance and compromised individual liberty. Forming the National Catholic Welfare Council (NCWC), they opposed federal aid to schools throughout the 1920s and 1930s and resisted state-level measures to restrict and prohibit private schools. Faced with a fierce onslaught of anti-Catholicism, Catholics positioned themselves as patriotic Americans and defenders of individual liberty and even ceded the right of the state to regulate private schools, which they had previously contested. However, they argued that the state had crossed a constitutional limit in dictating the content of private schools and regulating them out of existence. The NCWC argued that the Oregon law "sanctions by implication the Soviet claim to invade the home and substitute communal for parental care." It was also "an infringement of the liberty of conscience that has been the boast of our country," and a "triumph of bigotry." The Lutheran Schools Committee in Portland issued a pamphlet warning that the proposed referendum would be an "entering wedge of religious persecution." Lutherans argued that since "many private schools are maintained for a religious purpose and as a matter of conscience, to outlaw them would be a grave violation of religious liberty and an invasion of the freedom of conscience." In legal challenges that articulated a defense of minority rights against majority power, they pushed the U.S. Supreme Court to articulate new constitutional limits to the exploding state police power.[63]

In the 1923 case *Meyer v. Nebraska,* the U.S. Supreme Court considered whether state laws forbidding foreign language instruction in schools violated the federal constitution. State supreme courts in Nebraska, Iowa, and Ohio had applied precedents to uphold the laws as valid police power regulations; they served a legitimate public purpose and did not violate any express constitutional provisions, the courts argued. However, the U.S. Supreme Court disagreed and defined a Fourteenth Amendment constitutional guarantee of individual liberty. According to the court, "That the state may do much, go very far, indeed, in order to improve the quality of its citizens, physically, mentally and morally, is clear, but the *individual has certain fundamental rights which must be respected.*" These "certain fundamental rights" it declined to define with exactness but included "not merely freedom from bodily restraint but also the right of the individual to contract, to engage in any of the common occupations of life, to acquire useful knowledge, to marry, establish a home and bring up children, to worship God according to the dictates of his own conscience, and generally to enjoy those privileges long recognized at common law as essential to the orderly pursuit of happiness by free men." While it aimed for a laudable goal, the statute had gone too far to pursue it: "no emergency has arisen which renders knowledge by a child of some language other than English so clearly harmful as to justify its inhabitation with the consequent infringement of rights long freely enjoyed."[64]

In *Pierce v. Society of the Sisters* in 1925, the U.S. Supreme Court extended its arguments in *Meyer* to consider the realm of "fundamental rights" that the Fourteenth Amendment protected. Asked to consider the constitutionality of Oregon's new law to prohibit private schools, the court applied the reasoning in *Meyer* to argue that police powers must not unreasonably interfere with the rights of individuals. With no evidence that private schools were inherently harmful, the Court argued, destruction of private schools was an unreasonable abridgement of their property rights. It was also an invasion of the fundamental rights of parents. The Oregon law "unreasonably interferes with the liberty of parents and guardians to direct the upbringing and education of children under their control." The state did not have the power to "standardize its children by forcing them to accept instruction from public teachers only," for the "child is not the mere creature of the state" and "those who nurture him and direct his destiny have the right, coupled with the high duty, to recognize and prepare him for additional obligations." While it did not define these rights with any precision, the court argued that there were fundamental inviolate rights of parents protected by the U.S. Constitution that included at the very least the right to send children to a private school and instruct them in the family's moral and religious values. Parents' rights had a new foundation in constitutional law that could be used to set limits to state police power.[65]

In *Pierce* and *Meyer*, the Supreme Court both recognized the broad exercise of police power over schools and laid out significant new limitations for it. The court noted many areas where state authority to regulate was "unquestioned," citing as examples compulsory attendance laws, requirements for English instruction, minimum curriculum requirements, regulations of teachers' qualifications, mandatory loyalty oaths, and regulation of private schools. Yet, individuals held fundamental, inviolable rights that were protected by the Fourteenth Amendment, the Supreme Court held, and it located parents' right to some control over their children's education within it. In doing so, it expanded individual rights protections first articulated, ironically, in some of the most controversial and despised cases of the early twentieth century that struck down protective labor legislation as a violation of "liberty of contract."

The newly defined constitutional right of parents thus replaced the eroded rights of common law and set them on a firmer foundation, one that was absolute rather than relative. It was the beginning of a slow but major twentieth-century expansion of negative, absolute constitutional liberties protected against the state that were born in large part out of the growing conviction that untrammeled state power, even when representative of the democratic majority, should not be allowed to invade all domains. As one contemporary legal scholar astutely predicted, this interpretation of parental liberty under the Fourteenth Amendment would invite new kinds of constitutional claims, particularly cases of religious conscience of parents.[66]

At the same time that it outlined an important new limit to state police power, however, the Supreme Court's decision underscored just how far state regulation had extended in the past two decades. The need to offer a firmer constitutional basis for parental rights arose because the ground had shifted so far away from the expansive parental authority defined in common law and protected by the entire political system in the nineteenth century.

While the Supreme Court articulated an important limit to states' police power and protection for parents' rights, federal and state courts were slow and inconsistent in their elaboration of these fundamental rights under the Fourteenth Amendment. In a few cases, courts maintained that parents' rights included some control over educational content particularly for reasons of conscience. The Supreme Court of Colorado cited *Pierce* and *Meyer* to reject a child's expulsion for violating a school board rule that required children to read the Protestant King James Bible. Although the rule itself was reasonable, parents should be allowed to request their child be exempted, the court reasoned, because parents' rights deserved respect and the Bible reading was not so essential for good citizenship that it justified impinging on parents' values.[67]

Yet other courts and legal authorities did not agree that it gave parents license to resist school subjects or claim exemptions to school rules. In a series of cases in the 1930s and 1940s, state and federal courts upheld schools' authority to expel Jehovah's Witnesses who refused to salute the flag and recite the pledge of allegiance because they believed it violated their religion's prohibition against idol worship. Before the Supreme Court reversed itself in 1943, state and federal courts not only upheld the rules but allowed school officials to prosecute Jehovah's Witness parents for violating the compulsory attendance laws because of these expulsions. Courts continued to defer heavily to school officials' regulations and reject most parental objections, both in courts of record and by refusing to hear scores of other cases. In a Texas case in 1930, the court ruled that the school could expel a child who repeatedly left school grounds to eat lunch with her parents at their insistence and then prosecute the parents for violating the attendance law.[68]

Thus, while the Supreme Court recognized a fundamental right of parents to exert some control over the education of their children, what this meant in practice did not radically or immediately change relations between parents, schools, and the state. Parents had firmer ground on which to challenge school officials' regulations and state police power, but it was a much more circumscribed area than they had enjoyed in the voluntary school.

The rise and extension of compulsory attendance laws transformed the rights of parents and their relationship to the school. Under common law, parents' duty to educate their children was a moral one and they exercised nearly unlimited control over it, including whether, how, and where to provide education. Parents' rights to control the education of their children received both great legal and cultural deference, as it was part of an accepted right of households to liberty and self-government. Compulsory attendance statutes and enforcement, however, asserted a public interest in the education of children and transformed the duty to educate into a legal one that the state could enforce and regulate, which it did with increasing vigor over time. Courts defined attendance as a legitimate police power regulation on behalf of the public interest and in expansive language gave nearly carte blanche to state legislatures and local school officials to define conditions and standards for education.

Until the mid 1920s, courts recognized few limits to this police power in education and deferred heavily to school officials in day-to-day conflicts with parents over school rules. When parents challenged school policies, courts ruled that parents' rights under common law must be balanced with, and ultimately give way to, state regulation because the public interest trumped private rights. In the early 1920s, however, the U.S. Supreme Court laid a light finger on the scale when it rejected state police power regulations that it ruled were too broad and went too far to impinge the rights of parents. Locating parents' rights firmly in the Constitution rather than common law doctrine, it ruled that the Fourteenth Amendment protected the fundamental rights of individuals, including a parent's right to exert some control over the education of his or her child. While state police power was broad, the court ruled, it was not unlimited, and when it impinged on individual rights it had to have a compelling reason to do so. In grounding parental rights in an explicit constitutional provision, the court gave them firmer footing, although significantly more circumscribed than had existed under nineteenth-century common law and in the voluntary school. The compulsory school was thus a catalyst for redefining parental and individual rights, since it was a site where these were negotiated and contested on a regular basis.

This redefinition of parents' rights reflected a significant shift in the balance between home and school and the growing scope of public interest claims over children. Attendance became a mechanism and rationale for a host of new, and sometimes hidden, interventions that both policed individual families and applied new policies to all children. In home visitations and the surveillance of children in schools that was part of attendance service, public officials expanded their oversight of children and their families and weighed in on once private decisions about children's health, education, welfare, and work. Concerns about the quality of attendance, not merely the fact of it, led school reformers to extend school health and welfare policies. These policies, such as vaccination policies and medical treatment, became effectively compulsory for all children because of the legal requirement that they attend school.

In this way, attendance enforcement not only disciplined the resistant minority it brought into the school by force, but extended public power and oversight over all children in new ways. The compulsory school became the site for de facto regulations of children. Attendance laws justified, and even required, that public officials regulate private schools and home instruction to ensure that they satisfied the state's goals in requiring attendance. Attendance service also stimulated new techniques to monitor and regularize daily attendance, new systems for collecting and utilizing information about students, and new child services aimed to address the causes of irregular attendance. The combination of public relations work, persuasion and services, and threat of legal force all worked to pressure parents, and not only those who were confronted directly with attendance agents, to adjust their behavior and internalize new attitudes about attendance and health policy. Consequently, schooling was an important instrument of what Michel Foucault has called "governmentality," a modern mode of social governance that not only disciplines behavior but also shapes subjectivity by propelling individuals to internalize new norms and controls.[69]

School reformers tended to assume that the public welfare and individual benefits of education were compatible. Yet they did come into conflict. Schools could trample on the rights and welfare of individual parents and children in ways that we may find shocking in the twenty-first century. In one particularly egregious case, a court in Pennsylvania found parents guilty of violating the attendance law because they refused to send their child back to the classroom of a teacher who had been convicted of assaulting him and whom the school board had promised not to rehire.[70] The privileging of social goals, which justified the exclusion of a child with physical handicaps in Wisconsin or the expulsion of Jehovah's Witnesses who refused to salute the flag, could at times ride roughshod over individual rights and interests, particularly of minority groups.

Yet at other times the insistence on the public interest in children's education could bring greater opportunity and protection for children. Children who might have begun work at age thirteen at least had the opportunity to imagine a different life, and attendance service connected many families to needed health services and public resources. African American education reformers in the South challenged the failure of school officials to enforce attendance policies for black children because they recognized that compulsion reflected and intensified public responsibility for universal education that brought with it services and opportunities for many children. Coercion and opportunity were both deeply embedded in these new public interventions.

FIVE * *Creating Citizens and Workers: Curriculum Reform and the Aims of Education in a Democracy*

"The secondary schools of the United States, taken as a whole, do not exist for the purpose of preparing boys and girls for colleges," argued the National Education Association (NEA) Committee of Ten on Secondary School Studies in its 1894 report. Since "only an insignificant percentage of the graduates of these schools go to colleges or scientific schools," their "main function is to prepare for the duties of life that small proportion of all children in the country . . . who show themselves able to profit by an education prolonged to the eighteenth year." The committee had been appointed to deal with the problem of articulation between colleges and secondary schools, particularly the question of whether colleges should accept the ballooning "modern" subjects for admission—English, modern languages, history and civil government—or continue to insist on traditional subjects like Latin, Greek, and mathematics. The committee concluded that all subjects should be held in "equal rank for the purposes of admission to college," and it decisively rejected the idea of separate curriculums based on the destination of students. "Every subject which is taught at all in secondary school should be taught in the same way and to the same extent to every pupil so long as he pursues it, no matter what the probable estimation of the pupil may be, or at what point his education is to cease." The NEA assumed that both modern and classical subjects could contribute to the main goals of liberal education—mental discipline, general culture, and morality—and that this liberal education provided the best preparation for life for college-bound and non-college-bound youths alike.[1]

A quarter century later, the NEA sponsored a second major study of secondary school curriculum, the Commission on the Reorganization of Secondary Education (CRSE), which came to a very different conclusion and reflected the tremendous changes that had taken place in secondary education, including rising enrollments and a diversification of the school program. The commission articulated seven primary aims of the high school, all of which were oriented toward practical preparation for life:

health, command of fundamental processes, worthy home-membership, vocation, citizenship, worthy use of leisure, and ethical character. The CRSE explained that modern changes in society and the activities of the individual called "for a degree of intelligence and efficiency on the part of every citizen that cannot be secured through elementary education alone, or even through secondary education unless the scope of that education is broadened." All youths should attend high school, which should be further broadened to meet their practical needs. "Education in a democracy," the CRSE argued, "should develop in the individual the knowledge, interest, ideals, habits, and powers whereby he will find his place and use that place to shape both himself and society toward ever nobler aims." The high school must perform both specializing and unifying functions; it should discover and develop the aptitudes, abilities, and aspirations of each individual but also develop the "common knowledge, common ideals, and common interests essential to American democracy." This could best occur, the report concluded, in a comprehensive institution that differentiated instruction to meet student needs but also cultivated shared cultural and social experiences.[2]

The CRSE's "Cardinal Principles of Education" reflected important changes in the twentieth-century high school. Whereas the Committee of Ten in 1894 saw the high school as a relatively elite institution for students with above-average intelligence and resources, the CRSE viewed it as an institution that could and should serve all children. In 1890, 4 percent of children attended public high school, while by 1920 the percentage had grown to 24 percent and would reach 50 percent by the end of the 1930s, as a rising standard of living, cultural norms, and changes in the labor market including the expansion of white-collar work drove popular demand and attendance at high school. In addition to the growing size and reach of the high school, "Cardinal Principles" reflected a change in the aims and curriculum of the school. While both reports identified the goal of the high school as preparation for life rather than college, the assumptions about what this meant had clearly shifted. For the Committee of Ten, preparation for life derived from the intellectual and character training of liberal education, but for the CRSE, this preparation for life was more practical, instrumental, and connected to everyday social life including such things as worthy use of leisure and good health. While the Committee of Ten rejected a distinction between college-bound and non-college-bound students and sanctioned a common curriculum with free electives for all alike, the CRSE offered a democratic defense of differentiated curriculum. It argued that equality of opportunity meant a curriculum specialized to the needs of individuals rather than the same education imposed on all.[3]

The CRSE framed growing tendencies in education into an authoritative statement of purposes that shaped educational practice and discussion after World War I, when high schools further expanded, shaped their curriculums toward practical preparation for life, and embraced differentiation within a comprehensive high school. This chapter examines these curricular reforms and the changing aims of the school through the development of two new subjects that exemplified and shaped the new education: vocational education and civics. While nineteenth-century schools had purported to prepare for both work and citizenship through the entire curriculum, Americans pressed them to do this in more deliberate and systematic ways in the twentieth century. Both subjects enjoyed support from a range of groups outside the school that pressed school boards and administrators to develop classes and activities before World War I that were institutionalized and diffused more broadly after the war. Both subjects were concentrated initially and most centrally in the high school but filtered down to lower grades and influenced the larger conversation about schooling aims at all levels. Both subjects also reflected and furthered the high school's project of differentiating and socializing individuals; each viewed individual development as an inescapably social process shaped by social ends. And both subjects revealed tensions between the goal of adjusting individuals for the world as it was and the progressive demand that education equip them to transform it.

While the aims of the new education suffused all reforms—to remake school governance, expand state administration, extend the school's oversight, build educational expertise—it was in curriculum reform that Americans engaged most deliberately and self-consciously with the goals of the school and its relationship to society and state. In vocational education and civics, Americans struggled to make sense of modern changes and to define modern citizens and workers. They wrestled with the meaning and practice of democracy in a world of industrial capitalism, large-scale organization, and social interdependence, and in these new subjects they sought to deliberately accommodate individuals to these changes.

Americans committed themselves to expanding schooling, especially the high school or "people's college," to develop individuals to their fullest potential and equip them to navigate modern economy and society. They invested heavily in the American high school and celebrated it as an engine of democracy with its widespread access, its democratic attention to individual differences and needs, and its potential to unleash the talents of the individual. So strong was its power as a site of democratic imagination that even social critics who lambasted it for its democratic failures ultimately put their faith in schools to build a better democracy. This democratic image of the high school as an engine of equal opportunity and release of individual potential helped to quell anxieties about democracy in the new age and bolster individualism in a new context. Yet it also obscured the inequities embedded in the new education and shifted attention away from structural barriers to opportunity and structural limitations of schooling as a social policy strategy.

Vocational Education, Differentiation, and the Aims of the Modern School

Vocational education in the twentieth century developed out of the nineteenth-century movement for manual training. Americans had long imbued work with educational value and used work training as a tool to moralize and discipline criminals, delinquents, and so-called inferior peoples. In the late nineteenth century, manual training blossomed into a national reform movement for the public schools after demonstrations from abroad convinced American reformers to experiment with classes in woodworking, mechanical drawing, cooking, sewing, and other manual trades. John D. Runkle of Massachusetts Institute of Technology was an early supporter and argued that manual training could offer solutions to vexing problems of industrialization, including quelling labor unrest, supplying skilled labor necessary for industrial progress, and developing the capacity of the individual, which would "elevate and dignify the labor of our country." Other supporters argued manual training would improve education by infusing new life into the school and holding boys' interest. "Add the manual elements," one argued, "with their freshness and variety, their delightful shop exercises, their healthy intellectual and moral atmosphere, and the living reality of their work, and the *boys will stay in school*."[4]

Many of these arguments resonated with groups inside and outside the schools that supported manual training for the ways it seemed to respond to new needs and also reinforce old values. Supporters saw it as a solution to labor problems in an industrializing society; businessmen hoped it would weaken labor unions and feed the engines of industrial progress by expanding the supply of skilled labor while laborers themselves saw it as an opportunity for individual and collective economic advancement. Other supporters, including philanthropists and moral reformers, believed that manual training would exert a moralizing force over urban populations and would help to reinforce values of industry, discipline, and work that many feared were being undermined by transformations of economy and society. Progressive pedagogues saw it as an ideal way to put into practice new educational theories and methods, including the child-centered classroom that would build on the interest and self-activity of children. Other educators viewed manual training as an alternative method to accomplish traditional goals of character development, mental discipline, and liberal education. As one noted, "the co-operation of mind, hand and eye, all conduce to a broader mental culture."[5]

The myriad justifications for manual training helped to draw together a coalition of supporters with sometimes conflicting goals to support its spread in the public schools. In many cities, voluntary societies and interest groups pushed the public schools to introduce manual training. In Milwaukee, for example, clubwomen organized the Milwaukee Public School Cooking Association in 1887 to offer free instruction in cooking and domestic economy after school hours because of a concern about the declining state of the "housewifely arts." They successfully pressed the school board to take over and expand the courses and to introduce manual training for boys. School boards in other cities adopted new courses in the public schools when faced with similar lobbying and pressure, competition from private schools, and models from other cities. By 1890, the U.S. Bureau of Education reported that thousands of youths were enrolled in manual training classes in thirty-six cities, and a decade later the number had grown to over a hundred cities.[6]

However, as educators harmonized manual training with the traditional educational aims of the school, they diluted its economic value and frustrated the demands of some proponents for more practical, relevant training for work. The newly formed National Association of Manufacturers, for example, complained in 1905 that manual training had become too literary in focus and urged publicly supported trade training outside of the control of educators. It looked to Germany's system of trade schools as a model, arguing that this vocational training was "at once the admiration and fear of all countries" and was "the secret of her wonderful development in production and commerce." Farmers' advocates, including the Grange and the agricultural press, also urged agricultural instruction in the public schools and construction of special agricultural high schools in order to better prepare youths for lives on the farm, stem the drift to the city, and provide a pathway to agricultural colleges. For these groups, manual training's emphasis on handwork as a complement to headwork did not satisfy the need for practical instruction for work or meet the economic needs of individuals and society.[7]

These growing demands for practical trade training prompted the Massachusetts legislature to appoint the Massachusetts Commission on Industrial and Technical Education, commonly known as the Douglas Commission, to study the issue. Its 1906 report transformed the discussion of vocational education and helped stimulate a national movement for more practically oriented preparation for work. The commission hired a sociologist, consulted expert opinion and existing practice in other places, and held a series of well-attended public hearings that reflected the "widespread interest" in the subject. The report concluded that workers and manufacturers, as well as the state itself, had an interest in the wide distribution of technical skill, technical knowledge, and "industrial intelligence," which it defined as "mental power to see beyond the task which occupies the hands for the moment to the operations which have preceded and to those which will follow it" and "take in the whole process." Industrial skill, knowledge, and intelligence helped workers and manufacturers alike; it improved the self-respect and self-reliance of the individual worker and the overall productivity and competitiveness of business.[8]

Yet despite the importance of vocational education to the state, the commission observed that few opportunities existed for young people and adult workers to gain industrial skills and knowledge in any systematic way. Public and private trade training schools were limited in number, and the public schools did little to prepare students for work. Manual training had been framed as a cultural subject to stimulate intellectual effort rather than serve industrial ends and thus "has been severed from real life as completely as have the other school activities." This was part of a larger trend, the commission noted, in which the schools had become "too exclusively literary in their spirit, scope, and methods." Public schools had been founded to create intelligent citizens and favorably influence all the callings of life, but had come to privilege the former over the latter to such an extent that it now had a "one-sided sense of values, a one-sided view of life, and a wrong attitude toward labor." This literary focus failed to keep the interest of many adolescents who complained it did not meet their real needs, the investigating sociologist found, and was a significant factor in school-leaving before the completion of high school. Schools should embrace their vocational as well as cultural value, for "that which fits a child best for his place in the world as a producer, tends to his own highest development physically, intellectually, and morally." The commission recommended that public schools add vocational courses and emphasize the practical application of traditional subjects, and it urged the state to establish independent trade schools for adolescents.[9]

The Douglas Report was an important moment in which supporters of vocational education differentiated their aims from those of manual training and made a strong case for a public interest in technical skill and industrial intelligence. It reflected a shift in the terms of the debate, including a strong demand that schools provide more practical training and functional job preparation and embrace vocational aims alongside cultural ones. It also helped to stimulate an organized national movement for vocational education that brought together business, labor, farmers, social settlement workers, child welfare advocates, and educators, among others. These groups embraced and extended the rationales of the Douglas Commission to lobby for vocational education programs at local, state, and national levels. They established the National Society for the Promotion of Industrial Education (NSPIE) to organize publicity and lobbying campaigns for vocational education at state and federal levels. By 1913, NSPIE succeeded in securing state aid for vocational training in six states and state permission or mandate for vocational education in over a dozen more.[10]

In 1914, NSPIE turned its attention to federal aid for vocational education. It successfully lobbied Congress to appoint a federal commission to study the issue, which was staffed with four sympathetic congressmen and five members of NSPIE. The commission recommended federal matching aid to states for vocational education, which Congress adopted three years later. The Smith-Hughes Act of 1917 established a Federal Vocational Board to administer the aid and work with state officials. Over time it helped to diffuse vocational education nationally, bolster and expand state departments of education, and fuel backlash against general federal aid in the postwar period.[11]

In the years between the Douglas Commission Report and the Smith-Hughes Act, groups adopted and extended the arguments on behalf of vocational education and began to frame it as a democratic move to adapt the high school to the practical needs of the people. The American Federation of Labor (AFL) came out strongly on behalf of vocational education for its benefit to workers. A 1912 report on the subject declared that "we want a system which will develop the labor power of our people so that every worker may become interested in his work and approach the limits of human efficiency. Our public school system of to-day teaches too much and educates not enough, and fails entirely to prepare its pupils for productive labor." The AFL reasoned that "The 90 per cent who are going into manual occupations have the same right to the best preparation for their life's work that the State can give them as has the 10 per cent who go into the professions." Laborers made some of the strongest defenses of vocational education as a democratic reform. Testifying before Congress on the issue of federal aid, Leonora O'Reilly of the Woman's Trade Union League—who also argued for radical equality in the vocational training of girls and boys—claimed that vocational training was necessary for "industrial democracy" and an "opportunity for self-expression." According to O'Reilly, "every child is born with rich possibilities, which may be discovered and developed, and that is part of our work as a nation, to find out what the child can do, and give it its opportunity to do that."[12]

Although initially skeptical, most educators embraced vocational education and advocated its expansion in the public schools. The dean of Teachers College echoed the democratic claims of laborers, arguing that the American education system only "grants equality of opportunity to those who can go on to the college and university. It takes little account of the boy—and less still of the girl—who cannot have or does not wish for a higher education." Vocational training would grant equal opportunity to all by helping "the average man better to do his life-work and better realize the wealth of his inheritance as an American citizen." This position often had practical dimensions. Many educators saw vocational education as a curricular adaptation that could address problems of elimination and retardation in the schools as well as the growing diversity of the high school population.[13]

Vocational education was also essential, many educators argued, for redefining liberal education in the industrial age. While some educators critiqued vocational training as a threat to liberal education and culture, others argued it enhanced it. Liberal education was not a fixed, static set of cultural knowledge or intellectual skills, educators as diverse as Nicholas Murray Butler and John Dewey contended, but was intellectual development and individual efficacy within a particular social context. As one educational philosopher argued, "nobody can be liberally educated for life in a democracy who is not trained to use his powers in some one of the many possible vocations to contribute to human welfare." The "liberalizing value" of any study, he concluded, is in "what it does in setting free the best powers and capacities of the individual." Vocational education was not an alternative to liberal education but an expansion of the concept appropriate for the industrial age, a way of helping to equip individuals to navigate their world.[14]

Educators and other supporters also embraced vocational training in the public schools as an alternative to proposals for a separate system of trade training that would separate it from liberal education. The Douglas Commission recommended a "dual control" system in which vocational schools would be administered and funded separately from the existing public schools. Massachusetts and Wisconsin adopted this German model. Throughout the 1910s and early 1920s states wrestled with whether public funds for vocational education should go through the public school system or outside of it, an issue not settled by the Smith-Hughes Act, which gave states the discretion to decide how to spend federal money.

The debate in Illinois over a dual-control proposal illuminates some of the stakes of this debate. Underneath shared support for vocational policies, groups brought different aims and social assumptions about the goals of education that came to the fore during the public debate. It began in 1911 when the Commercial Club, a businessmen's reform organization, hired former city superintendent Edwin Cooley to study vocational training in Europe and formulate a plan for the state. The resulting legislative proposal, popularly known as the Cooley Bill, called for a public funding of vocational schools to be administered by state and local vocational boards composed of "practical men" of industry and separate from the public schools. Proponents argued that this dual system would foster efficiency and would be a "finishing school for the youth between 14 and 18 who are unable or unwilling to continue longer in the present elementary or secondary school." A separate system was necessary because the character, method, purposes, and scope of work for vocational schools should be different from that of public schools and because the school was currently failing youths over age fourteen, who dropped out in large numbers.[15]

David Snedden, commissioner of education in Massachusetts and later an educational sociologist at Teachers College, argued that the dual-control question "is merely one of securing the greatest efficiency." For Snedden, "vocational education is irreducibly and without unnecessary mystification, education for the pursuit of an occupation," and while it is "not all of education" it is "supremely important." Trade schools for boys over age fourteen who had already completed the common school should be under the control of practical men of industry, for "school men, however well intentioned, are apt to be impractical and to fail to appreciate actual conditions." Democracy, he argued, consists in "removing as far as practicable all artificial barriers (birth, rank, wealth) to the enjoyment of equal opportunities," and dual control helped to do this for boys who would otherwise not attend high school at all.[16]

Despite Snedden and other supporters' claims that separate trade schools would supplement rather than replace general education, many observers worried that it undermined the goals of public education. Workers were suspicious of the proposals by businessmen for a separate system under their own control. Margaret Haley of the Chicago Teachers Federation suspected it was driven by "commercial motive" and was a move "on the part of capital to fight the labor unions," while the president of the Illinois State Federation of Labor charged that businessmen "hope to gain an advantage in the labor market" and "want specialists that they can control, both in the shop and elsewhere." Many observers worried that separating working-class children into separate schools might lead to inferior education and create permanent class divisions. One educator warned that there was a "danger of removing all chance for general education from the growing tradesmen" with the dual system. Chicago superintendent Ella Flagg

Young supported vocational education but worried that the "great American vocational craze" was in danger "of making men factory workers and not teaching the joys of living." Schools had to do more than teach "accuracy and diligence," but should "open the door for individual growth" and "make it possible for them to advance beyond their environment and the circumstances into which they were born." In the vocational craze, schools must not lose sight of their ultimate goal to develop individual power and growth, not merely train workers.[17]

John Dewey made a similar appeal for vocational education that enhanced individual power and industrial intelligence and critiqued what he saw as the "narrow trade training" focus of many vocational supporters. In a series of articles in the *New Republic*, he attacked the Cooley Bill as an "undemocratic proposal" and took particular aim at David Snedden. "I object to regarding as vocational education any training which does not have as its supreme regard the development of such intelligent initiative, ingenuity and executive capacity as shall make workers, as far as they may be, the masters of their own industrial fate," Dewey argued. "The kind of vocational education in which I am interested is not one which will 'adapt' workers to the existing industrial regime; I am not sufficiently in love with the regime for that." Instead we should strive for a vocational education "which will first alter the existing industrial system, and ultimately transform it." In contrast to Snedden and other vocational education advocates, Dewey argued that vocational education should not aim just to prepare youths for specific jobs, which could "serve as a cloak conscious or unconscious, for measures calculated to promote the interests of the employing class" and "take for granted the perpetuity of the existing industrial regime." Vocational education should equip individuals with skills, intelligence, and commitments to adapt with and transform the economy, not accept the status quo.[18]

In the end, the Illinois legislature considered and rejected the Cooley Bill in three successive sessions before it finally abandoned it, and when federal aid became available the state directed it to the public schools. The debate over administrative control exposed some fissures within the coalition of reformers who supported vocational education, including differences in their aims and social assumptions. While many supporters of vocational education viewed it as preparation for specific jobs in the economy, others worried that this ran the danger of replicating the status quo and sought instead a more general vocational education that infused the school with practical interest and empowered individuals to succeed in the new economy. Reformers rarely acknowledged tension between these aims. Yet the resolution of the conflict in Illinois and in nearly every other state demonstrated that although most supporters viewed training for work as an important goal of the public school, they were not willing to abandon broader educational aims to do it as efficiently as possible, including training for citizenship and development of the individual's full range of powers.

In rejecting a separate system of vocational training, reformers and educators embraced vocational goals within the existing public school system. Supporters introduced new vocational classes and curriculums and allied organizational changes, such as the construction of prevocational junior high schools. Over the next decades, schools also embraced an expanded mission to prepare youths for lives of work by infusing vocational aims throughout the entire school program. The schools in Grand Rapids, Michigan, for example, brought vocational lessons into English course readings and assignments throughout the elementary and high school, such as assigned essays on blind-alley jobs, the economic value of high schooling, and students' own vocational interests and aptitudes. One Cincinnati school official explained the growing vocational focus of the high school, noting that "we are endeavoring to have the child select his high school course on the basis of the life career motive, and to use that motive as the impelling purpose which will keep him in school until graduation if possible."[19]

This vocational push did not come entirely from reformers and school officials. Parents and children had long considered the economic benefits of high schooling in their calculus of whether to attend, although it had not usually been the the sole or even guiding motivation. High schools became increasingly important gateways to the growing sector of white-collar jobs, however, and for women in particular, whose labor market participation was growing, they provided access to new clerical jobs and opportunities. Schools embraced more vocational aims in part because families saw vocational benefits of schooling, both in explicit commercial and vocational courses and in the general academic credentials and skills that the high school conferred. Over time, these utilitarian and instrumental rationales became increasingly prominent in the public debate about school aims and functions, and by the end of the century economic and vocational purposes would dominate discussion.[20]

The embrace of vocational education also advanced differentiation in theory and practice. Proponents of vocational education inverted the traditional common school argument about the democracy of the uniform curriculum for all. Democratic education and real equal opportunity, they argued, meant an education best suited to the needs, capacities, and interests of each individual and not the same education imposed on all. In *Democracy's High School* in 1914, Philadelphia principal William Lewis expressed the growing sentiment that "the boys in our schools cannot all be doctors, lawyers, preachers, and teachers. They are crying out for equal opportunities—a thing very different from identical opportunities." The education each child needs, Lewis argued, was the "type of training most likely to enable him to become the most intelligent, conscientious, and efficient citizen possible with his mental and physical endowments and limitations." Like in discussions of school finance and access, "equal educational opportunity" in curriculum did not mean the same education for all but rather an adequate and differentiated one. Vocational education helped to give curricular differentiation a democratic justification and to expand the practice as youths were encouraged to choose classes, a course of study, and extracurricular activities on the basis of vocation. Since these jobs were stratified by race, gender, and class it also expanded the differentiation in the school along these bases in subtle ways in the postwar era, as later sections will explore.[21]

Although supporters of vocational education spoke in terms of individual development, differentiation, and the needs of the individual child, their aims were inescapably social and their conception of the individual was situated in a social context. They worried about the economic competitiveness and progress of the nation, the needs of society and economy for skilled workers and harmonious labor relations, and the social benefits of human capital deployed in efficient ways. They fought to keep vocational training in public schools, where it could be situated within broader educational and social aims, including citizenship training. At the same time they were developing new vocational courses and embracing vocational aims, reformers wrestled with the individual's relationship to society and the larger social context, meaning, and significance of one's work and other life activities.

Citizenship Training and Social Education in the Modern World

"The signs of the times are unmistakable," professor James Vose announced in 1887 to the Massachusetts Council of the American Institute of Civics and the readers of the monthly journal *Education*. "In all our schemes of education, those studies that relate to citizenship are placed in the foremost rank" and hence "those things that fit a man for living in society, for doing intelligently and well his part in the body politic, are among the most vital and important that can come into his education," and yet "strangely enough, no subject has been more ignored in our schools." However, there had recently been "greatly increased interest in political studies among our people" and "I trust that the day is not distant when these courses, under the general name of civics, perhaps, will be as well and simply outlined, and as common, also, as those in mathematics or natural science." Vose noted that "Just what the new term *Civics* should include, and what exclude, has not yet been definitely settled," but he offered a tentative definition: "Civics is the Science of Citizenship" and its proper subject is "what the citizen of a free republic ought to know, that he may properly discharge his duties of citizenship," including ethics, civil polity, economics, history, and law. Vose's remarks on the emerging subject of civics came before the organization credited with originating the term just a few years before. The American Civics Institute was formed in 1885 by U.S. senators, Supreme Court justices, college presidents, and other "intelligent and patriotic citizens" with the goal of "promoting the qualities in citizenship which are essential to the integrity of our free institutions." To that end, it promoted patriotic holidays and displays, produced civics materials, and lobbied for their inclusion in the public schools and colleges.[22]

Educating for citizenship had been one of the primary justifications of public schools since their inception. Schools would preserve the republic by encouraging mass literacy, providing opportunities for leaders to rise, and cultivating widespread morality and character, which were essential attributes for a democratic society. Before the twentieth century, civic education for the masses came from the process of schooling itself rather than specific studies, and elements of civic pride and common culture were infused through the curriculum in spellers, readers, and lessons in history and geography. As Vose noted, training for citizenship was a fundamental goal of the school, but it offered little in the way of special instruction. Until the late nineteenth century, few thought that special instruction was needed. Democratic politics, practiced primarily as participation in community governance and in partisan political loyalty, was largely an exercise of character and civic spirit.[23]

As they did with education for work, reformers inside and outside of the school in the late nineteenth century argued that changes in modern life created new challenges for citizenship and necessitated more deliberate and systematic training. The American Institute of Civics and its allies were particularly concerned about urban political corruption and the need for good government in the nation's growing cities. They called for educated, independent voting by citizens rather than party loyalty, active support of municipal reforms, and a strong ethical commitment to public service and the common good above class interests. Concerns about immigrants fueled many of these discussions, one commentator noting that immigrants "swarm in our cities, and by their votes are largely responsible for the maintenance in power of the rings which plunder and misgovern so many American cities." They fueled crime, anarchism, and licentiousness, and they have "done much to lower the stand of American citizenship and degrade American politics." Immigration also threatened the unity of American national culture, and groups like the Daughters of the American Revolution (DAR) called for citizenship training as patriotism and assimilation to American culture, community, laws, and traditions.[24]

Immigrants were not the only threat to good government, and civics proponents criticized the apathy of native-born American citizens, one noting that "habitual indifference is threatening the nation." "We have in every community," a University of Chicago professor observed, "a large body of intelligent votes—large enough to turn the scales in favor of good government—who never attend a caucus, and who seldom exercise their right of suffrage except in state or national elections." These apathetic citizens are "not foreigners educated in Europe, nor are they representative of the criminal classes," but "native-born Americans, educated in our public schools" who "have not been properly trained in the duties of citizenship." A few observers recognized that this apathy might be structural. James Bryce observed that "in a vast population like ours, the individual feels swallowed up and obliterated, so that his own actions seem too small a unit in the sum of national action to be worth regarding." He mused that apathy might be due to the increasing size, complexity, and remoteness of modern governance, which alienated the individual and created barriers to the active participation that characterized small local communities.[25]

To most observers, however, this apathy was a failure of civic spirit, moral character, or knowledge and could be combated with efforts to awaken citizens to their responsibilities, including formal study in the schools. Consequently, early proponents of civics called for the study of government structure and operations, the political rights and obligations of citizenship, and cultivation of political ethics and patriotism. They urged the study of government in high school, for, as one civics author explained, "true political morality, and true patriotism must be based upon a knowledge of the real facts of government." Most commentators agreed that "good citizenship must be at its foundation intelligent citizenship. Patriotism, if it is to be more than a shallow sentiment, must be based on knowledge," the most important knowledge being "the necessity of government and the essential beneficence of its operations." In 1890, the NEA recommended that high schools add a course in civil government and that elementary schools infuse the study of government and patriotism in history courses. It estimated that one-third of high schools offered courses in government, but since these were usually given in the senior year they reached a fairly small and elite group of youths.[26]

In the early twentieth century, sociologists, educational theorists, and progressive thinkers began to press for an expanded conception of citizenship training in the school and in the process transformed the meaning of civics. Sociologist George Vincent argued that "the great problem of American education, then, is the problem of making better citizens" and the solution lie in efforts to "brin[g] the school into closer relation with life" and into "contact with the concrete social experience from which they sprang" in order to develop the "highest ideals of co-operation, loyalty, sacrifice." Philosopher John Dewey likewise argued that schools should be an "embryonic community life," which should foster democratic and moral values throughout their overall organization and pedagogy. "Society is a society of individuals and the individual is always a social individual. He lives in, for, and by society, just as society has no existence excepting in and through the individuals who constitute it," he argued in *Ethical Principles Underlying Education.* For Dewey, democracy was about this mutual constitution of the individual and society, and in many of his writings he argued that democratic citizens must be equipped with the "social intelligence, social power, and social interests" to navigate their world and recognize that their fate was bound with those of their fellows. Training of democratic citizens would not come from abstract study of government or political obligations but must be rooted in the social relations and experience of the school itself.[27]

Other intellectuals and reformers picked up this language of "social intelligence" and "social education" and urged that schools work consciously to cultivate these values. Changes in modern society rendered this social intelligence both more difficult and more important than ever before. The large-scale shift from a nation of agrarian self-governing island communities to urbanized, disconnected, and yet deeply interdependent mass society displaced older forms of authority, reshaped community, and eroded certainty. This left a deep malaise, Walter Lippmann noted in 1914, a "drift" of modern times, a "chaos of the new freedom," which created personal and social unease. "We are unsettled to the roots of our being," he argued, "we are not used to a complicated civilization, we don't know how to behave when personal contact and eternal authority have disappeared. There are no precedents to guide us, no wisdom that wasn't made for a simpler age. We have changed the environment more quickly than we know how to change ourselves" and "through it all our souls have become disorganized, for they have lost the ties which bind them."[28]

Sociologists and reformers of various ilk were concerned about social cohesion and community in modern life, particularly the problem of "social control"—how modern society exerted its norms and cultivated internal and external controls over the increasingly diverse and disconnected individuals that composed it. Individuals were less tied together and yet more interdependent than ever before. Some predicted the old individualism had passed and a new era of social organization was at hand.[29]

These anxieties fueled much of the new education discussion in which reformers called for schools to reform according to the needs of the new modern society and the new modern individual. As they worked to articulate the aims of the new education, pedagogical theorists and education reformers used a variety of terms—"adjustment," "development," "growth," "efficiency," "social intelligence," among others—that wrestled with how to educate individuals to be able to navigate the modern world. With varying degrees of emphasis, they all viewed individual development as a social process and the individual's efficacy and power to have meaning only in a social context. Harvard president Charles Eliot, like a growing number of educators, framed the goal of the school as "efficiency," which he defined as "effective power for work and service during a healthy and active life," including the ability to think, weigh evidence, make judgments, discern beauty, and use liberty wisely. Sociologist Michael O'Shea, who preferred the term "adjustment," argued that the goal of all education "must be to give the individual a mastery of the world," and to do this "we must regard a man as a member of a community rather than as an isolated individual," and hence "we must prepare him for his particular needs determined by the particular office he will fill in society." Still others, like Edward Hayes, argued that the goal of education was to develop and shape personality, for "within limits set by birth, individuality is a social product." They disagreed about how specifically the school should prepare for social roles—did it adapt individuals to particular social roles in the present or envision a more dynamic process?—but agreed that the modern school must pursue the linked projects of individual development and socialization.[30]

While many like Dewey and Vincent emphasized the ways in which the entire school program should be bent toward constructing socially minded and effective citizens for the new modern era, others began to experiment with ways in which the subject of civics could be used to concentrate these efforts and give them a special place in the curriculum. Arthur Dunn, who studied at the University of Chicago with Dewey and sociologists George Vincent and Albion Small, developed a landmark interdisciplinary program for elementary schools in Indianapolis in 1906 and then promoted it nationally through textbooks and consulting work for the U.S. Bureau of Education. Dunn emphasized the social basis of democratic citizenship, incorporated progressive pedagogical methods, and adapted civics for the elementary grades by defining it as "training in habits of good citizenship, rather than merely a study of government forms and machinery." For his practical training in citizenship, he articulated four main goals: "to help the child realize he is a responsible and helpful member of several social groups"; "to awaken and stimulate motives that will lead to the establishment of habits of order, cleanliness, cheerful cooperation, sympathetic service, and obedience to the law"; "to emphasize the intimate and reciprocal relations between the welfare of the individual and the welfare of the home and society"; and "to develop political intelligence and to prepare the young citizen for its exercise."[31]

Dunn's program in "community civics" used the community as a lens into the values, practices, and habits of citizenship and began with the environment close to the child—the home—and moved outward over time to the school, the neighborhood, the city, and the nation. In the lower grades, these lessons were infused throughout the curriculum in studies of literature, art, history, and geography. In eighth grade students were introduced to the formal study of civics to "give the pupil an organized conception of what his membership in the community means" and discuss government as "the supreme means by which the entire community may cooperate for the common welfare." Dunn elaborated these ideas and helped to popularize them with his 1907 textbook, *The Community and the Citizen*, which framed themes of civic obligation and government through the lens of community living, social welfare, and government provision of services to the community. He explained that the work of the school should be to "develop in the child the habit of thinking of himself as a member of a community, and the habit of acting with reference to community efficiency" and to establish "a consciousness of his civic relations in this broad sense." Dunn acknowledged that this gave civics a broader scope than was customary, but he argued that "good citizenship is nothing more nor less than efficient membership in the community in the relationships of neighbor, of family, of business, as well as in the political relationships."[32]

Educators in cities like New York, Philadelphia, and Cleveland experimented with community civics classes in the upper grades of the elementary school and filtered some lessons up to the high school. Like Dunn's program in Indianapolis, these experiments emphasized themes of community membership, social welfare, and government service and used the local community as a practical window into the habits, values, and practices of citizenship. By 1916, a host of groups, including several teachers' associations, the NEA, National Municipal League, and American Political Science Association, had studied and endorsed the new social approach to citizenship training.[33]

The NEA issued a laudatory report in 1915, *The Teaching of Community Civics*, which endorsed community civics and recommended its expansion as an eighth-grade course. It was a strong influence the following year for the CRSE's Committee on Social Studies, chaired by Arthur Dunn, which put forth the new term "social studies" to define subjects like civics that had as "their conscious and constant purpose the cultivation of good citizenship" through "development of an appreciation of the nature and laws of social life, a sense of the responsibility of the individual as a member of social groups, and the intelligence and the will to participate effectively in the promotion of the social well-being." It recommended the expansion of the social studies in the lower grades of the high school and stimulated experiments like the one in Milwaukee's Riverside High School, which created a new "socialized high-school civics" to give adolescents "a viewpoint from which they will get a vision, healthy and wholesome, of their responsibility and duty to society."[34]

Consequently, by the eve of American entry into the war, community civics had garnered acclaim as a progressive new model for civics at the elementary level and was starting to influence thinking at the secondary level. During and after the war, educators experimented with a "new civics" for the high school and expanded the social studies with civics at its center. This "new civics," the author of one of the new texts explained, was not the narrow study of government but rather "a study of the American nation as an organized group of citizens, with numerous public organizations, interests, and activities," and consequently it is "the heart, and in a sense the foundation, of the new course in the social sciences." It was becoming clear, another educator observed, that "the real subject of civics is the individual and his development in relation to the numerous units of social organization," and consequently the new civics course "focuses attention upon man, his responsibilities, his duties, and his obligations as a social being." Like community civics, this new civics emphasized the social dimensions of citizenship and redefined the subject as a social study rather than a political one.[35]

The development of social studies and new social civics was shaped not only by community civics experimentation and professional endorsement but also by wartime lessons and experiments with practical citizenship training. During World War I, many educators brought current events into the classroom through new materials or short ad-hoc courses encouraged by the federal government and voluntary associations. The U.S. Bureau of Education and Food Administration, for example, produced pamphlets for school children, *Lessons in National and Community Life,* which aimed to "lay the foundations for an intelligent enthusiasm of the United States," to "bring industry into the schools," and "to create a sense of responsibility" based on recognition of "interdependence" through discussion of current events like the war effort and conservation. It was one of many such efforts that educators reported helped infuse new life and interest into citizenship education.[36]

In addition to current events and discussion of contemporary social problems, classrooms fostered the war effort and good citizenship through student activities like Junior Red Cross, conservation drives, thrift clubs, student government, and fundraising. Franklin Johnson had argued as early as 1909 that extracurricular activities were a powerful, untapped resource for fostering social values. The war drove home the potential of student activities for practical citizenship, including developing character and promoting values like patriotism, cooperation, service, and leadership. In the postwar period, educators discussed at length how they could administer student extracurricular activities to best promote good citizenship, and activities became a central component of many new civics courses.[37]

The war provided a moment of reflection about citizenship and democracy, and the role of schooling in sustaining both, that spurred greater interest in civics and social studies. One educator observed in 1919 that Germany had given the world a "demonstration of the nearly limitless power of education" after which "no country henceforth can regard these instruments [schools] of national wellbeing or of national self-destruction, with indifference." John Dewey argued in 1918 that the war had made clear that effective organization of materials, munitions, food, and transportation "is absolutely dependent upon the underlying human capacity, upon inventive, cognizable, energetic human resources." The lesson of the war, he argued, was the need for "greater liberation of human power." Others came away with a similar sense of school's power and responsibility to shape individuals and society toward desired ends.[38]

Yet to many other observers, the war highlighted the failures and weaknesses of American citizenship and the challenges facing modern democracy. As chapter 3 explored, war mobilization and draft statistics showed higher than expected rates of illiteracy, poor health, and unassimilated immigrants and raised concerns about the education, health, and cohesion of the citizen body. Nationalist groups like the DAR and American Legion mobilized Americanization efforts, including private school controls, English-language regulations, aid and expansion of public schools, and Americanization programs for adults that promoted citizenship as loyalty, conformity, patriotism, and service. Concerned that "profound ignorance of the simple principles of American government is an ever-growing menace," these groups worked to promote "bedrock Americanism" through citizenship training inside and outside of the schools. As part of these efforts, they lobbied for state laws requiring civics, including an effort spearheaded by the American Bar Association (ABA) to require study of the Constitution that was adopted in over half of states by 1925.[39]

For some, the problem was less lack of social cohesion and national spirit than the structural challenges to democracy in the modern world highlighted by the war. Sociologist Charles Elwood argued that "the relative success of democracy under the simple, rural conditions of life in which our fathers lived is but little argument for the success of democracy in the complex, urban civilization in which we live." The war drove home the fact that "We have built a gigantic material civilization that resembles nothing so much as a mighty machine which requires almost infinite intelligence and good will to run it in such a way that will not bring disaster upon us," and it was uncertain, he noted, how we can secure this from the mass of citizens when the problems are so complex.[40]

Walter Lippmann was even more pessimistic. He was so disillusioned by his propaganda work for the government during the war that he argued that self-government in the modern world was a "fallacy" because public opinion was too easily manipulated, ill informed, and based on "fictions." The public lacked the ability to understand and weigh in on the complex governing issues of the day, which should be left to disinterested experts. He was part of a growing democratic realist movement in the interwar era that called into question the ability of the people to govern the modern nation-state directly and argued that Americans should give up the idea of democracy as self-government. According to Lippmann, if one redefines democracy so that "instead of hanging human dignity on the one assumption about self-government, you insist that man's dignity requires a standard of living, in which his capacities are properly exercised, the whole problem changes." While John Dewey responded to Lippmann with a defense of self-government, calling for the Great Community to find and organize itself, he also recognized the malaise and challenges of modern life. "The machine age has so enormously expanded, multiplied, intensified and complicated the scope of the indirect consequences, have formed such immense and consolidated unions in action, on an impersonal rather than a community basis, that the resultant public cannot identify and distinguish itself." Yet "the cure for the ailments of democracy," he argued, "is more democracy" and not a retreat from self-government.[41]

In this context of anxiety and reflection, state legislatures and local school boards embraced civics and social studies in the schools. While Americanization demands helped drive the spread of the laws, the new courses developed in practice tended to reflect the new social civics. In Iowa, for example, the 1919 state legislature required the teaching of American citizenship in all public and private schools as part of a wave of American-ization moves that included requiring instruction in English and prohib-iting foreign-language study under eighth grade. The state department of education prepared a recommended course of study that included the re-quired elements of patriotism and Constitution study but had an overall emphasis on social civics including community civics, economics, and so-ciology. Likewise, New Jersey's wartime legislation required all high school students to take two new courses, "Community Civics" and "Problems of American Democracy," in order to inculcate "the privileges and responsi-bilities of citizenship" and produce "the highest type of patriotic citizen-ship." The State Department of Education prepared a course of study that reflected social civics with goals of "self-reliant thinking" and knowledge of "civic obligations, present and future." By 1925, forty-six state legislatures required citizenship training through civics, history, and/or other social studies. A study of the content of civics courses conducted that year found that while the older political civics persisted in many places, the clear trend was toward civics as social study, and over 75 percent of schools offered one or more courses in the new civics.[42]

Social civics emerged not only because of professional endorsement and local experimentation but also because a variety of different groups and thinkers could find validation of their own particular vision of the good citizen and society in social civics' ambiguous messages. It also left space to bend practice in different directions at the local level. For groups like the American Legion and DAR, which saw the problem of citizenship primarily as one of patriotism and of forging common culture, social civics offered a way to emphasize values like civic spirit, cohesion, and community and was consistent with demands for assimilation. In practice, they could also infuse elements of loyalty, patriotism, and reverence for the nation into the study of society and its problems. Progressive pedagogues and democratic thinkers like John Dewey were committed to a definition of democratic citi-zenship as cultivation of the individual and meaningful participation in the social and political life of the nation. They saw potential in social civics' em-phasis on social cooperation, discussion of contemporary social issues and problems, and citizenship activities to build critical social intelligence.

Still for others who were concerned about declining community or a sense of moral crisis, social civics provided a place in the curriculum to em-phasize ethical and moral values. Country life reformers saw it as an ideal way to build up identification with the rural community and instill rural pride. For many urban moral reformers, including social gospel Chris-tians, peace and ethical society members, and religious groups concerned about the retreat of religion from the schools, social civics was a place on the curriculum to emphasize character and cultivate moral values like honesty, service, loyalty, integrity, brotherhood, and ethical standards in an ostensibly secular way. A wave of anxiety about the "moral breakdown of our times" in the 1920s prompted a movement for "character education" in Iowa, Nebraska, Utah, and a host of other states and cities that put social civics study and activities at its center.[43]

Social civics also obfuscated some of the uneasiness around democratic citizenship and modern governance by shifting the focus from individuals' political participation and self-government to citizen's everyday social roles and responsibilities. "Civic duty is not necessarily something outside of our everyday affairs, nor does it involve for most of us any but common virtues," one widely assigned text argued. It is a matter of "well-learned lessons, of honest work, of careful expenditure, and of upright living" as well as a "spirit of cooperation and mutual helpfulness in public as well as personal matters." Sociologist Ross Finney explained this focus on the individual's role in everyday life rather than political duties: "the most important social contribution that the typical citizen can make is to function normally in the ordinary relations of everyday life: in the family, in his work, as a neighbor, at the booth on election day, in support of the school and church, and with respect to the moral code. If all citizens could be depended upon to do those ordinary things effectively, our social problems would largely take care of themselves." Civics should thus explain to young people "how much they can contribute to the general welfare by merely taking their normal parts therein." This included their role as workers, and a spate of new books on "vocational civics" made this connection clear, highlighting opportunities for civic contributions by choosing and performing one's vocation well.[44]

While it emphasized study of social problems and one's social responsibilities, the new social civics deemphasized the role of the citizen in actually operating government. Civics "should train [the student's] judgment and develop his ability to discuss civic problems," one author noted, "yet it should emphasize continually the important fact that he is not solving these problems but is simply trying to weigh arguments and proposed solutions." A growing number of commentators stressed that the citizen's role was to be informed about social issues to help make up public opinion, but one's real efforts should be in the space of one's own life because governing issues were "technical in nature" and "no one but an expert is qualified to form an opinion of any value whatsoever." In demonstrating the complexity of social problems, social civics encouraged deference to experts and reverence for government's role in solving them. Most social civics texts portrayed government as the organized embodiment of the community that labored

on its behalf, framing it "not as a necessary evil, but as an instrument of social good." While the "old police theory of the government made it a power
to be feared," one educator noted, "the modern theory that the state is the
organization of all the people for public welfare makes it a thing to be loved
and patriotically served." Citizens should support the progressive expansion of government service on behalf of community welfare rather than
fear the activist state, for individual and community welfare came *through*
government service.[45]

The development of the subject of civics over time thus illustrates the
considerable interest and anxiety about modern citizenship, the divergent
views as to what constituted the good citizen and good society, and the
growing shared demand that the school develop and socialize individuals
in systematic ways. The socialized civics that emerged before the war and
was rapidly institutionalized after it emphasized one's everyday social responsibilities, like that of a worker, as having civic purpose and counseled
students to find their place in the world and perform their social roles well.
It therefore reflected and furthered the school's policies of differentiation
and individualization, investing one's individual development with social
value.

It also represented a profoundly inward turn in its framing of democratic citizenship. Democracy, social civics emphasized, was found in the
way that the community provided for the welfare of its members through
government and in the development of the individual in the everyday space
of the community. Reflecting a sense of individual impotence in the face of
the massive scale of public problems, it deemphasized self-government and
downplayed individuals as political actors to instead emphasize how one's
everyday activities were the real space of citizenship.

Adapting the School for Individual Differences

Preparing youths for good social citizenship was fundamentally tied to the
school's larger project of helping students to develop as individuals and
find their place in the world for both their benefit and the good of society.
Postwar schools not only embraced vocational education and curricular
differentiation, but other new forms of individualization that promised to
recognize individual differences and develop the individual to his or her
fullest potential: classes for atypical students, individualized methods of
instruction and promotion, grouping and classification schemes, guidance
services, and new measurement tools for assessing individuals. This democratic language of individual differences, however, obscured different social

assumptions and goals among educators and reformers. For some, it meant cultivating individuals to their fullest, unbounded potential, while for others it meant managing differences among youths of inherently unequal capacities. While in theory these educational adaptations to individual needs, interests, and abilities had democratic potential to help unleash the powers of the individual, they were often shaped in practice by organizational imperatives, social assumptions and prejudices of educators, and existing social barriers in ways that replicated, deepened, and obscured inequities.

High schools had begun to experiment with various ways to develop the individual and adapt the school to individual differences before the war. Vocational education was one major effort; new vocational classes and courses of study represented new forms of curricular differentiation and ostensibly enabled students to choose classes according to their vocational aspirations, talents, and interests. Educators in urban schools tried other forms of organizational differentiation to address the needs of special students, including those who struggled in the regular classroom: special classes for the deaf and blind, classes for mentally and physically handicapped students, open-air classrooms for tubercular students, special evening and part-time schools for working youths, accelerated classes for the gifted, and special ungraded classes for delinquent and truant children. Many of these children would once have been simply excluded from the school or lumped into regular classes until they dropped out. However, new attendance enforcement policies and social commitments to educating all students required teachers and school administrators to devise organizational solutions to manage the disruption of exceptional students and also consider how to offer them meaningful education.[46]

At the same time, a host of experiments with individualized instruction and flexible promotion plans sought ways to break the "lockstep" of mass education and adapt instruction for individual needs and differences. Many of these combined commitments to progressive pedagogical principles with practical administrative concerns about school failure and elimination. The Batavia Plan, for example, employed extra helping teachers in classrooms that assisted students who were struggling academically during daily sessions of individualized work. The Cambridge Plan reorganized students, grouping them by ability so that individuals could proceed through the curriculum at slower or faster rates according to their needs. Other efforts, like the Pueblo, Dalton, Gary, and Winnetka plans involved more fundamental changes in school organization. In the Pueblo Plan, for example, students worked at their own pace and used self-instruction bulletins; the individual and not the class was the unit of study, progress, and recitation, and it allowed for flexible promotion and individualized attention. These moves for flexible arrangements, individualized instruction, and special classes for exceptional students reflected in part creative efforts to include and adapt the school for groups that it was failing in the interests of recognizing, developing, and managing individuality. They also reflected school administrators' concerns with school management and efficiency; they could be used to separate out problem students who disrupted the progress of the classroom and to decrease elimination and retardation rates, which experts increasingly used to measure school effectiveness.[47]

World War I provided a major impetus to this project of recognizing individual differences and adapting the school to address them in the form of both powerful rationales for differentiation and new tools to accomplish it. On the eve of the war, proponents of vocational education argued that true equality of opportunity required schools to meet the needs of each individual in his or her life pursuits, rather than to impose the same education on all, and the war deepened this connection between differentiation and democracy. Many American commentators blamed Germany's public schools for inculcating a dangerous nationalism that subsumed individual identity in an overbroad conception of the state. In Germany, one Harvard professor warned, "we can see into what depths the human mind can fall if it bases its conception of the organization of society upon the state instead of upon the individual." In the United States, he argued, "we have a better, higher conception of citizenship which enlarges the individual and makes the state his creature, instead of making him the creature of the state." Germany "domesticated men into slaves," another educator charged, by stamping "false ideals through education," which served to "instill loyalty to autocracy." In contrast to Germany's autocracy, America's democratic education recognized and developed individuals.[48]

Wartime mobilization also provided a new set of tools to help assess and categorize individuals. During the war, the U.S. Army turned to a group of psychologists to develop and apply novel forms of testing to discern soldiers' abilities and match them efficiently with military roles. The Committee on Classification of Personnel in the Army adapted for group use the Stanford-Binet mental test, which purported to measure one's general intelligent quotient, or IQ. The committee used IQ tests to sort all recruits, select officers, and eliminate the feebleminded from service. It also developed vocational aptitude tests, personality tests, and occupational scales to identify the skills and ability required for each vocational role, evaluate recruits, and match them to jobs. The army effort was thus a major testing ground for new techniques of individual assessment and placement, which informed school practice for decades and stimulated rapid developments in pupil personnel management and educational guidance.[49]

The war was barely over before enterprising psychologists, aided by funding from the General Education Board and other philanthropies, adapted and marketed IQ tests for use in the schools. Psychologists like Guy Whipple envisioned the ways that tests could be used to measure students' general intelligence, classify them in the school, and guide them toward appropriate occupations. "Intelligence tests," he argued, "properly administered, and properly interpreted offer a feasible and valuable device for measuring these [inherited] differences in intellectual capacity" and making appropriate educational adjustments. It was a better means than individualized instruction plans, another advocate argued, to break "the 'lockstep' in public schools of children of widely different mental ability" and adapt to these individual differences. Dewey, while far from an enthusiastic advocate of IQ tests, acknowledged that they might have value as a starting point for "more intimate and intensive inquiry into individualized abilities and disabilities" with the ultimate goal to "discover and release individualized capacities."[50]

Testers frequently invoked the language of democracy in making their case for testing, but many were more concerned with managing student differences than with cultivating individuality. Since most ardent testers viewed intelligence as having a strong hereditary component, they believed that schools could do little to change the mental ablity of students and should therefore work to manage these inherent, immutable differences in ability and steer children toward classes and vocations for which they were intellectually suited. One testing proponent argued that "there can not be equality . . . where nature has made inequality. The best that can be done, and all that anybody wants to do, is furnish opportunity and means for each to do all that nature has made it possible for him to do." Tests can be "used to determine to a fairly good degree what part a child will probably be able to play, so far as his general intelligence goes, in the world of work" and can be used to guide children to "those spheres of activity in life where their powers of accomplishment will be called out most."[51]

Edward Thorndike predicted that IQ tests would enable psychologists to correlate mental traits with particular jobs so that "we shall be able to make up a bill of specifications of the sort of intellect and character required for a certain job, select men efficiently instead of haphazardly, and train them according to their individual needs instead of indiscriminately." He even went so far as to argue in 1932 that tests could determine how much and what kind of schooling individuals should receive, since extra education was "wasted" on those with low mental ability. It was time for "exercising careful discrimination in the distribution of education, giving the most to those who would use it best for the common good." While there were few other advocates of rationing education based on intelligence, many testers assumed that IQ tests could measure the limit of students' ability and thereby enable rational educational choices.[52]

These confident proclamations about the certainty of tests and the ways they should be used in education did not go unchallenged. Not all psychologists agreed about what the tests measured and how well they did it, and a host of other academics, educators, parents, and social commentators critiqued the social assumptions and arguments of testers. In a series of articles and addresses throughout the 1920s, for example, William Bagley of Teachers College lambasted the "educational determinism" of test advocates and critiqued their conception of intelligence as a fixed, hereditary, and measurable trait. The testers' philosophy that every man "can be taught to know his own place, appreciate his own limitations, and mind his own business" was profoundly antidemocratic, Bagley argued. Democracy was about elevating the common man, and it "required a high level of trained and informed intelligence as the basis of collective judgment and collective action" for all. Differences in intelligence did exist, he acknowledged, but he objected to the meaning that testers were giving to those differences.[53]

Walter Lippmann launched a series of attacks in the *New Republic* in the early 1920s about the reliability and implications of mental tests. Lippmann similarly rejected the idea that testing measured a fixed, innate quality, arguing that it "does not weigh or measure intelligence by any objective standards. It simply arranges a group of people in a series from best to worst by balancing their capacity to do certain arbitrarily selected puzzles against the ability of all others." In other words, he argued, it "is fundamentally an instrument for classifying a group of people." This might have some uses in the school, he acknowledged, but like Bagley he worried about popular "confusion about the spiritual meaning of the tests," namely that some would view the tests as a "scientific measurement of predestinated ability" and use it as rationale to write off people with "with low intelligence quotients as congenitally and hopelessly inferior." He charged testers with a "dogma which must lead to just such abuse" because of their claims that they were "measuring the capacity of a human being for all time and that this capacity is fatally fixed by the child's heredity." Such a view could lead to "an intellectual caste system in which the task of education had given way to the doctrine of predestination and infant damnation." There might be an important role for tests in classification and diagnosis, Lippmann acknowledged, so long as they were not held up as measuring an unchangeable intelligence or used to limit the education of those who performed poorly.

Like Dewey and Bagley, he did not reject tests outright but urged caution in how they were interpreted, and he rejected the assumption that they could be used to indicate the limits of human ability.[54]

IQ tests flourished in the postwar schools as administrators embraced them, less as wholesale endorsement of testers' vision than as a way to meet practical institutional needs. School administrators reported using IQ tests to diagnose individual students who were struggling academically; low test scores confirmed suspicions of low intelligence and could be used to make placement decisions while average or above average scores alerted school officials to look for other causes like personal maladjustment. In addition, administrators reported using IQ tests to help in career advising and to place students in school, including special classes for exceptional students, particular courses or curriculums, or homogenous instructional groups, also known as ability groups. In theory, this sorting was not just a tool of organizational management (to deal with failing students) but also an educational improvement that calibrated instruction to children's needs and abilities. In practice, however, it could have the effects that Lippmann and Bagley warned about, namely of diluting the education of low-performing students and marking them as inferior.[55]

The experience of Miami, Arizona, with testing and homogenous grouping reflects some of these tensions. Miami was a small mining town with a school population of 1,500, 50 percent of which was Mexican. Faced with high rates of retardation and school-leaving, the city superintendent tried reforms like smaller class sizes, increased professional supervision, and higher teacher salaries, and when they failed he hired a specialist to reclassify students into homogenous groups using IQ tests and teacher reports. In homogenous grouping, students were typically grouped together by ability—usually slow, average, and fast—in order to adjust the pace, amount, and character of instruction. It was a reform that rapidly spread in the postwar period, particularly in large schools; a 1932 U.S. Bureau of Education survey found 31 percent of reporting high schools used homogenous grouping, including 76 percent of schools with enrollments of over a thousand students.[56]

In Miami, tests and teachers placed most Mexican students in the lowest ability groups, which prompted the school board to build a new Mexican school oriented toward vocational subjects like homemaking and industrial training. In explaining the progressive nature of the reform, the city superintendent argued that most Mexican students dropped out of school after their sixth year to take up unskilled manual labor. The new system provided them training for practical pursuits "in place of condemning them to failure, discouragement, and early elimination," as the traditional course of study had done. This may have been an earnest attempt by school officials to improve school retention of Mexican students that were not being well served by the school, to provide an education that might open the doors to other choices besides unskilled labor, and to improve the overall effectiveness of the school. Yet these moves also intentionally or unintentionally segregated Mexican students and constrained their opportunities by steering them toward vocational training instead of academic subjects. It also reinforced stereotypes about their low intelligence, even as some may have placed poorly because of linguistic or cultural bias of the tests or teachers' racial perceptions.[57]

IQ tests and homogenous grouping were like many other postwar techniques for sorting, guiding, and individualizing students in the comprehensive high school that purported to meet individual needs and enhance democracy—and they had the potential to do so—but they often replicated, reinforced, and obscured subtle barriers and existing inequities. While IQ tests, if used judiciously, could be a diagnostic and classification aid, they often became a convenient way to adjust students to the school, segregate problem students, and blame individuals for educational failings. They also deepened the rationales for further differentiation and segregation in the school by providing supposedly scientific evidence of the widespread and pervasive differences in ability and intelligence among school pupils and confirming what people "knew" about individuals and groups. Despite growing evidence of class, cultural, and linguistic biases in the tests, for example, many commentators held them up as proof of the intellectual inferiority of racial and ethnic groups, which justified further segregation, including that of African American students in once relatively integrated Northern schools.[58]

Vocational guidance offers another example of a rapidly expanding postwar practice that was driven by democratic rationales and in many cases genuine commitments to child welfare but that subtly reinforced existing social barriers and inequities. Vocational guidance—career counseling to help students choose a vocation—grew out of child welfare impulses and the social settlement movement. In 1908, Frank Parsons of Boston's Civic House organized the nation's first bureau of vocational guidance to help immigrant youths avoid "blind-alley" or dead-end jobs. Within a year the Boston public schools asked him to organize vocational guidance in the city's schools and his work inspired other cities to follow suit. Parsons helped define the early goals and methods of vocational guidance, which he stated simply as "to aid young people in choosing an occupation, preparing themselves for it, finding an opening in it, and building up a career of efficiency and success." Boston's Vocation Bureau guided youths in self-study to discover their aptitudes, interests, and limitations and provide them information about the requirements, conditions, and opportunities in different lines of work. Parsons insisted that "the Bureau does not attempt to decide for any boy what occupation he should choose, but aims to help him investigate the subject and come to a conclusion on his own account."[59]

For Parsons and many supporters of vocational guidance, it was a democratic corollary to vocational education; if the school was going to assume responsibility for preparing children for work, it had an obligation to help them make wise choices. In vocational education and guidance, one commentator noted, "lies the salvation of the race and the safety of the nation," for it gives youths opportunity, "since by its means they may enjoy self-determination and self-selection in their life's work instead of being forced to accept haphazard employment at the whim of relatives or, in their desperation, to obtain employment in 'blind-alley' jobs which usually lead nowhere." Vocational guidance would empower children to make educated decisions about their life's work and open them to new possibilities and choices.[60]

Vocational guidance rapidly spread to other cities and developed as a professional field. By 1914, forty cities reported vocational guidance work and the number grew rapidly over the next two decades. In 1910, vocational counselors organized the first annual National Conference on Vocational Guidance and three years later founded a new professional organization, the National Vocational Guidance Association. Large cities developed guidance departments that offered career counseling, assessed and placed students in the school, advised students on classes and extracurricular activities, and addressed maladjustments in conversation with attendance departments, visiting teachers, and other pupil personnel workers. Smaller cities, towns, and county school systems performed some of these roles in less formal ways. As they did with so many other educational reforms, state departments of education promoted guidance work through a combination of leadership and service, including state guidance supervision, conferences, publications, and other supports for local effort.[61]

As they worked to professionalize, vocational guidance counselors extended and redefined Parson's principles. They deemphasized self-study as a means of choosing vocation and took a stronger role in advising and mediating between parents, teachers, and students. As one educator noted, "the destination of the particular child can not be left to his own immature judgment or whim; nor is the teacher alone a competent judge; nor can the decision be safely left to the parents alone—in whose hands it might seem to be most safely left." These groups must all confer "if the best possible chance is to be offered to the child." In the postwar period they turned to scientific measures like IQ, achievement, and personality tests to advise students, and they redefined their work as "educational guidance" to indicate not only vocational counseling but overall educational planning. Specialists asserted that guidance would give every child opportunity "to develop his own individuality." By the 1930s, guidance counselors emphasized the development of personality, with one National Society for the Study of Education Yearbook framing guidance work in part as an "effort to prevent all types of personality maladjustments" and promote "wholesome personality development."[62]

In theory, guidance in the high school was a benevolent application of the individuality of every child and reflected the democratic commitment of the school to help each child find and make his or her way in the world. However, in practice, guidance tended to reinforce the status quo as it was shaped by organizational imperatives of the school to manage students and minimize disruption, the social assumptions and prejudices of school officials, and existing inequities and barriers in the economy and society. Much of this was endemic in the project of vocational guidance counseling: it prepared youths for particular jobs and fields in the economy as it existed, and it thus replicated whatever assumptions and barriers structured them. It also assumed that youths could be educated away from low-wage, unskilled jobs or that education would elevate this work. It thus posited there was an educational solution for the structural problem of unskilled, low-paying, undesirable jobs.

Girls' vocational guidance and education offers one example of the overt and subtle ways in which guidance obscured and reified existing social assumptions and inequities. Vocational reformers had struggled with whether to prepare girls for wage labor or for their "ultimate vocation" as homemaker. They settled on preparing girls for their "double vocation" in household arts as well as appropriate female work, including female trades like textiles or millenary, female semiprofessions like teaching and social work, or female jobs in the expanding sector of white-collar service and office work like secretary or sales clerk. Some guidance counselors tried to remain open-minded about the definition of women's jobs. One 1934 manual, for example, offered a particularly wide berth of possible jobs for women. It listed chemical engineer, for example, noting that "the great field of chemistry has heretofore enrolled only men," but "just as women have entered other professions which have previously been considered the vocations of men, they are becoming interested in chemical engineering." It warned girls that "the most difficult task the woman chemical engineer will face will be convincing the employer that she can do the job" since it is "in the strictly pioneer stage" as a career for women. It therefore recommended any girl interested in the field attend an engineering school that placed students in the field so that she could make "actual contacts" to "give her a chance to prove that she can do the job."[63]

Most often manuals and vocational counselors, however, directed girls toward women's jobs and fields in which they would already find acceptance and emphasized above all else domestic arts and science for their roles as homemakers. Some of them did provide new opportunities for women by providing access to the growing sector of service and office jobs, but women tended to be contained within low-paying and supportive positions. Gendered assumptions about women's roles and the gendered divisions of the labor market thus conspired to steer all but the most precocious girls toward socially accepted female work. Preparation for "women's work" also introduced new gendered distinctions in coursework and school activities that had not previously existed since boys and girls prepared for different jobs. While they may have done so passively in the past, schools became active agents in reinforcing these gendered social assumptions and labor-market discriminations.[64]

Existing occupational opportunities and social assumptions similarly shaped how guidance counselors and school officials advised and educated African American students. The reality of labor market discrimination—the categorization of certain jobs as "Negro jobs" and the exclusion of African Americans from entire occupational fields in both the North and South—shaped the educational options available to black students. In Chicago, for example, few African American boys entered the Lane or Tilden technical high schools, which prepared for skilled trades, and in all of the supposedly integrated schools of the city, black students were tracked into classes that prepared them for the unskilled jobs open to them in the city. In much of the South, opportunities for vocational training and high schooling itself were so limited that W. E. B. DuBois, famous for his passionate critiques of industrial education earlier, argued for more vocational training for black children as a measure of equity in the 1930s.[65]

The racial discrimination of the job market presented a quandary for guidance counselors: should they advise black students to prepare for occupations that weren't open to them and thereby set them up for frustration and probable failure or guide them to "Negro jobs" and hence accommodate to the racial status quo and labor market discrimination? Many educators did the latter because of their own assumptions and prejudices about black student ability or because they thought it in the best interests of individual students to think realistically about the labor market. Some educators and students, however, did insist on training for the jobs of their choice and fighting for entry into the field. In Milwaukee, for example, some African American girls in the interwar years trained as teachers even though the city's public schools would not hire them. Most had to move away to secure teaching positions or leave the field, but over time pressure from the Urban League helped open up jobs for black teachers in the city. It was a slow process, however, and in the meantime many individuals undoubtedly found their personal ambitions frustrated, and untold others were dissuaded from ever embarking on the path to begin with. African American educators worried about the effect of labor-market discrimination on black students' educational motivation and aspirations, since it was clear that extended schooling did not provide the same economic and social benefits for black students as for white ones.[66]

Although the theory of guidance work stressed children's interest, aptitude, and personality as the guiding forces that shaped children's educational and vocational choices, in practice they were constrained by the stratification of the labor market, social assumptions and discrimination, and other structural impediments to free and equal access. These constraints also included geographic inequality and economic considerations that shaped who could afford to take advantage of extended schooling and who could not. Consequently, guidance work, like the other adaptations of the school on behalf of individual development, was steeped in language about democracy and opportunity, but the reality often fell far short and this rhetoric obscured that gulf.

This image of the high school as a democratic engine of opportunity shifted some of the attention away from structural impediments to individual success and equality in the industrial economy and located responsibility on the individual. Young people had ample opportunity, the reasoning went, to develop their talents and interests in the comprehensive high school, and consequently whether they succeeded or failed depended on their own effort, ability, and character. This was a profoundly limited view, however, as a group of social critics pointed out in the 1930s, but one with durable and significant power.

Schools and the Democratic Social Order

In 1928, Charles Judd, dean of the University of Chicago School of Education, wrote about the "unique character" of American secondary education. While elementary schools "are much alike in all civilized countries," Judd argued, "the secondary schools and the universities of a nation are the institutions which give distinctive character to its educational system" and reflect the "social system of which they are a part." America's high schools reflected the democratic conditions and aspirations of the nation, he argued, and were "one of the most expensive and most daring social experiments of our day." In contrast to Europe, where they were elite institutions, American high schools had grown up from the common schools to be part of the free public school system. They were accessible to the masses and oriented to their needs, particularly after the frantic high school building and deepening differentiation of the 1920s. They enrolled a far greater percentage of the population—nearly 50 percent by the late-1930s at the same time that European institutions typically served less than 20 percent of youths of high school age. The "people's college," as it was increasingly known, exhibited a "flexibility which no other secondary school in the world exhibits," Judd argued, for it "has been organized with a view to providing for pupils who do not expect to follow in the footsteps of their fathers." The American high school thus provided the opportunity for individuals to develop to their fullest potential and to transcend the conditions of their birth because of its widespread access, its flexibility and array of choices, and its commitment to individual development.[67]

Judd was one of many commentators who extolled the virtues of the American high school and viewed it as a reflection and engine of American democracy in the postwar era. Educator George Counts recognized this widespread faith in schooling, noting in 1930 that "Americans regard education as the means by which the inequalities among individuals are to be erased and by which every desirable end is to be achieved." This faith in education was one of the "fetishes of American society," he noted, and it gives schooling a kind of "magical power." Although Counts noted that American achievements in expanding education were "truly magnificent," he warned that to frame education as the whole of opportunity "is dangerous and calculated to blind the eyes to social injustice." It ignored real limitations to equality in practice and promoted a "false notion with regard to equality of opportunity." This faith in the democracy of the school obscured the fact that "racial discrimination mars opportunity not only for Negroes, but for Jews, Japanese, and other unpopular groups" and that "differences in wealth and family tradition mar the theory of a single system." Counts warned that the democratic discourse about the democracy of the school risked obscuring real, continuing inequalities and limiting the discussion about opportunity and democracy.[68]

George Counts was a leading figure in a radical social critique of schooling in the 1930s that took aim at the inherent conservatism of the school and the gap between the rhetoric and reality of its democracy. A group of "social reconstructionist thinkers," centered around but not exclusively located at

Columbia's Teachers College, called for systematic rethinking about the role of the school and its relationship to the social order. Some, like Counts and Dewey, had been making similar arguments for a decade or more, but they saw the material and ideological crisis of the Depression as an opportunity for major reconstruction. Their arguments reflected both critical insights about the conservative nature of the school as well as the power of the school in democratic imagination. While lambasting the school's tendency to reproduce the status quo, they ultimately put their faith in it as an agent for building a better democracy.[69]

Counts helped to galvanize this discussion in 1932 with his incendiary address to the Progressive Education Association, which posed the question: "Dare the schools build a new social order?" He argued that education was a form of indoctrination that was never neutral; "complete impartiality is utterly impossible" and the "school must shape attitudes, develop tastes, and even impose ideas." The school "is in the grip of conservative forces and is serving the cause of perpetuating ideas and institutions suited to an age that is gone," Counts charged, for it was indoctrinating economic individualism in an era of economic concentration. The time had come, Counts proclaimed, for schools to embrace real democracy, meaning the freedom and unhampered development of the individual. He argued that "the conscious and deliberate achievement of democracy under novel circumstances is the task of our generation," by which he meant using government to elevate and refine the lives of common men, provide genuine equality of opportunity, combat forces of social distinction, and democratize economic power through collective ownership. Teachers had a "heavy social obligation" to take a leading role in this "social regeneration" because they represented "not the interests of the moment or of any special class, but rather the common and abiding interests of the people." Counts concluded that "If schools are to be really effective, they must become centers for the building, and not merely for the contemplation, of our civilization."[70]

Counts's bold call accelerated a burgeoning discussion among academics and educators about the role of the school in a democratic society. Most social reconstructionist thinkers agreed with the central tenets of Counts's address: that schools were conservative institutions that replicated the status quo and obscured privilege and inequities built into it; that schools' dominant message was one of economic individualism and it should instead foster values of social cooperation and economic collectivism; that schools could and should be sites for cultivating values of democracy, namely the full development of individuality. Yet many also criticized Counts's analysis of "indoctrination," including philosophers like Horace Kallen and Boyd Bode, who rejected the idea that educators should impose a predetermined set of aims and social values and argued instead that they should cultivate critical intelligence and model democratic values, practices, and discussion.[71]

At the heart of the social reconstructionist critique was an argument that schools were inherently conservative institutions that tended to replicate the status quo because they fostered economic individualism that no longer made sense in the interdependent modern world. This economic individualism obscured and perpetuated inequalities and forestalled more fundamental reform. Although the schools had been embracing the language of socialization and social education, social reconstructionists like Dewey and Childs charged that they had actually maintained and reinforced the economic individualism of the past in only slightly new dress. Although social values "receive acceptance and words," they argued, they "are often merely plastered onto existing practices, being used to provide a new vocabulary for old practices and a new means for justifying them." Despite the language of social cooperation, schools were reinforcing egoistic individualism, pecuniary values, and laissez-faire government in their messages and methods, and this violated the true spirit of democracy: individual freedom.[72]

The school's emphasis on historic individualism, they argued, "favors and supports legal and economic institutions which encourage an exaggerated and one-sided development of the egoistic individuality in a privileged few, while mitigating against a full and fair opportunity for a normal individuality in the many." Individualism prevented Americans from acknowledging the need for more fundamental reforms like "social insurance which might mitigate insecurity" and planned government endeavors. According to Dewey and Childs, it was time to stop emphasizing the negative phrase of the democratic principle, namely the "overthrow of institutions that were autocratic," and to embrace the positive side: to extend democracy through "the creation of the kind of institutions that will effectively and constructively serve the development of all individuals."[73]

While social reconstructionists were critical of the school's conservatism and the ways in which it had functioned to reproduce the status quo in the past, they saw it as a potential instrument of change. The school may not have lived up to its democratic potential, but social reconstructionists had faith that it could. As Jesse Newlon optimistically argued, "The American people have never been afraid of change. They will welcome all change that will bring a fuller realization of the American dream of liberty and democracy, of social justice, economic security and a rich life for all." Social reconstructionists argued that schools should seek to build the commitments and skills of a truly democratic citizenship and be sites of democracy in action. To that end they argued for more discussion of critical social questions, including the economy and race relations, as well as democratic administration of the school and genuine equality of opportunity through better access across the nation. Many social reconstructionists endorsed federal aid and efforts to equalize funding and access geographically as well as other social welfare measures that targeted economic constraints to educational opportunity. Despite their limitations, social reconstructionists argued that schools were among the most accessible, far-reaching, and popular public institutions in the United States. As sites to transmit values, schools were potent instruments of either change or the status quo.[74]

The social reconstructionist critique influenced social studies discussions and materials in the 1930s. The AHA Commission on the Social Studies (1929–34) produced a series of texts that recommended that schools cultivate critical citizenship that privileged "the loyalty of reasoned affection, not the loyalty of tribal prejudice." Civic education should aim to "strengthen democratic institutions, make clear their workings, point out defects generally agreed upon, provide more effective leadership, illuminate every possible corner of the political scene, and promote habits of critical fairness among the electorate." Reflecting a clear social reconstructionist diagnosis of the current era, it argued that "the age of individualism and laissez-faire in economy and government is closing and a new age of collectivism is emerging." At the same time, Harold Rugg produced a series of bestselling social studies textbooks with a similar goal to cultivate critical inquiry into contemporary social questions and that took as a major assumption that the trend of the day was toward economic collectivism.[75]

These social reconstructionist arguments and assumptions did not go unchallenged. David Snedden scoffed at the romanticism of the AHA Commission on the Social Studies while curriculum specialist Franklin Bobbitt argued that despite "their frequent lip service to democracy . . . the whole tenor of their report is denial both of its legitimacy and its desirability." He charged them with throwing over individualism to make men "nurslings of the state" and argued that their project was to inculcate submission to "state paternalism, in which submissiveness and obedience are essential factors." Other critics challenged it as a communist attack on American capitalism and values of individualism. Hearst newspapers labeled the AHA Commission on the Social Studies a "red menace" and the DAR put the NEA on its list of organizations in "sympathy with communist ideas." The National Association of Manufacturers commissioned a series of textbooks to improve the image of capitalism and attack Rugg's series, and the American Legion spearheaded efforts to boycott Rugg's texts and combat teacher radicalism with loyalty oaths.[76]

As the crisis of the Depression passed, social reconstructionists' efforts to use the school to build a new social order waned. Most Americans did not want them to, for the reasons that social reconstructionists themselves acknowledged: most Americans believed the system was basically fair and they either did or would benefit from it. George Counts judged in 1930 that schools were conservative because the American people were conservative and "are less anxious to remove social and economic inequalities than to obscure the existence and moderate the effects of such inequalities." Support for modifying the social structure was low because it had "succeeded to an unprecedented degree in diffusing the goods and services of this world among the people," and although there were inequalities of wealth and dire poverty, "those with initiative and ability to organize and make their desires articulate are able to secure a share in the general prosperity" and those who do not "are unable to register effective protest." Counts reasoned that "many who are not prosperous to-day expect prosperity to-morrow and are therefore content." The "great masses of the people are therefore in no mood for radical political or economic doctrine" and they believed "the American social system is fundamentally sound." Most Americans believed in public schooling as they did the capitalist system itself, as an engine for social mobility and individual opportunity. Even the social reconstructionists, while railing against its democratic failings, ultimately put their faith in schooling as a democratic project.[77]

✳

Hence in the postwar era Americans celebrated the democracy of the comprehensive high school. The new subjects of civics and vocational education reflected the bottom-up demands that schools prepare individuals for life in the modern world and the anxieties about capitalism and democracy in it. In both subjects and in the more general adaptation of the postwar school to individual differences, schools wrestled with how to adjust and equip individuals to prosper in the new economy, keep open the gates of equal opportunity in a stratified industrial economy, and give meaning to democracy as traditional forms of community participation and individual efficacy were eroded by the growing scale of society, economy, and government. As they developed, civic and vocational education both ultimately encouraged youths to accept their social roles and responsibilities and adjust to prevailing economic and social relations, counseling them to find meaning for democratic citizenship in fulfilling these social obligations and in developing to their fullest individual potential in order to contribute to society.

Supporters came to these projects with different aims and social assumptions but shared the conviction that schools should do more to prepare individuals for the increasing demands and complexity of modern social roles and responsibilities. For some this meant primarily conforming to social norms and roles, while for others it meant equipping individuals with effective power to transform and navigate them. The very project of orienting individuals in more deliberate and systematic ways toward practical social roles, however, deepened the conservatism of the school by tying it more closely to arrangements as they already existed. The school became complicit in replicating social barriers, inequities, and discriminations of the economy and society at the very same time as its democratic language celebrated its unleashing of individual potential. This democratic language shifted blame for failure to rise to the individual and obscured the extent to which inequalities in educational access, discrimination in society and the labor market, and other structural factors systematically limited opportunity for many. It strengthened individualism and promised that social problems could be solved through education and individual effort. In the process it may have undermined support for more fundamental social and economic changes, as social reconstructionists charged, including more planned economic and social welfare measures and a public discussion about collective responsibility.

Yet while the school was a conservative institution it was not the instrument of wholesale domination that some critics have imagined, and it had spaces, however limited, for change, challenge, and opportunity. While it had a tendency, for example, to track immigrant youths in ways that reinforced class and ethnic backgrounds, it did not eliminate the potential for mobility and in fact helped many achieve it over generations. Although girls were usually directed toward homemaking and women's traditional work, some were able to use schooling as a gateway to push into new occupational fields and challenge traditional conceptions of women's work over time. Although Americans ignored subtle forms of privilege and discrimination built into the system, they also resisted curricular and organizational reforms that violated obvious norms of fair play or threatened to make schooling too castelike—at least for white children—such as dual control of schools or IQ test–based schooling allotments.

At a moment of profound unease about democracy and the changes of modern life, therefore, Americans embraced schooling as the new frontier of the twentieth century, a site of democratic imagination for the modern, industrial age. Like the frontier of the West, the modern school purported to offer equal opportunity for all to rise based on individual talent and effort, a guarantee of continued mobility and the efficacy of the individual in the new era. Yet, like the territorial frontier, the school's democracy was marred by hidden inequities, privileges, and coercions that systematically limited opportunity for some groups while advantaging others, and it obscured that fact under a powerful rhetoric about merit and individualism. Yet its power as a site of democratic imagination could bee seen in its widespread popularity and in the hopes that even the most marginalized groups—like African Americans in the segregated South—placed on schools to fulfill democratic opportunity and promote individual and collective advancement.

Conclusion: School, Society, and State

In 1899 on the second anniversary of the founding of his Laboratory School at the University of Chicago, philosopher John Dewey delivered a series of lectures, titled "School and Society," in which he explained the school's distinctive pedagogy and located it within a broader set of educational reforms. Not simply a fad or "mere changes of detail," Dewey argued, this "New Education" in the making was "part and parcel of the whole social evolution" and reflected a deliberate effort to "meet the needs of the new society that is forming." The great social and economic changes of the era had weakened older formal and informal means of education at the same moment that they had created complex new demands and challenges. In the span of his own lifetime, he noted, "one can hardly believe that there has been a revolution in all history so rapid, so extensive, so complete" and "only an equally radical change in education suffices." The school should assume a larger, more deliberate role in socializing individuals for this new world, Dewey argued. His active child-centered pedagogy aimed to do just that by training each child as a member of the community, "saturating him with the spirit of service, and providing him with the instruments of effective self-direction." At the heart of his pedagogy was an effort to cultivate the values of critical individualism and collective responsibility necessary for democratic community and the effective freedom of the individual in the modern world.[1]

Dewey's framing of the problem as "school and society" took for granted something at the very center of this relationship that helped to shape the educational changes of the period: the state. As reformers like Dewey defined schooling as a modern project of socialization, they turned to the state—state government and a host of other mechanisms of public power at all levels of the federal system—for the authority, coordination, and coercion necessary to enact reforms across space, make schooling an effective instrument of socialization, and address social problems through the school. In the process they expanded schooling and deepened its reach, extending the institutions and authority of government more deeply into the lives of millions of individuals. This great popular turn to schooling, enacted through top-down and bottom-up efforts by a wide range of groups, reflected a major national public response to the social and economic transformations of the era. It was a national social policy, but not a centralized or federal government one.

Putting the state back into the center of analysis of "school and society" offers significant new insights about education, American governance, and the period itself. First, it demonstrates the important role of state government and law in the educational transformations of the era. As a creature of state constitutions, public schools were legally state government projects from their inception, but what that meant changed over time. State constitutions and statutes shaped the legal framework of schooling, but in the nineteenth century legislatures delegated nearly every aspect of finance, control, and management to local districts. Beginning around 1890, state governments began to take back some of this authority, strengthened by state court definitions of schools as state institutions and education as an exercise of state police power. State legislatures and departments of education worked to articulate standards, disseminate research and models, advise local officials, use aid and accreditation to stoke local effort, and otherwise promote reform and integration of once largely independent local schools into coordinated systems.

In this and other periods, state law and policy are important for understanding the history of education and are too often neglected by scholars. State constitutions, statutes, case law, and administrative decisions create the incentives, constraints, and rules by which local schools operate and develop over time. State policies shape the distribution of power, and resources and are consequently essential to understand equity and power in education. These policies are not always in the form of statutory requirements, bureaucratic imposition, or direct state spending, nor do state policies always come by taking power away from districts. Histories of education must explore the wide range of state government strategies for shaping the framework of local schools. They should also recognize that this state government is not a monolithic force; different state agencies and branches can have different aims, assumptions, and agendas. In many Southern states, for example, state department of education professionals promoted African American school expansion at the same time that state legislatures or governors were often ambivalent or outright hostile to such efforts. Midwestern state department of education officials redefined legislative directives that required the study of patriotism to promote social civics in state courses of study and publications.[2]

State governments were also an important component of the national diffusion of policies in the period, a second major way that bringing the state back in to our studies of school and society helps us to view education reform and American governance in new ways. It raises an important but rarely examined question: how did schooling become a *national* policy in the absence of a strong *federal* government role? State governments played an important part in the construction of national policies by spreading reforms within their own borders and fashioning once independent schools into coordinated state systems. They also helped to diffuse reforms across the nation. State legislatures emulated, and sometimes outright copied, statutes and constitutional provisions from other states such as teacher salary schedules or equalization funds. State courts looked to one another to frame a national body of school case law in practice. In compulsory attendance, for example, state courts throughout the nation applied appellate decisions from Indiana, Ohio, and New Hampshire to decisively settle the issue of constitutionality of their own particular state laws under their own state constitutions. State department of education officials similarly engaged in close and ongoing communication with their counterparts in other states through correspondence, professional associations and conferences, educational literature, and professional networks.

National policies and a de facto national education system emerged from the complex interplay of top-down and bottom-up efforts. At the top, self-consciously national actors helped to define and diffuse models, including philanthropies like the General Education Board (GEB), universities of national stature like Columbia Teachers College, national professional and special interest organizations like the National Education Association and National Society for the Promotion of Industrial Education, and federal agencies like the U.S. Bureau of Education. Like many progressive reformers, these groups favored national reforms but were not enthusiastic federal state-builders; they preferred to pursue national reform through local policies and state-level legislation, voluntary associations, and national nonstate institutions such as philanthropic foundations. The GEB, for example, funded demonstration projects, supported state department of education officers and divisions to expand state capacity, held conferences for stakeholders to compare practices and discuss innovations, and sponsored and disseminated educational research including state surveys and IQ tests. Like other groups interested in promoting nationwide change, the GEB worked to shape a national conversation, foster new innovations

and diffuse them, lobby state and local governments for reforms, and institutionalize new practices directly.[3]

In addition to self-consciously national actors, reform was shaped at the
top by the standardizing effect of the science of education, which provided
both new experts and new expertise. The emerging, albeit contested, science of education helped to sanction particular norms, models, and goals
and to diffuse them through a burgeoning professional literature, growing schools of education and professional training, and emerging national
networks of educational experts and professionals. While it provided a
common reform language and exerted pressure toward standardization,
this science of education was far from unassailable. Expert sanction was no
guarantee that a given locality or state would adopt a practice. Educational
experts faced constant challenges to their legitimacy and authority, both at
the university level and in the politics of school reform. Nevertheless, educational expertise provided an important framework for reform efforts by
prioritizing and legitimating some reforms over others and diffusing them
among actors with a shared professional identity.

The nationalization of policies was also facilitated by a national debate
about the challenges that modern life posed for the individual and the
nation, particularly the growing scale and scope of economy and society.
Groups turned in piecemeal ways to address particular challenges stemming from the changes of the era. Some looked to schools to provide vocational education and guidance because of concerns about the changing
nature of work and economic competiveness. Others turned to the school to
Americanize immigrants and foster patriotism and social intelligence in all
citizens as they worried about the growing heterogeneity and declining social bonds of communities. A range of groups supported particular reforms
or the more general expansion of the school to address social problems including labor conflict, vice, racial control, rural depopulation, Americanization, political corruption, health, and poverty.

At the same time, social scientists, educational theorists, and other
commentators saw school reform as a more fundamental solution to over-
arching tensions of the era, particularly the problem of democracy in the
modern era. Observers like Dewey saw urban, industrial society as placing
unprecedented demands on the individual and society, and called for a "new
education" to develop individuals to their fullest potential and adjust them
to modern social life. The "new education" was a broad language obscuring very different assumptions and aims, but it reflected a shared sense of
crisis and anxiety about social changes, a sense that deepened significantly
after World War I highlighted the consequences of educational failures for
the nation-state. The war prompted greater state government and national

action as it drove home the problem of unequal educational access, need for minimum educational standards, and the importance of greater public oversight of citizens' education, health, and welfare.

This sense of problem also shaped reform activity at the grassroots level, without which these pressures and efforts from the top would have amounted to little. The tremendous popular appetite for education and the grassroots mobilization of reform efforts in communities across the nation pushed, supported, and shaped all school reforms in the era. Family demand for schooling access, for example, drove high school building and stimulated new state policies to increase high school access, make it affordable for communities, and articulate it with college. Adolescents and their parents looked to high schools to gain access to the growing sector of white-collar work and in the process helped push vocational aims and adaptations to the forefront of educational discussion. Families voted with their feet by the millions because they saw personal and social benefits in more and better schooling. This rising voluntary attendance also made it more feasible and legitimate to compel the attendance of those who refused.

The support of communities and mobilization of local groups were also essential to the diffusion of school reforms. Even as school administrators gained greater authority in cities and professional leaders mobilized reform in the countryside, community consent was necessary to enact most reforms. Local majorities had to vote for bond issues and spending increases, approve school consolidation and administrative changes, and support reform agendas by candidates for school board and elective administrative office including county and state superintendents. Furthermore, local interest groups, voluntary associations, and parents' associations were active in supporting reforms at the local level. Middle-class clubwomen sponsored kindergartens, afterschool programs, playgrounds, community use of the school, and health services and pushed schools to institutionalize them. Parent-teacher associations and local school improvement associations in both cities and the countryside helped to mobilize community support for revenue increases, school board elections, school improvements, and reforms like vocational education and clubwork.

Consequently, national school reform in the era was not the imposition of any one group, but was a messy, pluralistic project that engaged the efforts of a wide range of groups at all levels of American government. To say that reform was pluralistic is not to see all actors as having equal power to shape the conversation and outcomes; resources, organization, cultural authority, political clout, and a host of other factors shaped how much influence different groups and individuals exerted in local, state, and national level efforts and on different issues. In Chicago in the 1910s, for example, business associations had a strong voice in school administrative reforms, but their power was not unassailable, as the defeat of the business-backed dual-control proposal for vocational schools demonstrated. Likewise, the General Education Board was very successful at promoting state and county rural supervisors, among other reforms, but its efforts to demonstrate the county unit of school control in Indiana and promote the reform failed miserably. Simple explanations for education reform that emphasize social control or professional self-aggrandizement overstate the influence that any one group had to control the outcome in such a fragmented and diffuse system.[4]

They also give too much weight to conscious motivations and coherent ideologies. Much like other progressive reforms of the period, educational changes often reflected compromises, complex negotiations, and the mobilization of social languages that could obscure the diversity and complexity of motivations. "Social efficiency," for example, was a slogan deployed by thinkers as different as Albion Small and John Dewey to argue for the full development of individuality on the one hand, and David Snedden and Lewis Terman to argue for recognizing innate limits to individual capacity on the other. Likewise, a variety of groups came together to support social civics instruction in the schools, but this shared advocacy obscured some radically different goals in citizenship training that motivated reformers. As in other progressive reforms, social languages in education were pliable and political coalitions were shifting and diverse.[5]

This story of national education policy through decentralized means offers insights for other Progressive Era social policies. It shows some of the myriad alternative ways in which progressive reformers pursued national policies, including coordinated state-level legislation, national networks and voluntary organizations of state and local government actors, and federated grassroots campaigns at all levels of government. Federated lobbying organizations like women's clubs that had local, state, and national affiliates could be particularly powerful agents for national reform by working simultaneously at multiple levels. Philanthropic foundations similarly used their resources to facilitate coordinated action at different levels of government and across the nation and to spur reform energy within the federalist system through targeted experimentation and demonstration.[6]

While scholars have emphasized economic competition as a major motor of and limit to interstate diffusion of social policy, there were other factors at work that deserve further analysis. Normative and cultural pressure from experts, national actors, and other states could prompt reform by playing to state governments' self-image or interests beyond purely economic ones. New England states guarded their reputations as educational leaders, for example, and reformers were able to marshal statistical comparisons with other places, such as the Ayres index or U.S. Bureau of Education data, to shame, pressure, and incentivize state action. Furthermore, the threat of federal action could stimulate state-level reforms; Southern states that had resisted child labor and compulsory attendance regulations passed them as a campaign for federal legislation developed. World War I–era campaigns for federal aid to education likewise convinced state legislatures to provide state-level aid and equalization policies to both address the inequalities exposed and to stave off federal intervention.[7]

Bringing the state back in to studies of school and society consequently also offers insights for American political development. It demonstrates how national policies could emerge without an overt federal government role through the American system of federalism, providing a model of decentralized nationalism. Our dominant narratives of government in the period tend to tell the story of the growth of federal government administration and to look for federal policies; the dominant themes are often those of centralization, professionalization, bureaucratization, and upward shifts of power to the federal level. Education, however, demonstrates the continued importance of state-level government in social policy and the ways that state governments pursued their goals through a range of alternatives to bureaucratic imposition, including cooperation with and delegation to local districts.[8]

It also demonstrates how decentralization could be a source of strong state-building. Local control, for example, was not simply an obstacle to be overcome or an impediment to centralization, but rather was a constitutive part of educational state-building and provided reform energy, innovation, and popular support that contributed to the spread of policies. State governments expanded their own influence and authority by working with and through local districts, and local control contributed in important ways to the nationalization of policies. Scholars need to think beyond simple models of centralization and decentralization and instead look at mechanics of cooperative federalism and intergovernmental cooperation. Far from a zero-sum game, power could grow simultaneously at each level, as well as through the mobilization of private actors. This may appear on the surface to be simply weak state-building, but that misses how effective it could be at achieving its goals over time.[9]

In compulsory attendance, for example, state legislatures defined statutory requirements but invested enforcement in local districts. Some localities embraced the goal of universal attendance and worked to develop new techniques of enforcement that pushed state legislatures to tighten loopholes and strengthen the law's requirements over time. Other districts lagged behind, selectively enforced it, or ignored it altogether. States legislatures and departments of education disseminated information about successful attendance enforcement, provided services and leadership to localities, offered incentives to encourage enforcement, and over time increased pressure on lagging districts through new statutory requirements and penalties. More and more localities invested in state attendance policies as the examples of their neighbors, incentives and coercion from state government, and public opinion within and outside the community pressured local officials to act.

This kind of cooperative federalism in which state policies were pursued through local districts involved tradeoffs. Working with local control brought flexibility and adaptability to local needs and conditions. It built on local consent and support, which gave reforms greater legitimacy and more durability and strength and which avoided the hostility often directed at "state centralization." In addition, local pride was a strong string on which to pull for greater investment, and the sense of ownership by the local community in the school built a strong expansionist dynamic into school reform. Communities that might resist other forms of taxation were willing to spend for "their" school, and local pride and self-image could lead districts to try to keep up with their neighbors or experiment with new practices. This flexibility and experimentation produced innovations that then spread across the state and nation. Local control of schools could be a font of creative energy.

However, this approach was also slow and uneven as some localities could not or would not embrace state policies, and it accepted a great deal of inequality. Differences in local effort were often shaped by structural constraints, including geographic differences in wealth; although state policies attempted to lessen some of the impact of these differences with state aid, they left vastly unequal structures in place and tolerated significant disparities. This approach also did not challenge local power structures or discrimination. Localism did not always foster democratic participation, and localism could just as easily foster exclusion, parochialism, and inequity. Deference to local control could thus exacerbate inequalities even as states defined particular policies and equalization itself as an important state interest. To some extent, this was consistent with contemporaries' definition of the goals of education: "equalization" was not a project of closing gaps or offering the same opportunities to all, but of guaranteeing a satisfactory minimum education based on one's differentiated needs and social roles; race, gender, and location shaped the definition of this minimum education. The tradeoff between innovation and equity did not concern most reformers so long as all localities and students received an adequate minimum education to make them productive and successful citizens.[10]

The historical study of education policymaking and its tradeoffs raises questions for education policy in the present. Although there have been major changes in the relationship between levels of government in education, most notably the stronger role of Congress and federal courts over the past half century, it remains a fragmented, relatively decentralized system in which education reformers try to find points to leverage and diffuse change. The increasing presence of the federal government in education policy means there is not the same vacuum at the national level as in the earlier period, however, philanthropic foundations, policy institutes, and other private entities with resources and reach can still have a strong impact on national reform by working in similar ways to stimulate and disseminate local and state educational experiments. In some ways, the contemporary federal-state relationship mirrors the state-local relationship of the early twentieth century, with federal grants-in-aid, standards, and leadership attempting to push, prod, and incentivize state-level reforms according to federally defined priorities. The history of state-local reform suggests that these efforts will be most successful when they give some autonomy to states and enable them to invest in the reforms as their own, fiscally and emotionally. It also suggests promise for efforts like charter school reform that marshal reform energy and local investment around individual schools to foster change. Decentralization can be a profound motor for innovation and reform energy.

This history also suggests a tradeoff, however, that often remains unacknowledged in these and other reform efforts: the embrace of innovation through decentralization often tolerates and exacerbates inequalities within the system overall. It encourages the most able districts to improve while often doing little to help the others left behind, widening the gap between them, and leaves intact significant differences in fiscal and human resources between districts. Early twentieth-century reformers did not find this tradeoff inconsistent with their goals of cultivating good citizens according to differentiated criteria, because they aimed for a satisfactory minimum standard for good citizenship. However, these systemwide disparities seem to run counter to our contemporary discourse about closing gaps, achieving greater equity, and ensuring that no child is left behind in the preparation for work and life in a context where the quality and duration of schooling affect one's economic prospects and social mobility more than ever before. The civil rights movement widened our conceptions of equal educational opportunity and invited scrutiny into social and economic barriers to its enjoyment. Yet our contemporary policy conversations are often imprecise about what we mean by equality as a goal and ignore some of the challenges that decentralization poses to its realization. Current discussions about closing educational achievement gaps, for example, suggests a robust definition of equality that considers not only a satisfactory minimum education but also grapples with systemic differences in meaningful opportunity and how they shape educational outcomes. However, policy solutions tend to focus on targeting low-performing schools and students without addressing the larger patterns of economic and social disparities in which they operate. They also seem to overpromise, since the most advantaged schools and students continue to accrue advantages that make closing gaps a receding target. Our current policy conversations often evade the tension between innovation and equity within a decentralized system of unequal resources and may consequently set us up for repeated disappointment and failure.

Putting the state back into the center of analysis of school and society also highlights schools as state-building projects, places where public aims and power are exercised over children. State attendance and child labor policies worked over time to transform schooling from a casual, voluntary institution governed by parental and community needs into a mandatory, full-time, state-supervised endeavor for nearly all youths. Not only were more kids brought under the control of the school for longer than ever before, but school professionals and state officials exercised much greater authority over them as the expansive public interest in the new education consistently outweighed local and familial interests. In obvious ways, state-approved texts, courses of study, and standards intended to directly proscribe and shape the knowledge, skills, and values taught to children in the public schools, and new tools like IQ testing, grouping, and guidance reached more deeply into shaping their subjectivity. The modern state school defined more ambitious and invasive aims than had the community school of the nineteenth century. It aimed to develop and adjust the individual for all of his or her social roles in more systematic and deliberate ways, including preparation as citizen, worker, family member, consumer, and neighbor. As schools became increasingly powerful credentialing and sorting institutions for the economy over the course of the twentieth century, these school policies to manage, sort, and allocate students would take on even greater social power.

In less obvious ways, the modern state school was a place where regulations, surveillance, and policies were extended over children in new ways. Public officials applied medical inspection, vaccination, physical training, dietary and sanitation practices, child labor regulations, poor relief, job training and guidance, morals policing, and birth-registration and record-keeping systems to children in the compulsory school. State compulsory attendance statutes applied public school standards and policies to private schools and home instruction and thereby served as a means for the state to proscribe educational goals and policies for *all* children in the state. Attendance enforcement also gave the school the authority and responsibility to monitor and intervene in the household, from supervising children's health and morals to serving as an entry point for social services and public interventions. Schools were at the center of deep Progressive Era conflicts over the relationship between children, parents, and the state. Studies of child welfare, social policy, and family history have consequently often overlooked an important place where states asserted new responsibility and power over children and where crucial questions of parental authority and individual rights were negotiated.

Schooling was also at the center of early twentieth-century efforts to reconcile democracy with industrial capitalism, social interdependence, and the changing scale of economic and social life. This is a final way in which thinking about school, society, and state helps us to ask new questions about the period: it highlights schooling as a major national social policy to address tensions between democracy and industrial capitalism. Concerns about democratic opportunity animated many of the major school reform efforts: the expansion of school access; the articulation of minimum standards, aid policies, and equalization; the differentiation and individualization of school curriculum and services. Reformers were anxious about the social and political impact of concentrated wealth, changes in the nature and stability of work, deepening economic and social divides, and the massive scale and interdependence of society and economy, which disrupted traditional institutions.

They looked to schools to safeguard democracy and humanize industrial capitalism. Reformers argued that it would elevate and dignify all labor, producing economic development that benefited all while lessening the discontent of workers. It would also keep the gates of equal opportunity propped open in a time of closing frontier and deepening economic cleavages by empowering individuals to navigate the new world of work. While industrial capitalism might produce winners and losers, reformers asserted that the wide diffusion of state schooling would ensure that all had the opportunity to be winners. European nations pursued more collectivist solutions, working to socialize risk and create the foundations of social safety nets for all citizens. American investment in schooling instead bolstered individualism by investing in schooling to provide a new pathway to democratic opportunity and freedom of the individual in the modern world. It reflected a large public commitment and social welfare transfer on behalf of parents, but one rarely regarded as such.

When compared to the centralized systems of social insurance constructed in European welfare-states, this public investment in education might be easy to overlook as a national social policy. Education was a decentralized, diffuse project that operated through state and local governments and bubbled up from below in piecemeal ways, rather than a centralized federal government project. It aimed less to compensate for the risks of industrial capitalism and more to widen access to its benefits and empower individuals to succeed in the system. Furthermore, reformers rarely talked about education as social policy nor did they emphasize it as governance at all; on the contrary, school reformers actively sought to separate education from "politics" and frame it as a project of civic protection rather than social welfare. Public schooling is also easy to overlook as a national social policy because of its history: it predated the period in which scholars have examined the origins of welfare states, it grew out of and remained tied to local and private efforts, and it was bound up with other goals including citizenship training. The long and messy history of public schooling has caused many studies of social policy and comparative welfare states to simply set it aside in their analysis.[11]

Most of all, schooling has been easy to overlook as a national social policy response because of the way that social science scholarship has framed the problem of comparative welfare development. Social scientists tend to uncritically accept European nation-states as the normative model for the welfare state: direct social spending, centralized bureaucratic administration, socialization of risk, and income transfers. They have been primarily concerned with theorizing the essence of the welfare state and explaining differences across nations. Starting with a theoretical definition of the welfare state, they have asked why the United States looks so laggard, stingy, and weak and more generally what accounts for variations across nations. Scholarship on the "hidden" American welfare state has taken aim at some of these assumptions, demonstrating the need to think about social policies as a series of historically, contextually grounded choices about policy priorities and means that are shaped by political culture, institutional arrangements, politics, and values. This scholarship has expanded the analytical categories and tools to apply to the welfare state but has rarely added schooling.[12]

If we take seriously the generous fiscal investment in education and the heavy burdens Americans placed on schools to address the social consequences of industrialization, it forces us to reshape this question: Why did

Americans chose education and with what consequences? Part of the answer to the question of why Americans invested in education may be found
in how it resonated with American political culture and values, including
long-cherished myths about progress, individualism, merit, and opportunity. It was an individualistic project of self-improvement, an avenue for
individual and collective progress. Schooling was not a form of charity or
relief; it was an enabling institution that purported to maintain fairness and
opportunity so that any individual could rise through his or her own effort
and talent. In a nation where most people were invested in the American
Dream of mobility, the popular demand was for government to safeguard
this promise rather than compensate for its failures.

In addition, American political structures and development may help
to explain some of this turn to schooling. By the late nineteenth century
when progressive reformers began to wrestle with social and economic
changes, public schooling was already a popular, widespread institution in
the United States. Elementary schooling reached into every state and nearly
every community by the turn of the century and had strong popular support and legitimacy across the political spectrum, making it easier to attach
new goals and projects to schooling than to pursue them in other ways. This
early and extensive institutional development of public schooling may have
channeled or shaped social reform efforts in that direction. As this book
has explored, federalism and decentralization could fuel bottom-up investment and popular support for schooling; local communities identified with
and took ownership of "their" local schools and they invested in schooling
both as a conscious and unconscious social policy strategy.[13]

Schooling was a profoundly individualist approach to addressing social
problems, and this had myriad consequences. Schooling shifted attention
away from structural challenges and inequities and framed social problems
as individual ones with individual solutions. The problem of so-called blind-
alley or dead-end jobs, for example, could be solved through vocational
education and guidance, according to reformers, even though these low-
paying, low-skill jobs were structural features of emerging industrial capitalism. In giving every individual the opportunity to rise above blind-alley
jobs through hard work and talent, it located the blame for those trapped
in them to the individuals themselves. Consequently one of the fundamental consequences of this investment in education as a social policy strategy
has been to individualize and educationalize larger social and structural
problems stemming from industrialization, to redefine them as problems
that can be solved through education and individual effort. In doing so,
it obscures structural dimensions of social problems and hides the extent

to which beneath the rhetoric of democratic opportunity for all, schools structure opportunity differently for different groups. While schools could provide avenues for mobility and individual security, they did so unevenly; economic and social barriers, discrimination, and structures systematically limited opportunities for some groups, such as African Americans.

It also perpetuates a narrative about individual effort and merit that undermines arguments for collective responsibility and more overt social transfers. This dynamic growth of education and its popular appeal as a solution to industrial inequalities and insecurities may have weakened potential support for other, more redistributionist social policies, either by monopolizing financial support or seeming to render them less necessary. The rhetorical separation of education from other social welfare policies may also have robbed the "hidden" welfare state of potential sources of support; public schooling is a big, expensive, popular project, and even in moments of antitax politics or antigovernment rhetoric, Americans have tended to invest generously in it. By obscuring the public welfare aims and collective responsibility inherent in education and separating it from other social welfare policies, we have perpetuated misleading myths about individualism and American hostility to social welfare and obscured the true size and orientation of the American welfare state. Education is like other aspects of the American welfare state: it has a strong orientation toward middle-class benefits and aspirations rather than benefits for the poor or working class; it privileges equality of opportunity over equality of results; it emphasizes preventative rather than curative approaches; and it is far more comfortable with inequalities in the distribution of benefits, particularly along geographic and racial lines, than most European welfare states.

American public schooling was not simply one more progressive reform. It was one of the fundamental public projects of the early twentieth century to reconcile democracy and industrial capitalism. While some progressive reformers and social reconstructionists saw in schools the realization of the socialized individual and new claims of collective responsibility, much of schooling's broad popular appeal came from the ways in which it reinforced values of individualism in a new context and legitimated powerful myths about the American Dream. In doing so, however, it obscured continuing inequities and structural constraints to opportunity and promoted an emphasis on individualism over collective welfare and responsibility that has reverberated into the twenty-first century.

Today we face attacks on the welfare state and political discourse that paints it as a European invention. Our political discourse fails to recognize the true size, scope, orientation, and history of American social policies and tends to denigrate collective responsibility and redistributionist policies as un-American. This attack on public policies is even beginning to spill into public schooling, which is today facing some of the most serious attacks on it as a public good and responsibility in its almost two-hundred-year history. Scholars and public commentators alike should recognize schooling as a social welfare project and consider the strengths, weaknesses, and trade-offs involved in this choice.

NOTES

Abbreviations

AAAPSS	*Annals of the American Academy of Political and Social Science*
AHR	*American Historical Review*
AJS	*American Journal of Sociology*
APNEA	*Addresses and Proceedings of the National Education Association*
CDT	*Chicago Daily Tribune*
Coon Papers	Charles L. Coon papers, group no. 177, Southern Historical Collection, The Wilson Library, University of North Carolina at Chapel Hill
CSM	*Christian Science Monitor*
ER	*Educational Review*
ESJ	*Elementary School Journal*
GEB	General Education Board
GEB Papers	General Education Board Archives, Rockefeller Archive Center, Sleepy Hollow, NY
HEQ	*History of Education Quarterly*
HO	*Historical Outlook*
JAH	*Journal of American History*
JPH	*Journal of Policy History*
NAM	National Association of Manufacturers
NCEA Papers	National Catholic Education Association papers, Catholic University of America, Washington, D.C.
NCSA	North Carolina State Archives, Raleigh.
NCWC	National Catholic Welfare Council
NCWC Papers	National Catholic Welfare Council papers, Catholic University, Washington, D.C.
NEA	National Education Association
NR	*New Republic*
NSSE	National Society for the Study of Education
NYT	*New York Times*
SEB	Southern Education Board
SEB Papers	Southern Education Board papers, coll. 680, Southern Historical Collection, The Wilson Library, University of North Carolina at Chapel Hill

SF   *Social Frontier*
SR   *The School Review*
SS   *School and Society*
USBE   United States Bureau of Education (after 1929, U.S. Office of
              Education)
USBE CSL   *United States Bureau of Education City School Leaflets*
USBE Papers   United States Office of Education papers, record group 12, Office of
              the Commissioner, entry 6: historical file, 1870–1950, NARA II, Col-
              lege Park, MD
USBE RSL   *United States Bureau of Education Rural School Leaflets*
USCB   United States Children's Bureau
USDA   United States Department of Agriculture

Introduction

1. *De Lease v. Nolan*, 185 A.D. 52; 172 NYS 552 (1918).
2. Thomas Snyder, ed., *120 Years of American Education: A Statistical Portrait* (Wash-
    ington, D.C.: National Center for Education Statistics, 1993), 6–14, 32–37, 57; James
    Anderson, *The Education of Blacks in the South, 1860–1935* (Chapel Hill: University
    of North Carolina Press, 1988); Claudia Goldin, "The Human-Capital Century and
    American Leadership: Virtues of the Past," *Journal of Economic History* 61 (June
    2001): 268; *Biennial Survey of Education in the United States*, 1938–40, vol. 2, 20.
3. For attempts to explain America's "weak" social policies and welfare state in com-
    parative perspective, see, for example, Edwin Amenta and Theda Skocpol, "Taking
    Exception: Explaining the Distinctiveness of American Public Policies in the Last
    Century," in *The Comparative History of Public Policy*, ed. Francis G. Castles (New
    York: Oxford University Press, 1989): 292–333; Gosta Esping-Anderson, *Three Worlds
    of Welfare Capitalism* (Princeton: Princeton University Press, 1990); Edwin Amenta,
    Bold Relief: Institutional Politics and the Origins of Modern American Social Policy
    (Princeton: Princeton University Press, 1998); Edward Berkowitz and Kim Mc-
    Quaid, *Creating the Welfare State: The Political Economy of Twentieth-Century Reform*
    (Lawrence: University Press of Kansas, 1988); Neil Gilbert and Barbara Gilbert, *The
    Enabling State: Modern Welfare Capitalism in America* (New York: Oxford University
    Press, 1989); Seth Koven and Sonya Michel, eds., *Mothers of a New World: Maternal-
    ist Politics and the Origins of Welfare States* (New York: Routledge, 1993); Linda Gor-
    don, ed., *The Women, the State, and Welfare* (Madison: University of Wisconsin Press,
    1990); Suzzane Mettler, *Dividing Citizens: Gender and Federalism in New Deal Public
    Policy* (Ithaca: Cornell University Press, 1998); Daniel Levine, *Poverty and Society:
    The Growth of the American Welfare State in International Comparison* (New Bruns-
    wick: Rutgers University Press, 1988).
4. Snyder, *120 Years of American Education*, 93; *Historical Statistics of the United States*,
    vol. 1 supplement (series H 1–31): 340–41; Goldin, "The Human-Capital Century and
    American Leadership," 268; *Europe's Needs and Resources: Trends and Prospects in
    Eighteen Countries* (Twentieth Century Fund, 1961).

5. John Dewey, *The School and Society* (1900; repr., Chicago: University of Chicago Press, 1990), 28, 8.

6. On "bringing the state back in" as a social science effort, see, for example, Peter B. Evans, Dietrich Rueschemeyer, and Theda Skocpol, eds., *Bringing the State Back In* (New York: Cambridge University Press, 1985); Dietrich Rueschemeyer and Theda Skocpol, eds., *States, Social Knowledge, and the Origins of Modern Social Policies* (Princeton: Princeton University Press, 1996); Theda Skocpol, *Protecting Soldiers and Mothers: The Political Origins of Social Policy in the United States* (Cambridge, MA: Belknap Press, 1992); Stephen Skowronek, *Building A New American State: The Expansion of National Adminstrative Capacities 1877-1920* (Cambridge: Cambridge University Press, 1982).

7. For important exceptions to this general neglect of the state role by historians of education, see David Tyack, Thomas James, and Aaron Benavot, *Law and the Shaping of Public Education, 1785-1954* (Madison: University of Wisconsin Press, 1987); David Tyack and Thomas James, "State Government and American Public Education: Exploring the 'Primeval Forest,'" HEQ 26 (Spring 1986): 39-69; Benjamin Justice, *The War That Wasn't: Religious Conflict and Compromise in the Common Schools of New York State, 1865-1900* (Albany: State University of New York Press, 2005); Maris Vinovskis, "Gubernatorial Leadership and American K-12 Education Reform," in *A Legacy of Innovation: Governors and Public Policy*, ed. Ethan G. Sribnick (Philadelphia: University of Pennsylvania Press, 2008); Edgar Fuller and Jim B. Pearson, eds., *Education in the States: Historical Development and Outlook* (Washington, D.C.: Council of Chief State School Officers, 1969).

8. A few historical essays have pointed to this puzzle of educational nationalization: William W. Cutler III, "The Systematization of American Education," HEQ 16 (1976): 79-92; David B. Tyack, "The Spread of Public Schooling in Victorian America: In Search of a Reinterpretation." *History of Education 7*, no. 3 (1978): 173-82.

9. Brian Balogh, *A Government out of Sight: The Mystery of National Authority in Nineteenth-Century America* (Cambridge: Cambridge University Press, 2009); William J. Novak, "The Myth of the 'Weak' American State," AHR 113 (June 2008): 752-72; Peter Baldwin, "Beyond Weak and Strong: Rethinking the State in Comparative Policy History," JPH 17 (2005): 12-33; Ann Shola Orloff, "Social Provision and Regulation: Theories of States, Social Policies, and Modernity," in *Rethinking Modernity: Politics, History, and Sociology*, ed. Julia Adams, Elisabeth S. Clemens, and Ann Shola Orloff (Durham: Duke University Press, 2005): 190-224; Elisabeth S. Clemens, "Lineages of the Rube Goldberg State: Building and Blurring Public Programs, 1900-1940," in *Rethinking Political Institutions: The Art of the State*, ed. Ian Shapiro, Stephen Skowronek, and Daniel Galvin (New York: New York University Press, 2006), 187-215; William J. Novak, "The American Law of Association: The Legal-Political Construction of Civil Society," *Studies in American Political Development* 15, no. 2 (Oct. 2002): 163-82. Sociological literature on isomorphism and policy diffusion also offers some guides, such as Paul J. DiMaggio and Walter W. Powell, "The Iron Cage Revisited: Institutional Isomorphism and Collective Rationality in Organizational Fields," in *The New Institutionalism as Organizational Analysis*, ed.

Walter W. Powell and Paul J. DiMaggio (Chicago: University of Chicago Press, 1991): 63–82; Mark H. Leff, "Consensus for Reform: The Mothers'-Pension Movement in the Progressive Era," *Social Science Review* 47, no. 3 (1973): 397–417; Sarah Soule, "Runaway Train?: The Diffusion of State-Level Reform in the ADC/AFDC Eligibility Requirements, 1950–1967," AJS 103 (Nov. 1997): 733–62; Eliza K. Pavalko, "State Timing of Policy Adoption: Workman's Compensation in the United States, 1909–1929," AJS 95 (Nov. 1989): 592–615.

10. For examples of this emphasis on the bureaucratic ambitions of school reformers and the conflicts over centralization, see David B. Tyack, *The One Best System: A History of American Urban Education* (Cambridge, MA: Harvard University Press, 1974); William A. Bullough, *Cities and Schools in the Gilded Age: The Evolution of an Urban Institution* (Port Washington, NY: Kennikat Press, 1974); Raymond E. Callahan, *Education and the Cult of Efficiency: A Study of the Social Forces That Have Shaped the Administration of the Public Schools* (Chicago: University of Chicago Press, 1962); Samuel Bowles and Herbert Gintis, *Schooling in Capitalist America: Educational Reform and the Contradictions of Economic Life* (New York: Basic Books, 1976); Wayne E. Fuller, *The Old Country School: The Story of Rural Education in the Middle West* (Chicago: University of Chicago Press, 1982); William A. Link, *A Hard Country and a Lonely Place: Schooling, Society, and Reform in Rural Virginia, 1870–1920* (Chapel Hill: University of North Carolina Press, 1986). Accounts of grassroots politics, shifting reform coalitions, and pliable reform languages should make us rethink this top-down story, such as William J. Reese, *Power and the Promise of School Reform: Grassroots Movements during the Progressive Era*, 2nd ed. (New York: Teachers College Press, 2002); Jeffrey Mirel, "Progressive School Reform in Comparative Perspective," in *Southern Cities, Southern Schools: Public Education in the Urban South*, ed. David N. Plank and Rick Ginsberg (New York: Greenwood Press, 1990); Daniel Rodgers, "In Search of Progressivism," *Reviews in American History* 10 (Dec. 1982): 113–32.

11. Lawrence A. Cremin, *The Transformation of the School: Progressivism in American Education, 1876–1957* (New York: Alfred A. Knopf, 1961); Robert H. Wiebe, *The Search for Order, 1877–1920* (New York: Hill and Wang, 1967); Daniel T. Rodgers, *Atlantic Crossings: Social Politics in a Progressive Age* (Cambridge, MA: Belknap Press, 1998).

12. Tensions between capitalism and democracy are a central theme in many major studies of progressive reform and thought. See, for example, Richard Hofstdadter, *The Age of Reform: From Bryan to F. D. R.* (New York: Knopf, 1955); Samuel P. Hayes, *The Response to Industrialism, 1885–1914*, 2nd ed. (Chicago: University of Chicago Press, 1995); Weibe, *The Search for Order*; Rodgers, *Atlantic Crossings*; Eldon J. Eisenach, *The Lost Promise of Progressivism* (Lawrence: University Press of Kansas, 1994); Jackson Lears, *Rebirth of a Nation: The Making of Modern America, 1877–1920* (New York: Harper Collins, 2009); James T. Kloppenberg, *Uncertain Victory: Social Democracy and Progressivism in European and American Thought, 1870–1920* (New York: Oxford University Press, 1986).

13. On federalism, see Daniel J. Elazar, *The American Partnership: Intergovernmental Cooperation in the Nineteenth-Century United States* (Chicago: University of Chicago

Press, 1962); William Graebner, "Federalism in the Progressive Era: A Structural Interpretation of Reform," JAH 64 (Sept. 1977): 331–57; Harry N. Scheiber, "Federalism and the American Economic Order, 1789–1910," *Law and Society Review* 10 (Autumn 1975): 57–118; David Brian Robertson, "The Bias of American Federalism: The Limits of Welfare-State Development in the Progressive Era," JPH 1, no. 3 (1989): 261–91; Martha Derthick, ed., *Dilemmas of Scale in America's Federal Democracy* (Cambridge: Cambridge University Press, 1999).

14. Margaret Weir, Ann Shola Orloff, and Theda Skocpol, eds., *The Politics of Social Policy in the United States* (Princeton: Princeton University Press, 1988). Other studies that acknowledge, but then largely set aside, education for analysis include Morris Janowitz, *Social Control of the Welfare State* (Chicago: University of Chicago Press, 1976); Peter Flora and Arnold J. Heidenheimer, eds., *The Development of Welfare States in Europe and America* (New Brunswick: Transaction Books, 1984); Harold L. Wilensky, *The Welfare State and Equality: Structural and Ideological Roots of Public Expenditures* (Berkeley: University of California Press, 1975). On the hidden welfare state, see Christopher Howard, *Hidden Welfare State: Tax Expenditures and Social Policy in the United States* (Princeton: Princeton University Press, 1997); Christopher Howard, *The Welfare State Nobody Knows: Debunking Myths about U.S. Social Policy* (Princeton: Princeton University Press, 2007); Jacob Hacker, *The Divided Welfare State: The Battle over Public and Private Social Benefits in the United States* (Cambridge: Cambridge University Press, 2002); Michael Katz, *The Price of Citizenship: Redefining the American Welfare State* (New York: Metropolitan Books, 2001); Jennifer Klein, *For All These Rights: Business, Labor, and the Shaping of America's Public-Private Welfare State* (Princeton: Princeton University Press, 2003).

15. A few recent studies have argued more forcefully for the inclusion of education in analysis of the welfare state: Irwin Garfinkel, Lee Rainwater, and Timothy Smeeding, *Wealth and Welfare States: Is America a Laggard or Leader?* (New York: Oxford University Press, 2010); Michael B. Katz, "Public Education as Welfare," *Dissent* (Summer 2010): 52–56; Miriam Cohen, "Reconsidering Schools and the American Welfare State," HEQ 45 (Winter 2005): 512–53; Michael B. Katz, *Improving Poor People: The Welfare State, the "Underclass," and Urban Schools as History* (Princeton: Princeton University Press, 1995).

Chapter One

1. The articles appeared in *Forum* throughout 1892 and were published in book form the following year. Joseph M. Rice, *The Public-School System of the United States* (New York: Arno Press, 1969; repr., New York: Century Co., 1893), 98–100; 9–27.

2. For interpretations that stress the top-down imposition of business elites and/or professional educators, see, for example, David B. Tyack, *The One Best System: A History of American Urban Education* (Cambridge, MA: Harvard University Press, 1974); Raymond E. Callahan, *Education and the Cult of Efficiency: A Study of the Social Forces That Have Shaped the Administration of the Public Schools* (Chicago: University

of Chicago Press, 1962); Samuel Bowles and Herbert Gintis, *Schooling in Capitalist America: Educational Reform and the Contradictions of Economic Life* (New York: Basic Books, 1976). For accounts that instead emphasize pluralism, working-class support for reforms, and other challenges, see Paul E. Peterson, *The Politics of School Reform, 1870–1940* (Chicago: University of Chicago Press, 1985); Ira Katznelson and Margaret Weir, *Schooling for All: Class, Race, and the Decline of the Democratic Ideal* (New York: Basic Books, 1985); Jeffrey Mirel, *The Rise and Fall of an Urban School System: Detroit, 1907–1981* (Ann Arbor: University of Michigan Press, 1993); Selwyn K. Troen, *The Public and the Schools: Shaping the St. Louis System, 1838–1920* (Columbia: University of Missouri Press, 1975); William J. Reese, *Power and the Promise of School Reform: Grassroots Movements during the Progressive Era*, 2nd ed. (New York: Teachers College Press, 2002).

3. For a good overview of the intellectual roots of this effort, see William J. Reese, "The Origins of Progressive Education," HEQ 41 (Spring 2001): 1–24; William J. Reese, *America's Public Schools: From the Common School to "No Child Left Behind"* (Baltimore: Johns Hopkins University Press, 2005), chap. 3.

4. For contemporary accounts of these municipal reform efforts, see William Howe Tolman, *Municipal Reform Movements in the United States* (New York: Fleming H. Revell Co., 1895); Frederic C. Howe, *The City: The Hope of Democracy* (New York: Scribner's Sons, 1905); Charles Zueblin, *American Municipal Progress*, rev. ed (New York: Macmillan Co., 1916).

5. Peter G. Filene, "An Obituary for 'The Progressive Movement,'" *American Quarterly* 22 (Spring 1970): 20–34; Daniel T. Rodgers, "In Search of Progressivism" *Reviews in American History* 10 (Dec. 1982): 113–32; Jeffrey Mirel, "Progressive School Reform in Comparative Perspective," in *Southern Cities, Southern Schools*, ed. David N. Plank and Rick Ginsberg (New York: Greenwood Press, 1990), 151–74. "Island communities" is a phrase from Robert H. Wiebe, *The Search for Order, 1877–1920* (New York: Hill and Wang, 1967), and Daniel T. Rodgers, *Atlantic Crossings: Social Politics in a Progressive Age* (Cambridge, MA: Belknap Press, 1998), explores transatlantic social politics. On these changes, see also Alfred D. Chandler Jr., *The Visible Hand: The Managerial Revolution in American Business* (Cambridge, MA: Belknap Press, 1993); Morton Keller, *Regulating a New Economy* (Cambridge, MA: Harvard University Press, 1990); Morton Keller, *Regulating a New Society: Public Policy and Social Change in America, 1900–1933* (Cambridge, MA: Harvard University Press, 1994); Alan Dawley, *Struggles for Justice: Social Responsibility and the Liberal State* (Cambridge, MA: Belknap Press, 1993).

6. Walter Lippmann, *Drift and Mastery* (1914; repr., Madison: University of Wisconsin Press, 1985), 17; Jackson Lears, *Rebirth of a Nation: The Making of Modern America, 1877–1920* (New York: Harper Collins, 2009); Robert M. Crunden, *Ministers of Reform: The Progressives' Achievement in American Civilization, 1889–1920* (New York: Basic Books, 1972); Thomas L. Haskell, *The Emergence of the Professional Social Science: The American Social Science Association and the Nineteenth-Century Crisis of Authority* (Urbana: University of Illinois Press, 1977); James T. Kloppenberg, *Uncertain Victory: Social Democracy and Progressivism in European and American Thought,*

1870–1920 (New York: Oxford University Press, 1986); Dorothy Ross, *The Origins of American Social Science* (Cambridge: Cambridge University Press, 1991).

7. Elisabeth S. Clemens, *The People's Lobby: Organizational Innovation and the Rise of Interest Group Politics in the United States, 1890–1925* (Chicago: University of Chicago Press, 1997); Michael E. McGerr, *The Decline of Popular Politics: The American North, 1865–1928* (New York: Oxford University Press, 1986); Michael Schudson, *The Good Citizen: A History of American Civic Life* (New York: Free Press, 1998); Rodgers, "In Search of Progressivism."

8. John Dewey, *The School and Society* (1900; repr., Chicago: University of Chicago Press, 1990), 28; Albion W. Small, "Some Demands of Sociology upon Pedagogy," AJS 2 (May 1897): 851, 839. For examples of this sociological discussion, see Edward A. Ross, *Social Control: A Survey of the Foundations of Order* (New York: Macmillan Co., 1901); I. W. Howerth, "Education and the Social Ideal," ER 24 (Sept. 1902): 150–65; Ira W. Howerth, "Education and Social Progress," ER 23 (Apr. 1902): 355–70; M. V. O'Shea, *Education as Adjustment: Educational Theory Viewed in Light of Contemporary Thought* (New York: Longmans, Green, and Co., 1903); David Snedden, *Problems of Educational Readjustment* (Boston: Houghton Mifflin Co., 1913); Arnold Tompkins, "The Relation of Sociology and Pedagogy," AJS 1 (Nov. 1895): 353–58; M. V. O'Shea, "Notes on Education for Social Efficiency," AJS 11 (Mar. 1906): 646–54; Charles Ellwood, "The Educational Theory of Social Progress," *Scientific Monthly* 5 (Nov. 1917): 439–50.

9. Scott Nearing, *The New Education: A Review of Progressive Educational Movements of the Day* (New York: Arno Press, 1969; repr., New York: Row, Peterson, & Co., 1915), 25–31; Walter Barnes, "The New Education: An Interpretation," ER 64 (Sept. 1922): 124–34. See also Nicholas Murray Butler, "Is There a New Education?," ER 11 (Jan. 1896): 58–71; Herman H. Horne, "Again the New Education," ER 75 (Feb. 1928): 91–98; Herman Harrell Horne, *This New Education* (New York: Abingdon Press, 1931).

10. R. J. W. Selleck, *The New Education: The English Background 1870–1914* (London: Sir Isaac Pitman & Sons, 1968), makes a similar argument about the new education in England, which he argues transcends pedagogy to be a reform spirit that reshaped all aspects of school goals, curriculum, and governance.

11. Barbara Beatty, " 'The Letter Killeth': Americanization and Multicultural Education in Kindergartens in the United States, 1856–1920," in *Kindergartens and Cultures: The Global Diffusion of an Idea*, ed. Roberta Wollons (New Haven: Yale University Press, 2000), 42–58; Barbara Beatty, *Preschool Education in America: The Culture of Young Children from the Colonial Era to the Present* (New Haven: Yale University Press, 1995); Marvin Lazerson, *Origins of the Urban School: Public Education in Massachusetts, 1870–1915* (Cambridge, MA: Harvard University Press, 1971), chap. 2.

12. Paula Baker, "The Domestication of Politics: Women and American Political Society, 1780–1920" AHR 89 (June 1984): 620–47; Reese, *The Power and the Promise of School Reform*; Theda Skocpol, *Protecting Soldiers and Mothers: The Political Origins of Social Policy in the United States* (Cambridge, MA: Belknap Press, 1992); Seth Koven and Sonya Michel, eds., *Mothers of a New World: Maternalist Politics and the Origins of Welfare States* (New York: Routledge, 1993); Michael McGerr, "Political Style

and Women's Power, 1830–1930," JAH 77 (Dec. 1990): 864–85; Molly Ladd-Taylor, *Mother-Work: Women, Child Welfare, and the State, 1890–1930* (Urbana: University of Illinois Press, 1994).

13. William J. Reese, "Between Home and School: Organized Parents, Clubwomen, and Urban Education in the Progressive Era," SR 87 (Sept. 1978): 3–28; Reese, *The Power and Promise of School Reform*. On the role of grassroots reform, see also Ronald D. Cohen, *Children of the Mill: Schooling and Society in Gary, Indiana, 1906–1960* (Bloomington: Indiana University Press, 1990); Sol Cohen, *Progressives and Urban School Reform: The Public Education Association of New York City, 1895–1954* (New York: Teachers College, 1964); Judith Rosenberg Raftery, *Land of Fair Promise: Politics and Reform in Los Angeles Schools, 1885–1941* (Stanford: Stanford University Press, 1992).

14. For overviews of vocational education, see Sol Cohen, "The Industrial Education Movement, 1906–7," *American Quarterly* 20 (Spring 1968): 95–110; Harvey Kantor, "Work, Education, and Vocational Reform: The Ideological Origins of Vocational Education, 1890–1920," *American Journal of Education* 94 (Aug. 1986): 401–26; Harvey A. Kantor, *Learning to Earn: School, Work, and Vocational Reform in California, 1880–1930* (Madison: University of Wisconsin Press, 1988); Herbert M. Kliebard, *Schooled to Work: Vocationalism and American Culture, 1876–1946*, 2nd ed. (New York: Teachers College Press, 1999); Lazerson, *Origins of the Urban School*.

15. On the broadening of the curriculum, see Herbert M. Kliebard, *The Struggle for the American Curriculum, 1893–1958*, 3rd ed. (New York: RoutledgeFalmer, 2004); Edward A. Krug, *The Shaping of the American High School* (New York: Harper & Row, 1964); Reese, *America's Public Schools*, chaps. 4–6; Commission on the Reorganization of Secondary Education, "Cardinal Principles of Secondary Education," *USBE Bulletin*, no. 35 (1918).

16. Cohen, *Progressives and Urban School Reform*; A. R. Mead, "Functions of Parent-Teacher Associations," *Educational Administration and Supervision* 8 (1922): 505; J. C. Hanna, "Discussion" in Nathaniel Butler, "Parents' Associations," SR 16 (1908): 87. On the history of PTAs, see Christine A. Woyshner, *The National PTA, Race, and Civic Engagement, 1897–1970* (Columbus: Ohio State University Press, 2009); Steven L. Schlossman, "Before Home Start: Notes toward a History of Parent Education in America, 1897–1929," *Harvard Educational Review* 46, no. 3 (1976): 436–67; Julian E. Butterworth, *The Parent-Teacher Association and Its Work* (New York: Macmillan Company, 1928); Ellen C. Lombard, "Recent Developments of Parent-Teacher Associations," *USBE Bulletin*, no. 5 (1923); *A New Force in Education* (Washington, D.C.: National Congress of Parents and Teachers, 1930); *The Parent-Teacher Organization: Its Origins and Development* (Chicago: National Congress of Parents and Teachers, 1944); Elmer S. Holbeck, *An Analysis of the Activities and Potentialities for Achievement of the Parent-Teacher Association with Recommendations* (New York: Teachers College, 1934).

17. On the importance of demand in shaping school reform, see David Angus, "The Origins of Urban Schools in Comparative Perspective," in Plank and Ginsberg, *Southern Cities, Southern Schools*, 59–78; Charles Strickland, "The Rise of Public Schooling and the Attitude of Parents: The Case of Atlanta, 1872 to 1897," in *Schools in Cities:*

Consensus and Conflict in American Educational History, ed. Ronald K. Goodenow and Diane Ravitch (New York: Holmes & Meier, 1982), 249-62.

18. John D. Philbrick, "City School Systems in the United States," *USBE Circulars of Information,* no. 1 (1885): 155; William A. Bullough, *Cities and Schools in the Gilded Age: The Evolution of an Urban Institution* (Port Washington, NY: Kennikat Press, 1974), 22-25.

19. Jon C. Teaford, *The Unheralded Triumph: City Government in America, 1870-1900* (Baltimore: Johns Hopkins University Press, 1984). As the title suggests, Teaford argues that city machines did a better job governing than their critics at the time and many historians since have acknowledged, including, for example, Clifford W. Patton, *The Battle for Municipal Reform: Mobilization and Attack, 1875 to 1900* (Washington, D.C.: American Council on Public Affairs, 1940).

20. On good government efforts, see Kenneth Fox, *Better City Government: Innovation in American Urban Politics, 1850-1937* (Philadelphia: Temple University Press, 1977); Frank Mann Stewart, *A Half Century of Municipal Reform: The History of the National Municipal League* (Berkeley: University of California Press, 1950); Martin J. Schiesl, *The Politics of Efficiency: Municipal Administration and Reform in America, 1800-1920* (Berkeley: University of California Press, 1977); John G. Sproat, *"The Best Men": Liberal Reforms in the Gilded Age,* 2nd ed. (Chicago: University of Chicago Press, 1982); Camilla Stivers, *Bureau Men, Settlement Women: Constructing Public Administration in the Progressive Era* (Lawrence: University Press of Kansas, 2000); Samuel P. Hayes, "The Politics of Reform in Municipal Government in the Progressive Era," in *American Political History as Social Analysis* (Knoxville: University of Tennessee Press, 1980).

21. Tyack, *The One Best System,* 89; Frank Rollins, "School Administration in Municipal Government" (Ph.D. diss., Columbia University, 1902).

22. These examples of corruption are recounted in Bullough, *Cities and Schools in the Gilded Age,* 67, and Troen, *The Public and the Schools,* 212-14. See also Diane Ravitch, *The Great School Wars: A History of the New York City Public Schools,* 2nd ed. (Baltimore: Johns Hopkins University Press, 2000).

23. Joseph M. Cronin, *The Control of Urban Schools: Perspective on the Power of Educational Reformers* (New York: Free Press, 1973), 70-71; Andrew Draper, "Plans of Organization for School Purposes in Large Cities," *ER* 6 (June 1893): 1-16; B. A. Hinsdale, "Recent School Legislation for Cities," *Dial* 26 (Feb. 1899): 107-9; S. P. Orth, "The Cleveland Plan of School Administration," *Political Science Quarterly* 19 (Sept. 1904): 402-16. The Cleveland Plan was endorsed by the NEA in 1895: Edwin P. Seaver, "Committee of Fifteen: Report of the Subcommittee on the Organization of City School System,s" *ER* 9 (Mar. 1895): 304-12.

24. For discussions of particular administrative experiments, see, for example, E. E. White, B. A. Hinsdale, J. C. Dougherty, "Report of the Committee on City School Systems: School Superintendence in Cities," *APNEA* (1890): 312; Nicholas Murray Butler, "The Educational System of Greater New York," *Independent* 49 (Mar. 1897): 5-7; Charles W. Eliot, "A Good Urban School Organization," *US Commissioner of Education Report* 2 (1903): 1356-62; Edward C. Eliot, "A Nonpartisan School Law," *APNEA*

(1905): 223–31; Ellwood P. Cubberley, "The School Situation in San Francisco," ER (Apr. 1901): 364–81; P. W. Horn, "City Schools under the Commission Form of City Government," ER 37 (Apr. 1909): 362–74; B. A. Hinsdale, "Recent School Legislation for Cities," *Dial* 26 (Feb. 1899): 107–9.

25. For discussion of these emerging principles at the time, see B. A. Hinsdale, "City School Systems," *Dial* 25 (Oct. 1898): 251–53; James C. Boykin, "Organization of City School Boards," ER 13 (Mar. 1897): 232–45; Truman A. Deweese, "Better City School Administration," ER 20 (June 1900): 61–71; Calvin W. Edwards, "School Boards, Number of Members, Terms of Service, and Mode of Selection," APNEA (1903): 898–905; Washington Gladden, "The Perils of Public Schools," *Independent* 51 (Aug. 1899): 2125–28; A. Lawrence Lowell, "The Professional and Non-Professional Bodies in Our School System, and the Proper Function of Each," APNEA (1898): 999–1004; James M. Greenwood, "The Superintendent and the Board of Education," ER 21 (Nov. 1899); Aaron Gove, "City School Supervision I," ER 2 (Oct. 1891): 256–61 (the first of five ruminations by superintendents on the city supervision over the next year); E. C. Moore, "Indispensable Requirements in City School Administration," ER 46 (Sept. 1913): 143–56.

26. *Report of the Educational Commission of the City of Chicago*, 2nd ed. (Chicago: University of Chicago Press, 1900); "The Report of the Chicago Educational Commission," *Dial* 26 (Jan. 1899): 2–5.

27. On Chicago, see Julia Wrigley, *Class Politics and Public Schools: Chicago 1900–1950* (New Brunswick: Rutgers University Press, 1982); David John Hogan, *Class and Reform: School and Society in Chicago, 1880–1930* (Philadelphia: University of Pennsylvania Press, 1985); Wayne Urban, "Organized Teachers and Educational Reform during the Progressive Era: 1890–1920," HEQ 16 (Spring 1976): 35–52; George S. Counts, *School and Society in Chicago* (New York: Harcourt, Brace, & Co., 1928). For examples in other cities, see William H. Issel, "Teachers and Educational Reform during the Progressive Era: A Case Study of the Pittsburgh Teachers Association," HEQ 7 (Summer 1967): 220–33; Victor L. Shradar, "Ethnicity, Religion, and Class: Progressive School Reform in San Francisco," HEQ 20 (1980): 385–401; Troen, *The Public and the Schools*.

28. Ellwood P. Cubberley, "The Baltimore School Situation," ER 42 (Nov. 1911): 325–45.

29. For research studies that charted these changes at the time, see Thomas McDowell Gilland, *The Origin and Development of the Power and Duties of the City-School Superintendent* (Chicago: University of Chicago Press, 1935); Grover Cleveland Morehart, *The Legal Status of City School Boards* (New York City: Teacher's College, 1927); John Cayce Morrison, *The Legal Status of the City School Superintendent* (Baltimore: Warwick & York, 1922); W. S. Deffenbaugh, "Current Practice in City School Administration," *USBE Bulletin*, no. 8 (1917); Hans C. Olsen, *The Work of Boards of Education* (New York: Teachers College, 1926); William Walter Theisen, *The City Superintendent and the Board of Education* (New York: Teachers College, 1917); Theodore Lee Reller, *The Development of the City Superintendency of Schools in the United States* (Philadelphia: self-published, 1935).

30. George D. Strayer et. al., *Report of the Survey of the Schools of Chicago, Illinois*, 5 vols.

(New York: Teachers College, Division of Field Studies, 1932). For a breakdown of enrollment, personnel, and finances in several cities, see "Statistics of City School Systems for the Year 1931–32, Being Chapter 2 of the Biennial Survey of the Education in the United States: 1930–32," *USBE Bulletin*, no. 2 (1933). For analysis and examples of increasing specializations, see Harry S. Ganders, "Personnel and Organization of Schools in Small Cities," *USBE Bulletin*, no. 6 (1926); William C. McGinnis, *School Administrative and Supervisory Organizations in Cities of 20,000 to 50,000 Population* (New York: Teachers College, 1929); David Tyack and Elisabeth Hansot, *Managers of Virtue: Public School Leadership in America, 1820–1980* (New York: Basic Books, 1982); John D. Wolcott, "A Handbook of Educational Associations and Foundations in the United States," *USBE Bulletin*, no. 16 (1926).

31. Studies at the time and since have emphasized the "elite" nature of school governance reforms and noted that civic-business elites dominated reorganized city government and school boards. See Hayes, "The Politics of Reform in Municipal Government;" Scott Nearing, "Who's Who on Our Boards of Education," SS 5 (Jan. 1917): 89–90; George C. Counts, *The Social Composition of Boards of Education: A Study in the Social Control of Public Education* (Chicago: University of Chicago Press, 1927). However, William Reese and Jeffrey Mirel have argued that the shift represented not one from working class representation to elite takeover, but rather a shift in the kinds of elites that dominated school boards, from neighborhood to metropolitan elites. William Reese, "The Control of Urban School Boards during the Progressive Era: A Reconsideration" *Pacific Northwest Quarterly* (Oct. 1977): 164–74; Jeffrey Mirel, *The Rise and Fall of an Urban School System*, 1907–81, 2nd ed. (Ann Arbor: University of Michigan Press, 1999).

32. Peterson, *The Politics of School Reform*; Reese, *The Power and Promise of School Reform*.

33. Rollins, "School Administration in Municipal Government" 59. See Tyack and Hansot, *Managers of Virtue*, for an excellent overview and contrast of educational leadership in the nineteenth and twentieth centuries.

34. Leigh G. Hubbell, "The Development of University Departments of Education in Six States of the Middle West" (Ph.D. diss, Catholic University, 1924); Timothy F. O'Leary, *An Inquiry into the General Purposes, Functions, and Organization of Selected University Schools of Education With Special Reference to Certain Aspects of their Growth and Development* (Washington, D.C.: Catholic University of America Press, 1941); Allen S. Whitney, *History of the Professional Training of Teachers at the University of Michigan for the First Half-Century, 1879–1929* (Ann Arbor: George Wahr Publisher, 1931); Edwin Augustus Lee, "The Development of Professional Programs in Education in Six Selected Universities of the United States" (Ph. D. diss, Columbia University, 1925); W. S. Sutton, "The Organization of the Department of Education in Relation to the Other Departments in Colleges and Universities," *Journal of Pedagogy* 19 (Dec. 1906–Mar. 1907): 81–136.

35. For analysis of the institutional tensions and dynamics of university education programs (in addition to the sources above), see Geraldine Joncich Clifford, *Ed School: A Brief for Professional Education* (Chicago: University of Chicago Press, 1988); David

F. Labaree, *The Trouble with Ed Schools* (New Haven: Yale University Press, 2006); Ellen Condliffe Lagemann, *An Elusive Science: The Troubling History of Education Research* (Chicago: University of Chicago Press, 2000); Arthur G. Powell, *The Uncertain Profession: Harvard and the Search for Educational Authority* (Cambridge, MA: Harvard University Press, 1980); Jesse B. Sears and Adin D. Henderson, *Cubberley of Stanford and His Contribution to American Education* (Stanford: Stanford University Press, 1957). On normal schools, see Christine A. Ogren, *The American State Normal School: "An Instrument of Great Good"* (New York: Palgrave Macmillan, 2005); Jurgen Herbst, *And Sadly Teach: Teacher Education and Professionalization in American Culture* (Madison: University of Wisconsin Press, 1989).

36. William H. Payne, *Contributions to the Science of Education* (New York: American Book Co., 1886), 13.

37. For enrollment statistics, O'Leary, *An Inquiry into the General Purposes*; Frederick E. Bolton, "The Relation of the Department of Education to Other Departments in Colleges and Universities," *Journal of Pedagogy* 19 (1907): 137–76, contains detailed data on enrollment at over twenty institutions. Arthur G. Powell, "University Schools of Education in the Twentieth Century," *Peabody Journal of Education* 54 (Oct. 1976): 3–20; David F. Labaree, "Career Ladders and the Early Public High-School Teacher: A Study of Inequality and Opportunity," in *American Teachers: Histories of a Profession at Work*, ed. Donald Warren (New York: Macmillan, 1989).

38. On the history of Teachers College, see Lawrence A. Cremin, David A. Shannon, and Mary Evelyn Townsend, *A History of Teachers College Columbia University* (New York: Columbia University Press: 1954); James E. Russell, *Founding Teachers College: Reminiscences of the Dean Emeritus* (New York: Teachers College, 1937); O'Leary, *An Inquiry into the General Purposes*; Eleanor M. Witmer and May B. Van Arsdale, *Introducing Teachers College: Some Notes and Recollections* (New York: Teachers College, 1948). Chicago's *Announcement of the School of Education* quoted in Lee, "The Development of Professional Programs," 60.

39. For discussions at the time of whether there was a science of education and what it looked like, see Josiah Royce, "Is there a Science of Education?," ER 1 (Jan. 1891): 15–25; James E. Russell, "The Function of the University in the Training of Teachers," *Teachers College Record* 1 (Jan. 1900): 1–11; Richard Gause Boone, *Science of Education* (New York: Charles Scribner's Sons, 1904); Samuel Bower Sinclair, *The Possibility of a Science of Education* (Chicago: University of Chicago Press, 1903).

40. Walter S. Monroe, "Ten Years of Educational Research, 1918–1928," *University of Illinois Bulletin*, no. 25 (Aug. 1928): 114. For overviews of early educational research, including Thorndike's influence, see Lagemann, *An Elusive Science*; Robert M. W. Travers, *How Research Has Changed American Schools: A History from 1840 to the Present* (Kalamazoo: Mythos Press, 1983); Monroe, "Ten Years of Educational Research, 1918–1928"; Geraldine M. Joncich, ed., *Psychology and the Science of Education: Selected Writings of Edward L. Thorndike* (New York: Teachers College, 1962); Edward L. Thorndike, *An Introduction to the Theory of Mental and Social Measurements* (New York: Science Press, 1904).

41. For Thorndike's work on school-leaving and its impact, see, for example, Edward Thorndike, "The Elimination of Pupils from Our Schools," *USBE Bulletin*, no. 4 (1907); Leonard P. Ayres, *Laggards in Our Schools: A Study of Retardation and Elimination in City School Systems* (New York: Russell Sage Foundation, 1909); George Strayer, "A Study in Retardation and Elimination," *USBE Bulletin*, no. 5 (1911); Ronald P. Faulkner, "Retardation: Its Significance and its Measurement," ER 38 (Sept. 1909): 122–31; Roland P. Falkner, "Elimination of Pupils from Schools: A Review of Recent Investigations," *Psychological Clinic* 2 (Feb. 1909): 255–75; Leonard P. Ayres, *An Index Number for State School Systems* (New York: Russell Sage Foundation, 1920).

42. Leonard P. Ayres, "Measuring Educational Processes through Educational Results," SR 20 (May 1912): 300–309; Edward C. Elliot, "Discussion: Report of the Committee of Tests and Standards of Efficiency in Schools and School Systems," APNEA (1913): 398; Stratton Brooks, "Discussion," SR 20 (May 1912): 318.

43. On the authority of numbers and quantification as a social process, see Theodore M. Porter, *Trust in Numbers: The Pursuit of Objectivity in Science and Public Life* (Princeton: Princeton University Press, 1995); Patricia Cline Cohen, *A Calculating People: The Spread of Numeracy in Early America* (New York: Routledge, 1999); Sarah E. Igo, *The Averaged American: Surveys, Citizens, and the Making of a Mass Public* (Cambridge, MA: Harvard University Press, 2007); Wendy Nelson Espeland and Mitchell L. Stevens, "A Sociology of Quantification," *European Journal of Sociology* 48 (2008): 401–36; Wendy Nelson Espeland and Mitchell Stevens, "Commensuration as a Social Process," *Annual Review of Sociology* 24 (1998): 313–43. On the shift from philosophical and normative inquiry in the field of education to rigid empiricism and study of the status quo, see Michael B. Katz, "From Theory to Survey in Graduate Schools of Education," *Journal of Higher Education* 37 (June 1966): 325–34.

44. There was an intense conversation about the value of measurement and some occasional cautions, particularly from 1912 to 1918, at NEA meetings, special conferences, and in the pages of educational journals. See, for example, Edward Thorndike, "The Measurement of Educational Products," SR 20 (May 1912): 289–99; Fred N. Scott, "Efficiency for Efficiency's Sake," SR 23 (Jan. 1915); "Topic: By What Standards or Tests Shall the Efficiency of a School or System of Schools be Measured?," APNEA (1912): 560–74; George Strayer, "Report of the Committee on Tests and Standards of Efficiency in Schools and School Systems," APNEA (1913): 392–406; NSSE fifteenth yearbook, part 1, *Standards and Tests for the Measurement of the Efficiency of Schools and School Systems* (1916); NSSE seventeenth yearbook, part 2, *The Measurement of Educational Products* (1918). On the development of programs of school administration, see Clifford, *Ed School*; Fred Englehardt, "Educating School Administrators," in *The Changing Educational World, 1905–1930*, ed. Alvin C. Eurich (Minneapolis: University of Minnesota Press, 1931), 279–304; George Strayer, "Professional Training for Superintendents of Schools," *Teachers College Record* 26 (June 1925): 815–26; Edward C. Elliott, "University Courses in Educational Administration" pamphlet (Iowa City: National Society of College Teachers of Education, 1910); Tyack and Hansot, *Managers of Virtue*.

45. For discussions of teacher professionalization, including some of the tensions within it, see Kate Rousmaniere, *City Teachers: Teaching and School Reform in Historical Perspective* (New York: Teachers College Press, 1997); Urban, "Organized Teachers and Educational Reform"; Wayne J. Urban, *Gender, Race, and the National Education Association: Professionalism and Its Limitations* (New York: Routledge Falmer, 2000); Willard S. Elsbree, *The American Teacher: Evolution of a Profession in a Democracy* (New York: American Book Co., 1939); James Fraser, *Preparing America's Teachers: A History* (New York: Teachers College Press, 2007).

46. For examples of administrators' interest in teacher professionalization and its tensions, see Walter R. Smith, "The Professional Status of Teaching," ER 63 (Jan. 1922): 35–49; Harvey C. Lehman and Paul A. Witty, "Some Suggestions for Making Teaching a Profession," ER 74 (Dec. 1927): 258–69; I. M. Allen, "Improving the Professional Stature of Teachers," ESJ 26 (Feb. 1926): 430–40.

47. Martin Bulmer, Kevin Bales, and Kathryn Kish Sklar, *The Social Survey in Historical Perspective 1880–1940* (Cambridge: Cambridge University Press, 1991).

48. For analysis of the Boise, Montclair, and East Orange surveys, see Edward Franklin Buchner, "School Surveys," *U.S. Commissioner of Education Report* 1 (1914): 516–18; Hollis Leland Caswell, *City School Surveys: An Interpretation and Appraisal* (New York City: Teacher's College, 1929), 18–20; Ernest Carroll Moore, *Report of the Examination of the School System of East Orange, New Jersey* (East Orange Board of Education, 1912).

49. Edward Buchner summarized the key techniques, personnel, and findings of every survey from 1910 to 1923 for the U.S. Bureau of Education. Buchner, "School Surveys" (1914): 513–96; Edward Franklin Buchner, "School Surveys," *U.S. Commissioner of Education Report* 1 (1915): 433–92; Edward Franklin Buchner, "Educational Surveys," *U.S. Commissioner of Education Report* 1 (1916): 353–71; Edward Franklin Buchner, "Educational Surveys," *USBE Bulletin*, no. 45 (1918); Edward Franklin Buchner, "Educational Surveys," *USBE Bulletin*, no. 17 (1923). For other overviews of the trends and principles in surveying, see Arthur J. Klein et al., "Educational Surveys," *USBE Bulletin*, no. 11 (1928); George D. Strayer, Isaac L. Kandel, and Carter Alexander, "Selected Bibliography of Recent School Surveys," in *Rating, Placing, and Promotion of Teachers; Educational Surveys; List of Educational Investigations by Members*, School Review Monographs, no. 5 (Chicago: University of Chicago Press, 1914); Don C. Bliss, *Methods and Standards for Local School Surveys* (Boston: D. C. Heath, 1918); Jesse B. Sears, *The School Survey: A Textbook on the Use of School Surveying in the Administration of Public Schools* (Cambridge, MA: Riverside Press, 1925); H. L. Smith and Charles H. Judd, NSSE thirteenth yearbook, part 2, *Plans for Organizing School Surveys with a Summary of Typical School Surveys* (1914).

50. Charles Hubbard Judd, *Measuring the Work of the Public Schools*, Cleveland Education Survey (Cleveland: Survey Committee, 1917); Leonard Ayres, *The Cleveland School Survey (Summary Volume)* (Cleveland: Survey Committee, 1917); Leonard Ayres, "Significant Developments in Educational Surveying," APNEA (1918): 994–1001; Caswell, *City School Surveys* , 95–98. On research bureaus in city school systems, see Harold Benjamin Chapman, *Organized Research in Education with Special Reference*

to the Bureau of Educational Research (Columbus: Ohio State University Press, 1927); W. S. Deffenbaugh, "Research Bureaus in City School Systems," *USBE CSL*, no. 5 (Jan. 1923); Elise H. Martens, "Organization of Research Bureaus in City School Systems," *USBE CSL*, no. 14 (Jan. 1924); Frank W. Ballou, "General Organization of Educational Measurement Work in City School Systems," in NSSE seventeenth yearbook (1918): 41–51.

51. Caswell, *City School Surveys*, chap. 5; George Drayton Strayer, "Score Card for City School Buildings," NSSE fifteenth yearbook (1916): 41–51; N. L. Engelhardt, *A School Building Program for Cities* (New York: Teachers College, 1918). For examples with recommended forms and new measures, see George D. Strayer, *Some Problems in City School Administration* (Yonkers-on-Hudson, NY: World Book Inc., 1916); George D. Strayer, "Report of the Survey of the Schools of Tampa, Florida," Division of Field Studies School Survey Series (New York: Teachers College, 1926); George D. Strayer and N. L. Engelhardt, *A Scorecard and Standards for the Records and Reports of City School Systems* (New York: Teachers College, 1923). On efforts at uniform statistics, see "Final Report of the Committee on Uniform Records and Reports," APNEA (1912); Frank M. Phillips, "Influence of Statistics in Unifying American Education," *School Life* (May 1924): 222–23.

52. Ellwood P. Cubberley, *The Portland Survey: A Textbook on City School Administration Based on a Concrete Study* (Yonkers-on-Hudson, NY: World Book Co., 1915). Caswell identified health work as one of the major innovations introduced into city schools as a result of surveys; Caswell, *City School Surveys*.

53. Nancy E. Adelman, "Sphere of Influence: Factors in the Development of Three New Jersey Communities in the Progressive Era," in Goodenow and Ravitch, *Schools in Cities*, 111–62. The quote is Harold Caswell to Nancy Adelman April 6, 1979, quoted in Adelman, "Spheres of Influence," 114.

54. On professional networks and career sponsorship, see Tyack and Hansot, *Managers of Virtue*; Tyack, *The One Best System*; Lagemann, *An Elusive Science*, chap. 3; Robert Louis Rose, "Career Sponsorship in the School Superintendency" (Ph.D. diss, University of Oregon, 1969); Sears and Henderson, *Cubberley of Stanford*.

55. On the local effects of school surveys in general, see Caswell, *City School Surveys*; Leonard P. Ayres, "School Surveys," SS 1 (April 1915): 577–81; Leonard V. Koos, "The Fruits of School Surveys," SS 5 (Jan. 1917): 35–41; R. E. Garlin, "Factors Conditioning the Success of School Surveys," SS 28 (Sept. 1928): 337–40. On Portland and Wilmington, see USBE Papers, historical file 501, local school surveys, boxes 53–59, including: "Results of Educational Surveys Conducted by the U.S. Bureau of Education," memo 26266, Sept. 1928, box 54; W. S. Deffenbaugh, "Results of Some City School Surveys Made by the Bureau of Education," undated, box 54; letter from Portland school director to J. Tigert, 16 February 1924, box 58; memo from Alice Borrows to Commissioner Tigert on "The results of the Portland, Oregon school building survey," 29 June 1924, box 58; Robert Osborne to John Tigert, 23 May 1923, box 58; "Why Is a School Survey Needed?," *Portland City Club Bulletin*, 24 May 1923, box 58; "That School Survey," editorial from (Wilmington) *Advocate*, 7 February 1920, in box 56; Commissioner Claxton to Joseph Bancroft, 2 July 1920, box 56.

56. Adelman, "Spheres of Influence," 127–37.

57. Strayer, *Some Problems in City School Administration*. For discussions of public rela-
tions and the role of school surveys and reports, see Carter Alexander and W. W.
Theisen, *Publicity Campaigns for Better School Support* (Yonkers-on-Hudson, NY:
World Book Co., 1921); R. E. Garlin, "Giving Publicity to City School Surveys,"
SS 26 (Aug. 1927): 277–80; Arthur B. Moehlman, *Public School Relations* (Chicago:
Rand McNally & Co., 1927); Mervin Gordon Neale, *School Reports as a Means
of Securing Additional Support for Education in American Cities* (Columbia: Mis-
souri Book Co., 1921); Clyde R. Miller and Fred Charles, *Publicity and the Public
School* (Boston: Houghton Mifflin Co., 1924); Ward G. Reeder, *An Introduction to
Public-School Relations* (New York: Macmillan Co., 1937).

58. Buchner, "Educational Surveys" (1918),15–16; Buchner, "School Surveys," 489–90.

59. Abraham Flexner and Frank P. Bachman, *The Gary Schools: A General Account* (New
York: General Education Board, 1918); Stuart A. Courtis, *The Gary Public Schools:
Measurement of Classroom Products* (New York: General Education Board, 1919). On
Gary, see also Cohen, *Children of the Mill*; Ronald Cohen and Raymond Mohl, *The
Paradox of Progressive Education: The Gary Plan and Urban Schooling* (Port Washing-
ton, NY: Kennikat Press, 1979).

60. George D. Strayer and N. L. Engelhardt, "Score Card for High School Buildings"
(New York: Teachers College, 1924), 3–5; Adelman, "Spheres of Influence."

61. Ernest Carroll Moore, *How New York City Administers Its Schools: A Constructive
Study* (Yonkers-on-Hudson, NY: World Book Co., 1913); Cubberley, *The Portland
Survey.*

Chapter Two

1. J. W. Olsen, "Progress in Consolidation of Rural Schools," APNEA (1902): 793.

2. David B. Tyack, "The Tribe and the Common School: Community Control in Rural
Education," *American Quarterly* 24 (Mar. 1972): 3–19; Spencer J. Maxcy, "Progressiv-
ism and Rural Education in the Deep South, 1900–1950," in *Education and the Rise of
the New South*, ed. Ronald K. Goodeow and Arthur O. White (Boston: G. K. Hall and
Co., 1982), 61. On bureaucratic ambitions of rural reformers, see David B. Tyack, *The
One Best System: A History of American Urban Education* (Cambridge, MA: Harvard
University Press, 1974); Wayne E. Fuller, *The Old Country School: The Story of Rural
Education in the Middle West* (Chicago: University of Chicago Press, 1982); William
A. Link, *A Hard Country and a Lonely Place: Schooling, Society, and Reform in Rural
Virginia, 1870–1920* (Chapel Hill: University of North Carolina Press, 1986); William
L. Bowers, *The Country Life Movement in America, 1900–1920* (Port Washington, NY:
Kennikat Press, 1974); David B. Danbom, *The Resisted Revolution: Urban America and
the Industrialization of Agriculture, 1900–1930* (Ames: Iowa State University Press,
1979).

3. For studies of American government that explore some of these dynamics in other
contexts, see, for example, William J. Novak, "The Myth of the 'Weak' American
State," AHR 113 (June 2008): 752–72; Peter Baldwin, "Beyond Weak and Strong:

Rethinking the State in Comparative Policy History," JPH 17 (2005): 12–33; Brian Balogh, *A Government Out of Sight: The Mystery of National Authority in Nineteenth-Century America* (Cambridge: Cambridge University Press, 2009); Christopher Howard, *The Welfare State Nobody Knows: Debunking Myths about U.S. Social Policy* (Princeton: Princeton University Press, 2007); Michael B. Katz, *The Price of Citizenship: Redefining the American Welfare State* (New York: Metropolitan Books, 2001); Elisabeth S. Clemens, "Lineages of the Rube Goldberg State: Building and Blurring Public Programs, 1900–1940," in *Rethinking Political Institutions: The Art of the State*, ed. Ian Shapiro, Stephen Skowronek, and Daniel Galvin (New York: New York University Press, 2006), 187–215; William J. Novak, "The Legal Origins of the Modern American State," in *Looking Back at Law's Century*, ed. Austin Sarat, Bryant Garth, and Robert A. Kagan (Ithaca: Cornell University Press, 2002), 249–83; Jacob Hacker, *The Divided Welfare State: The Battle over Public and Private Social Benefits in the United States* (Cambridge: Cambridge University Press, 2002).

4. Fuller, *The Old Country School*; Carl F. Kaestle, *Pillars of the Republic: Common Schools and American Society, 1780–1860* (New York: Hill and Wang, 1983); Jonathan Zimmerman, *Small Wonder: The Little Red Schoolhouse in History and Memory* (New Haven: Yale University Press, 2009); John G. Richardson, "Settlement Patterns and the Governing Structures of Nineteenth-Century School Systems," HEQ 92 (Feb. 1984): 178–206; Hilary J. Moss, *Schooling Citizens: The Struggle for African American Education in Antebellum America* (Chicago: University of Chicago Press, 2009); Paul Theobald, *Call School: Rural Education in the Midwest to 1918* (Carbondale: Southern Illinois University Press, 1995).

5. James D. Anderson, *The Education of Blacks in the South, 1860–1935* (Chapel Hill: University of North Carolina Press, 1988); Adam Fairclough, *A Class of Their Own: Black Teachers in the Segregated South* (Cambridge, MA: Belknap Press, 2007); Henry Allen Bullock, *A History of Negro Education in the South: From 1619 to the Present* (Cambridge, MA: Harvard University Press, 1967); Horace Mann Bond, *The Education of the Negro in the American Social Order* (New York: Prentice-Hall Inc., 1934); Heather Andrea Williams, *Self-Taught: African-American Education in Slavery and Freedom* (Chapel Hill: University of North Carolina Press, 2005); Richard Barry Westin, "The State and the Segregated Schools: Negro Public Education in North Carolina, 1863–1923" (Ph.D. diss., University of North Carolina, 1966).

6. Caleb Mills, *Biennial Report of State Superintendent* (1856), quoted in Fassett A. Cotton, *Biennial Report of State Superintendent of Public Instruction* (1903–4): 271–72.

7. Fassett A. Cotton, *Biennial Report of State Superintendent of Public Instruction* (1905–6): 618–19; "The Rural Schools," *Outlook* 64 (Jan. 1900): 207; Lewis D. Bonebrake, "The Centralization of Rural Schools," APNEA (1901): 805. See also E. T. Fairchild, "Bulletin of Information Regarding Consolidation of Rural Schools" (Topeka: State Printing Office, 1908); John T. Prince, "Consolidation of Rural Schools," APNEA (1903): 929–35; J. Y. Joyner, "Consolidation of Schools" APNEA (1904): 313–16; Charles A. Van Matre, "The Financial Phase of the Consolidation of Rural Schools," APNEA (1902): 224–30. For a bibliography of other state superintendent reports, see William K. Fowler, "The Consolidation of School Districts, The Centralization

of Rural Schools, and the Transportation of Pupils at Public Expense" (Nebraska Department of Public Instruction, 1903); William Fowler, "Consolidation of Rural Schools," APNEA (1903): 919-29. On the demographic shifts of rural life, see Hal S. Barron, *Those Who Stayed Behind: Rural Society in Nineteenth-Century New England* (New York: Cambridge University Press, 1984); Hal S Barron, *Mixed Harvest: The Second Great Transformation in the Rural North, 1870-1930* (Chapel Hill: University of North Carolina Press, 1997).

8. "Report of the Committee of Twelve on Rural Schools," APNEA (1897): 391, 440.

9. "The Country Child's Right," *Prairie Farmer*, 29 June 1905, 6; *Hoard's Dairyman*, 19 July 1895, 419, quoted in Lawrence A. Cremin, *The Transformation of the School: Progressivism in American Education, 1876-1957* (New York: Alfred A. Knopf, 1961), 45.

10. "Agriculture in Rural Schools," *Prairie Farmer*, 7 Apr. 1904, 1; "Teach Agriculture Now," *Prairie Farmer*, 24 Dec. 1903, 1; "Agriculture in the Public Schools," *Prairie Farmer*, 12 Mar. 1903; John M. Gillette, "The Drift to the City in Relation to the Rural Problem," AJS 16 (Mar. 1911): 645-67; Sir Horace Plunkett, *The Rural Life Problem in the United States: Notes of an Irish Observer* (New York: Macmillan Co., 1911), 132; Rex Beresford, "Give the Farm Boy a Chance in the Country School," *Prairie Farmer*, 1 Apr. 1912, 11. See also "Why Boys Leave the Farm," *Prairie Farmer*, 5 Jan. 1905, 2; "The Boy and the Farm," *Prairie Farmer*, 18 May 1905, 6. For a good discussion of farmers' advocacy of agricultural education, see Cremin, *The Transformation of the School*, 41-50.

11. Daniel T. Rodgers, *Atlantic Crossings: Social Politics in a Progressive Age* (Cambridge, MA: Belknap Press, 1998), chap. 8; Theodore Roosevelt, "Special Message" in "Report of the Country Life Commission," Senate doc. no. 75, 60th Congress, 2nd sess., 1909, 6-9. See also Theodore Roosevelt, "Progressive Democracy: Country Life and Conservation," *Outlook* 102 (Sept. 7, 1912): 20-21; "Roosevelt to the Farmers: Betterment of Rural Life One of Nation's Great Needs," NYT, 24 Aug. 1910, 2.

12. Plunkett, *The Rural Life Problem in the United States*, 47-48; Liberty Hyde Bailey, *Country-Life Movement in the United States* (New York: Macmillan Co., 1911), 20; T. N. Carver, "Economic Significance of Changes in Country Population," AAAPSS 40 (Mar. 1912): 21, 22. See also John M. Gillette, "Conditions and Needs of Country Life," AAAPSS 40 (Mar. 1912): 3-11; Gillette, "The Drift to the City in Relation to the Rural Problem."

13. Theodore Roosevelt to L. H. Bailey, 10 Aug. 1908, in "Report of the Country Life Commission," 22-24. On the formation, methodology, and findings of the Country Life Commission, see Clayton S. Ellsworth, "Theodore Roosevelt's Country Life Commission," *Agricultural History* 34 (Oct. 1960): 155-72; Bowers, *The Country Life Movement in America*; Olaf F. Larson and Thomas B. Jones, "The Unpublished Data from Roosevelt's Commission on Country Life," *Agricultural History* 50 (July 1976): 583-99; Scott J. Peters and Paul A. Morgan, "The Country Life Commission: Reconsidering a Milestone in American Agricultural History," *Agricultural History* 78 (Summer 2004): 289-316; Paul G. Theobold, "Country Lifers Reconsidered: Educational Reform for Rural America," *Journal of Research in Rural Education* 7 (Winter

1991): 21–28. On the public hearings, see, for example, "Dr. Bailey Was Well Pleased," *Atlanta Constitution*, 12 Nov. 1908, 5; "Country Life Has No Problems Here," *LA Times*, 26 Nov. 1908, 1; "Mothers Pledge Aid to South," *Atlanta Constitution*, 23 Dec. 1908, 7; "Farm Board in Virginia," *Washington Post*, 11 Nov. 1908, 5; "Board Discusses Farm Life," *Washington Post*, 12 Nov. 1908, 3.

14. "Report of the Country Life Commission," 53–54.

15. Ellsworth, "Theodore Roosevelt's Country Life Commission"; Mabel Carney, *Country Life and the Country School* (Chicago: Row, Petterson and Company, 1912), appendix; N. J. Backener, presidential address to 42nd National Grange Meeting, Nov. 1908, quoted in Thomas Clark Atkeson, *Semi-Centennial History of the Patrons of Husbandry* (New York: Orange Judd Co., 1916), 255–56.

16. Julius Bernhard Arp, *Rural Education and the Consolidated School* (New York: World Book Co., 1918), 70; William B. Aspinwall, "The New Conception of the Rural School Problem," *Education* 37 (May 1917): 541–44; R. L. Countryman, "How Rural Schools Can Better Meet the Needs of Rural Life" *Education* 36 (Mar. 1916): 425–36.

17. O. J. Kern, *Among Country Schools* (Boston: Ginn & Company, 1906), 13, chaps. 3, 4, 6, 7.

18. Ibid. , chaps. 6, 7, 15; Wickliffe Rose, "Report on Educational Progress in Southern States during the Past five Years" [ca. 1906–7], SEB Papers, series 2.1, folder 116. For a few discussions of this work after the CLC, see NSSE tenth yearbook, part 2, *The Rural School as a Community Center* (1911); E. E. Davis, *Twentieth-Century Rural School* (Indianapolis: Bobbs-Merrill Company, 1920); Harold Waldstein Foght, *The American Rural School: Its Characteristics, Its Future, and Its Problems* (New York: Macmillan Company, 1910); Carney, *Country Life and the Country School*; James E. Delzell, "The Betterment of Rural Schools thru Boys' and Girls' Clubs: The Nebraska Plan," APNEA (1912): 1373–75; Josephine C. Preston, "Some Conditions in Rural Schools and Their Improvement," APNEA (1914): 190–91; F. W. Miller, "The Betterment of Rural Schools thru Agriculture: The Ohio Plan," APNEA (1912): 1366–74; Mary A Grupe, "How the Problems of the Rural Schools are Being Met," *Popular Science Monthly* 83 (Nov. 1913): 484–90; W. T. Hodges, "Important Features in Rural School Improvement," *USBE Bulletin*, no. 25 (1914).

19. On Southern education reform, see Louis R. Harlan, *Separate and Unequal: Public School Campaigns and Racism in the Southern Seaboard States, 1901–1915* (Chapel Hill: University of North Carolina Press, 1958); James L. Leloudis, *Schooling the New South: Pedagogy, Self, and Society in North Carolina, 1880–1920* (Chapel Hill: University of North Carolina Press, 1996); Link, *A Hard Country and a Lonely Place*; Raymond B. Fosdick, *Adventure in Giving: The Story of the General Education Board* (New York: Harper & Row, 1962); Anderson, *The Education of Blacks in the South*.

20. Leloudis, *Schooling the New South*, chap. 5.

21. *Biennial Report of the Superintendent of Public Instruction of Kentucky* (1909–11). For other examples, see Link, *A Hard Country and a Lonely Place*; "Summary of Reports of Educational Progress in Southern States, July 1–December 31, 1909," SEB Papers, series 2.1, folder 116.

22. W. K. Tate, "Country Schools for Country Children," *World's Work* 24 (May 1912): 102–7; Jessie Field, *The Corn Lady: The Story of a Country Teacher's Work* (Chicago: A. Flanagan Co., 1911).

23. Tate, "Country Schools for Country Children," 102–7.

24. For an excellent study of county superintendents' reform influence, see Dina L. Stephens, "The Role of County Superintendents in Rural School Reform in Late Nineteenth and Early Twentieth Century Wisconsin" (Ph.D. diss., University of Wisconsin–Madison, 1996).

25. Katherine M. Cook and A. C. Monahan, "Rural School Supervision," *USBE Bulletin*, no. 48 (1916): 57; A. C. Monahan, "The Status of Rural Education in the United States," *USBE Bulletin*, no. 8 (1913): 51; Cook and Monahan, "Rural School Supervision," 57, 31. The average supervisory district in 1916, the USBE reported, was 1,672 square miles. For excellent data about school supervision at different points in time, see also Katherine M. Cook, "Supervision of Rural Schools," *USBE Bulletin*, no. 10 (1922); William E. Cole, *The Status of Rural Supervisors of Instruction in the United States* (Ithaca: New York State College of Agriculture, 1930); N. William Newsom, "The Legal Status of the County Superintendent," *USBE Bulletin*, no. 7 (1932); "Status of Rural-School Supervision in the United States in 1935–1936," *USBE Pamphlet*, no. 72 (1936).

26. Cook, "Supervision of Rural Schools," 41–49. For other good descriptions of the work of rural school supervisors, see Hodges, "Important Features in Rural School Improvement"; Annie Reynolds, "Some Lessons from a Decade of Rural Supervision," *USBE Bulletin*, no. 9 (1925); Annie Reynolds, "Supervision and Rural School Improvement," *USBE Bulletin*, no. 31 (1930); H. E. Hall, "A Study of School Supervision in the County Districts of Ohio," *Journal of Rural Education* 5 (Jan.–Feb. 1926): 231–36. The SEB and GEB archives also contain a host of reports from county and state rural supervisors. For example, in SEB Papers, series 2.1, folders 92–108, and series 2.3, folders 119–25, 169–74.

27. Cook, "Rural Supervision" (1922), 20; Julian E. Butterworth, "The County Superintendent in the United States," *USBE Bulletin*, no. 6 (1932): 39–40. For discussions on the challenges of rural supervision, see W. C. Hoppes, "Supervision of Rural Schools," *Journal of Rural Education* 3 (Feb. 1924): 261–72; NSSE twelfth yearbook, part 2, *The Supervision of Rural Schools* (1913); "Leadership in Rural Education," *Educational Leadership: Progress and Possibilities*, eleventh yearbook (NEA Department of Superintendence, 1933).

28. N. O. Nelson, "Industrial Supervisors in Georgia" (1909), SEB Papers, series 2.1, folder 95; W. K. Tate, "To the County Rural School Supervisors," circular letter, 13 Sept. 1912, GEB Papers, series 1.1, box 131, folder 1198. See also "Summary of Reports of Educational Progress in Southern States, July 1–December 31, 1909," SEB Papers, series 2.1, folder 116; "Reports of Supervisors of Rural Elementary Schools for the Quarter Ending December 31, 1910," SEB Papers, series 2.1, folder 119; county supervisors reports, SEB Papers, series 2.1, folder 107.

29. Harlan, *Separate and Unequal*, 15; "The Educational Equipment and Needs of North

Carolina," confidential to members of the GEB, Jan. 1904, SEB Papers, series 2.1, folder 104: 27–28.

30. Extract from letter, Walter Page to Wickliffe Rose, 24 Feb. 1910, attached to "confidential" letter, Ellsworth Brown to Walter Page, 24 Feb. 1910, SEB Papers, series 1.2, folder 13. The literature on the motives of philanthropists in promoting industrial education is large and often highly critical. See, for example, James D. Anderson, "Northern Foundations and the Shaping of Southern Black Rural Education, 1902–1935," HEQ 18 (Winter 1978): 371–96; Anderson, *The Education of Blacks in the South*; Donald Spivey, *Schooling for the New Slavery: Black Industrial Education, 1868–1915* (Westport, CT: Greenwood Press, 1978); William H. Watkins, *The White Architects of Black Education: Ideology and Power in America, 1865–1954* (New York: Teachers College Press, 2001); Fairclough, *A Class of Their Own*.

31. On black communities using philanthropic aid for their own purposes, see, for example, Anderson, *The Education of Blacks in the South*; Link, *A Hard Country and a Lonely Place*; Fairclough, *A Class of Their Own*.

32. Mrs. N. Lee Butler, "The Awakening in Caroline County" (1914), GEB Papers, series 1.1, box 187, folder 1753. On Jeanes teachers, see Lance G. E. Jones, *The Jeanes Teachers of the Southern States* (Chapel Hill: University of North Carolina Press, 1937); Ann Short Chirhart, *Torches of Light: Georgia Teachers and the Coming of the Modern South* (Athens: University of Georgia Press, 2005); Ambrose Caliver, "Rural Elementary Education among Negroes under Jeanes Supervising Teachers," *USBE Bulletin*, no. 5 (1933); Fairclough, *A Class of Their Own*.

33. "Jeanes Teachers—Superintendent Testimonials, 1926," Department of Public Instruction Records, special subject file box 2, NCSA; Anderson, *The Education of Blacks in the South*; Mary S. Hoffschwelle, *The Rosenwald Schools of the American South* (Gainesville: University Press of Florida, 2006); Dennis Hargrove Cooke, *The White Superintendent and the Negro Schools in North Carolina* (Nashville: George Peabody College for Teachers, 1930).

34. S. L. Smith, *Builders of Goodwill: The Story of the State Agents of Negro Education in the South, 1910 to 1950* (Nashville: Tennessee Book Company, 1950); Fosdick, *Adventures in Giving*; Joan Malczewski, "Weak State, Stronger Schools: Northern Philanthropy and Organizational Change in the Jim Crow South," *Journal of Southern History* 75 (Nov. 2009): 963–1000.

35. A. J. Bourland, "Plan of Work of Southern Education Board," 23 July 1904, SEB Papers, series 2.3, folder 185.

36. R. H. Powell Jr., "Georgia" in "Reports of Supervisors of Rural Elementary Schools for Quarter Ending June 30, 1910," SEB Papers, series 3.2, folder 119; W. K. Tate, "South Carolina" in "Report of Supervisors of Rural Elementary Schools for Quarter Ending March 31, 1912", SEB Papers, series 2.1, folder 122; A. P. Bourland, "Report of General Agent to the Trustees of the Peabody Fund," ca. 1911, SEB Papers. series 2.3, folder, 168, 8.

37. "Report of N. C. Newbold, State Supervisor of Rural Schools for negroes in North Carolina, for the Month of Jan. 1914," GEB Papers, series 1.1, box 115, folder 1042.

38. Leo Favrot to Wallace Buttrick, 28 Aug. 1913, GEB Papers, series 1.1, box 24, folder 213; J. B. Felton to Leo Favrot, 17 Jan. 1938, GEB Papers, series 1.1, box 131, folder 1201; C. L. Coon to N. C. Newbold, 18 July 1919, Coon Papers, box 5, folder 60. For the fairly innocuous exchange that preceded Coon's critique, see N. C. Newbold to C. L. Coon, 15 July 1919, and N. C. Newbold to C. L. Coon, 17 July 1919, box 5, folder 60, Coon Papers. N. C. Newbold's correspondence contains many other examples of this delicate relationship with white superintendents: see especially boxes 1–3, Division of Negro Education, General Correspondence of the Director, NCSA.

39. L. C. Brogden to Wickliffe Rose, 1 Jan. 1910, SEB Papers, series 2.1, folder 104; Katherine M. Cook, "Supervision of Instruction as a Function of State Departments of Education," *USBE Bulletin*, no. 6, monograph no. 7, Studies of State Departments of Education (1940): 16. See also Katherine M. Cook, "Rural Education," *USBE Bulletin*, no. 36 (1923); Annie Reynolds, "Certain State Programs for the Improvement of Rural Instruction," *USBE Bulletin*, no. 18 (1931).

40. On women's roles as rural supervisors, see Jackie M. Blount, *Destined to Rule the Schools: Women and the Superintendency, 1873–1995* (Albany: State University of New York Press, 1998); Kathleen Weiler, *Country Schoolwomen: Teaching in Rural California, 1850–1950* (Stanford: Stanford University Press, 1998); Michael Pisapia, "The Authority of Women in the Political Development of Public Education in the American States, 1860–1930," *Studies in American Political Development* 24, no. 2 (2010): 24–56.

41. Arp, *Rural Education and the Consolidated School*, 194.

42. Ibid., 189–94; Clayton S. Ellsworth, "The Coming of Rural Consolidated Schools to the Ohio Valley, 1892–1912," *Agricultural History* 30 (July 1956): 119–28.

43. Van Matre, "The Financial Phase of the Consolidation of Rural Schools," 227–28.

44. George Herbert Betts and Otis Earle Hall, *Better Rural Schools* (Indianapolis: Bobbs-Merrill Company, 1914), 215–16; Louis W. Rapeer, "School Administration and Consolidation," in *The Consolidated Rural School* (New York: Charles Scribner's Sons, 1920), 94; Foght, *The American Rural School*, 302; Ellwood P. Cubberley, *Rural Life and Education: A Study of the Rural-School Problem as a Phase of the Rural-Life Problem* (Boston: Houghton Mifflin Co., 1914), 229.

45. Fairchild, "Bulletin of Information Regarding Consolidation," 46; Carney, *Country Life and the Country School*, 133–36.

46. Katherine M. Cook, "A Visit to a Consolidated School," in *The Consolidated Rural School*, 130–48, 147.

47. George W. Knorr, "A Study of 15 Consolidated Rural Schools; Their Organization, Cost, Efficiency, and Affiliated Interests," in *Southern Education Board Publication*, no. 6 (1911).

48. On the legal authority of state legislatures, see Lee O. Garber, *Education as a Function of the State* (Minneapolis: Educational Test Bureau Inc., 1934); Newton Edwards, *The Courts and the Public Schools: The Legal Basis of School Organization and Administration* (Chicago: University of Chicago Press, 1933); H. H. Schroeder, *Legal Opinion on the Public School as a State Institution* (Bloomington: Public School Publishing Com-

pany, 1928). For examples of state incentives for consolidation, see A. C. Monahan, "Consolidation of Rural Schools and Transportation of Pupils at Public Expense," *USBE Bulletin*, no. 30 (1914); Edith Lathrup, "How Laws Providing for the Distribution of State School Funds Affect Consolidation," *USBE RSL*, no. 5 (Aug. 1922); J. F. Abel, "Consolidation of Schools and Transportation of Pupils," *USBE Bulletin*, no. 41 (1923).

49. "School Consolidation: Delegations Appear in Opposition before the Montgomery Board," *Washington Post*, 1 June 1904, 4.

50. "To Comply with Law," *Richfield Reaper*, 6 Feb. 1908; "Consolidation," *Richfield Reaper*, 10 Feb. 1911; "Consolidation a Dead Duck," *Richfield Reaper*, 28 Mar. 1911; "Consolidation Bobs up Again," *Richfield Reaper*, 12 Oct. 1911; "Advancement Made Under Consolidation," *Richfield Reaper*, 18 Dec. 1913. See also Monahan, "Consolidation of Rural Schools and Transportation of Pupils," 26–34; *Chester Tp. Rural School Dist. (Bd of Ed) v. Morrow Co. (Bd of Ed)*, 1919 WL 1002 (Ohio Com. Pl.) (1919); *Brook Park Board of Education v. Cuyahoga Co. Bd of Ed*, 1924 WL 2652 (Ohio App. 8 Dist.) (1924).

51. Carney, *Country Life and the Country School*, 150–59; W. S. Fogarty, "Methods and Facts of Consolidation," in *The Consolidated Rural School*, 239–41.

52. Lee F. Driver, "Methods and Facts of Consolidation," in *The Consolidated Rural School*, 260–70; L. L. Driver, "Consolidation of Schools in Randolph County," in State of Indiana, Department of Public Instruction, *Twenty-Sixth Biennial Report of the State Superintendent of Public Instruction* (1911–12): 124–47; O. H. Griest, "Consolidation of Schools in Randolph County, Indiana," *USBE RSL*, no. 12 (1923).

53. David R. Reynolds, *There Goes the Neighborhood: Rural School Consolidation at the Grass Roots in Early Twentieth-Century Iowa* (Iowa City: University of Iowa Press, 1999), chaps. 8 and 9.

54. Timon Covert, "Rural School Consolidation: Decade of School Consolidation with Detailed Information from 105 Consolidated Schools," *USBE Pamphlet*, no. 6 (June 1930): 2–8; A. C. Monahan, "Growth of Consolidation," in *The Consolidated Rural School*, 113–14.

55. For consolidation statistics and regional analysis, see also Abel, "Consolidation and Schools and Transportation of Pupils," 52–56; Katherine M. Cook, "Rural Education"; James F. Abel, "Recent Data on Consolidation of Schools and Transportation of Pupils," *USBE Bulletin*, no. 22 (1925); Monahan, "Consolidation of Rural Schools and Transportation of Pupils at Public Expense," *USBE RSL*, no. 4 (ME and CT), 19 (LA), 22 (NM); C. G. Sargent, "Consolidated Schools of the Mountains, Valleys and Plains of Colorado," in *Colorado Agricultural College Bulletin*, no. 5 (1921).

56. William Link, "Making the Inarticulate Speak: A Reassessment of Public Education in the Rural South, 1870–1920," *Journal of Thought* 18 (Fall 1983): 63–75; Reynolds, *There Goes the Neighborhood*. As Link and Reynolds note, reformers' voices are the ones preserved in most sources. For discussions of rural resistance by reformers, see, for example, Albert Frederick Probst, "Consolidation and Transportation: A Rural School Problem," *The Elementary School Teacher* 9 (Sept. 1908): 1–16; L. J. Hanifan,

"The Difficulties of Consolidation," in *The Consolidated Rural School*; J. W. Jarnigan, "Some Things We Have Learned about Rural School Consolidation" (roundtable), *Bulletin of the Iowa State Teachers College*, no. 20 (June 1920).

57. "Regenerating the County School," *Nation* 88 (18 Mar. 1909): 271–72.

58. Benjamin J. Burris, "The County School System: How Organized and Administered," *State of Indiana Department of Public Instruction Educational Bulletin*, no. 24 (1924), 34. For other arguments on behalf of the county system, see Ellwood P. Cubberley, *Public School Administration: A Statement of the Fundamental Principles Underlying the Organization and Administration of Public Education* (New York: Houghton Mifflin, 1916); Ellwood P. Cubberley, *State School Administration: A Textbook of Principles* (Cambridge, MA: Riverside Press, 1927); Albert S. Cook, "Centralizing Tendencies in Educational Administration: The County as a Unit for Local Administration," *Educational Administration and Supervision* 4 (1918): 133–40; George W. Knorr, "Consolidated Rural Schools and Organization of a County System," *USDA Office of Experiment Stations Bulletin*, no. 282 (1910); A. G. Yaberg, "The County Unit," *Journal of Rural Education* 4 (Feb./Mar. 1925): 269–72; J. Harold Williams, "Reorganizing a County System of Rural Schools: Report of the Study of the Schools of San Mateo County, California," *USBE Bulletin*, no. 16 (1916); A. C. Monahan, "County-Unit Organization for the Administration of Rural Schools," in *USBE Bulletin*, no. 44 (1914).

59. Frank Bachman to Abraham Flexner, 10 Jan. 1923, GEB Papers, series 1.2, box 311, folder 3246; Hilda Hughes to Frank Bachman, 19 Mar. 1923, GEB Papers, series 1.2, box 311, folder 3250. For an overview of the project, see James H. Madison, "John D. Rockefeller's General Education Board and the Rural School Problem in the Midwest, 1900–1930," HEQ 24 (Summer 1984): 181–99.

60. Frank Bachman, "For the Attention of the Executive Committee" memo, 30 Aug. 1923, GEB Papers, series 1.2, box 311, folder 3250. On the plan of work and its results, see Frank Bachman, "County Unit Demonstration in Indiana" memo, 29 June 1923; Frank Bachman to Abraham Flexner, 1 June 1923; Frank Bachman, "Memorandum re: Indiana County Demonstrations," 30 Aug. 1923, GEB Papers, series 1.2, box 311, folder 3250; Hilda Hughes, "Lessons in Supervision of Rural Schools from the Indiana Experiment," *Journal of Rural Education* 5 (Sept./Oct. 1925): 39–50; "Indiana School Survey," in *Annual Report of the General Education Board 1922–1923* (New York: GEB, 1924), 24–27; "County Units in Indiana," in *Annual Report of the General Education Board 1923–1924* (New York: GEB, 1925), 26–27.

61. "The County Unit Not Accepted" (ESJ, Apr. 1923), in Carr, ed., *County Unit of School Administration*, 131.

62. "A County Unit of School Administration," *Bulletin of the Extension Division, Indiana University* (1926), in Carr, *County Unit of School Administration*, 144; Arp, *Rural Education and the Consolidated School*, 97–98, 26–27.

63. Monahan, "County-Unit Organization for the Administration of Rural Schools," 42–43. For some of these trends in county administration in the 1920s, see Cubberley, *State School Administration: A Textbook of Principles*; Richard E. Jaggers, *Administering the County School System* (New York: American Book Co., 1934); Julian E. Butterworth, *Principles of Rural School Administration* (New York: Macmillan Co., 1926);

Burris, "The County School System: How Organized and Administered"; Walter S. Deffenbaugh and Timon Covert, "School Administrative Units with Special Reference to the County Unit," *USBE Bulletin*, no. 34 (1933); Warren C. Coxe, "County School Administration," *Review of Educational Research* 4 (Oct. 1934): 417–25; William A. Cook, *Federal and State School Administration* (New York: Thomas Y. Crowell Company, 1927).

64. Foght, *The American Rural School*, 115.

65. On the political strength of federated women's organizations, see Elisabeth S. Clemens, *The People's Lobby: Organizational Innovation and the Rise of Interest Group Politics in the United States, 1890–1925* (Chicago: University of Chicago Press, 1997); Theda Skocpol, *Protecting Soldiers and Mothers: The Political Origins of Social Policy in the United States* (Cambridge, MA: Belknap Press, 1992).

66. Kern, *Among Country Schools*; Roy V. Scott, *The Reluctant Farmer: The Rise of Agricultural Extension to 1914* (Urbana: University of Illinois Press, 1970); Mary S. Hoffschwelle, *Rebuilding Rural Southern Community: Reformers, Schools, and Homes in Tennessee, 1900–1930* (Knoxville: University of Tennessee Press, 1998).

67. On philanthropies and national policymaking, see Eldon J. Eisenach, *The Lost Promise of Progressivism* (Lawrence: University Press of Kansas, 1994); Barry D. Karl and Stanley N. Katz, "The American Private Philanthropic Foundation and the Public Sphere 1890–1930," *Minerva* 19, no. 2 (1981): 236–70; Barry D. Karl and Stanley N. Katz, "Foundations and Ruling Class Elites," *Daedalus* 116, no. 1 (1987): 1–40; Robert H. Bremner, *American Philanthropy* (Chicago: University of Chicago Press, 1960); Judith Sealander, *Private Wealth and Public Life: Foundation Philanthropy and the Reshaping of American Social Policy from the Progressive Era to the New Deal* (Baltimore: Johns Hopkins Press, 1997); Ellen Condliffe Lagemann, "The Politics of Knowledge: The Carnegie Corporation and the Formulation of Public Policy," HEQ 27 (Summer 1987): 205–20; Ellen Condliffe Lagemann, *Private Power for the Public Good: A History of the Carnegie Foundation for the Advancement of Teaching*, 2nd ed. (New York: College Entrance Examination Board, 1999).

68. W. N. Sheats to Abraham Flexner, 12 Nov. 1917, GEB Papers, series 1.1, box 36, folder 326. On the role of philanthropies in building Southern capacity, see Ullin Whitney Leavell, *Philanthropy in Negro Education* (Nashville: George Peabody College for Teachers, 1930); Fosdick, *Adventure in Giving*; Hoffschwelle, *The Rosenwald Schools of the American South*; Malczewski, "Weak State, Stronger Schools."

69. Harlan Updegraff and William R. Hood, "A Comparison of Urban and Rural Common-School Statistics," *USBE Bulletin*, no. 21 (1912); Covert, "Rural School Consolidation"; Darrell Hevenor Smith, *The Bureau of Education: Its History, Activities, and Organization* (Baltimore: Johns Hopkins Press, 1923); Donald R. Warren, *To Enforce Education: A History of the Founding Years of the United States Office of Education* (Detroit: Wayne State University Press, 1974).

70. The USBE archives also has useful information on its organization, functions, and history including its efforts to foster standardized forms and reporting. See USBE Papers, file 100, boxes 1–5; file 500, box 49. Cook and Monahan's bulletins have been cited throughout this chapter.

Chapter Three

1. Payson Smith, "Limitations of State Control in Education," APNEA (1918): 490–97.
2. Ibid.
3. J. Joyner, C.P. Carey, et. al, "Centralizing Tendencies in Educational Administration: Discussion," APNEA (1918): 504–7.
4. Ibid.
5. On the power of a government "out of sight," see Brian Balogh, *A Government Out of Sight: The Mystery of National Authority in Nineteenth-Century America* (Cambridge: Cambridge University Press, 2009).
6. *State v. Haworth*, 23 N.E. 946 (Ind. 1890); Adam Shappiro, "Losing the Word: The Scopes Trial, Biology Textbooks, and the Evolution of Biblical Literalism" (Ph.D. diss., University of Chicago, 2007), chaps. 2–3; A. C. Monahan, "Free Textbooks and State Uniformity," *USBE Bulletin*, no. 36 (1915); David Tyack, Thomas James, and Aaron Benavot, *Law and the Shaping of Public Education, 1785–1954* (Madison: University of Wisconsin Press, 1987); William Clarence Webster, "Recent Centralizing Tendencies in State Educational Administration" (Ph.D. diss., Columbia University, 1897), chap. 6; Ward W. Keesecker, "Legislation Concerning Free Textbooks," *USBE Pamphlet*, no. 59 (1935); Clyde J. Tidwell, *State Control of Textbooks, with Special Reference to Florida* (New York: Teachers College, 1928); Wilford L. Coffey, *Legislative Enactments and Judicial Decisions Affecting the Adoption, Sale, and Use of Textbooks* (Detroit: self-published, 1931).
7. See, for example, John Lambert Flokstra, *The Legal Basis of School Organization and Administration in Wisconsin* (Ph.D. diss., University of Chicago, 1944); James Bartlett Edmonson, *The Legal and Constitutional Basis of a State School System: An Analysis of the Constitutional Provisions, Laws, and the Supreme Court Decisions Affecting the School System of the State of Michigan* (Bloomington, IL: Public School Publishing Co., 1926); Carl Graydon Leech, *The Constitutional and Legal Basis of Education in New Jersey* (Lancaster, PA: Science Press Printing Company, 1932).
8. On the role of law in releasing local energy, see James Willard Hurst, *Law and the Conditions of Freedom in the Nineteenth-Century United States* (Madison: University of Wisconsin Press, 1964); Morton J. Horowitz, *The Transformation of American Law, 1780–1860* (Cambridge, MA: Harvard University Press, 1979).
9. Carl F. Kaestle, *Pillars of the Republic: Common Schools and American Society, 1780–1860* (New York: Hill and Wang, 1983); Edgar Fuller and Jim B Pearson, eds., *Education in the States: Historical Development and Outlook* (Washington, D.C.: Council of Chief State School Officers, 1969). Fuller and Pearson's text, a substantial history of the state department of education in every state, is an invaluable resource and excellent starting point for any study of these agencies.
10. Forest Chester Ensign, *Compulsory School Attendance and Child Labor: A Study of the Historical Development of Regulations Compelling Attendance and Limiting the Labor of Children in a Selected Group of States* (Iowa City: Athens Press, 1921); William T. Harris, "Compulsory Attendance Laws in the United States," in *Report of the Commissioner of Education for the Year 1888–89* (Washington, D.C.: U.S. Government Print-

ing Office, 1891), 470–531; August William Weber, "State Control of Instruction: A Study of Centralization in Public Education" (Ph.D. diss., University of Wisconsin, 1911); Webster, "Recent Centralizing Tendencies in State Educational Administration"; Jonathan Zimmerman, *Distilling Democracy: Alcohol Education in America's Public Schools, 1880–1925* (Lawrence: University of Kansas Press, 1999).

11. *State v. Haworth*, 23 N.E. 946 (Ind. 1890).

12. *School Dist. No. 17 of Garfield County v. Zediker*, 47 P. 482 (Okla. 1896); *Kennedy v. Miller*, 97 Cal. 429, 32 P. 558 (Calif. 1893). See also *Attorney General v. Lowrey*, 131 Mich. 639, 92 N.W. 289 (Mich. 1902); *Ford v. School District of Kendall Borough*, 121 Pa. 543, 15 A. 812 (Pa. 1888); *State v. Hine*, 21 A. 1024 (Conn. 1890); *City of Louisville v. Board of Education of City of Louisville*, 157 S.W. 379 (Kent. 1913); Edward Claude Bolmeier, "Legal Basis of City and School Relationships" (Ph.D. diss., University of Chicago, 1936); Joachim Frederick Weltzin, *The Legal Authority of the American Public School as Developed by a Study of Liabilities to Damages* (Grand Forks, ND: Mid-West Book Concern, 1931).

13. *Leeper v. State*, 53 S.W. 962 (Tenn. 1899); *City of Louisville v. Commonwealth*, 121 S.W. 411 (Kent. 1909).

14. Charles Warren, "The Progressiveness of the United States Supreme Court," 13 *Columbia Law Review* 294 (1913); Charles Warren, "A Bulwark to the State Police Power—the United States Supreme Court," 13 *Columbia Law Review* 667 (1913). For historians on this point, see William R. Brock, *Investigation and Responsibility: Public Responsibility in the United States, 1865–1900* (Cambridge: Cambridge University Press, 1984); William J. Novak, "The Legal Origins of the Modern American State," in *Looking Back at Law's Century*, ed. Austin Sarat, Bryant Garth, and Robert A. Kagan (Ithaca: Cornell University Press, 2002), 249–83; Howard Gillman, *The Constitution Besieged: The Rise and Demise of Lochner Era Police Powers Jurisprudence* (Durham: Duke University Press, 1993).

15. Lee O. Garber, *Education as a Function of the State* (Minneapolis: Educational Test Bureau Inc., 1934); Newton Edwards, *The Courts and the Public Schools: The Legal Basis of School Organization and Administration* (Chicago: University of Chicago Press, 1933); H. H. Schroeder, *Legal Opinion on the Public School as a State Institution* (Bloomington, IN: Public School Publishing Company, 1928); Harry Raymond Trusler, *Essentials of School Law* (Milwaukee: Bruce Publishing Company, 1927).

16. Katherine M. Cook and A. C. Monahan, "Rural School Supervision," *USBE Bulletin*, no. 48 (1916); Edith A. Lathrup, "State Direction of Rural School Library Service," *USBE Bulletin*, no. 6 (1930); Edith A. Lathrop and Ward W. Keesecker, "Laws Affecting School Libraries," *USBE Bulletin*, no. 7 (1940).

17. "Virginia State Department of Public Instruction Score Card for Country Schools" (1915), GEB Papers, series 1.1, box 188, folder 1765; summary of reports of J. H. Binford [VA], 1 July 1915 to 1 Jan. 1916, GEB Papers, series 1.1, box 26, folder 230; Edith Lathrop, "The Improvement of Rural Schools by Standardization," *USBE RSL*, no. 32 (1925); A. D. Mueller, "Standardization of Rural Schools," *Journal of Rural Education* 3 (Jan. 1924): 225–31; William L. Sherman and Paul Theobald, "Progressive Era Rural Reform: Creating Standard Schools in the Midwest," *Journal of Research in*

Rural Education 17 (Fall 2001): 84–91. For additional examples, see W. D. Ross, *Standardization of Rural Schools in Kansas* (Topeka: State Printing Plant, 1917); Wyoming State Dept. of Education, "Standardization of Rural Schools: Score Cards, Minimal Requirements and Specifications," *Bulletin*, no. 2, series B (1919); Agnes Samuelsson and Jessie M. Parker, *Standardization of Rural Schools* (Des Moines: State of Iowa, 1928).

18. Julian E. Butterworth, *Problems in State High School Finance* (Yonkers-on-Hudson, NY: World Book Co., 1918), 31–37; William R. Hood, "Legal Provisions for Rural High Schools," *USBE Bulletin*, no. 40 (1924); Edwin R. Snyder, *The Legal Status of Rural High Schools in the United States* (New York: Press of Brandown Printing Company, 1909); Henry R. Corbett, "Free High Schools for Rural Pupils," SR 8 (June 1900): 335–63.

19. William H. Hand, "School Progress in South Carolina to the Year 1913," GEB Papers, series 1.1, box 128, folder 1174; William H. Hand to Wallace Buttrick, 12 Mar. 1907, GEB Papers, series 1.1, box 128, folder 1173; Bruce R. Payne, "Five Years of High School Progress in Virginia," GEB Papers, series 1.1, box 181, folder 1687.

20. Marc A. VanOverbeke, *The Standardization of American Schooling: Linking Secondary and Higher Education, 1870–1910* (New York: Palgrave Macmillan, 2008); Calvin Olin Davis, *A History of the North Central Association of Colleges and Secondary Schools, 1895–1945* (Ann Arbor: North Central Association of Colleges and Secondary Schools, 1945); Edward A. Krug, *The Shaping of the American High School* (New York: Harper & Row, 1964).

21. Carl A. Jessen and W. T. Spanton, "Supervision of Secondary Education as a Function of State Departments of Education," *USBE Bulletin*, no. 6, monograph no. 9 (1940): 2–3.

22. Wallace Buttrick to Edwin A. Alderman, 1 Apr. 1905, GEB Papers, series 1.1, box 180, folder 1680; Bruce R. Payne, "Secondary Education in Virginia: Report for the Month of April [1906]," GEB Papers, series 1.1, box 180, folder 1653; Charles Maphis to E. C. Sage, 15 Dec. 1914, GEB Papers, series 1.1, box 180, folder 1686. Detailed monthly reports of the professors of secondary education in Virginia and other states can be found in the GEB archives.

23. T. C. Engum, "Minnesota," in *Education in the States*, 626–27; John Levi Manahan, "State Classification and Standardization of High Schools" (Ph.D. diss., Harvard University, 1918); C. Ross Dean, "The Development of State Control of Secondary Education in Indiana" (Ph.D. diss., Indiana University, 1947); James W. Underwood, "A History of Secondary School Accreditation in the State of Missouri" (Ed.D. diss., University of Missouri-Columbia, 1987); J. D. Falls, *Job Analysis of State High School Supervisor in the United States* (Nashville: George Peabody College, 1926).

24. James S. Cookston et al., "Louisiana," in *Education in the States*, 495. On high school standardization more generally, see Henry H. Hill, "State High School Standardization," *Bulletin of the Bureau of School Service* 2 (University of Kentucky,), no. 3 (Mar. 1930); Ward Keesecker, "Legal and Regulatory Provisions Affecting Secondary Education," *USBE Bulletin*, no. 17 National Survey of Secondary Education, monograph no. 9 (1932); Fred Engledhardt, William H. Zeigel, and Roy O. Billett, "Administration and Supervision," *USBE Bulletin*, no. 17 National Survey of Secondary Educa-

tion, monograph no. 11 (1932); Oliver Leonard Troxel, *State Control of Secondary Education* (Baltimore: Warwick and York, 1928); Willlard Walter Patty, *Legal Basis of the Public Secondary Education Program of the United States* (Fred A. Williams, 1927); Emmett Ellis, *An Evaluation of State Programs of Secondary Education* (Nashville: George Peabody College for Teachers, 1932).

25. William B. Guitteau, "What the War Should Do for Our Methods in Civics and Economics," APNEA (1919): 553.

26. For discussions of the war's educational lessons, see Christopher Capozzola, *Uncle Sam Wants You: World War I and the Making of the Modern American Citizen* (New York: Oxford University Press, 2008); Douglas J. Slawson, *The Department of Education Battle, 1918–1932: Public Schools, Catholic Schools, and the Social Order* (Notre Dame: University of Notre Dame, 2005), 6–8; Ernest Carroll Moore, *What the War Teaches about Education and Other Papers and Addresses* (New York: Macmillam Co., 1919); John A. H. Keith and William C. Bagley, *The Nation and the Schools: A Study in the Application of the Principle of Federal Aid to Education in the United States* (New York: Macmillan Co., 1920); Charles W. Eliot, "Defects in American Education Revealed by the War," SS 9 (1919): 1–10; P. P. Claxton, "Education for the Establishment of a Democracy in the World," APNEA (1919): 81–88; Frank E. Spaulding, "Educating the Nation," *Atlantic Monthly* 125 (Apr. 1920): 528–38.

27. "The Towner-Sterling Bill: An Analysis of the Provisions of the Bill; a Discussion of the Principles and Policies Involved; and a Presentation of the Facts and Figures Relating to the Subject," Legislative Commission series no. 3 (Washington, D.C.: NEA, 1922): 51; I. L. Kandell, "Federal Aid to Education," NR 15 (June 1918): 252–53; Will C. Wood, "New Occasions and New Duties," SS 10 (Nov. 1919): 624.

28. Keith and Bagley, *The Nation and the Schools*, 124–25.

29. Hoke Smith quoted in Aaron H. Ulm, "National Education and Its Pilot," *Forum* 61 (Mar. 1919): 292–93; E. C. Hartwell, "Financing the Public Schools," APNEA (1918): 606.

30. Slawson, *The Department of Education Battle, 1918–1932*; Lynn Dumenil, "'The Insatiable Maw of Bureaucracy': Antistatism and Education Reform in the 1920s," JAH 77 (Sept. 1990): 499–524; Gilbert E. Smith, *The Limits of Reform: Politics and Federal Aid to Education, 1937–1950* (New York: Garland Publishing Inc., 1982).

31. William Bagley, "A Federal Department of Education," APNEA (1920): 449; John K. Norton, *The Ability of States to Support Education* (Washington, D.C.: NEA, 1926), 71; George D. Strayer, "Financing Education on a Scientific Basis," SS 21 (1925): 247.

32. Paul H. Douglas, "Federal Aid for Education," ER 64 (June 1922): 41–42. See also William C. Bagley, "Federal Aid for Public Schools," APNEA (1921): 618; J. H. Beveridge et Al., "A National Program for Education," APNEA (1919): 509–24; George D. Strayer, "A National Program for Education: A Final Report of the Commission on the Emergency in Education," APNEA (1920): 41–48; Horace Mann Towner, "National Aid for Education," APNEA (1921): 786–95; Ellwood P. Cubberley, "The American School Program from the Standpoint of the Nation," APNEA (1923): 180–88; William C. Bagley, "How Shall Opportunity Be Equalized?," *NEA Journal* (Dec. 1924): 315–16; George D. Strayer, "What Shall Be the Nation's Part?," APNEA (1924):

254–65; Elmer H. Staffelbach, "Some Facts Concerning the Need of Federal Aid in Support of Public Education," SS 21 (Jan. 1925): 147–52; Mabel V. Wilson, "Federal Aid to Education," APNEA (1925): 388–94; Austin F. MacDonald, "Federal Subsidies for Education," AAAPSS 129 (Jan. 1927): 102–5.

33. Slawson, *The Department of Education Battle, 1918–1932*; Dumenil, "'The Insatiable Maw of Bureaucracy'"; David B. Tyack, "The Perils of Pluralism: The Background of the Pierce Case," AHR 74 (Oct. 1968): 74–98.

34. Edward A. Fitzpatrick, "Federalization and State Educational Bankruptcy," ER 63 (1922): 402–3; Alexander Inglis, "The Need of a National Organization for Educational Service," APNEA (1922): 1326. See also H. A. Hollister, "Why and How Should We Federalize Education?," SS 10 (Nov. 1919): 591–94; Rufus S. Tucker, "The Financial Argument for Federal Aid to Education: A Criticism," *American Economics Review* 13 (Mar. 1923): 34–47; "Opposition to the Federal Education Bill," SS 19 (Apr. 1924): 457–58.

35. "Documents on the Towner-Sterling Bill," SS 16 (July 1922): 133, 137; W. P. Burris, "A Federal Department of Education," APNEA (1920): 448–49.

36. James H. Ryan, "Dangers of Federalized Education," *Current History Magazine* (Sept. 1924): 926–31; Robert H. Mahoney, "The Federal Government and Education: An Examination of the Federalization Movement in Light of the Educational Demands of a Democracy" (Ph.D. diss., Catholic University of America, 1922), 70.

37. "A Manual of Educational Legislation: For the Guidance of Committees on Education in the State Legislatures," *USBE Bulletin*, no. 4 (1919); "A Manual of Educational Legislation: For the Guidance of Committees on Education in the State Legislatures," *USBE Bulletin*, no. 36 (1924).

38. On early equalization and aid to weak districts, see Elwood P. Cubberley, *School Funds and Their Apportionment* (New York: Teachers College, 1906); Theodore L. Mac-Dowell, "State versus Local Control of Elementary Education (Finance)," *USBE Bulletin*, no. 22 (1915); J. F. Abel, "State Aid to Weak Districts," USBE RSL, no. 7 (Sept. 1922). For major postwar research studies, see George D. Strayer and Robert Murray Haig, *The Financing of Education in the State of New York*, Educational Finance Inquiry, vol. 1 (New York: Macmillan Co, 1923); Fletcher H. Swift, *Studies in Public School Finance*, 4 vols. (Minneapolis: University of Minnesota, 1922–25); Paul R. Mort, *The Measurement of Educational Need: A Basis for Distributing State Aid* (New York: Teachers College, 1924); Paul R. Mort, *State Support for Public Schools*, School Administration series (New York: Teachers College, 1926); Paul Mort, *State Support for Public Education*, National Survey of School Finance (Washington, D.C.: American Council on Education, 1933); A. W. Schmidt, *Development of a State's Minimum Educational Program* (New York: Teachers College, 1932); Leslie L. Chism, *The Economic Ability of the States to Finance Public Schools* (New York: Teachers College, 1936); Mabel Newcomer, *An Index of the Tax-Paying Ability of State and Local Governments* (New York: Teachers College, 1935).

39. Fletcher Swift, "State Policies in Public School Finance," *USBE Bulletin*, no. 7 (1922): 13–15; Gordon G. Singleton, *State Responsibility for the Support of Education in Georgia* (New York: Teachers College, 1925), 36. See also Harlan Updegraff, *Rural School Sur-*

vey of New York State: Financial Support (Ithaca: Joint Committee on Rural Schools, 1922); Fred Wilson Morrison, *Equalization of the Financial Burden of Education among Counties in North Carolina: A Study of the Equalizing Fund* (New York: Teachers College, 1925); Joseph Kindred Long, *Trends in the Equalization of Educational Opportunity in North Carolina* (Nashville: George Peabody College for Teachers, 1936).

40. Paul R. Mort, "Equalization of Educational Opportunity," *Journal of Educational Research* 13 (Feb. 1926): 90; T. H. Harris, "The State's Financial Responsibility to the Public Schools," APNEA (1925): 549–54.

41. Samuel Harrison McGuire, *Trends in Principles and Practices of Equalization of Educational Opportunity* (Nashville: George Peabody College for Teachers, 1934), 24–28.

42. Mort, *State Support for Public Education*, 151; M. P. Shawkey, "Financial Support of the Public Schools," SS 1 (Mar. 1915): 361.

43. Nolen Meaders Irby, *A Program for the Equalization of Educational Opportunities in the State of Arkansas* (Nashville: George Peabody College for Teachers, 1930); Ambrose Caliver, "Availability of Education to Negroes in Rural Communities," *USBE Bulletin*, no. 12 (1935); Ambrose Caliver, "Fundamentals in the Education of the Negroes," *USBE Bulletin*, no. 6 (1935); Doxey A. Wilkerson, "Special Problems in Negro Education," staff study, no. 12, Advisory Committee on Education (Washington, D.C.: U.S. Government Printing Office, 1939); Paula S. Fass, "Without Design: Education Policy in the New Deal," *American Journal of Education* 91, no. 1 (Nov. 1982): 36–64.

44. McGuire, *Trends in Principles and Practices of Equalization*, 52; Robert Moyer and David W. Zimmerman, "Maryland," in *Education in the States*, 545.

45. Wayne W. Soper, "Development of State Support of Education in New York State," *University of the State of New York Bulletin* 1019 (1933); George Dayton Strayer Jr., *Centralizing Tendencies in the Administration of Public Education: A Study of Legislation for Schools in North Carolina, Maryland, and New York since 1900* (New York: Teachers College, 1934).

46. Timon Covert, "State Provisions for Equalizing the Cost of Public Education," *USBE Bulletin*, no. 4 (1936); Fletcher H. Swift and Bruce Lewis Zimmerman, "State School Taxes and Their Apportionment," *USBE Bulletin*, no. 29 (1928); Fletcher H. Swift, *Federal and State Policies in Public School Finance in the United States* (Boston: Ginn & Co., 1931), 252–53.

47. On the fiscal crisis, see David Tyack, Robert Lowe, and Elisabeth Hansot, *Public Schools in Hard Times: The Great Depression and Recent Years* (Cambridge, MA: Harvard University Press, 1984); "Forum on the Emergency in the States," APNEA (1932): 151–62; William John Cooper, "The Crisis in Education: Are We Taking It Out on Our Children?," *Scribner's Magazine* 93 (Feb. 1933): 129–31; Timon Covert, "Financial Situation in the Public Schools," *School Life* (June 1936): 283–84.

48. Covert, "State Provisions for Equalizing," 18–21, 37–40, 4–5; "State Support of Schools," SS (Nov. 1932): 701; "An Ohio Equalization Fund," SS 36 (Dec. 1932): 827–28; R. Merele Eyman and Earl Metz, "Ohio," in *Education in the States*, 955–56.

49. Newton Edwards and Herman G. Richey, *The Extent of Equalization Secured through State School Funds*, staff study, no. 6, Prepared for the Advisory Committee on Education (Washington, D.C.: U.S. Government Printing Office, 1938); Ward W.

Keesecker, "Nation-Wide Trends in State Legislation," *School Life* (Oct. 1936): 39; Betty K. Whitelaw, "State Centralization: A Trend in the Administration of Public Elementary and Secondary Education, 1930–1940" (M.A. thesis, University of Chicago, 1940), chap. 3. See also Ambrose Perrin, "The Administration of Equalization Funds in States Having Recent Administrative Legislation," ESJ 33 (Dec. 1932): 286–92; "New Sources of Revenue for School Support," ESJ 34 (Apr. 1934): 568–70; E. C. Bolmeier, "Recent Tendencies in Taxation for Public-School Support," ESJ 35 (Feb. 1935): 415–22.

50. Tyack, Lowe, and Hansot, *Public Schools in Hard Times*; Smith, *The Limits of Reform*.

51. John K. Norton, "A National Outlook on Education," APNEA (1934): 664; William F. Russell, "Federal Financing of Education," SS 38 (Aug. 1933): 232. See also Alfred P. James, "Federal Aid for Public Schools," SS 39 (Feb. 1934): 225–31; Jesse B. Sears, "Federal Support for Public Schools," SS 40 (Oct. 1934): 433–37; George F. Zook, "Federal Aid to Education," SS 40 (Jul. 1934): 41–48; Ernest Lundeen, "Federal Aid to Meet the Emergency in Education," SS 42 (May 1935): 177–86; Edward P. Costigan, "Education and the General Welfare," APNEA (1935): 73–83; Charles H. Judd, "Federal Support of Public Education," ESJ 36 (Mar. 1936): 497–512; Paul R. Mort, "Symposium on Federal Support of Public Education," APNEA (1936): 401–12; Agnes Samuelson, "Rural Education and the National Welfare," SS 43 (Feb. 1936): 273–78; Newton Edwards, *Equal Educational Opportunity for Youth: A National Responsibility*, Report to American Youth Commission (Washington, D.C.: American Council on Education, 1939).

52. William F. Russell, "Federal Aid—Boon or Bane?," SS 39 (Feb. 1934): 289; R. A. Kent, "The Implications of Federal Aid to Education," SS (Sept. 1934): 342; "Federal Control of Education," SS 46 (Oct. 1937): 443. For other arguments against federal aid, see John J. Tigert, "Federal Aid for the Schools," SS 40 (Jul. 1934): 98–100; S. M. Brownell, "Shall It Be 'Yes' or 'No' on Federal Aid?," SS 49 (May 1939): 668–71. Several debate handbooks collected documents on both sides of the debate. See Bower Aly, ed., *Equalizing Educational Opportunity by Means of Federal Aid to Education: The Debate Handbook, 1934–1935* (Columbia, MO: Herald-Statesman Pub. Co., 1934); E. C. Buehler, ed., *Federal Aid for Education,* High School Debater's Help Book (New York: Noble and Noble, 1934); Julia E. Johnson, ed., *Federal Aid for Education,* Reference Shelf, vol. 14 (New York: H. W. Wilson Co., 1941); Helen M. Muller, ed., *Federal Aid for the Equalization of Educational Opportunity,* Reference Shelf, vol. 9 (New York: H. W. Wilson, 1934).

53. Eugene Alfred Bishop, *The Development of a State School System: New Hampshire* (New York: Teachers College, 1930); *Report of the State Board of Education* [New Hampshire] (1919–20); "School Progress in New Hampshire in Five Years," New Hampshire State Board of Education, institute circular, no. 109 (1924); "An Educational Study of Alabama," *USBE Bulletin*, no. 41 (1919); Austin R. Meadows, "Alabama," in *Education in the States*, 5–6.

54. Robert F. Will and Louise R. Murphy, "State School Administration: 1900–1957; Reports of Major Surveys and Studies," *USBE Circular*, no. 580 (1958); Leonard P. Ayres, *An Index Number for State School Systems* (New York: Russell Sage Foundation,

1920); Harlan Updegraff and Leroy A. King, *A Survey of the Fiscal Policies of the State of Pennsylvania in the Field of Education* (1922). Correspondence and findings from GEB surveys of Maryland (1916), Delaware (1919), North Carolina (1920–21), Kentucky (1921), Indiana (1923), and Florida (1926) are located in the GEB archives.

55. Edward Franklin Buchner, "Educational Surveys," *USBE Bulletin*, no. 17 (1923); W. S. Deffenbaugh, "School Administration in State Educational Survey Reports," *USBE Bulletin*, no 35 (1930); "State Leadership in Education," *Educational Leadership: Progress and Possibilities*, eleventh yearbook, NEA Department of Superintendence (1933).

56. Abraham Flexner to Frank Bachman, 28 Mar. 1919, GEB Papers, series 1.2, box 308, folder 3219; Frank Bachman to Abraham Flexner, 23 Apr. 1921, GEB Papers, series 1.2, box 308, folder 3220; *Public Education in Delaware: A Report to the Public School Commission of Delaware with an Appendix Containing the New School Code* (New York: General Education Board, 1919); Paul H. Johnston, "Delaware," in *Education in the States*, 205–31; *Annual Report of the State Board of Education* [Delaware] (1919–20); *Public Education in Indiana* (New York: General Education Board, 1923); Frank Bachman to Abraham Flexner, 20 Jan. 1923, GEB Papers, series 1.2, box 311, folder 3246; L. P. Benezet to Bachman, GEB Papers, series 1.2, box 311, folder 3246; Charles M. Curry to Bachman, 15 Feb. 1923, GEB Papers, series 1.2, box 311, folder 3246.

57. Katherine Amelia Frederic, *State Personnel Administration: With Special Reference to Departments of Education* (Washington, D.C.: U.S. Government Printing Office, 1940).

58. NEA Research Division, "Staffs and Salaries in State Departments of Education," *Studies in State School Administration*, no. 9 (Mar. 1931): 5–6; Frederic, *State Personnel Administration*, 62–65; Raymond B. Fosdick, *Adventure in Giving: The Story of the General Education Board* (New York: Harper & Row Publishers, 1962); "Divisions of Schoolhouse Planning" in *Annual Report of the General Education Board, 1924–1925*, 20–21; "Divisions of Information and Statistics and Divisions of School Buildings," *Annual Report of the General Education Board, 1925–1926*, 33–34.

59. Jessen and Spanton, "Supervision of Secondary Education," 7; H. Edgar Williams, "Colorado," in *Education in the States*, 145–76.

60. Doak S. Campbell, Frederick H. Bair, and Oswald L. Harvey, "Educational Activities of the Works Progress Administration," Advisory Committee on Education, staff study, no. 14 (Washington, D.C.: U.S. Government Printing Office, 1939); *Annual Report of the Director of Education, 1933–1935* [Ohio], 110–17; Fendall R. Ellis et al., "Virginia," in *Education in the States*, 1301; Whitelaw, "State Centralization," chap. 4; Harry Zeitlin, "Federal Relations in American Education, 1933–1943: A Study of New Deal Efforts and Innovation" (Ph.D. diss., Columbia University, 1958).

61. On organization and functions of state departments, see Henry E. Schrammel, *The Organization of State Departments of Education*, Bureau of Educational Research, monograph no. 6 (Columbus: Ohio State University Press, 1926), 49; Arthur Wesley Ferguson, "Professional Staff of State Departments of Education," *USBE Bulletin*, no. 17 (1925): 6–7; L. A. Kalbach and A. O. Neal, "Organization of State Departments of Education," *USBE Bulletin*, no. 46 (1920): 39–48; Herbert M. Carle, "Organization,

Housing, and Staffing of State Departments of Education, 1923–4," *USBE Statistical Circular*, no. 5 (1925): 8–9; Ward G. Reeder, "The Chief State School Officer," *USBE Bulletin*, no. 5 (1924); Katherine M. Cook, "Supervision of Instruction as a Function of State Departments of Education," *USBE Bulletin*, no. 6 Studies of State Departments of Education, monograph no. 7 (1940).

62. Smith, "Limitations of State Control in Education," 504.

63. William A. Cook, *Federal and State School Administration* (New York: Thomas Y. Crowell Company, 1927), 140; Ellwood P. Cubberley, *State School Administration: A Textbook of Principles* (Cambridge, MA: Riverside Press, 1927), 715; Cook, *Federal and State School Administration*, 140. See also Fred Engelhardt, *Public School Organization and Administration* (Boston: Ginn and Company, 1931); Clyde Milton Hill, ed., *Educational Progress and School Administration* (New Haven: Yale University Press, 1936); Samuel Train Dutton and David Snedden, *The Administration of Public Education in the United States*, rev. ed. (New York: Macmillan Company, 1916); Ralph Hewett Smith, "The Legal Basis of Educational Control: A Study of Centralization" (Ph.D. diss., University of Kansas, 1933); Whitelaw, "State Centralization"; Charles Haywood Gilmore, "Distribution among State Agencies of the Control of Public Education" (Ph.D. diss., George Peabody College for Teachers, 1938); Lewis Cass Tidball, "A Study of the Functions of State Departments of Education" (Ph.D. diss., University of Washington, 1930); Paul R. Mort and Francis G. Cornell, *Adaptability of Public School Systems* (New York: Teachers College, 1938); William M. Alexander, *State Leadership in Improving Instruction: A Study of the Leadership Function of State Education Departments, with Special Reference to Louisiana, Tennessee, and Virginia* (New York: Teachers College, 1940).

64. David Tyack and Michael Berkowitz, "The Man Nobody Liked: Toward a Social History of the Truant Officer, 1840–1940," *American Quarterly* 29 (Spring 1977): 31–54; Ensign, *Compulsory Attendance and Child Labor*; Walter I. Trattner, *Crusade for the Children: A History of the National Child Labor Committee and Child Labor Reform in America* (Chicago: Quadrangle Books, 1970); Grace Abbott, ed., *The Child and the State*, vol. 1, *Legal Status in the Family, Apprenticeship and Child Labor* (Chicago: University of Chicago Press, 1938).

65. F. V. Bermejo, *The School Attendance Service in American Cities* (Menasha, WI: George Banta Publishing Company, 1923); Frederick Earle Emmons, *City School Attendance Service* (New York: Teachers College, 1926); Whittier Lorenz Hanson, *The Costs of Compulsory Attendance Service in the State of New York and Some Factors Affecting Cost* (New York: Teachers College, 1924)

66. Ward W. Keesecker, "Laws Relating to Compulsory Education," *USBE Bulletin*, no. 20 (1928); W. S. Deffenbaugh et al., "Compulsory School Attendance," *USBE Bulletin*, no. 2 (1914); W. S. Deffenbaugh and Ward Keesecker, "Compulsory School Attendance Laws and Their Administration" *USBE Bulletin*, no. 4 (1935); Maris M. Proffitt and David Segel, "School Census, Compulsory Education, Child Labor: State Laws and Regulations," *USBE Bulletin*, no. 1 (1945).

67. David Segel and Maris Proffitt, "Pupil Personnel Services as a Function of State Departments of Education," *USBE Bulletin*, no. 6, monograph no. 5 (1940).

68. "Home and School Visitor—A Manual," *Pennsylvania State Department of Education Bulletin*, no. 72 (1939), and "School Census and Attendance Administration," *Education Bulletin* 2, no. 7 (Sept. 1934), quoted in Segel and Proffit, "Pupil Personnel Services," 17, 21–22; Timon Covert, "Financing of Schools as a Function of State Departments of Education," *USBE Bulletin*, no. 6, monograph no. 3 (1940).

69. Irvin Simon Noall, "Administration of Compulsory School Attendance" (Ed.D. diss., University of California, 1935), 149–50; "Survey of Education in Utah," *USBE Bulletin*, no. 18 (1926); "Utah's Educational Program" (Utah Educational Campaign Committee, 1920); John Clifton Moffitt, "The Development of Centralizing Tendencies in Educational Organization and Administration in Utah" (Ph.D. diss, University of Chicago, 1940).

70. Noall, "Administration of Compulsory School Attendance."

71. George H. Chatfield, "What Provisions Should a Compulsory-Education Law Include from the Viewpoint of Aim and the Viewpoint of Enforcement," APNEA (1917): 828; John Leslie Lawing, *Standards for State and Local Compulsory School Attendance Service* (Maryville, MO: Forum Print Shop, 1934).

72. Noall, "Administration of Compulsory School Attendance"; Richard Watson Cooper and Hermann Cooper, *Negro School Attendance in Delaware: A Report to the State Board of Education of Delaware*, Bureau of Education, Service Citizens of Delaware (Newark: University of Delaware Press, 1923).

Chapter Four

1. *Commonwealth v. Roberts*, 59 Mass. 372, 34 N.E. 402 (1893) (italics mine).

2. *Stephens v. Bongart*, 15 N.J. Misc. 80, 189 A. 131 (1937) (italics mine).

3. The literature on Progressive Era child welfare is extensive. See Anthony M. Platt, *The Child Savers: The Invention of Delinquency* (Chicago: University of Chicago Press, 1969); Davis S. Tanenhaus, *Juvenile Justice in the Making* (New York: Oxford University Press, 2004); Judith Sealander, *The Failed Century of the Child: Governing America's Young in the Twentieth Century* (Cambridge: Cambridge University Press, 2003); Michael Grossberg, "Changing Conceptions of Child Welfare in the United States, 1820–1935," in *A Century of Juvenile Justice*, ed. Margaret K. Rosenheim et al. (Chicago: University of Chicago Press, 2002), 3–41; Steven L. Scholossman, *Love and the American Delinquent: The Theory and Practice of 'Progressive' Juvenile Justice, 1825–1920* (Chicago: University of Chicago Press, 1977); Susan Tiffin, *In Whose Best Interest?: Child Welfare Reform in the Progressive Era* (Westport, CT: Greenwood Press, 1982); Kriste Lindenmeyer, *"A Right to Childhood": The U.S. Children's Bureau and Child Welfare, 1912–46* (Urbana: University of Illinois Press, 1997).

4. Christopher G. Tiedeman, *A Treatise on the Limitations of Police Power in the United States* (St. Louis: F. H. Thomas Law Book Co., 1886), 561. On the connections between the household and republican liberty, see Stephanie McCurry, *Masters of Small Worlds: Yeoman Households, Gender Relations, and the Political Culture of the Antebellum South Carolina Low Country* (New York: Oxford University Press, 1995); Laura F. Edwards, *Gendered Strife and Confusion: The Political Culture of Reconstruction*

(Urbana: University of Illinois Press, 1997); Carole Shammas, *A History of Household Government in America* (Charlottesville: University of Virginia Press, 2002); Michael Grossberg, *Governing the Hearth: Law and Family in Nineteenth-Century America* (Chapel Hill: University of North Carolina Press, 1985).

5. *Board of Education v. Purse*, 28. S.E. 896 (Ga. 1897). On parents' duties under common law as moral rather than legal responsibilities and modifications to common law, see also *Stephenson v. Hall*, 14 Barb. 222 (N.Y. 1852); *People v. Olmstead*, 27 Barb. 9 (N.Y. 1857); *Bennet v. Bennet*, 1860 WL 3110 (N.J. Ch.) (1860); *Huke v. Huke*, 1891 WL 2545 (Mo. App., 1891); Harvey Cortland Voorhees, *The Law of the Public School System of the United States* (Boston: Little, Brown & Co., 1916), chap. 1.

6. *Morrow v. Wood*, 1874 WL 3360 (Wis. 1874). See also *Rulison v. Post*, 1875 WL 8690 (Ill. 1875); *Trustees of Schools v. People ex rel. Martin Van Allen*, 1877 WL 9862 (Ill. 1877); *State ex rel. Sheibley v. School District No. 1 of Dixon County*, 48 N.W. 393 (Neb. 1891). Courts were not unanimous in upholding a parental right to select studies; some courts ruled that it interfered with the good government of the school. For example, *Kidder v. Chellis*, 1879 WL 4275 (N.H. 1879); *State ex rel. Andrews v. Webber*, 8 N.E. 708 (Ind. 1886); Otto Templar Hamilton, *The Courts and the Curriculum* (New York: Teachers' College, 1927).

7. Ward M. McAfee, *Religion, Race, and Reconstruction: The Public School in the Politics of the 1870s* (Albany: State University of New York Press, 1998).

8. Birdsey Grant Northrop, "Obligatory Education," *Annual Report of the Board of Education of the State of Connecticut* (1872): 29–48.

9. Thomas Conway, report (1871) quoted in Samuel Fallows, "Special Report on Compulsory Education," *Annual Report of the Superintendent of Public Instruction of the State of Wisconsin* (1873): 56; Newton Bateman, *Biennial Report* (1871–72), quoted in Fallows, "Special Report on Compulsory Education," 51. On the turn to state law, see, for example, Morton Keller, *Affairs of State: Public Life in Late Nineteenth Century America* (Cambridge, MA: Harvard University Press, 1977); William J. Novak, *The People's Welfare: Law and Regulation in Nineteenth-Century America*. (Chapel Hill: University of North Carolina Press), 1996.

10. Richard Edwards, *Eighteenth Biennial Report of the Superintendent of Public Instruction of the State of Illinois* (1888–90): 85; Z. F. Smith, *Annual Report* (1871), quoted in Fallows, "Special Report on Compulsory Education," 55. On *parens patriae* and the changing legal rights of households, see Florence Kelley, "On Some Changes in the Legal Status of the Child since Blackstone," *International Review* 13 (Aug. 1882): 83–98; David Dudley Field, "The Child and the State," *Forum* 1 (Apr. 1886): 105–13; Helen Clarke, *Social Legislation: American Laws Dealing with Family, Child, and Dependent* (New York: Appleton-Century Co., 1940); Peter W. Bardaglio, *Reconstructing the Household: Families, Sex, and the Law in the Nineteenth-Century South* (Chapel Hill: University of North Carolina Press, 1995); Mary Ann Mason, *From Father's Property to Children's Rights: The History of Child Custody in the United States* (New York: Columbia University Press, 1994); David Spinoza Tanenhaus, "Policing the Child: Juvenile Justice in Chicago, 1870–1925" (Ph.D. diss., University of Chicago, 1997), chap. 2; Michael Grossberg, "'A Protected Childhood': The Emergence of Child Protection in

America," in *American Public Life and the Historical Imagination*, ed. Wendy Gambler, Michael Grossberg, and Hendrick Hartog (Notre Dame: University of Notre Dame Press, 2003), 213–39.

11. M. A. Newell, *Annual Report* (1872), quoted in Fallows, "Special Report on Compulsory Education," 57.

12. Oscar H. Cooper, "Compulsory Laws and Their Enforcement," APNEA (1890): 186–91, 191; Zachary Montgomery, *The Poison Fountain; or, Anti-Parental Education* (San Francisco: self-published, 1878), 13.

13. N. C. Dougherty, "Recent Legislation upon Compulsory Education in Illinois and Wisconsin," APNEA (1891): 396–97; John MacDonald in "Discussion," APNEA (1891): 402; E. M. Winston, "The School Controversy in Illinois," *Forum* 12 (Oct. 1891): 213; J. P. Meibohm, "Voice of the People: Compulsory School Laws," NYT, 25 May 1890, 11; J. D. Roth, "Letter to the Editor: Lutherans and the Schools," NYT, 1 June 1890, 11. See also William Villas, "The Bennett Law in Wisconsin," *Forum* 12 (Oct. 1891): 198; "The Schools in Politics," NYT, 26 May 1890, 1; James C. Carper and Thomas C. Hunt, *The Dissenting Tradition in American Education* (New York: Peter Lang, 2007), chap. 4; Lloyd P. Jorgenson, *The State and the Non-Public School, 1825–1925* (Columbia: University of Missouri Press, 1987).

14. William T. Harris, "Compulsory Attendance Laws in the United States," in *Report of the Commissioner of Education for the Year 1888–89* (Washington, D.C.: U.S. Government Printing Office, 1891), 470–531; Aaron Gove, "Discussion," APNEA (1890): 192. On difficulties of enforcement, see also "Report," public document no. 2, in *59th Annual Report of the Board of Education* (Mass., 1894–95): 529–601; George Walton, "Report," in *50th Annual Report of the Board of Education* (Mass., 1885–86): 163–85; "Attendance" and "Report of the Agent of the Board," in *Annual Report of the Board of Education of the State of Connecticut* (1885–86): 31–70; "Compulsory Education," report prepared for the Public Education Association and Civic Club (Philadelphia, 1898); "Compulsory Education," NYT, 6 Mar. 1875, 4; "The Board of Education, Condition of the Public Schools," NYT, 8 Feb. 1877, 2; "Compulsory Education," NYT, 1 Nov. 1878, 4.

15. Harris, "Compulsory Attendance Laws in the United States," 523–24.

16. "Second Annual Report of the Factory Inspectors of Illinois, 1894," in *The Child and the State* vol. 1, *Legal Status in the Family, Apprenticeship and Child Labor*, ed. Grace Abbott (Chicago: University of Chicago Press, 1938), 423; "Fourth Annual Report of the Factory Inspectors of Illinois, 1896," in Edith Abbott and Sophonisba P. Breckenridge, *Truancy and Non-Attendance in the Chicago Schools: A Study of the Social Aspects of the Compulsory Education and Child Labor Legislation of Illinois* (Chicago: University of Chicago Press, 1917), 426; "The Child Labor Law in New Jersey," NYT, 10 July 1883, 5; Florence Kelley, "An Effective Child-Labor Law: A Program for the Current Decade," AAAPSS 21 (May 1903): 96–103. On the child labor reform movement, see Raymond G. Fuller, *Child Labor and the Constitution* (New York: Thomas Y. Crowell Co., 1923); "White Child Slavery: A Symposium," *Arena* 1 (Apr. 1890): 589–603; AAAPSS 25, Child Labor (May 1905): 1–232; AAAPSS 27, Child Labor (Mar. 1906): 1–141; AAAPSS 29, Child Labor (Jan. 1907): 1–243; AAAPSS 32, supp. 22: Child

Labor and Social Progress (July 1908): 1–177; Edna D. Bullock, ed., *Selected Articles on Child Labor*, 2nd ed. (New York: H. W. Wilson Co., 1915); John Spargo, *The Bitter Cry of the Children* (New York: Macmillan Co., 1906); Mrs. John Van Vorst, *The Cry of the Children: A Study of Child-Labor* (New York: Moffat, Yard and Co., 1908); Julia E. Johnson, ed., *Selected Articles on Child Labor*, Handbook Series (New York: H. W. Wilson Co., 1925); Hugh D. Hindman, *Child Labor: An American History* (Armonk, NY: Sharpe Publishers, 2002); Walter I. Trattner, *Crusade for the Children: A History of the National Child Labor Committee and Child Labor Reform in America* (Chicago: Quadrangle Books, 1970); Sam Beal Barton, "Factors and Forces in the Movement for the Abolition of Child Labor in the United States" (Ph.D. diss., University of Texas, 1938); Elizabeth H. Davidson, *Child Labor Legislation in the Southern Textile States* (Chapel Hill: University of North Carolina Press, 1939).

17. Jeremy P. Felt, *Hostages of Fortune: Child Labor Reform in New York State* (Syracuse: Syracuse University Press, 1965), 109. On child labor laws, enforcement, and relation to attendance, see Helen Thompson Woolley, "The Issuing of Working Permits and Its Bearing on Other School Problems," SS 1 (May 1915): 726–33; Helen L. Sumner and Ella A. Merritt, "Child Labor Legislation in the United States," USCB, Industrial Series, no. 1, bureau pub. no. 10 (1915); Helen L. Sumner and Ethel E. Hanks, "Administration of Child Labor Laws: Part 2, Employment-Certificate Systems in New York," USCB, Industrial Series, no. 2, part 2, bureau pub. no. 17 (1917); Forest Chester Ensign, *Compulsory School Attendance and Child Labor: A Study of the Historical Development of Regulations Compelling Attendance and Limiting the Labor of Children in a Selected Group of States* (Iowa City: Athens Press, 1921); Arch O. Heck, *A Study of the Ohio Compulsory Education and Child Labor Law*, Bureau of Educational Research Monographs, no. 9 (1931).

18. Historians have noted that the laws passed from a symbolic phase to a bureaucratic one in the early twentieth century and explained it largely in terms of new urban school bureaucracies. However, this ignores the broadening constituency and commitments of reformers, inside and outside the schools, who supported attendance policy. David B. Tyack, "Ways of Seeing: An Essay on the History of Compulsory Schooling," *Harvard Educational Review* 46 (Aug. 1976): 355–389; David Tyack and Michael Berkowitz, "The Man Nobody Liked: Toward a Social History of the Truant Officer, 1840–1940," *American Quarterly* 29 (Spring 1977): 31–54; Michael S. Katz, "The Concepts of Compulsory Education and Compulsory Schooling: A Philosophical Inquiry" (Ph.D. diss., Stanford University, 1974); Stephen J. Provasnik, "Compulsory Schooling, From Idea to Institution: A Case Study of the Development of Compulsory Attendance in Illinois, 1857–1907" (Ph.D. diss., University of Chicago, 1999).

19. H. R. Bonner, "Waste in Education," *American School Board Journal* 63 (July 1921): 33–35, 124; Moses Stambler, "The Effect of Compulsory Education and Child Labor Laws on High School Attendance in New York City, 1898–1917," HEQ 8 (Summer 1968): 189–214.

20. On compulsory attendance statutes over time, see W. S. Deffenbaugh et al., "Compulsory School Attendance," *USBE Bulletin*, no. 2 (1914); Ward W. Keesecker, "Laws

Relating to Compulsory Education," *USBE Bulletin*, no. 20 (1928); Walter S. Deffenbaugh and Ward W. Keesecker, "Compulsory School Attendance Laws and Their Enforcement," *USBE Bulletin*, no. 4 (1935); John Harrison Hutchinson, *The Legal Basis of Public School Attendance in the United States* (Chicago: University of Chicago Libraries, 1941); Frank Alexander Ross, *School Attendance in 1920: An Analysis of School Attendance in the United States and in the Several States, with a Discussion of the Factors Involved*, census monographs 5 (Washington, D.C.: U.S. Government Printing Office, 1924); Ensign, *Compulsory School Attendance and Child Labor*.

21. "Runaway School Boys: Amusing Features of Truancy Agents' Efforts to Find Them," NYT, 7 Apr. 1881, 8; Tyack and Berkowitz, "The Man Nobody Liked."

22. Arch O. Heck, "The Development of Various Pupil-Personnel Services," *Educational Research Bulletin* 14 (Apr. 1935): 98–102, 98; George H. Chatfield et al., *Problems of School Attendance and Pupil Adjustment* (Albany: University of the State of New York Press, 1932); Tyack and Berkowitz, "The Man Nobody Liked."

23. On the school census and its adaptation for use in attendance services (as well as the myriad challenges it posed), see John Dearling Haney, *Registration of City School Children: A Consideration of the Subject of the City School Census* (New York: Teachers College, 1910); Arch O. Heck, *Administration of Pupil Personnel: A Book on Pupil-Accounting Written from the Point of View of the Classroom Teacher* (Boston: Ginn and Company, 1929); Arthur B. Moehlman, *Child Accounting: A Discussion of the General Principles Underlying Educational Child Accounting Together with the Development of a Uniform Procedure* (Detroit: Friesema Bros. Press, 1924); Paul B. Habans, "The Factors of an Adequate School Census—How They May Be Realized," APNEA (1917): 835–37; Maris M. Proffitt and David Segel, "School Census, Compulsory Education, Child Labor: State Laws and Regulations," *USBE Bulletin*, no. 1 (1945); William A. Greeson, "The School Census and Its Use in School Administration," ESJ 19 (Sept. 1918): 14–23; David Segel and Maris M. Proffitt, "Pupil Personnel Services as a Function of State Departments of Education," *USBE Bulletin*, no. 6, monograph no. 5 (1940).

24. For studies of attendance service, see F. V. Bermejo, *The School Attendance Service in American Cities* (Menasha, WI: George Banta Publishing Company, 1923); Frederick Earle Emmons, *City School Attendance Service* (New York: Teachers College, 1926); Joseph LeMart Schultz, "An Analysis of Present Practices in City Attendance Work" (Ph.D. diss., University of Pennsylvania, 1938); Whittier Lorenz Hanson, *The Costs of Compulsory Attendance Service in the State of New York and Some Factors Affecting Cost* (New York: Teachers College, 1924); S. O. Hartwell, "The Enforcement of Compulsory Attendance Laws," SS 2 (July 1915): 49–55; M. Bates Stephens, "One Year of Compulsory School Attendance in Maryland, 1916–1917" (Baltimore: State Board of Education, 1918); Edward Clinton Bixler, "An Investigation to Determine the Efficiency with Which the Compulsory Attendance Law Is Enforced in Philadelphia" (Ph.D. diss., University of Pennsylvania, 1913); Hermann Cooper, *An Accounting of Progress and Attendance of Rural School Children in Delaware* (New York: Teachers College, 1930).

25. John W. Davis, *First Annual Report of the Director of Attendance for the Year Ending July 31, 1915* (New York: Department of Education, Bureau of Attendance, 1916), 49, 147.

26. Abbott and Breckinridge, *Truancy and Non-Attendance in the Chicago Schools*, 274, 140–43.

27. Ibid., 123–36; John W. Davis, *Report of the Bureau of Attendance for the Period between July 31, 1915, to July 31, 1918* (New York: Department of Education, Bureau of Attendance, 1919), 143. For other case studies, see Mary B. Sayles, *The Problem Child in the School: Narratives from Case Records of Visiting Teachers* (New York: Joint Committee on Methods of Preventing Delinquency, 1925); Elisabeth A. Irwin, *Truancy: A Study of the Mental, Physical, and Social Factors of the Problem of Non-Attendance at School* (New York: Public Education Association, 1915).

28. Davis, *Report of the Bureau of Attendance*, 164–66.

29. Ibid., 154–57. Schools were access points for courts: Bernadine Dohrn, "The School, the Child, and the Court," *A Century of Juvenile Justice*, 267–308. On the service and coercion embedded in social work, see Regina G. Kunzel, *Fallen Women, Problem Girls: Unmarried Mothers and the Professionalization of Social Work, 1890–1945* (New Haven: Yale University Press, 1993); Michael Willrich, *City of Courts: Socializing Justice in Progressive Era Chicago* (Cambridge: Cambridge University Press, 2003); Gwendolyn Mink, *The Wages of Motherhood: Inequality in the Welfare State, 1917–1942* (Ithaca: Cornell University Press, 1996).

30. H. R. Bonner, "Compulsory Attendance Laws," *American School Board Journal* 59 (Dec. 1919): 37.

31. Arch O. Heck, "School Attendance," *Review of Educational Research* 3 (June 1933): 186–93; Thomas Snyder, *120 Years of American Education: A Statistical Portrait* (Washington, D.C.: National Center for Education Statistics, 1993), 57. However, attendance statistics for the earlier period were notoriously unreliable, given both record-keeping practices and the tendency to drop from the roll students who were absent longer than a week. For a discussion, see Moehlman, *Child Accounting*, chap. 2.

32. Heck, *Administration of Pupil Personnel*, 12.

33. Moehlman, *Child Accounting*, 41; Deffenbaugh and Keesecker, "Compulsory School Attendance Laws," 57, 64–65.

34. May Ayres, Jesse F. Williams, and Thomas D. Wood, *Healthful Schools: How to Build, Equip, and Maintain Them* (Boston: Houghton Mifflin Co., 1918), 208.

35. Thomas D. Wood and Hugh Grant Rowell, *Health Supervision and Medical Inspection of Schools* (Philadelphia: W. B. Saunders Co., 1927), 23; Williard Small, "Educational Hygiene," *USBE Bulletin*, no. 33 (1923): 5; James Frederick Rogers, "School Health Activities in 1930," *USBE Pamphlet*, no. 21 (1931): 31–33. For examinations of medical inspection and health supervision in urban and rural schools, see Luther Halsey Gulick and Leonard P. Ayres, *Medical Inspection of Schools* (New York: Russell Sage Foundation, 1913); Ernest Bryant Hoag and Lewis M. Terman, *Health Work in the Schools* (Boston: Houghton Mifflin Co., 1914); Ernest B. Hoag, "Organized Health Work in the Schools," *USBE Bulletin*, no. 44 (1913); C. P. Knight, "Health Supervision of School Children on a State-Wide Basis," *APNEA* (1921): 379–83; Charles H. Keene, "A State Program in Education for Health," *SS* 20 (Oct. 1924): 415–29; "Current Educational Topics No. 3," *USBE Bulletin*, no. 24 (1912); James Frederick Rogers,

"Supervision of Health and Physical Education as a Function of State Departments of Education," *USBE Bulletin*, no. 6, monograph no. 14 (1940).

36. *Division of Medical Inspection of Public Schools: Report for the Year Ending June 30, 1930* (Philadelphia: Board of Public Education, 1930).

37. A. J. Philpott, "Guarding the Health of 110,000 Children," *Boston Daily Globe*, 2 Nov. 1913, 61; Abbott and Breckinridge, *Truancy and Non-Attendance in the Chicago Schools*, 130. On school nurses as social workers, see Hoag, "Organized Health Work in Schools," 12–16; "She Is Angel of the Schools," *LA Times*, 24 Mar. 1907, sec. 2, 11.

38. Judith Walzer Leavitt, *The Healthiest City: Milwaukee and the Politics of Health Reform* (Princeton: Princeton University Press, 1982); William J. Reese, *Power and the Promise of School Reform: Grassroots Movements during the Progressive Era*, 2nd ed. (New York: Teachers College Press, 2002). On health education and hygiene, see Fletcher B. Dresslar, *School Hygiene* (New York: Macmillan Co., 1917); J. Mace Andress, *Health Education in Rural Schools*, rev. ed. (Boston: Houghton Mifflin Co., 1925); Edward R. Shaw, *School Hygiene* (New York: Macmillan Co., 1901); Jesse Feiring Williams and Clifford Lee Brownell, *The Administration of Health and Physical Education* (Philadelphia: W. B. Saunders Co., 1937); Louis W. Rapeer, ed., *Educational Hygiene from the Pre-School Period to the University* (New York: Charles Scribner's Sons, 1915).

39. S. W. Newmayer, *Medical and Sanitary Inspection of Schools: For the Health Officer, the Physician, the Nurse and the Teacher*, 2nd ed. (Philadelphia: Lea & Febiger, 1924), 64–67; Walter S. Cornell, *Health and Medical Inspection of School Children* (Philadelphia: F. A. Davis Co., 1912); Frances Williston Burks and Jesse D. Burks, *Health and the School: A Round Table* (New York: D. Appleton and Co., 1913); Davis, *Report of the Bureau of Attendance*, 167–68; James A. Tobey, *Public Health Law: A Manual for Sanitarians* (Baltimore: Williams & Williams Co., 1926).

40. *Sprague v. Baldwin*, 1896 WL 3756 (Pa.Com.Pl) (1896); *Mathews v. Board of Education*, 127 Mich. 530, 86 N.W. 1036 (1901); *State v. Zimmerman*, 86 Minn. 353, 90 N.W. 783 (1902); *Jacobson v. Massachusetts*, 197 U.S. 11, 25 S.Ct. 358 (1905); J. W. Kerr, "Vaccination," *Public Health Bulletin*, no. 52 (1912): 7; John Fredrick Bender, *The Functions of the Courts in Enforcing School Attendance Laws* (New York: Teachers College, 1927); William Fowler, "Smallpox Vaccination Laws, Regulation, and Court Decisions," *Public Health Report*, supp. no. 60 (1927). On the politics around vaccination, see James Colgrove, "Between Persuasion and Compulsion: Smallpox Control in Brooklyn and New York, 1894–1902," *Bulletin of the History of Medicine* 78 (2004): 349–78; James Colgrove, *State of Immunity: The Politics of Vaccination in Twentieth-Century America* (Berkeley: University of California Press, 2006); Michael Willrich, "'The Least Vaccinated of Any Civilized Country': Personal Liberty and Public Health in the Progressive Era," *JPH* 20, no. 1 (2008): 76–93; Robert D. Johnston, *The Radical Middle Class: Populist Democracy and the Question of Capitalism in Progressive Era Portland, Oregon* (Princeton: Princeton University Press, 2003); Martin Kaufman, "The American Anti-Vaccinationists and Their Arguments," *Bulletin of the History of Medicine* 41 (Sept./Oct. 1967): 463–78.

41. *Commonwealth v. Smith*, 1900 WL 4587 (Pa. Quart.Sess.) (1900); *Shappee v. Curtis*, 127 N.Y.S. 33 (1911). See also *Compulsory School-Attendance v. Vaccination*, 1906 WL 3035

(Pa.Atty.Gen, 1906); *Ohio v. L.M. Tourney,* 1909 WL 1144 (Ohio Circ., 1909); *State v. Cole,* 119 S.W. 424 (Mo. 1909).

42. *New York v. Ekerold,* 211 N.Y. 386, 105 N.E. 670 (1914). For subsequent cases, many of which cited *Ekerold,* see *People v. McIlwain,* 151 N.Y.S. 366 (1915); *Commonwealth v. Aiken,* 1916 WL 4644 (Pa.Super.) (1916); *Commonwealth v. Wilkins,* 1920 WL 2164 (Pa. Quar.Sess.) (1920); *In Re Martha G. Hargy and Harry E. Hargy Jr.,* 1920 WL 571 (Ohio Com Pl.) (1920); *Barber v. School Board of Rochester,* 135 A. 159 (N.H. 1926); *State v. Drew* 192 A. 629 (N.H. 1937); *Marsh v. Earle,* 24 F. Supp. 385 (Pa. 1938).

43. *Commonwealth v. Gillen,* 1916 WL 5152 (Pa.Qaur.Sess.); *Commonwealth v. Gillen,* 65 Pa. Super.31 (1916). A similar case in New York, with the same result, was covered at length by the Christian Science Monitor: "Parochial School Bars Child," CSM, 8 Jan. 1921, 2; "Decision Rendered in Vaccination Case," CSM, 14 Jan. 1921, 8; "Vaccination Case Outcome Awaited," CSM, 17 Mar. 1921, 5; "MacCullom-More Case to be Appealed," CSM, 1 Apr. 1921, 4; "Vaccination Case to Be Fought Out," CSM, 16 May 1921, 1.

44. "Parents Win Their Fight," *LA Times,* 5 Apr. 1911, 4; "School Boys Revolt," *LA Times,* 26 Jan. 1912, 15.

45. Raymond McLaughlin, *A History of State Legislation Affecting Private Elementary and Secondary Schools in the United States, 1870-1945* (Washington, D.C.: Catholic University of America Press, 1946), 66–68; John Bascom, "A New Policy for the Public Schools," *Forum* (Mar. 1891): 64.

46. McLaughlin, *A History of State Legislation,* 90–102, 189; Charles N. Lischka, "Private Schools and State Laws," *NCWC Education Bulletins,* no. 4 (1924): 103–8; "Some Laws and Regulations Relating to the Qualifications and Certification of Teachers" [ca. 1926], box 9, NCWC Papers; Crowly to James H. Ryan, NCWC interoffice memo, 10 Dec. 1924, NCWC Dept. of Ed., box 12, folder "Education and the State, 1919–1938," NCWC Papers; John Elson, "State Regulation of Nonpublic Schools: The Legal Framework," in *Public Controls for Nonpublic Schools,* ed. Donald A. Erikson (Chicago: University of Chicago Press, 1969): 103–34.

47. *Commonwealth v. Snyder,* 1906 WL 3024 (Pa.Quar.Sess) (1906); *State v. Counort,* 69 Wash. 361, 124 P. 910 (1912); *Wright v. State,* 209 P. 179 (Okla. 1922); *State v. Hoyt,* 146 A. 170 (N.H. 1929); Bender, *The Function of Courts.*

48. Hoag and Terman, *Health Work in the Schools,* 4; Hollis P. Allen, *Universal Free Education* (Stanford: Stanford University Press, 1934), 52.

49. "Memorandum of Educational Policy" [ca. 1905], series 1.1, box 1, NCEA Papers; "Parents—Their Rights and Duties" [ca. 1937], box 11, NCWC Papers; "State Monopoly of Education Is Firmly Opposed," 23 Apr. 1923, box 106, gen. sec., NCWC Papers; Rev. N. N. McKinnon to Archbishop John M. Farley, 6 June 1905, series 1.1, box 1, NCEA Papers; J. A. Burns, *The Growth and Development of the Catholic School System in the United States* (New York: Benziger Brothers, 1912), chap. 9; James H. Ryan, "The Proposed Monopoly in Education," *Atlantic Monthly* 133 (Feb. 1924): 172–79.

50. Mrs. S. B. Readle, "Letters: Medical Control of the People," CSM, 1 Mar. 1918, 3; W. Stephenson, "Letters to the Times: Vaccination and the Schools," *LA Times,* 21 Sept. 1899, 7; "Municipal Socialism," *Boston Daily Globe,* 22 Mar. 1909, 10; Edgar J. Levey,

"Municipal Socialism and its Economic Limitations," *Political Science Quarterly* 24 (Mar. 1909): 23–56; "How the School Robs the Home," NYT, 11 June 1909, 8.

51. *Quigley v. Ohio*, 1891 WL 289 (Ohio Cir.) (1891).

52. *State v. Bailey*, 61 N.E. 730 (Ind. 1901) (italics mine).

53. *State v. Jackson*, 53 A. 1021 (N.H. 1902); *Commonwealth v. Edsall*, 1903 WL 2585 (Pa. Quar.Sess.) (1903); Stephen Provasnik, "Judicial Activism and the Origins of Parental Choice: The Court's Role in the Institutionalization of Compulsory Education in the United States, 1891–1925," 46 HEQ (Fall 2006): 311–47.

54. Lee O. Garber, *Education as a Function of the State* (Minneapolis: Educational Test Bureau Inc., 1934); Newton Edwards, *The Courts and the Public Schools: The Legal Basis of School Organization and Administration* (Chicago: University of Chicago Press, 1933); H. H. Schroeder, *Legal Opinion on the Public School as a State Institution* (Bloomington: Public School Publishing Co., 1928).

55. *Bissel v. Davison*, 32 A. 348 (Conn.1894). See also *In Re Walters*, 84 Hun 457 (N.Y. 1895); *Viemeister v. White*, 70 L.R.A. 796, 72 N.E. 97 (N.Y. 1904); *Stull v. Reber*, 215 Pa. 156, 64 A. 410 (PA, 1906); *State v. Board of Education of Barberton*, 76 Ohio St. 297, 81 N.E. 568 (1907). On racial assignment and exclusion, see Harry Raymond Trusler, *Essentials of School Law* (Milwaukee: Bruce Publishing Company, 1927), chap. 2; *People v. Gallagher*, 93 N.Y. 438, 1883 WL 12689 (1883); *Lehew v. Brummel*, 15 S.W. 765 (Mo. 1891); *Ward v. Flood*, 48 Cal. 36 (1874); *People v. School Board*, 44 A.D. 469, 61 NYS 330 (1899); *Reynolds v. Board of Education*, 66 Kan. 672, 72 P.274 (1903); *Piper v. Big Pine School District*, 193 Cal. 664, 226 P. 926 (1924).

56. *Fogg v. Board of Education*, 82 A. 173 (N.H. 1912).

57. *State v. Board of Education of Antigo*, 172 N.W. 153 (Wis. 1919).

58. *State v. Board of Education of Fond du Lac*, 23 N.W. 102 (Wis. 1885). For additional examples of courts defining the boundaries of "reasonable" rules in the nineteenth century, see *Burdick v. Babcock*, 1871 WL 293 (Iowa, 1871); *King v. Jefferson City School Board*, 1880 WL 9741 (Mo. 1880); *Sewell v Board of Education of Defiance Union School*, 9 Ohio St. 89, 1876 WL 47 (1876); *Ferriter v. Tyler*, 1876 WL 7490 (Vt. 1876); *Stevens v. Fassett*, 847 WL 1440 (Maine 1847); *Lander v. Seaver*, 1859 WL 5454 (Vt. 1859); *State v. Mizner*, 1876 WL 888 (Iowa 1876); *State v. Burton*, 1878 WL 3286 (Wis. 1878); *Vanvactor v. State*, 5 N.E. 341 (Ind. 1888); *State v. Vanverbilt*, 18 N.E. 266 (Ind. 1888); *Holman v. School Trustees of Avon*, 77 Mich. 605, 43 N.W. 996 (1889); *Feritch v. Michener*, 11 N.E. 605 (Ind. 1887).

59. For an overview of school rules and regulations, see Newton Edwards's three-part series, "Legal Authority of Boards of Education to Enforce Rules and Regulations," ESJ 31 (Feb. 1931): 446–59; ESJ 31 (Mar. 1931): 504–13; ESJ 31 (Apr. 1931): 619–27; M. M. Chambers, "The Legal Status of Pupils," *Review of Educational Research* 3 (Dec. 1933): 428–33; Trussler, *Essentials of School Law*; William Graebner, "Outlawing Teenage Populism: The Campaign against Secret Societies in the American High School, 1900–1960," JAH 74 (Sept. 1987): 411–35. For representative cases, see *Puglsey v. Sellmeyer*, 250 S.W. 538 (Ark. 1923); *Valentine v. Independent School Dist. of Casey*, 183 N.W. 434 (Iowa 1923); *Stromberg v. French*, 136 N.W. 477 (S. Dak. 1931); *Favorite v. Board of Education*, 235 Ill. 314, 85 N.E. 402 (Ill., 1908); *Bradford v. Board of Education*

of San Francisco, 18 Cal.App. 19, 121 P. 929 (1912); *Lee v. Hoffman*, 166 N.W. 565 (Iowa 1918); *Sutton v. Board of Education of City of Springfield*, 306 Ill. 507, 138 N.E. 131 (Ill. 1923); *Douglas v. Campbell*, 116 S.W. 211 (Ark. 1909); *Flory v. Smith*, 145 Va 164, 134 S.E. 360 (1926); *Bozeman v. Morrow*, 34 S.W.2d 654 (Tex. 1931).

60. *Dresser v. District Board*, 116 N.W. 232 (Wis. 1908); *Kinzer v. Directors of Independent School District of Marion*, 105 N.W. 686 (Iowa 1906); *Douglas v. Campbell*, 116 S.W. 211 (Ark. 1909); *Jones v. Day*, 89 So. 906 (Miss. 1921).

61. *Hobbs v. Germany*, 49 So. 515 (MS, 1909); *Magnum v. Keith*, 95 S.E. 1 (Ga., 1918).

62. William G. Ross, *Forging New Freedoms: Nativism, Education, and the Constitution, 1917–1927* (Lincoln: University of Nebraska Press, 1994); David B. Tyack, "The Perils of Pluralism: The Background of the Pierce Case," *AHR* 74 (Oct. 1968): 74–98; *The Oregon School Fight: A True History* (Portland: A. B. Cain, 1924); Jorgensen, *The State and the Non-Public School*; Douglas J. Slawson, *The Department of Education Battle, 1918–1932: Public Schools, Catholic Schools, and the Social Order* (Notre Dame: University of Notre Dame Press, 2005).

63. NCWC News Service, 13 Nov. 1922, box 14, NCWC Papers; "The Truth about the So-Called Compulsory Education Bill" (Portland: Lutheran Schools Committee), box 14, NCWC Papers. See also, for example, NCWC News Service, "State Monopoly of Education Is Firmly Opposed," 23 Apr. 1923, NCWC gen. sec., box 106, NCWC Papers; Justin McGrath, memo for Father Burke, 2 Nov. 1925, box 78, NCWC Papers; "Sixteen Reasons Why Every American Should Oppose a State Monopoly of Education," *NCWC Education Bulletin*, no. 3 (Feb. 1923), in NCWC Dept. of Ed., box 15, NCWC Papers.

64. *Meyer v. Nebraska*, 262 U.S. 390, 43 S.Ct. 625 (1923) (italics mine); *Pohl v. State*, 102 Ohio St. 474, 132 N.E. 20 (1921); *Meyer v. State*, 187 N.W. 100 (Neb. 1922); *State v. Bartels*, 181 N.W. 508 (Iowa 1921).

65. *Pierce v. Society of Sisters*, 268 U.S. 510, 5 S.Ct. 571 (1925); "State Control of Private Schools and Parochial Schools," *SS* 17 (1923): 426–29; Clifford E. McDonald, "Compulsory Public School Attendance," *Marquette Law Review* 7 (1922): 96–104; "The Oregon Compulsory School Law," *Constitutional Review* 8 (1924): 241–45.

66. Carl Zollmann, "Parental Rights and the Fourteenth Amendment," *Marquette Law Review* 8 (1923–24): 53–60.

67. *People v. Stanley*, 81 Colo. 276, 255 P. 610 (1927).

68. On flag salute, see *People v. Sandstrom*, 279 N.Y. 523, 18 N.E. 2d 840 (1939); *Nicholls v. Mayor and School Committee of Lynn*, 297 Mass. 65, 7 N.E.2d577 (1937); *Leoles v. Landers*, 184 Ga 580, 192 S.E. 318 (1937); *Hering v. State Board of Education*, 117 N.J.L. 455, 189 A. 629 (1937); *Johnson v. Deerfield*, 25 F. Supp. 918 (Mass. 1939); *Minersville School District v. Gobitis*, 310 U.S. 586, 60 S.Ct. 1010 (1940). Contrary opinions in *Zavilla v. Masse*, 112 Colo. 183, 147 P.2d 823 (1944); *West Virginia State Board of Education v. Barnette*, 319 U.S. 624, 63 S.Ct. 1178 (1943). M. M. Chambers, "The Youth, the Schools, and the Laws: Court Decisions in the Nineteen Thirties Touching Public Education" (Washington, D.C.: by author, 1940); James W. Fraser, *Between Church and State: Religion and Public Education in a Multicultural Society* (New York: St. Martins, 1999); Clark Spurlock, *Education and the Supreme Court* (Urbana: University of

Illinois, 1955); William G. Fennell, *Compulsory Flag Salute in Schools: A Survey of the Statutes and an Examination of Their Constitutionality* (New York: ACLU, 1938). On school lunch and other rejections of parents' Fourteenth Amendment claims, see *Bishop v. Houston Independent School District*, 119 Tex. 403, 29 S.W.2d 312 (1930); *State v. Drew*, 192 A. 629 (N.H. 1937); *Marsh v. Earle* 24 F. Supp. 385 (Pa. 1938).

69. Michel Foucault, "Governmentality," in *The Foucault Effect: Studies in Governmentality*, eds. Graham Burchell, Colin Gordon, and Peter Miller (Chicago: University of Chicago Press, 1991); Michel Foucault, *Discipline and Punish: The Birth of the Prison* (New York: Vintage Books, 1995).

70. *Commonwealth v. Holben*, 8 Pa. D. & C. 396 (1926).

Chapter Five

1. National Education Association, *Report of the Committee of Ten on Secondary School Studies, with the Reports of the Conferences Arranged by Committee* (New York: American Book Co., 1894), 51–52, 17.

2. "Cardinal Principles of Secondary Education: A Report of the Commission on the Reorganization of Secondary Education," in *USBE Bulletin*, no. 35 (1918): 9, 21.

3. Leonard V. Koos, *The American Secondary School* (Boston: Ginn & Co., 1927), 5; Thomas D. Synder, ed., *120 Years of American Education: A Statistical Portrait* (Washington, D.C.: National Center for Education Statistics, 1993), 6–14; Robert Wiebe, "The Social Functions of Public Education," *American Quarterly* 21 (Summer 1969): 147–64; Edward A. Krug, *The Shaping of the American High School* (New York: Harper & Row, 1964).

4. John D. Runkle, "The Manual Element in Education," in *American Education and Vocationalism: A Documentary History 1870–1970*, ed. Marvin Lazerson and W. Norton Grubb (New York: Teachers College Press, 1974), 57; Calvin M. Woodward, *The Manual Training School, Comprising a Full Statement of Its Aims, Methods, and Results* (Boston: D. C. Heath, 1887), 204; Charles A. Bennett, *History of Manual and Industrial Education Up to 1870* (Peoria, IL: Manual Arts Press, 1926).

5. James MacAlister, *Manual Training in the Public Schools of Philadelphia*, Educational Monographs of NY College for the Training of Teachers 3, no. 2 (Mar. 1890): 10. See also Felix Adler, *The Moral Instruction of Children* (New York: D. Appleton and Company, 1893); Charles H. Ham, *Manual Training: The Solution of Social and Industrial Problems* (New York: Harper & Brothers, 1886); Calvin M. Woodward, *Manual Training in Education* (New York: Charles Scribner's Sons, 1898).

6. Herbert M. Kliebard, *Schooled to Work: Vocationalism and American Culture, 1876–1946*, 2nd ed. (New York: Teachers College Press, 1999), 62–68; Lawrence A. Cremin, *The Transformation of the School: Progressivism in American Education, 1876–1957* (New York: Alfred A. Knopf, 1961), 32–33; Charles A. Bennett, *History of Manual and Industrial Education, 1870 to 1917* (Peoria, IL: Manual Arts Press, 1937), 397.

7. "Report on Industrial Education," *NAM Proceedings* 10 (1905): 141–51; "Needs of Organization and Education," *NAM Proceedings* 9 (1904): 107–23; Cremin, *Transformation of the School*, chap. 2.

8. *Report of the Commission on Industrial and Technical Education*, Teachers College Educational Reprints 1 (New York: Teachers College, 1906): 1–5.

9. Ibid., 7–9, 19–23.

10. C. A. Prosser, "Progress in Vocational Education," in *U.S. Commissioner of Education Report* 1 (1912): 281–97; William T. Bawden, "Progress in Vocational Education," in *U.S. Commissioner of Education Report* 1 (1913): 249–76. On the history of manual training and vocational education, see also Harvey A. Kantor, *Learning to Earn: School, Work, and Vocational Reform in California, 1880–1930* (Madison: University of Wisconsin Press, 1988); Marvin Lazerson, *Origins of the Urban School: Public Education in Massachusetts, 1870–1915* (Cambridge, MA: Harvard University Press, 1971); Kliebard, *Schooled to Work*; Harvey Kantor and David B. Tyack, *Work, Youth, and Schooling: Historical Perspectives on Vocationalism in American Education* (Stanford: Stanford University Press, 1982); Sol Cohen, "The Industrial Education Movement, 1906–7," *American Quarterly* 20 (Spring 1968): 95–110; Arthur G. Wirth, *Education in the Technological Society: The Vocational-Liberal Studies Controversy in the Early Twentieth Century* (Scranton: Intext Educational Publishers, 1972).

11. Arthur F. Payne, *Administration of Vocational Education: With Special Emphasis on the Administration of Vocational Industrial Education under the Federal Vocational Education Law* (New York: McGraw-Hill, 1924); W. Stull Holt, *The Federal Board for Vocational Education: Its History, Activities, and Organization* (New York: D. Appleton and Company, 1922).

12. Charles H. Winslow, "Industrial Education: Report of Committee on Industrial Education of the American Federation of Labor" (Washington, D.C.: 62nd Congress, 2nd Session, Senate doc. no. 936, 1912): 19; *Industrial Education* (Washington, D.C.: AFL, 1910); "Report of the Commission on National Aid to Vocational Education Together with the Hearings Held on the Subject" (Washington, D.C.: House of Representatives, 63rd Congress, 2nd session, doc no. 1004, 1914): 187.

13. James E. Russell, "Democracy and Education: Equal Opportunity for All," APNEA (1908): 156–57.

14. Irving Elgar Miller, *Education for the Needs of Life: A Textbook in the Principles of Education*, 2nd ed. (New York: Macmillan Co., 1919), 187–88; Nicholas Murray Butler, *The Meaning of Education and Other Essays and Addresses* (New York: Macmillan Co., 1898). See also Ellwood P. Cubberley and Robert A. Woods, "Does the Present Trend toward Vocational Education Threaten Liberal Culture?," SR 19 (Sept. 1911): 454–88; E. Davenport, *Education for Efficiency: A Discussion of Certain Phases of the Problem of Universal Education with Special Reference to Academic Ideals and Methods* (Boston: D. C. Heath & Co., 1909); "Topic: Harmonizing Vocational and Cultural Education," APNEA (1914): 375–86; David Snedden and William C. Bagley, "Fundamental Distinctions between Liberal and Vocational Education," APNEA (1914): 150–70; Charles W. Eliot, "The Value during Education of the Life-Career Motive," APNEA (1910): 133–41.

15. Edwin Cooley, "A Plan for Vocational Training," CDT, 15 Dec. 1912, 1; Edwin G. Cooley, "Professor Dewey's Criticism of the Chicago Commercial Club and Its Vocational Education Bill," *Vocational Education* 3 (Sept. 1913): 24–29; John Hogan, *Class and*

Reform: School and Society in Chicago, 1880–1930 (Philadelphia: University of Pennsylvania Press, 1985); Julia Wrigley, *Class Politics and Public Schools: Chicago, 1900–1950* (New Brunswick: Rutgers University Press, 1982). Cooley's findings for the Commercial Club were published as *Some Continuation Schools of Europe* (Chicago, 1912) and *Vocational Education in Europe: Report to the Commercial Club of Chicago* (Chicago, 1912).

16. David Snedden, "Vocational Education," NR 3 (15 May 1915): 40–42; David Snedden, *Vocational Education* (New York: Macmillan Company, 1920), 64. See also David Snedden, *The Problem of Vocational Education* (Boston: Houghton Mifflin Co., 1910); David Snedden, "Democratic Vocational Education," SR 36 (Sept 1928): 522–27; Walter H. Drost, *David Snedden and Education for Social Efficiency* (Madison: University of Wisconsin Press, 1967).

17. "For Vocational Work: But in Present Schools," CDT, 14 Dec. 1912, 14; Edwin R. Wright, "Union Chief on Trade Training: Edwin R. Wright Considers the Problem from the Standpoint of the Worker," CDT, 29 Dec. 1912, A2; "Bill Providing Trade Schools Doomed to Die?," CDT, 15 Apr. 1915, 7; Ella Adams Moore, "Trade Training Emphasized," CDT, 25 Dec. 1912, 8; "For Vocational Work: But in Present Schools," CDT, 14 Dec. 1912, 14; "Gives Plan for Trade Schools," CDT, 16 Dec. 1912, 4; "Fears Craze for Teaching Crafts: Mrs. Ella Flagg Young Sees Perils in Turning Schools into Mere Workshops," CDT, 4 Dec. 1912, 2.

18. John Dewey, "An Undemocratic Proposal," (1913) in Lazerson and Grubb, *American Education and Vocationalism*, 143–47; John Dewey, "Education vs. Trade Training—Dr. Dewey's Reply," NR 3 (May 1915): 42–43; John Dewey, "A Policy of Industrial Education," NR 1 (Dec. 1914): 11–12. See also Walter H. Drost, "Social Efficiency Reexamined: The Dewey-Snedden Controversy," *Curriculum Inquiry* 7 (Spring 1977): 19–32; John Dewey, "Splitting up the School System," NR 2 (Apr. 1915): 283–84; John Dewey, "Industrial Education—A Wrong Kind," NR 2 (Feb. 1915): 71–73.

19. Jesse Buttrick Davis, *Vocational and Moral Guidance* (Boston: Ginn and Company, 1914); Frank P. Goodwin, "Vocational Guidance in Cincinnati," *Vocational Education* 3 (Mar. 1914): 250.

20. Kliebard, *Schooled to Work*; W. Norton Grubb and Marvin Lazerson, *The Education Gospel: The Economic Power of Schooling* (Cambridge, MA: Harvard University Press, 2004); John L. Rury, *Education and Women's Work: Female Schooling and the Division of Labor in Urban America, 1870–1930* (Albany: SUNY Press, 1991).

21. William D. Lewis, *Democracy's High School* (Boston: Houghton Mifflin Co., 1914), 49.

22. James E. Vose, "Methods of Instruction in Civics," *Education* 7 (April 1887): 529–31; James E. Vose, "Methods of Instruction in Civics," *Education* 12 (May 1887): 617–27; Henry Randall Waite, "American Institute of Civics," *American Journal of Politics* 5 (July 1894): 56–57; Henry Randall Waite, "Civics: A Science for Citizens and a Creed for Patriots," *American Magazine of Civics*: 202–5. For early definitions of "civics," see C. F. Crehore, "The Teaching of Civics in the Schools," *Education* 7 (Dec. 1886): 264–65; Jesse Macy, "Practical Instruction in Civics," *Journal of Social Science* 32 (Nov. 1894): 151–59; Rev. Clarence Greeley, "Civics and the Public Schools," *Lend a Hand* 13

(Sept. 1894): 189–92; S. E. Forman, "The Aim and Scope of Civics," SR 11 (Mar. 1903): 288–304.

23. On nineteenth-century civic education, see Michael Schudson, *The Good Citizen: A History of American Civic Life* (New York: Free Press, 1998); Lori Ann Alvarez Parker, "American Civic Education (1607–1925)" (Ph.D. diss., University of California Irvine, 1992); Michael V. Belok, "The Instructed Citizen: Civic Education in the United States during the Nineteenth Century," *Paedagogica Historica* 18, no. 2 (1978): 257–74.

24. Ira H. Evans, "Good Citizenship," *American Journal of Politics* 5 (Sept. 1894): 12.

25. Jesse Macy, *First Lessons in Civil Government* (Boston: Ginn & Company, 1896), 178; Chauncey P. Colegrove, "Patriotism in Our Public Schools," *American Magazine of Civics* 9 (1896): 121; James Bryce, "The Teaching of Civic Duty," ER 6 (Sept. 1893): 169.

26. Macy, *First Lessons in Civil Government*, iv–v; Geroge H. Martin, *Hints on Teaching Civics* (New York: Silver, Burdett and Company, 1898), 7, 60; "Civics," in Paul Monroe, ed., *Cyclopedia of Education*, vol. 2 (New York: Macmillan Co., 1911), 24–28; Sidney C. Sivertson, "Community Civics: Education for Social Efficiency" (Ph.D. diss., University of Wisconsin, 1972), chap. 2.

27. George E. Vincent, "Social Science and the Curriculum," SR 10 (1902): 193–94; John Dewey, *School and Society* (1900; repr., Chicago: University of Chicago Press, 1990), 44; John Dewey, *Ethical Principles Underlying Education* (1897; repr., Chicago: University of Chicago Press, 1903), 8, 26. See also John Dewey, *Moral Principles in Education* (Boston: Houghton Mifflin Co., 1909); John Dewey, *Democracy and Education: An Introduction to the Philosophy of Education* (New York: Free Press, 1916).

28. Walter Lippmann, *Drift and Mastery: An Attempt to Diagnose the Current Unrest* (1914; repr., Madison: University of Wisconson Press, 1985), 17, 92, 100. On social education, see Henry W. Thurston, "Civics in the Elementary School," *Elementary School Teacher* 4 (Mar. 1907): 471–76; Samuel T. Dutton, *Social Phases of Education in the School and Home* (New York: Macmillan Co., 1899); Colin A. Scott, *Social Education* (Boston: Ginn & Co., 1908); Ira W. Howerth, "Education and Social Progress," ER 23 (Apr. 1902): 355–70; Jeremiah W. Jenks, "The Social Basis of Education," ER 30 (Dec. 1905): 442–63; William E. Chancellor, "Education for Social Control," APNEA (1901): 619–26; Henry Suzzallo, "Education as Social Study," SR 5 (May 1908): 330–40; William Bishop Owen, "Social Education through the School," SR 15 (Jan. 1907): 11–26; John M. Gillette, "An Outline of Social Study for Elementary Schools," AJS 19 (Jan. 1914): 491.

29. For discussions of social control and interdependence, see Edward A. Ross, *Social Control: A Survey of the Foundations of Order* (New York: Macmillan Co., 1901); Robert MacDougall, "The Social Basis of Individuality," AJS 18 (July 1912): 1–20; Edward A. Ross, "Socialization," AJS 24 (May 1919): 652–71; Albion W. Small and George E. Vincent, *An Introduction to the Study of Society* (New York: American Book Co., 1894); Lester F. Ward, *Dynamic Sociology* (New York: D. Appleton and Co., 1898); Emile Durkheim, *The Division of Labor in Society* (New York: Free Press, 1984); Max Weber, *Economy and Society: An Outline of Interpretative Sociology*, ed. Guenther Roth and Claus Wittich (New York: Bedminster Press, 1968); Thomas L. Haskell,

The Emergence of the Professional Social Science: The American Social Science Association and the Ninteenth Century Crisis of Authority (Urbana: University of Illinois Press, 1977); James T. Kloppenberg, *Uncertain Victory: Social Democracy and Progressivism in European and American Thought, 1870–1920* (New York: Oxford University Press, 1986); Dorothy Ross, *The Origins of American Social Science* (Cambridge: Cambridge University Press, 1991).

30. Charles Eliot, *Education for Efficiency and the New Definition of the Cultivated Man* (Boston: Houghton Mifflin Co., 1909), 1, 29; M. V. O'Shea, *Education as Adjustment: Educational Theory Viewed in Light of Contemporary Thought* (New York: Longmans, Green, and Co., 1903), 286–87; Edward C. Hayes, "Education for Personality," ER 48 (Dec. 1914): 476. For examples of different uses of "social efficiency" and its cognates, see W. H. Maxwell, "Education for Efficiency," *Popular Science Monthly* 67 (Aug. 1905): 363–71; Albion W. Small, "A Vision of Social Efficiency," AJS 19 (Jan. 1914): 433–45; M. V. O'Shea, "Notes on Education for Social Efficiency," AJS 11 (Mar. 1906): 646–54; Stephen S. Colvin, "Discussions: The Conception of Adjustment as Applied to Education," ER 29 (May 1905): 510–15; Edward T. Devine, "Education and Social Economy," APNEA (1914): 142–50; George S. Counts, "Education for Vocational Efficiency," SR 30 (Sept. 1922): 493–513.

31. Arthur Dunn, "Civic Education in Elementary Schools as Illustrated in Indianapolis," *USBE Bulletin*, no. 17 (1915): 8.

32. Arthur W. Dunn, *The Community and the Citizen* (Boston: D. C. Heath & Co., 1907); Arthur Dunn, "The Civic Value of Local History," *Indiana Magazine of History* 4 (1908): 175–76. See also Arthur Dunn, "Community Civics—What It Means," *History Teacher's Magazine* 6 (1915): 52; Sivertson, "Community Civics," chaps. 4–5; Julie A. Reuben, "Beyond Politics: Community Civics and the Redefinition of Citizenship in the Progressive Era," HEQ 37 (Winter 1997): 399–420.

33. For examples, see Sivertson, "Community Civics," chap. 5; Madison Gathany, "Practical Aims and Methods in the Teaching of Civics," *History Teacher's Magazine* 4 (Jan. 1913): 20–22; Howard C. Hill, "The Social Sciences in the University High School," SR 27 (Nov. 1919); James J. Sheppard, "Municipal Civics in Elementary and High Schools," *History Teacher's Magazine* 2 (Nov. 1910): 56–57; Mabel Hill, *The Teaching of Civics* (Boston: Houghton Mifflin, 1914); Jesse Field and Scott Nearing, *Community Civics* (New York: Macmillan Co., 1916).

34. "The Teaching of Community Civics" (Washington, D.C.: NEA, 1915); William Dunn, "The Social Studies in Secondary Education: Report of the Committee on Social Studies of the Commission of the Reorganization of Secondary Education of the National Education Association," *USBE Bulletin*, no. 28 (1916): 9; W. H. Hathaway, "A Course in Socialized High-School Civics," SR 25 (1917): 743; Ronald W. Evans, *The Social Studies Wars: What Should We Teach the Children?* (New York: Teachers College Press, 2004); David Warren Saxe, *Social Studies in Schools: A History of the Early Years* (Albany: State University of New York Press, 1991).

35. R. L. Ashley, "The Social Sciences in the High School (The Pasadena Plan)," HO 10 (June 1919): 332; Ira S. Wile, "Civics in the Schools," SS 6 (Sept. 1917): 311–12; D. W. Horton, "Standards for Community Civics," *History Teacher's Magazine* 7 (Feb. 1916):

57–63. On the "new civics," see also Thomas Warrington Gosling, "A High-School Program for Training in Citizenship," SR 28 (1920): 57–65; Howard C. Hill, "The New Civics: Its Evolution and Meaning," HO 14 (June 1923): 223–27; William Bennett Munro and Charles Eugene Ozanne, *Social Civics* (New York: MacMillan Co., 1922); R. M. Tryon, "Current Literature on Civics and Other Social Studies in Junior and Senior High Schools," SR 25 (Apr. 1917): 293–99; Howard C. Hill, "Recent Literature on Civics and other Social Studies," SR 26 (Nov. 1918): 705–14; NSSE twenty-second yearbook, part 2, *The Social Studies in the Elementary and Secondary Schools* (1923).

36. Charles H. Judd, "Introduction," in *Lessons in Community and National Life* (Washington, D.C.: GPO, 1918), 7; Charles H. Judd, "The Teaching of Civics," SR 26 (1918): 511–32.

37. Franklin Winslow Johnson, "The Social Organization of the High School," SR 17 (Dec. 1909): 665–80; Lewis Paul Todd, *Wartime Relations of the Federal Government and the Public Schools, 1917–1918* (New York: Arno Press, 1971). See also J. Lynn Barnard, "A Program of Civics Teaching for War Times and After," HO 9 (Dec. 1918): 492–500; H. B. Wilson, "Training for Efficient American Citizenship through the Junior Red Cross," APNEA (1928): 91–103; Roscoe Ashley, *The Practice of Citizenship in Home, School, Business, and Community* (New York: Macmillan Co., 1922); William B. Aspinwall, "Making Citizenship Training Effective," *Education* 38 (June 1918): 733–39; Frank G. Pickell, "Training for Citizenship through Practice," SR 28 (Sept. 1920): 518–28; Will E. Wiley, "Organization of Extra-Curricula Activities as a Device for Training in Citizenship," SR 33 (Jan. 1925): 62–66; Jesse H. Newlon, "Social Studies and Citizenship" APNEA (1927): 684–92; Thomas M. Deam and Olive M. Bear, *Socializing the Pupil through Extra-Curricular Activities* (New York: Benj. H. Sanborn & Co., 1928).

38. Ernest Carroll Moore, *What the War Teaches about Education and Other Papers and Addresses* (New York: Macmillan Co., 1919), 215–16, 235; John Dewey, "Vocational Education in the Light of the World War," *Vocational Education Association of the Middle West Bulletin*, no. 4 (1918): 2.

39. "American Citizenship Committee's Report," *ABA Journal* 9 (1923): 654, 653; R. E. L. Saner, "American Citizenship," *Constitutional Review* 7 (1923): 179; Christopher Capozzola, *Uncle Sam Wants You: World War I and the Making of the Modern American Citizen* (New York: Oxford University Press, 2008); Douglas J. Slawson, *The Department of Education Battle, 1918–1932: Public Schools, Catholic Schools, and the Social Order* (Notre Dame: University of Notre Dame, 2005).

40. Charles A. Ellwood, "Education for Citizenship in a Democracy," AJS 26 (July 1920): 73–74.

41. Walter Lippmann, *Public Opinion* (1922; repr., New York: Free Press, 1997),195–96, 10, 147; John Dewey, *The Public and Its Problems*, (1927; repr., Chicago: Gateway Books, 1946), 126, 144; Edward A. Purcell Jr., *The Crisis of Democratic Theory: Scientific Naturalism and the Problem of Value* (Lexington: University Press of Kentucky, 1973); Wilfred M. McClay, *The Masterless: Self and Society in Modern America* (Chapel Hill: University of North Carolina Press, 1994).

42. Carroll Engelhardt, "Citizenship Training and Community Civics in Iowa Schools: Modern Methods for Traditional Ends, 1876–1928," *Mid-America* 65 (1983): 55–69; "Problems in American Democracy," State of New Jersey Department of Public Instruction High School Series, no. 8 (Trenton: State Board of Education, 1920): 9–10; Bessie Pierce, "The Social Studies in the Eighth Grade," HO 16 (Nov. 1925): 315–31; Sivertson, "Community Civics," chap. 7. See also City of Baltimore, *The Social Studies: Course of Study for Senior and Junior High Schools* (Baltimore: Department of Education, 1925); Grace Raymond Hebard, *Civics: For Use in the Wyoming Public Schools* (San Francisco: C. F. Weber and Col, 1926); *Syllabus in Civic Activities for High Schools* (New York: Board of Education, 1926); Harry H. Moore, "Status of Certain Social Studies in High Schools," *USBE Bulletin*, no. 45 (1922): 3; Walter S. Monroe and I. O. Foster, "The Status of the Social Sciences in the High Schools of the North Central Association," *University of Illinois Bureau of Educational Research Bulletin*, no. 13 (1922).

43. F. M. Gregg, "Symposium on Citizenship Training—the Nebraska Plan," APNEA (1928): 68. On character education, see also Stephen M. Yulish, *The Search for a Civic Religion: A History of the Character Education Movement in America, 1890–1935* (Washington, D.C.: University Press of America Inc., 1980); "Character Education," *USBE Bulletin*, no. 7 (1926); John W. Carr, "Moral Education thru the Agency of the Public Schools," APNEA (1911): 353–77; A. P. James, "Teaching Morals through the Social Studies," SS 21 (Jan. 1925): 89–95.

44. Roscoe Lewis Ashley, *The New Civics: A Textbook for Seconday Schools* (New York: Macmillan Co., 1918), 32; Ross L. Finney, "What Do We Mean by 'Community Civics' and 'Problems of Democracy'?," SR 32 (1924): 528. On vocational civics, see R. O. Hughes, *Economic and Vocational Civics* (Boston: Allyn and Bacon, 1921); R. O. Hughes, *A Text-Book in Citizenship: Community Civics, Economic Civics, Vocational Civics* (Boston: Allyn and Bacon, 1923); Cloyd Heck Marvin, "Vocational Civics," SS 5 (June 1917): 696–701; Frederick Mayor Giles, *Vocational Civics: A Study of Occupations as Background for the Consideration of a Life-Career* (New York: Macmillan Co., 1922).

45. Ashley, *The New Civics*, v–vi; Charles Grove Haines, *The Teaching of Government: Report to the American Political Science Association by the Committee on Instruction* (New York: Macmillan Co., 1916), 34; Charles Merriam, *Civic Education in the United States*, report of the Commission on the Social Studies 6 (New York: Charles Scribner's Sons, 1934), 22; William O. Thompson, "Education for Political and Moral Service," APNEA (1914): 108.

46. See, for example, "Provision for Exceptional Children in the Public Schools," *USBE Bulletin*, no. 14 (1911); Meta L. Anderson, *Education of Defectives in the Public Schools* (Yonkers-on-Hudson, NY: World Book Co., 1917); John Louis Horn, *The Education of Exceptional Children* (New York: Century Co., 1924); Robert Alexander Fyfe McDonald, *Adjustment of School Organization to Various Population Groups* (New York: Teachers College, 1915); "Schools and Classes for Feeble-Minded and Subnormal Children 1918," *USBE Bulletin*, no. 70 (1919).

47. For descriptions, see William H. Holmes, *School Organization and the Individual Child* (Worcester, MA: Davis Press, 1912); NSSE twenty-fourth yearbook, part 2, *Adapting the School to Individual Differences* (1925); Roy O. Billet, "Provisions for Individual Differences Marking, and Promotion," *USBE Bulletin*, no. 17, monograph no. 13 (1932); Arthur Zilversmit, *Changing Schools: Progressive Education Theory and Practice, 1930-1960* (Chicago: University of Chicago Press, 1993).

48. Albert Bushnell Hart, "The Lesson of the Obligation of Citizenship," *Education* 38 (June 1918): 741–42; J. E. Bodin, "Education for Democracy," SS 7 (1918): 726–27.

49. Paul Davis Chapman, *Schools as Sorters: Lewis M. Terman, Applied Pyschology, and the Intelligence Testing Movement, 1890-1930* (New York: New York University Press, 1988); Daniel J. Kevles, "Testing the Army's Intelligence: Psychologists and the Military in World War I," *JAH* 55 (Dec. 1968): 565–81; Arthur F. Payne, *Organization of Vocational Guidance* (New York: McGraw-Hill, 1925); Arch O. Heck, *Administration of Pupil Personnel: A Book on Pupil-Accounting Written from the Point of View of the Classroom Teacher* (Boston: Ginn and Co., 1929).

50. Guy M. Whipple, "Educational Determinism: A Discussion of Professor Bagley's Address at Chicago," SS 15 (June 1922): 602; I. W. Cole, "Prevention of the Lockstep in Schools," SS 15 (Feb. 1922): 211–17; John Dewey, "Mediocrity and Individuality," NR 33 (Dec. 1922): 36; John Dewey, "Individuality Equality and Superiority," NR 33 (Dec. 1922): 61.

51. Thomas M. Thomson, "Intelligence Tests and Democracy in Education," ER 67 (Jan. 1924): 10–11. See also "Intelligence and Its Measurement: A Symposium," *Journal of Educational Psychology* 12 (Mar. 1921): 123–47; NSSE twenty-first yearbook, Guy Whipple, ed., *Intelligence Tests and Their Use* (1922); Guy Whipple, "The Intelligence Testing Program and Its Objectors—Conscientious and Otherwise," SS 17 (May 1923): 561–68; J. McKeen Cattell, "The Interpretation of Intelligence Tests," *Scientific Monthly* 18 (May 1924): 508–16; Walter Dearborn, *Intelligence Tests: Their Significance for School and Society* (Boston: Houghton Mifflin Co., 1928); Virgil E. Dickson, *Mental Tests and the Classroom Teacher* (Yonkers-on-Hudson, NY: World Book Co., 1923); Lewis M. Terman, *The Measurement of Intelligence* (Boston: Houghton Mifflin Co., 1916).

52. Edward L. Thorndike, "Intelligence and Its Uses," *Harper's Magazine* 140 (Jan. 1920): 234; Edward Thorndike, "America's School Policy Challenged," NYT, 20 Mar. 1932, E7.

53. William C. Bagley, "Educational Determinism; or, Democracy and the IQ," *Educational Administration and Supervision* 8 (May 1922): 266–67; William C. Bagley, *Determinism in Education: A Series of Papers on the Relative Influence of Inherited and Acquired Traits in Determining Intelligence, Achievement, and Character* (Baltimore: Warwick & York, 1925).

54. Walter Lippmann, "The Mystery of the 'A' Men," NR 32 (Nov. 1922): 247; Walter Lippmann, "The Reliability of Intelligence Tests," NR 32 (Nov. 1922): 277; Walter Lippmann, "The Abuse of the Tests," NR 32 (Nov. 1922): 297–98. For other critiques, see Thomas J. McCormack, "A Critique of Mental Measurements," SS 15 (June 1922): 686–92; Warren W. Coxe, "The Problem of the Intelligence Test," ER 67 (Feb. 1924):

73–77; Marion E. Macdonald, "The I.Q. and Democracy," SS 25 (May 1927): 631–34; Harry Miles Johnson, "Science and Sorcery in Mental Tests," Forum 82 (Dec. 1929): 366–72; Alice V. Keliher, A Critical Study of Homogeneous Grouping with a Critique of Measurement as the Basis for Classification (New York: Teachers College, 1931).

55. For examples of how the tests were used, see Chapman, Schools as Sorters; Hobart M. Corning, After Testing—What?: The Practical Use of Test Results in One School System (Chicago: Scott, Foresman and Co., 1926); Cecile White Flemming, Pupil Adjustment in the Modern School (New York: Teachers College, 1931); W. S. Deffenbaugh, "Uses of Intelligence and Achievement Tests in 215 Cities," USBE CSL 20 (Mar. 1925); Philip Albert Boyer, "The Adjustment of a School to Individual and Community Needs" (Ph.D. diss., University of Pennsylvania, 1920); I. N. Madsen, "The Contribution of Intelligence Tests to Educational Guidance in High School," SR 30 (Nov. 1922): 692–701.

56. Billet, "Provisions for Individual Differences," 43; C. R. Tupper, "The Use of Intelligence Tests in the Schools of a Small City," in Lewis M. Terman et al., Intelligence Tests and School Reorganization (Yonkers-on-Hudson, NY: World Book Co., 1923).

57. Tupper, "The Use of Intelligence Tests in the Schools of a Small City," 102.

58. For discussions of the racial and cultural bias of tests, see Walter Lippmann, "Rich and Poor, Girls and Boys," NR 34 (May 1923): 295–96; Herbert Sidney Langfeld, "The Value of Intelligence Tests," Forum 76 (Aug. 1926): 276–79; James L. Mursell, "Mental Testing: A Protest" Harper's Magazine 180 (Apr. 1940): 526–34. On how tests were used to make conclusions about the intelligence of racial groups, see William H. Sheldon, "The Intelligence of Mexican Children," SS 19 (1924): 139–42; Gregory D. Walcott, "The Intelligence of Chinese Students," SS 11 (Aug. 1920): 474–80; Thomas Garth and Calvin A. Whatley, "The Intelligence of Southern Negro Children," SS 22 (Oct. 1925): 501–4; Morris S. Viteles, "The Mental Status of the Negro," AAPSS 140 (Nov. 1928): 166–77; Raymond G. Fuller, "Intelligence of Our Immigrants," NYT, 18 Mar. 1923, BR18.

59. Frank Parsons, "The Vocation Bureau: Part I," Arena 40 (July 1908): 3–4; Frank Parsons, "The Vocation Bureau: Part II," Arena 40 (Sept. 1908): 171–83; Frank Parsons, Choosing a Vocation (Boston: Houghton Mifflin Co., 1909).

60. James J. Davis, "The Worker's Attitude toward Vocational Education," in Edwin A. Lee, ed., Objectives and Problems of Vocational Education (New York: McGraw-Hill, 1928), 355.

61. On the history of vocational guidance, see John M. Brewer, The Vocational-Guidance Movement: Its Problems and Possibilities (New York: Macmillan Co., 1919); John M. Brewer, History of Vocational Guidance: Origins and Early Development (New York: Harper & Brothers Publishers, 1942); Charles A. Prosser and Charles R. Allen, Vocational Education in a Democracy (New York: Century Co., 1925); Arthur F. Payne, Organization of Vocational Guidance (New York: McGraw Hill, 1925); W. Carson Ryan Jr., "Vocational Guidance and the Public Schools," USBE Bulletin, no. 24 (1918); David Segel and Maris M. Proffitt, "Pupil Personnel Services as a Function of State Departments of Education," USBE Bulletin, no. 6, monograph no. 5 (1940); Maris M. Proffitt, "State Guidance Programs," USBE Pamphlet, no. 35 (1933); "Vocational

Guidance and Junior Placement: Ten Cities in the Unites States," USCB pub. no. 149 (1925).

62. George Herbert Mead, "The Larger Educational Bearings of Vocational Guidance," in "Vocational Guidance," *USBE Bulletin*, no. 14 (1914): 22; Leonard Righter, "The Curriculum and Vocational Guidance," ESJ 16 (Mar. 1916): 370; Arthur Jones and Harold C. Hand, "Guidance and Purposeful Living," in NSSE thirty-seventh yearbook, Guy M. Whipple, ed., *Guidance in Educational Institutions* (1938), 3; Ruth Strang, "Guidance in Personality Development," *Guidance in Educational Institutions*, 197–228. See also "Vocational Guidance in Secondary Education," *USBE Bulletin*, no. 19 (1918); John M. Brewer, ed., *Case Studies in Educational and Vocational Guidance* (Boston: Ginn & Co. , 1926); Leonard V. Koos and Grayson N. Kefauver, *Guidance in Secondary Schools* (New York: Macmillan Co., 1932); Leonard V. Koos and Grayson N. Kefauver, "The Concept of Guidance," SR 40 (Mar. 1932): 204–12.

63. Marguerite Stockman Dickson, *Vocational Guidance for Girls* (Chicago: Rand McNally & Co., 1919), 14–16; Catherine Filene, *Careers for Women: New Ideas, New Methods, New Opportunities—To Fit a New World*, rev. ed. (Cambridge, MA: Riverside Press, 1934), 242–45.

64. Rury, *Education and Women's Work*; Karen Graves, *Girls' Schooling during the Progressive Era: From Female Scholar to Domesticated Citizen* (New York: Garland Publishing Inc., 1998); Jane Bernard Powers, *The 'Girl Question' in Education: Vocational Education for Young Women in the Progressive Era* (Washington, D.C.: Falmer Press, 1992); Albert H. Leake, *The Vocational Education of Girls and Women* (New York: Macmillan Co., 1918).

65. Chicago Commission on Race Relations, *The Negro in Chicago: A Study of Race Relations and a Race Riot* (Chicago: University of Chicago Press, 1922), chap. 6; Michael W. Homel, *Down from Equality: Black Chicagoans and the Public Schools, 1920–41* (Urbana: University of Illinois Press, 1984); W. E. B. DuBois, "Education and Work" (1930), in *The Education of Black People: Ten Critiques, 1906–1960*, ed. Herbert Aptheker (New York: Monthly Review Press, 1973).

66. Marechal-Neil E. Young, "Some Sociological Aspects of Vocational Guidance of Negro Children" (Ph.D. diss., University of Pennslyvania, 1944); Fred D. Patterson, "Avenues of Redirection in Vocational Education," *Journal of Negro Education* 5 (July 1936): 495–501; D. O. W. Holmes, "Does Negro Education Need Reorganization and Redirection?—A State of the Problem," *Journal of Negro Education* 5 (July 1936): 314–23; Ambrose Caliver, "Vocational Education and Guidance of Negroes: Report of a Survey Conducted by the Office of Education," *USBE Bulletin*, no. 38 (1937); Jack Doughtery, *More Than One Struggle: The Evolution of Black School Reform in Milwaukee* (Chapel Hill: University of North Carolina Press, 2003), chap. 1; Anderson, *The Education of Blacks in the South*, chap. 6.

67. Charles H. Judd, "The Unique Character of American Secondary Education," SR 36 (Feb. 1928): 99, 113, 110; Snyder, *120 Years of American Education*, 6–14; Claudia Goldin, "The Human-Capital Century and American Leadership: Virtues of the Past," *Journal of Economic History* 61 (June 2001): 263–91.

68. George S. Counts, *The American Road to Culture: A Social Interpretation of Education in the United States* (New York: John Day Co., 1930), 16–17, 19, 86.

69. C. A. Bowers, *The Progressive Educator and the Depression: The Radical Years* (New York: Random House, 1969); David Tyack, Robert Lowe, and Elisabeth Hansot, *Public Schools in Hard Times: The Great Depression and Recent Years* (Cambridge, MA: Harvard University Press, 1984).

70. George Counts, *Dare the School Build a New Social Order?* (New York: John Day Co., 1932), 19, 5, 40, 29, 37.

71. Horace M. Kallen, *Education versus Indoctrination* (Chicago, University of Chicago Press, 1934); Boyd H. Bode, "Education and Social Reconstruction," SF1 (Jan. 1934): 18–22; Boyd H. Bode, "Dr. Childs and Education for Democracy," SF 5 (Nov. 1938): 38–40; John L. Childs, "Dr. Bode on 'Authentic' Democracy," SF 5 (Nov. 1938): 40–42; John Dewey, "Education, Democracy, and Socialized Economy," SF5 (Dec. 1938): 71–72; John Dewey, "Education and Social Change," SF 3 (May 1937): 235–38; William Heard Kilpatrick, *Education and the Social Crisis: A Proposed Program* (New York: Liveright Publishing Corp., 1932); Carleton Washburne, "Indoctrination versus Education," SF 2 (April 1936): 212–15.

72. John Dewey and John L. Childs, "The Social-Economic Situation and Education," in William H. Kilpatrick, ed., *The Educational Frontier* (New York: Century Co., 1933), 33, 54.

73. John Dewey, "Can Education Share in Social Reconstruction?," SF 1 (Oct. 1934): 11–12; John Dewey and John L. Childs, "The Underlying Philosophy of Education," in Kilpatrick, *Educational Frontier*, 291–92. See also William H. Kilpatrick, "Educational Ideals and the Profit Motive," SF 2 (Nov. 1934): 9–13; Boyd H. Bode, "Education and Social Reconstruction," SF 1 (Jan. 1934): 18; Lawrence Dennis, "Education—The Tool of the Dominant Elite," SF 1 (Jan. 1934): 11–15; Normal Boardman, "Are We Moving toward a New Social Order?," SF 1 (June 1935): 21–25.

74. Jesse H. Newlon, "The Place of the Educational Profession in the National Life," SS 42 (July 1935): 84. See also George A. Coe, "Defending Democracy," SF 3 (Oct. 1936): 10; Ordway Tread, "Democracy in Administration," SF 22 (Jan. 1937): 105; Jesse H. Newlon, *Education for Democracy in Our Time* (New York: McGraw-Hill Co., 1939); E. L. Curtis, "Democracy in Education," SS 35 (Mar. 1932): 429–31; Rabbi Abba Hillel Silver, "Educating the Children for the New Deal," *Journal of the NEA* 23 (Apr. 1934): 97–99; Carroll D. Champlin, "Education Rebuilding our Social Order," SS (Nov. 1935): 709–10; Alexander J. Stoddard, "The Function of the Schools in this Democracy," SS 42 (Aug. 1935): 241–47; William F. Russell, "Education for Democracy," SS 48 (Dec. 1938): 862–65; Harry Elmer Barnes, "The Responsibility of Education to Society," *Scientific Monthly* 51 (Sept. 1940): 248–60; William Heard Kilpatrick, *Education for a Changing Civilization* (New York: Macmillan Co., 1929).

75. Charles A. Beard, *A Charter for the Social Sciences in the Schools* (New York: Charles Scribner's Sons, 1932), 104–5, 48; *Conclusions and Recommendations: Report of the Commission on the Social Studies* (New York: Charles Scribner's Sons, 1934), 16. From the series, see also Jesse H. Newlon, *Educational Administration as Social Policy* (New

York: Charles Scribner's Sons, 1934); George S. Counts, *The Social Foundations of Education* (New York: Charles Scribner's Sons, 1934).

76. David Snedden, "The Social Studies—for What?," SS 36 (Sept. 1932): 358–62; Franklin Bobbitt, "Questionable Recommendations of the Commission on the Social Studies," SS 40 (Aug. 1934): 205–6; Evans, *The Social Studies Wars*, 50–66; Edward A. Krug, *The Shaping of the American High School, 1920–1941* (Madison: University of Wisconsin Press, 1972), 238–39; Philip W. L. Cox, "Are the Conclusions and Recommendations of the Commission on the Social Studies 'Startling' or 'Alarming'?," SS 40 (Oct. 1934): 554–57; Joseph Moreau, *School Book Nation: Conflicts over American History Textbooks from the Civil War to the Present* (Ann Arbor: University of Michigan Press, 2003), chap. 6; Jonathan Zimmerman, *Whose America?: Culture Wars in the Public Schools* (Cambridge, MA: Harvard University Press, 2002), chap. 3.

77. Counts, *The American Road to Culture*, 134–35, 86.

Conclusion

1. John Dewey, *The School and Society* (1900; repr., Chicago: University of Chicago, 1990), 8, 18, 28–29.

2. Exceptions to the general neglect of state government in education include David Tyack and Thomas James, "State Government and American Public Education: Exploring the 'Primeval Forest,'" HEQ 26 (Spring 1986): 39–69; David Tyack, Thomas James, and Aaron Benavot, *Law and the Shaping of Public Education, 1785–1954* (Madison: University of Wisconsin Press, 1987); Maris Vinovskis, "Gubernatorial Leadership and American K-12 Education Reform," in *A Legacy of Innovation: Governors and Public Policy*, ed., Ethan G. Sribnick (Philadelphia: University of Pennsylvania Press, 2008); Edgar Fuller and Jim B. Pearson, eds., *Education in the States: Historical Development and Outlook* (Washington. D.C.: Council of Chief State School Officers, 1969).

3. On philanthropies and other nonstate actors in national policymaking, see Eldon J. Eisenach, *The Lost Promise of Progressivism* (Lawrence: University Press of Kansas, 1994); Barry D. Karl and Stanley N. Katz, "The American Private Philanthropic Foundation and the Public Sphere, 1890–1930," *Minerva* 19, no. 2 (1981): 236–70; Barry D. Karl and Stanley N. Katz, "Foundations and Ruling Class Elites," *Daedalus* 116, no. 1 (1987): 1–40; Judith Sealander, *Private Wealth and Public Life: Foundation Philanthropy and the Reshaping of American Social Policy from the Progressive Era to the New Deal* (Baltimore: Johns Hopkins Press, 1997); Ellen Condliffe Lagemann, *Private Power for the Public Good: A History of the Carnegie Foundation for the Advancement of Teaching*, 2nd ed. (New York: College Entrance Examination Board, 1999); Brian Balogh, *A Government Out of Sight: The Mystery of National Authority in Nineteenth-Century America* (Cambridge: Cambridge University Press, 2009).

4. On pluralism and grassroots reform, see, for example, William J. Reese, *Power and the Promise of School Reform: Grassroots Movements during the Progressive Era*, 2nd ed. (New York: Teachers College Press, 2002); Judith Rosenberg Raferty, *Land of Fair Promise: Politics and Reform in Los Angeles Schools, 1885–1941* (Stanford: Stanford

University Press, 1992); Ira Katznelson and Margaret Weir, *Schooling for All: Class, Race, and the Decline of the Democratic Ideal* (New York: Basic Books Inc., 1985); Julia Wrigley, *Class Politics and Public Schools: Chicago, 1900–1950* (New Brunswick: Rutgers University Press, 1982).

5. "Social efficiency" offers one of many examples in which historians have assumed a coherent ideology or philosophy and tried to divide reformers into rigid camps; I think this obscures more than it reveals. See Herbert Kliebard, *The Struggle for the American Curriculum, 1893–1958* (New York: Routledge, 1987); Joel Spring, "Education and Progressivism," HEQ 10 (Spring 1970): 53–71; Barry M. Franklin, "The Social Efficiency Movement Reconsidered: Curriculum Change in Minneapolis, 1917–1950," *Curriculum Inquiry* 12 (Spring 1982): 9–33. I find it more useful to see social efficiency and other slogans as pliable social languages that had different meanings to different actors in different contexts: Daniel T. Rodgers, "In Search of Progressivism," *Reviews in American History* 10 (Dec. 1982): 113–32; Jeffrey Mirel, "Progressive School Reform in Comparative Perspective," in *Southern Cities, Southern Schools: Public Education in the Urban South*, ed. David N. Plank and Rick Ginsberg (New York: Greenwood Press, 1990).

6. On the power of federated interest groups, see Theda Skocpol, *Protecting Soldiers and Mothers: The Political Origins of Social Policy in the United States* (Cambridge, MA: Belknap Press, 1992).

7. On federalism as an impediment to social policy, see David Brian Robertson, "The Bias of American Federalism: The Limits of Welfare-State Development in the Progressive Era," *Journal of Policy History* 1, no. 3 (1989): 261–91; William Graebner, "Federalism in the Progressive Era: A Structural Interpretation of Reform," JAH 64 (Sept. 1977): 331–57; Harry N. Schreiber, "Federalism and the American Economic Order, 1789–1910," *Law and Society Review* 10 (Autumn 1975): 57–118.

8. For excellent but all too rare studies of state governments in the period, see William Brook, *Investigation and Responsibility: Public Responsibility in the United States, 1865–1900* (Cambridge: Cambridge University Press, 1984); Jon Teaford, *The Rise of the States: Evolution of American State Government* (Baltimore: Johns Hopkins Press, 2002); Morton Keller, *Regulating a New Society: Public Policy and Social Change in America, 1900–1933* (Cambridge, MA: Harvard University Press, 1994).

9. On the strength of decentralization and federalism in state-building, see, for example, Daniel J. Elazar, *The American Partnership: Intergovernmental Co-Operation in the Nineteenth-Century United States* (Chicago: University of Chicago Press, 1962); William J. Novak, "The Myth of the 'Weak' American State," AHR 113 (June 2008): 752–72; Elisabeth S. Clemens, "Lineages of the Rube Goldberg State: Building and Blurring Public Programs, 1900–1940," in *Rethinking Political Institutions: The Art of the State*, ed. Ian Shapiro, Stephen Skowronek, and Daniel Galvin (New York: New York University Press, 2006), 187–215; Elisabeth Clemens, *The People's Lobby: Organizational Innovation and the Rise of Interest Group Politics in the United States, 1890–1925* (Chicago: University of Chicago Press, 1997).

10. On the inegalitarian dimensions of localism, see, for example, Martha Derthick, ed., *Dilemmas of Scale in America's Federal Democracy* (Cambridge: Cambridge

University Press, 1999); Paul Theobald, *Call School: Rural Education in the Midwest to 1918* (Carbondale: Southern Illinois University Press, 1995); Thomas J. Sugrue, "All Politics Is Local: The Persistence of Localism in Twentieth-Century America," in *The Democratic Experiment: New Directions in American Political History,* ed. Meg Jacobs, William J. Novak, and Julian E. Zelizer (Princeton: Princeton University Press, 2003).

11. A few recent studies have argued more forcefully for the inclusion of education in analysis of the welfare state: Irwin Garfinkel, Lee Rainwater, and Timothy Smeeding, *Wealth and Welfare States: Is America a Laggard or Leader?* (New York: Oxford University Press, 2010); Michael B. Katz, "Public Education as Welfare," *Dissent* (Summer 2010): 52–56; Miriam Cohen, "Reconsidering Schools and the American Welfare State," HEQ 45 (Winter 2005): 512–53; Michael B. Katz, *Improving Poor People: The Welfare State, the "Underclass," and Urban Schools as History* (Princeton: Princeton University Press, 1995).

12. For examples of this comparative welfare state scholarship, see Gosta Esping-Anderson, *Three Worlds of Welfare Capitalism* (Princeton: Princeton University Press, 1990); Harold L. Wilensky, *The Welfare State and Equality: Structural and Ideological Roots of Public Expenditures* (Berkeley: University of California Press, 1975); Margaret Weir, Ann Shola Orloff, and Theda Skocpol, eds., *The Politics of Social Policy in the United States* (Princeton: Princenton University Press, 1988). For scholarship on the hidden welfare state and American political development that challenges some of these assumptions, see Peter Baldwin, "Beyond Weak and Strong: Rethinking the State in Comparative Policy History," JPH 17 (2005): 12–33; Peter Baldwin, "The Welfare State for Historians: A Review Article," *Comparative Studies in Society and History* 34 (Oct. 1992): 695–707; Christopher Howard, *Hidden Welfare State: Tax Expenditures and Social Policy in the United States* (Princeton: Princeton University Press, 1997); Christopher Howard, *The Welfare State Nobody Knows: Debunking Myths about U.S. Social Policy* (Princeton: Princeton University Press, 2007); Michael Katz, *The Price of Citizenship: Redefining the American Welfare State* (New York: Metropolitan Books, 2001); Jacob Hacker, *The Divided Welfare State: The Battle over Public and Private Social Benefits in the United States* (Cambridge: Cambridge University Press, 2002); Jennifer Klein, *For All These Rights: Business, Labor, and the Shaping of America's Public-Private Welfare State* (Princeton: Princeton University Press, 2003).

13. Theda Skocpol has argued that civil war pensions and public education were the two great American social policies of the nineteenth century. While she analyzed the "policy feedback" loop of pensions on the development of welfare policy in the early twentieth century, this analysis has not been applied to public schooling. Skocpol, *Protecting Soldiers and Mothers*; Margaret Weir, Ann Shola Orloff, and Theda Skocpol, eds., *The Politics of Social Policy in the United States* (Princeton: Princenton University Press, 1988); Edwin Amenta and Theda Skocpol, "Taking Exception: Explaining the Distinctiveness of American Public Policies in the Last Century," in *The Comparative History of Public Policy*, ed. Francis G. Castles (New York: Oxford University Press, 1989), 292–333.

INDEX